Presidential Accountability in Wartime

Presidential Accountability in Wartime

President Bush, the Treatment of Detainees, and the Laws of War

Stuart Streichler

University of Michigan Press
Ann Arbor

For questions or permissions, please contact um.press.perms@umich.edu

Published in the United States of America by the
University of Michigan Press
Manufactured in the United States of America
Printed on acid-free paper
First published November 2023

A CIP catalog record for this book is available from the British Library.

Library of Congress Cataloging-in-Publication Data

Names: Streichler, Stuart, 1957– author. | Michigan Publishing (University of Michigan), publisher.
Title: Presidential accountability in wartime : President Bush, the treatment of detainees, and the laws of war / Stuart Alan Streichler.
Other titles: President Bush, the treatment of detainees, and the laws of war
Description: Ann Arbor [Michigan] : University of Michigan Press, [2023] | Includes bibliographical references (pages 253–272) and index.
Identifiers: LCCN 2023020929 (print) | LCCN 2023020930 (ebook) | ISBN 9780472076499 (hardcover) | ISBN 9780472056491 (paperback) | ISBN 9780472903900 (ebook other)
Subjects: LCSH: War and emergency powers—United States—History. | Executive power—United States—History. | Bush, George W. (George Walker), 1946– | Prisoners of war—Abuse of—United States. | Terrorism—Prevention—Law and legislation—United States—History. | Legislative power—United States—History. | Political questions and judicial power—United States—History. | Torture—Law and legislation—United States. | Torture (International law) | Humanitarian law.
Classification: LCC KF5060 .S87 2023 (print) | LCC KF5060 (ebook) | DDC 342.73/062—dc23/eng/20230609
LC record available at https://lccn.loc.gov/2023020929
LC ebook record available at https://lccn.loc.gov/2023020930

DOI: https://doi.org/10.3998/mpub.12407071

The University of Michigan Press's open access publishing program is made possible thanks to additional funding from the University of Michigan Office of the Provost and the generous support of contributing libraries.

CONTENTS

PREFACE

This book explores the complexities in holding US presidents accountable for violating the laws of armed conflict through an in-depth analysis of the treatment of detainees under President George W. Bush during the war against terrorism. Perhaps nothing better illustrates why I felt compelled to take on this project than some remarks made not by President Bush but rather by his successor. In April 2009, three months after his inauguration, President Barack Obama issued a brief statement announcing the release of four previously classified legal opinions prepared by the Bush Justice Department. These opinions had reviewed the Central Intelligence Agency's so-called enhanced interrogation techniques and approved them for use in the war against terrorism. The lurid details of these memoranda—with precise step-by-step descriptions of the interrogation procedures—left the new president little choice but to concede that Bush era interrogations marked "a dark and painful chapter" in American history.

It might have been thought that there was likewise little choice but to prosecute those involved, but President Obama resisted the idea. Having banned the use of the enhanced interrogation methods shortly after taking office, President Obama pronounced the Bush administration's interrogation program "a thing of the past." He believed that "at a time of great challenges and disturbing disunity, nothing will be gained by spending our time and energy laying blame for the past." It was "a time for reflection," he said, "not retribution."

Several years have gone by since then. Americans by now, it might be thought, have heard quite enough of waterboarding and torture; they have reached their conclusions; and history will judge President Bush accordingly.

Yet the more I reflect on this accountability failure, the more I see at stake. It is difficult for me to reconcile the conception of accountability implicit in President Obama's remarks with what actually happened during the Bush presidency. In effect, President Bush laid down a challenge to explain why the laws of war matter, and President Obama laid down a challenge to explain why accountability matters. This book takes up both challenges.

It is a pleasure to thank everyone who assisted me in this endeavor. Among those who offered comments after reading related conference papers or chapter drafts, I would like to single out Lisa Hajjar, Jamie Mayerfeld, and Daniel Tichenor. I am grateful for the time, thought, and care two anonymous referees gave the entire manuscript. I would also like to express my gratitude to Elizabeth Demers of the University of Michigan Press for shepherding this project through the publication process. Several students provided research and administrative assistance, including Ariana Bengtsston, Quinn Russell Brown, Elijah Nicholson, and Sarah Pennington. My idea for this work grew out of an invitation I received from the *University of San Francisco Law Review* to contribute to a symposium on war crimes accountability and to speak at the 13th Annual Trina Grillo Public Interest and Social Justice Retreat. This provided me with a forum to work out preliminary thoughts on the subject. See "The War Crimes Trial That Never Was: An Inquiry into the War on Terrorism, the Laws of War, and Presidential Accountability," *University of San Francisco Law Review* 45 (2011): 959–1004. I am also thankful for comments I received at colloquia at the School of Law and the Law, Societies, and Justice Department at the University of Washington as well as annual meetings of the Law and Society Association and the Western Political Science Association.

Introduction

For many Americans, it may be difficult to take seriously any suggestion that a US president committed war crimes. This is partly due to the popular understanding of this class of crimes. They bring to mind unspeakable atrocities—the like of killing fields, ethnic cleansing, and genocide.[1] War criminals are seen as bad actors without any redeeming virtue. To Americans, crimes of war are most often associated with authoritarian regimes or war-torn countries—that is, someplace else, a place where the rule of law has not taken hold or where military forces lack a professional ethos. Criticizing presidents may be a favorite pastime in the United States, but talk of presidential war crimes is bound to be greeted with skepticism.

The early years of America's war against terrorism raised unsettling questions on this subject. A substantial body of evidence has accumulated that suggests that President George W. Bush committed war crimes, not under some amorphous standard of what constitutes an atrocity, but rather as those criminal offenses are defined by the laws of war. The most egregious infractions involved the mistreatment of terrorism suspects taken prisoner by the United States. The Geneva Conventions set forth binding standards for the protection of persons detained in the course of an armed conflict, whatever they have done and whether or not they qualify as prisoners of war. At a minimum, the conventions mandate the humane treatment of wartime captives.[2] President Bush violated this basic rule.

The mistreatment of detainees in US custody was the inevitable result of the interrogation program the president approved for use in the war against terrorism. Questioning captured enemy soldiers is nothing new. The laws of war permit interrogation. In earlier conflicts like World War II, the American military had scored valuable intelligence coups by conducting interrogations in accordance with the laws of war.[3] At the time of the terrorist attacks on September 11, 2001, every branch of the US armed services had in place detailed regulations governing the treatment of detainees. Army Field Manual 34-52 made it clear that interrogations involving "inhumane treatment" and "physical or mental torture" were "criminal acts" in violation of the laws of war and US law.[4]

Five years after the September 11 attacks, President Bush spoke publicly for the first time about an "alternative set of procedures" he had authorized for the interrogation of terrorism suspects. "These procedures," the president noted, "were designed to be safe, to comply with our laws, our Constitution, and our treaty obligations." At that time, President Bush declined to provide further details about the interrogation methods used. "I think you understand why," he told an audience gathered in the East Room of the White House. "If I did, it would help the terrorists learn how to resist questioning."[5]

It is now known that these alternative procedures were derived from a US military training program called Survival, Evasion, Resistance, Escape (SERE). That program was not set up to train military interrogators. As its name implies, SERE was designed instead to prepare American servicemembers in case they were captured by enemy forces. One part of the curriculum, designated Level C, provided resistance training by simulating conditions of prisoner abuse. Trainees were hooded, stripped naked, slapped, deprived of sleep, slammed into walls, forced to hold stress positions, exposed to extreme temperatures, and placed in small boxes. Degradation—treating mock prisoners like animals—was a key part of this training. It was thought that anyone treated like this under controlled conditions would be better prepared to withstand mistreatment by an enemy that did not comply with international law.[6]

The SERE program was not the product of "what if" contingency planning. Its origins can be traced to the actual experience of American POWs in the Korean War. Chinese Communists had got dozens of captured US airmen to make confessions that were so patently false that the American public came to accept some mysterious form of "brainwashing" as a plausible explanation of their behavior. Investigations by the Air Force, along with Central Intelligence Agency (CIA) studies of Soviet police practices, revealed something else at work. It became clear that coercive techniques as seemingly innocuous as sleep deprivation—techniques that might be considered psychological torture—had a devastating effect on prisoners, even more than physical violence did. One Air Force study, "Communist Attempts to Elicit False Confessions from Air Force Prisoners of War," identified several methods used to break down the airmen. Besides sleep deprivation, these included isolation, sensory manipulation (darkness, bright light, restricted movement), exposure to cold, and prolonged constraint. The Chinese also used something the Air Force called "degradation" to strip their American captives of any shred of dignity and bring them down to "animal level" concerns. Guards taunted the prisoners, prevented them from cleaning themselves, denied them bathroom privacy, and imposed demeaning punishments.[7]

Despite SERE's purpose and origins, the Bush administration "imported" its techniques for use in the war against terrorism.[8] The overall goal was to create "a state of learned helplessness"—a concept drawn from psychological experiments that administered electric shocks to dogs in cages.[9] Before questioning began, prisoners were subjected to baseline conditioning to make clear to them that they had "no control over basic human needs."[10] Forced nudity and sleep deprivation were considered essential to the conditioning process. Interrogators kept some prisoners naked for months at a time. Sleep deprivation was approved for 180 consecutive hours (seven and one-half days). The "primary method" used to stop detainees from sleeping was to shackle them to the ceiling and the floor with their hands outstretched in front.[11]

Government documents marked "TOP SECRET" describe the interrogation procedures with bureaucratic precision. One, called "walling," involved slamming prisoners into walls to induce a feeling of "dread." There was no stated limit to the number of times this could be done, though thirty in a row was not considered too many.[12] "Water dousing" was another technique. Interrogators were authorized to douse detainees in cold water as low as 41° for twenty minutes without a break—ten minutes shy of the time hypothermia would be expected for a healthy person immersed in water at that temperature. The process could be repeated once the prisoner was dried and rewarmed.[13] "Cramped confinement" involved placing the detainee in a small dark box that one government official described as "a dog crate."[14] If the prisoner had room to stand, confinement could last for eight consecutive hours.[15] Several stress positions were approved to "humiliate" detainees. For example, they could be forced to hold themselves in place while kneeling on the floor and leaning back at a 45° angle (the Army Field Manual in effect then defined "physical torture" to include "forcing an individual to stand, sit, or kneel in abnormal positions for prolonged periods of time").[16] Additional interrogation procedures went by the names of insult slap, abdominal slap, facial hold, and attention grasp.[17]

Of all the Bush administration's interrogation tactics, waterboarding has received the most publicity. This may have been partly due to its history, with the Gestapo and the Khmer Rouge among its most notorious practitioners. The Bush Justice Department recognized waterboarding as "the most traumatic" of the approved interrogation methods. The aim was to produce the "sensation of drowning."[18] The gag reflex induced can be intense—so intense that Justice Department lawyers had at one time concluded that waterboarding constituted "a threat of imminent death," which can be one element in the criminal offense of torture under US law. "Any reasonable person undergoing this procedure," one Justice Department memorandum stated, "would feel as if he is drowning at the very moment of the procedure due to the uncontrollable physiological sensation he is experiencing."[19] Among the medical risks, waterboarding can cause "spasms of the larynx," rendering the prisoner incapable of resuming breathing without an emergency tracheotomy.[20]

It was obvious to everyone involved in planning the interrogation program that these tactics brought up significant legal issues. Internal administration documents reveal the extent of their concern. Attorney General John Ashcroft sent a letter to President Bush warning him that there could be "substantial criminal liability" for "involved U.S. officials." A draft memorandum for the president bearing the name of White House counsel Alberto R. Gonzales recommended that President Bush declare the Geneva Conventions inapplicable in order to mitigate the "threat of domestic criminal prosecution" under a US law called the War Crimes Act.[21]

On February 7, 2002, President Bush issued a classified memorandum to his top national security officials that was titled "Humane Treatment of al Qaeda and Taliban Detainees" (see appendix A). Citing his authority as commander in chief, President Bush declared that "none of the provisions of Geneva" applied in the conflict with Al Qaeda. He made a blanket determination that Al Qaeda and Taliban fighters could not qualify as prisoners of war; hence, they were not legally entitled to the protections Geneva provided POWs. While the memorandum stated that detainees would be treated humanely as a matter of policy, the president decided that Common Article 3 of the Geneva Conventions—a crucial provision that sets out minimum requisites for the humane treatment of "persons taking no active part in the hostilities" during non-international conflicts—did not apply either. In the words of Jack Goldsmith, President Bush "rejected any binding legal constraints on detainee treatment under the laws of war." If there was any question of the president's understanding of his power in relation to this body of law, that was laid to rest when he asserted plainly that he had the "authority under the Constitution to suspend Geneva."[22]

To the general public, the first sign of something amiss came in the spring of 2004, when graphic reports and photographs surfaced showing the abuse of prisoners in the custody of the US Army at Abu Ghraib Prison in Iraq.[23] The Bush administration attributed the problems there to "a few bad apples," but with a succession of revelations about Justice Department "torture memos," the use of "enhanced interrogation techniques," and a global network of secret prisons run by the CIA called "black sites," it became increasingly difficult to single out a handful of wayward soldiers for censure.[24]

The extent of President Bush's involvement remained unclear while he was in office. After news broke about Abu Ghraib, the White House indicated that he had little to do with the specifics of the administration's interrogations. His press secretary said that the president had set forth general guidelines, all the while insisting that the treatment of detainees must be "consistent with our laws." White House counsel Gonzales told reporters that President Bush had "not directed the use of specific interrogation techniques."[25] It was not until 2008 that news accounts began to link harsh interrogations to the highest-ranking members of President Bush's national security team. ABC News found out that Vice President Dick Cheney, the CIA director, the national security advisor, and several cabinet secretaries had met repeatedly to approve detailed interrogation plans for particular detainees. At one point, Attorney General Ashcroft reportedly asked his colleagues, "Why are we talking about this in the White House? History will not judge this kindly." Still, President Bush appeared in news accounts to have kept his distance. The ABC News report went no further than to say that the president knew that his national security principals met to discuss interrogations and he approved of their doing so.[26]

Nearly two years after leaving office, President Bush disclosed that he had played a far greater role than was previously known. In his memoir *Decision Points*, published in November 2010, the former president wrote that he had reviewed proposed interrogation methods, directed lawyers at the Justice Department and the CIA to assess their legality, and then authorized their use. The president noted, evidently with some pride, that he had personally directed the CIA to waterboard particular terrorism suspects.[27] President Bush related that, when the agency asked for permission to waterboard Khalid Shaikh Mohammed, his reply consisted of two words: "Damn right." To those who considered waterboarding torture, this was a stunning admission, by itself prima facie evidence of the former president's criminal liability.[28]

Even before the memoir's publication, a retired US Army general had concluded that there was "no longer any doubt as to whether the current administration committed war crimes." The man who made that statement, Major General Antonio M. Taguba (Ret.) ought to know. He had spearheaded the Army's investigation of the 800th Military Police Brigade, the unit at the center of the Abu Ghraib scandal. The general did not mince words about the president's overall responsibility: "The Commander-in-Chief and those under him authorized a systematic regime of torture." The "only question that remains to be answered," Taguba added, was "whether those who ordered the use of torture will be held to account."[29]

As the Bush presidency recedes in memory, the answer to that question has become clear. While the military court-martialed several servicemembers, no one in the highest ranks was prosecuted.[30] Of all those outside the military who might be implicated, the Justice Department brought charges against only one (a CIA contractor named David Passaro), and that was while President Bush was still in office.[31] During President Barack Obama's administration, federal prosecutors conducted a limited criminal investigation that began when Attorney General Eric Holder opened "a preliminary review" of selected CIA interrogations. Holder confined the investigation to the use of unauthorized methods. That meant that interrogation tactics like waterboarding were not part of the inquiry so long as interrogators followed the procedures approved by the Bush Justice Department. The attorney general emphasized that charges would not "necessarily follow."[32] It was a prophetic remark. After looking into approximately one hundred cases, prosecutors closed the preliminary review, conducted criminal investigations in two cases, and then concluded the inquiry without indicting anyone.[33] In announcing the end of the investigation, Attorney General Holder said that it "was not intended to, and does not resolve, broader questions regarding the propriety of the examined conduct."[34]

The Justice Department never focused on President Bush's role in the mistreatment of detainees, and it is evident by now, if it was not previously, that he was never going to be tried for war crimes in the United States or anywhere else. In theory, prosecutors in other countries could have filed charges against President Bush, but the odds were always stacked against any other nation exercising jurisdiction over him.[35] Other prosecutorial options were simply inconceivable. The UN Security Council was never going to establish a special international criminal tribunal as it had for Rwanda and the former Yugoslavia. Nor was President Bush ever going to be hauled before the International Criminal Court in the Netherlands, even with a slowly developing investigation of war crimes committed in Afghanistan.[36]

While this record of prosecutorial nonfeasance is remarkable enough, the discussion of accountability in the public debate seems no less so. To sum up the zeitgeist on this, it seemed unclear why accountability mattered. As President Bush's second term came to a close, a critical mass of commentators (including many dismayed by reports of torture) peremptorily dismissed the idea of prosecuting anyone involved, let alone the president. Americans were told that the legal obstacles were insurmountable and the political consequences ruinous. Jack M. Balkin thought that criminal prosecutions might be "the least effective" mechanism to achieve accountability for prisoner abuse. Jack Goldsmith considered any "insistence" on criminal trials "misplaced." Jeffrey Rosen summed up the prevailing view: "even staunch advocates of legal accountability for the Bush administration's interrogation policy don't believe that a straight war-crimes approach has a high chance of success."[37]

If the legal obstacles appeared formidable, political considerations loomed even larger. As the public debate over the Bush administration's interrogation regime unfolded, there emerged something that might be called a discourse of accountability. That discourse provided a vocabulary of what could be done and, more to the point, what could not be done to hold individuals accountable for the mistreatment of detainees. The message was clear from the language used: "criminalizing policy differences," "stop scapegoating," and "partisan witch hunt."[38] Prosecuting here, *Washington Post* columnist David S. Broder warned, would turn "all future policy disagreements" into "criminal vendettas." Perhaps it was inevitable that no one in authority would be prosecuted, but the sentiments expressed in language like that appear to have gone a long way to rationalize that result. President Obama did not favor prosecutions either, as he told Americans that "nothing will be gained by spending our time and energy laying blame for the past."[39]

Although the Constitution's framers contemplated the prosecution of former presidents, putting President Bush on trial was so obviously out of the question that it got hardly any argument. Some thought that the American political system could not withstand the strain of such a trial. There seemed to be an implicit consensus, sometimes explicitly stated, that while his actions were really bad—criminal in fact—it would be impossible to prosecute him. "We're not just talking about 'enhanced interrogations,'" said Thomas L. Friedman, but "sheer brutality" and "homicides." Yet justice "taken to its logical end" would lead to trying President Bush, and that, Friedman thought, would "rip our country apart." Likewise, Andrew Sullivan believed there was "flagrant evidence of war crimes" committed by the president "on down," but prosecuting him would "tear this already polarized society apart." Michael Walzer, who established his reputation for work on ethical conduct in warfare, did not doubt that the president had "authorized" torture, but he suggested that prosecuting him would be "radically imprudent."[40]

This book takes issue with the notion that a US president can commit war crimes with impunity. It proceeds from the view that the misconduct in question—holding individuals incommunicado, depriving them of any sort of hearing, torturing them—reflects the most visceral concerns over the abuse of executive power and that prosecuting the president was the only alternative comporting with international law. With that in mind, it might be tempting to present a straight-line argument that President Bush committed war crimes and that he should have been prosecuted.

This study takes a different approach. While it has seemed necessary to examine what President Bush did in violation of the laws of war in the course of laying out this book's argument, this work was not conceived as a call to action for federal prosecutors to indict the former president. This book does more than lay out a case against him, and no attempt is made to canvass every technical question of law that might have been brought up in criminal proceedings. Using the Bush administration's mistreatment of detainees in the war against terrorism as a crucial case study, this book is designed to reflect more broadly on the American presidency and its relationship to the law—in this case the laws of war—and the complexities surrounding presidential accountability in wartime. By framing the question of President Bush's conduct around the laws of war, this study merges constitutional analysis with international humanitarian law. In doing so, it adds to a large body of work that takes the US Constitution as the principal source of law for judging the exercise of presidential power.

Given the interpretive approach taken in this work, it will be useful to provide a summary introduction of its guiding assumptions regarding accountability, the presidency, and the laws of war.

"Accountability" is a term so often used that it would seem to require no clarification. In the context of this discussion of war crimes, the first thought that may spring to mind is holding individuals responsible for their behavior through the criminal process to determine whether they are blameworthy and how they should be punished. That can be the most fitting alternative in many situations, but there is more to the concept of accountability than that. At its core, accountability means that persons (or organizations or states) are answerable to others for their actions. Often this is described in terms of a baseline obligation to explain or justify conduct. Transparency is a necessary element of accountability. Following the rules—whether strictly defined laws or unwritten social norms—is another key aspect of accountability. So too is liability for violating the rules. Besides criminal sanctions, liability can take various forms, ranging from disciplinary proceedings to financial audits. As this book defines it, accountability includes prospective or before-the-fact accountability (the idea being to constrain someone to prevent misconduct from occurring in the first place) as well as retrospective or after-the-fact accountability (which necessarily comes into play after misdeeds have already taken place).[41]

This inquiry into the Bush administration's mistreatment of detainees provides an opportunity to observe how presidential accountability intersects with the concerns animating human rights accountability. In recent years, considerable thought has been given to accountability in the emerging field of transitional justice.[42] Prosecution remains an important alternative, befitting the nomenclature of war crimes and crimes against humanity, but the question of how to enable societies moving from authoritarian rule or intercommunal conflict to a peaceful democracy respectful of human rights has led to an expanded set of accountability options. These include truth commissions, civil litigation, immigration measures (deportation, denaturalization), financial sanctions, reparations, memorialization, and measures geared toward a successful transition (reconstituting the judiciary or barring human rights violators from public office, for example). Some of these human rights accountability mechanisms may be relevant to consider for presidential accountability in the United States; others clearly are not germane.[43]

On paper, the options Americans have for holding their presidents accountable make for an impressive list. The obligation to face voters at the polls should probably count as the most basic accountability mechanism, not only through quadrennial elections but also by virtue of the ongoing force of public opinion. Then there is the familiar system of checks and balances. Congress has a reservoir of powers that can be brought to bear against the president, whether through ordinary legislation, oversight hearings, budgetary controls, the appointments process, or impeachment. The Supreme Court has built up its authority to invalidate actions taken by the president. State governments provide an additional counterweight against the nation's chief executive, as illustrated by recent high-profile lawsuits filed by state attorneys general contesting presidential policy initiatives. The president may encounter pushback from within the executive branch as well. An assortment of individuals and institutions outside the government can also play a part in checking the president, usually by exposing executive overreach. Some, like the press, have long standing; others are of more recent origin (for example, public advocacy groups). Independent commissions can be set up to investigate White House activities. In theory, criminal prosecution affords yet another avenue to hold presidents accountable, although no one who served in that office had ever been charged with a criminal offense until a Manhattan grand jury indicted President Donald J. Trump.[44]

It goes without saying that accountability is an intrinsic feature of a functioning democracy.[45] A central premise underlying this book's argument is that presidential accountability is likewise an indispensable feature of the constitutional system of government devised at the nation's founding. This proposition should not stir controversy. Individuals across the political spectrum have said something to that effect. According to Arthur M. Schlesinger Jr., the Constitution's framers sought to couple "a strong presidency" with "an equally strong system of accountability." Or, as Justice Antonin Scalia explained, the founders "established a single Chief Executive accountable to the people" so that "the blame can be assigned to someone who can be punished."[46] As unobjectionable as this point may be, a brief history will help to set the stage for this book's argument.

To the framers of the Constitution, presidential accountability was the key to solving a problem that was, in their eyes, one of the most challenging they faced: the problem of executive power. When the delegates gathered at the Constitutional Convention in Philadelphia in 1787, they had two models before them. One was the example provided by King George. The other was the experience of their own governments under the Articles of Confederation. It had become clear by then that each suffered from serious disadvantages.

Regarding the British Crown, it would not be accurate to say that, under the prevailing theory of the English constitution at the time, the king was an absolute ruler with unlimited power. But to the American revolutionaries, there was nothing to distinguish His Majesty's conduct from that of a sovereign who was above the law—one who exercised power without limitation. That sentiment was expressed in the Declaration of Independence, which described the king's "direct object" as "the establishment of an absolute Tyranny." This lesson on executive power was not lost on Americans as they formed their own governments during the Revolutionary War. "They seem never for a moment," James Madison reflected, "to have turned their eyes from the danger" presented by an "overgrown and all-grasping prerogative of an hereditary magistrate."[47] Generalizing from their particular case, Americans had drawn a broader conclusion from the exercise of Crown authority. It was not just the monarchy that was at issue. They questioned executive power itself, seen by its nature to be all too easily subject to abuse, a ripe vehicle for corruption, and fundamentally at odds with individual liberty. "Executive power," wrote one observer from Delaware, was "ever restless, ambitious, and ever grasping at encrease of power."[48]

Perhaps there is no better indication of how deeply this concern ran than the efforts made to expunge any trace of executive power from the newly formed governments under the Articles of Confederation. The central government had no independent executive branch. Members of the Continental Congress could not even bring themselves to entertain a proposal for an executive council composed of persons they selected. Congress retained executive power, which it was compelled by necessity to exercise, but it did so haphazardly by delegating administrative tasks first to ad hoc committees and private individuals, then standing committees and executive departments.[49] As for the new state governments, it is true that almost every one of their constitutions adopted during the Revolutionary War had a governor (with the exception of Pennsylvania's twelve-member Executive Council), but the office was typically little more than an empty title, with sharply limited powers, short terms (many no longer than one year), no veto power, and no discretionary authority to take action without preapproval of a council whose members were appointed by the legislature.[50] The chaos that ensued laid bare the problems in taking this concern over executive power too far.

With Americans wary of creating a strong executive like the English monarchy and frustrated with their own dysfunctional governments, the framers' constitutional solution may seem obvious in retrospect. They sought to create a powerful and independent executive adapted, so they thought, to fit republican government. This was something new in the history of politics. During the ratification debates, some questioned whether that was even possible. "There is an idea, which is not without its advocates," Alexander Hamilton admitted, that "a vigorous executive is inconsistent with the genius of republican government."[51]

It fell to Hamilton, who was always for a broad reading of executive

power, to convince a skeptical public that the Constitution neatly reconciled the two. Responding to arguments comparing the American presidency with the English monarchy, he pointed out several distinctions. The
president held office for a defined term while the king was a *"hereditary
prince."* Congress could override presidential vetoes; the British sovereign
had an absolute veto. The Senate could reject treaties negotiated by the
president. The king, by contrast, had the authority to conclude treaties with
foreign states on his own. The president's nominees had to be approved by
the Senate. There was no similar restriction on the Crown's appointment
powers. Both held title as commander in chief, but the king had the authority to declare war and raise armies—powers that the Constitution placed
with Congress. And unlike the king of England, the president was subject
to impeachment and removal from office.[52]

What emerges from Hamilton's *Federalist* essays is something more than
this point-by-point comparison suggests, however. Perhaps it does not go
too far to say that his justification of the presidency, presented at the crucial moment when the Constitution was submitted to the people for their
consideration, was essentially a statement on presidential accountability. In
Federalist no. 70, Hamilton noted that the king was "unaccountable for his
administration" while every officeholder in a republic "ought to be personally responsible for his behavior in office." To show that the presidency satisfied this objective, Hamilton made passing reference to the election cycle.
He drew attention to the way in which the president's powers were interwoven with those of Congress and therefore held in check (with the exception
of the pardon power that was given over to the president's discretion). The
"restraints of public opinion" had an important role in this. A major reason
for having a single president instead of a multimember council was to enable
the public to hold the president accountable. "It often becomes impossible"
with a council, Hamilton explained, for people "to determine on whom the
blame or the punishment of a pernicious measure" ought "really to fall,"
leaving public opinion "in suspense."[53] He also noted that, for any president
who abused the power of the office, the Constitution provided a remedy in
impeachment. Reiterating the Constitution's language, Hamilton pointed out
that any president removed from office by impeachment "would afterwards
be liable to prosecution and punishment in the ordinary course of law."[54]
His conclusion was emphatic: the president would be "at all times liable to
impeachment, trial, dismissal from office, incapacity to serve in any other,
and to the forfeiture of life and estate by subsequent prosecution in the com-

mon course of law." What more, he asked, "can an enlightened and reasonable people desire?"[55]

Alas, while the presidency has grown stronger since the founding, presidential accountability has diminished over the years. Perhaps the best way to introduce this point is by reference to the concept of the "imperial presidency"—a loaded phrase no doubt, but one that clearly echoes the founding generation's anxiety stemming from the colonial experience with the British monarchy. Arthur M. Schlesinger Jr. popularized this concept in his book titled, naturally enough, *The Imperial Presidency*. Writing at the close of the Vietnam War and in the midst of the Watergate scandal, he argued that the accumulation of unchecked power in the presidency was radically different from the founders' original design. An imperial presidency, he suggested, had displaced the "constitutional Presidency" set up in 1787 which subjected executive power to the rule of law and the countervailing powers of Congress and the courts.[56] Not everyone agrees with Schlesinger,[57] but it is possible to apply his overall thesis without embracing every detail of his argument. In any event, his catchy phrase entered the political lexicon, and the "imperial presidency" has become synonymous with unilateral decision-making, excessive secrecy, and the abuse of executive power.[58]

Schlesinger's book was published at a key moment in presidential history, but the matter no longer seemed to be of pressing concern after Congress reasserted its authority in the aftermath of Watergate. With the impeachment of President Bill Clinton, even Schlesinger was ready to concede the issue with an op-ed in the *New York Times* titled "So Much for the Imperial Presidency."[59]

Any such concession was premature, Schlesinger thought midway through the Bush presidency, when he wrote about "the imperial presidency redux." There was talk of a "new imperial presidency" and "the return of the imperial presidency,"[60] though the problem, as it now appeared to those who shared Schlesinger's concern, had never really gone away.[61] If the characteristics of the imperial presidency were more obvious with some administrations than others, the defect was seen to be institutional in nature, with the imperial presidency many years in the making. Perhaps the most compelling explanation of its development was given by Stephen Skowronek. He attributed the rise of the imperial presidency to a succession of reform-minded constituencies that looked to the White House to "break through the system of checks and balances" that was skewed to preserve the status quo.[62] He traced this pattern back to the early 1800s when the Jeffersonians and then the Jacksonians reconfigured national party politics around the presidency, though presidents continued to play a secondary role in domestic policymaking until the Progressive Era. Then, in the face of entrenched congressional opposition and the federal judiciary's reliably conservative bent, Progressives turned to the White House to promote their reform agenda. Liberal New Dealers followed suit, and with FDR's extraordinary personality, the shift of power in the federal system to the national government, the growth of administrative agencies, and America's emergence as a superpower, the presidency's hold on the nation's public affairs was solidified. By the 1980s, this path had been so well trod that Reagan conservatives managed to overcome traditional Whiggish suspicions of executive power in their effort to dismantle the New Deal.[63]

In short, even when individual presidents failed, so the "imperial presidency" argument goes, the presidency continued to accumulate powers that the Constitution had placed elsewhere (particularly with Congress).[64] Some observers used the term "presidentialism" or, in case the point might be lost, "aggressive presidentialism" to describe the result: executive supremacy in place of the original system of checks and balances; presidents unconstrained by the rule of law; presidentialism in lieu of constitutionalism.[65] By the time President Bush left office, Bruce Ackerman thought the presidency had become "far more dangerous" than when Schlesinger first issued his warnings.[66]

Wars can make matters worse. Of all the powers presidents wield, perhaps none presents a greater challenge to constitutional limitations than the war power, which Justice Robert H. Jackson once described as the "Achilles Heel of our constitutional system."[67] Presidents have invoked this power to do many things over the years. In the past, constitutional questions arose mainly in two areas. One, the driving force behind the emergence of the imperial presidency in Schlesinger's view, has to do with the power presidents had assumed to use military force abroad without congressional authorization.[68] This has been the subject of considerable debate since World War II regarding military engagements large and small, from President Harry S. Truman's police action in Korea to an assortment of air strikes, deployments, invasions, missile attacks, and humanitarian missions.[69] The other involves presidents infringing upon civil liberties at home as, for example, when President Abraham Lincoln suspended habeas corpus during the Civil War and the Union Army arrested thousands of civilians.[70]

This book suggests that President Bush's actions in the war against terrorism brought into relief yet another area of concern regarding presidential war powers—this one arising when the president becomes directly involved in making law-of-war decisions concerning the conduct of hostilities.

The law of war—in today's parlance the law of armed conflict—is typically divided into two categories. One, called *jus ad bellum* (justice of war), has to do with the propriety of going to war—the question of whether the use of force is legitimate. The other, *jus in bello* (justice in war), concerns the conduct of warfare. This latter category, which also goes by the name of international humanitarian law, can be further subdivided into two parts, though there is some overlap. What has come to be known as the Law of The Hague (in reference to international treaties negotiated in that city) focuses on the means and methods of combat. The Law of Geneva, codified in successive versions of the Geneva Conventions and subsequent protocols, spells out protections for prisoners of war, wounded soldiers, civilians, and others caught up in hostilities.[71]

When dealing with a sworn enemy in time of war, especially one whose modus operandi is to target civilians in plain violation of international law, it is no doubt tempting to act without restraint. Perhaps there is no greater test of the capacity of law to regulate social behavior. Yet so far as the historical record goes, people have felt the need to recognize rules of warfare as long as they have fought wars.[72] Modern treaties regulating the conduct of warfare sprang from a humanitarian impulse, to be sure, but one tempered by a practical understanding that people would continue to resort to war, that war is inherently cruel, and that it inevitably brings suffering. The overall aim, which found expression in prefatory language of treaties on the subject, was to moderate war's effects. The St. Petersburg Declaration of 1868, one of the earliest of these international agreements, linked the "progress of civilization" to "alleviating as much as possible the calamities of war." Hague Convention IV of 1907 pointed to "the desire to diminish the evils of war."[73]

This nascent international movement was put to the test in the first half of the twentieth century, as one world war followed another, culminating in the horrors of World War II, with its grotesque medical experiments, massacres, mass starvation, and genocide. Still there persisted a stubborn faith in the capacity of law to supply meaningful constraints on the conduct of warfare, and the story of this historical period is one of a deepening international commitment to the laws of war, thanks in no small part to the efforts of the United States.[74]

In the aftermath of World War II, the idea began to take hold that all persons committing war crimes—from soldiers in the lowest ranks to heads of state—were criminally liable for their actions. As part of the human rights revolution that followed that conflict, a legal framework was put in place with enforcement machinery to prosecute war crimes unlike anything that had previously existed. The Nuremberg trials of Nazi war criminals along with the Tokyo war crimes trials established individual criminal responsibility as the norm. The Geneva Conventions of 1949 set up an apparatus for enforcing it. The conventions required nations to prosecute or extradite for prosecution anyone who committed serious violations called "grave breaches." These included torture and inhuman treatment. If the conventions' mandate were fulfilled, war criminals would find no sanctuary. Even nations having no connection to an armed conflict have a legal obligation to bring those accused of such offenses to trial.[75]

For various reasons (the Cold War chief among them), it was not until the end of the twentieth century that this Nuremberg/Geneva model of accountability came of age. In the 1990s, the United Nations established ad hoc international tribunals first for the former Yugoslavia and then for Rwanda. Empowered to try individuals for committing war crimes, genocide, and crimes against humanity,[76] these tribunals provided the impetus for the establishment of the International Criminal Court, a permanent court with jurisdiction over the same types of cases plus the crime of aggression.[77] Some countries (e.g., Cambodia, East Timor, and Sierra Leone) set up special hybrid tribunals composed of national and international judges to address human rights abuses committed within their borders. The principle of universal jurisdiction seemed on the verge of becoming a reality after Spanish judges charged officials from Chile, Argentina, and Guatemala, with the most famous case involving General Augusto Pinochet, Chile's former head of state. In the meantime, a growing number of nations resorted to domestic prosecutions for human rights violations—a trend that got its start in Greece in the 1970s, with Argentina's prosecutions relating to its so-called dirty war among the most influential.[78] So dramatic were these developments that scholars have been led to describe them as a "justice cascade" and an "age of human rights accountability."[79] Gone were the days when powerful leaders could claim immunity from prosecution for war crimes and crimes against humanity.

Or so it seemed. As fate would have it, it was at this point in time that the war against terrorism began. It goes too far to say that the failure to prosecute those responsible for the Bush administration's interrogation program single-handedly reversed the progress that had been made on so many fronts. At the very least, this conspicuous failure in accountability cast a pall over the various efforts to enforce international humanitarian law and human rights laws at a critical stage in their development.

A point on the terminology used in international humanitarian law should be addressed before going further. In this book, the basic legal rule in question is phrased as a requirement for "humane treatment." That is the language of Common Article 3, the most relevant treaty provision, which states that "persons taking no active part in the hostilities . . . shall in all circumstances be treated humanely." That wording also appears in President Bush's critical memorandum of February 7, 2002, even its title. Following the logic of that word construction, this book also refers to the rule as a prohibition against "inhumane" treatment. At the same time, it should be noted that several human rights treaties, including other provisions of the Geneva Conventions, speak of "inhuman treatment," usually in a catch-all provision forbidding "cruel, inhuman, and degrading treatment." Accordingly, when this book takes up treaties or legislation that incorporate the word "inhuman," the corresponding discussion follows that word usage. The question that naturally arises is whether using one and not the other makes a difference, especially as a matter of law. This book posits that it does: a rule requiring humane treatment sets forth a more exacting standard of conduct. Without plumbing all the definitional complexities, suffice it to say that the distinction applied here accords with what might be taken to be the ordinary meaning of these words. "Inhumane" refers to cruel treatment that causes suffering while "inhuman" treatment necessarily involves extremely cruel behavior.[80]

Although the task of writing this book was not undertaken in order to respond directly to other works, it can be viewed as entering into a dialogue with *Power and Constraint: The Accountable Presidency after 9/11*, written by Harvard law professor Jack Goldsmith. He believed that the war against terrorism led to an "unnoticed revolution" in "wartime presidential accountability," as Congress, the courts, and the press "pushed back far harder against the Commander in Chief than in any other war" in US history. "Never before," Goldsmith said, had a wartime president "been so influenced, and constrained, by law."[81] The key in his view was how an extended network of untraditional accountability mechanisms (national security lawyers, human rights organizations, and even bloggers) worked in combination with long-established checks on the president: a well-sourced news report here, a Freedom of Information Act disclosure there, a blogger's critical analysis follows, an inspector general conducts an investigation, and Congress and the courts are compelled to weigh in. It would be impossible, Goldsmith suggested, for any president to withstand the scrutiny of so many actors.[82]

This book takes a different view. It contends that, for all the apparent novelty of President Bush's interrogation program, his actions fit a larger historical pattern of presidential behavior. It further suggests that the accountability breakdown that occurred here reflects fundamental problems with the American constitutional system and its checks on the presidency. Without going so far as to say that the various accountability checks can never moderate presidential conduct, the findings derived from this episode may be generalized to suggest how and why they provide an unreliable counterweight against the abuse of executive power in wartime. While the administration's interrogation policy did not go unchallenged, none of the accountability mechanisms stopped President Bush from violating the Geneva Conventions. Hardly anything of consequence was done to hold those involved to account afterwards. It is difficult to see how anyone could claim that President Bush was held personally accountable.

This book's argument is presented in five chapters. Chapter 1 frames the analysis by examining the development of the laws of war and the modern concept of war crimes accountability. Chapter 2 reconstructs the Bush administration's internal decision-making process on the Geneva Conventions and explains how his conception of presidential power factored into his decision on the laws of war. The remaining chapters assess the breakdown of the principal accountability mechanisms in the American system of government. Chapter 3 examines Congress's actions while chapter 4 looks at the judiciary, with the focus placed on the Supreme Court. Chapter 5 explores the public's reaction through a close analysis of the torture debate.

The aim in laying out this book's argument, it bears emphasizing, is not to spur prosecutors to reopen investigations or take action against President Bush, but rather to explore the complexities of presidential accountability in wartime. If it is naive to expect that a US president could be prosecuted, no matter how grievous the crime, what does that say about the presidency? And what does it reveal about the state of American constitutional democracy today if it has become practically impossible to hold a president accountable for serious crimes of war?

CHAPTER ONE

The Law of War

The usual reasons given to justify prosecuting those involved in the mistreatment of detainees—the conventional arguments as they might be called—had a linear logic. "Criminal justice for criminal policy," it was said. Passing reference was made to the rule of law. The nation's "legal duty to prosecute" under treaties was duly noted. The most frequently cited was the Convention Against Torture, which requires nations to prosecute offenders or extradite them to countries that will. Those in favor of criminal accountability suggested that prosecutions best served the purpose of deterrence.[1]

These arguments were not necessarily wrong, but they did not fully capture what was at stake. This chapter offers a rationale for holding President Bush accountable that is grounded in the laws of war. One way to do that would be to undertake a detailed legal analysis of selected provisions of the Geneva Conventions. This chapter approaches this question differently. On the view that the president by his actions presented a serious challenge to the laws of war—a challenge, more fundamentally, to the very idea of having a law of war—the aim here is to provide a broader historical perspective. The chapter begins by sketching the overall development of the laws of war in order to offer some sense of why people throughout recorded history have recognized the laws of war and what they were meant to do. It then puts President Bush's actions in the context of the human rights revolution following World War II. The focus there is placed on the adoption of the 1949 Geneva Conventions, the central value of which, it is argued, was the humane treatment of anyone not actively engaged in hostilities. To convey something of what was lost by the failure to hold President Bush accountable, the chapter explains the meaning and significance of the Nuremberg principle of individual criminal accountability by tracing the evolution of war crimes accountability. It closes with a summary analysis of the Geneva Conventions' applicability to the war against terrorism.

I

Given the Bush administration's cavalier attitude toward the laws of war,[2] the first point to be made is simply to reflect on the fact that there is a law of war and what that means at its most basic level. The animating principle behind this body of law, as restated in the Hague Regulations of 1907, is that the "right of belligerents to adopt means of injuring the enemy is not unlimited."[3] By itself this language does not identify what is permissible and what is prohibited (other provisions in the Hague Regulations do some of that work), but it is important on its own as an assertion that there are limits in war. Behind this language is a crucial idea—a conviction no less—that law can regulate the use of force and supply meaningful constraints when the temptation is greatest to ignore all restraints.

So far as can be determined, there have always been rules regulating the conduct of warfare. For centuries these rules were mostly unwritten, drawn from practical experience and passed from one generation to the next in the form of custom. By the time of the Peloponnesian War, ancient Greeks could point to the rules of combat established by the "common customs" of the Hellenes.[4] In many places around the world, rules governing warfare found expression in premodern codes of conduct for warriors such as India's Code of Manu, the Japanese samurai's Bushido, and the Islamic law of nations.[5]

Notwithstanding regional variation, the laws of war shared some basic features. There were rules regulating the use of weapons. Poison was almost universally condemned. Religious sites often had protected status.[6] Issues regarding tactics were addressed if not fully resolved. Deception may well be a time-honored aspect of warfare, but it was generally acknowledged that there must be some limit to its use, though the line between perfidy and legitimate ruse was not always clear.[7] A number of cultural traditions proscribed the killing of prisoners and enemy wounded, as well as women and children not engaged in fighting—in essence providing some minimal standard for the protection of individuals not engaged in combat.[8]

While such practices might appear to anticipate modern humanitarian concerns, the rules of war were for a long time limited in scope and unenforceable in practice. And just as the laws of war have an ancient pedigree, so too do accounts of their violation. Indeed, if one central theme stands out in the history of warfare, it is the difficulty of relying on the law to constrain conduct in battle.

The Middle Ages is often regarded as a formative stage in the history of the laws of war.[9] The law of chivalry covered an impressive range of issues (immunity of pages, grounds for reprisal, use of poison, activities during a truce, for example). An elaborate legal system came into being, complete with courts like England's Court of Chivalry that specialized in the "law of arms." While cases often involved contractual claims concerning prisoners' ransoms and the spoils of war, that does not detract from the image of knights submitting to legal process to resolve their disputes. Perhaps above all else, the law of arms in the age of chivalry affirmed two key points: first, that there were limits to what was acceptable in warfare, and second, that standards could be established to judge the conduct of those engaged in battle.[10]

Yet from the standpoint of today's standards, the code of chivalry left much to be desired. Its rigid hierarchy did not prohibit the killing of common soldiers captured or wounded in battle, and there could be many in that category (archers, gunners, town militias, armed peasants—essentially anyone on foot). Knights could be denied quarter so long as their enemy had given proper notice that they would be engaged in a war to the death, a task easily accomplished by displaying a red banner before battle. In siege warfare, a major part of wars then, an army besieging a city was entitled to kill all of its inhabitants unless they surrendered. There was no legal prohibition against the rape of women by the victors. Whether under siege or not, average laborers fared poorly in the wars of the Middle Ages.[11]

It is difficult to say that the lot of the general population had improved by the time of the Thirty Years' War (1618–48), which left several million dead. In the midst of that conflict, Dutch lawyer Hugo Grotius complained of "a lack of restraint" in warfare. "When arms have once been taken up there is no longer any respect for law," he wrote, "as if, in accordance with a general decree, frenzy had openly been let loose for the committing of all crimes."[12]

This state of affairs prompted Grotius to write a massive treatise on the subject, *De Jure Belli ac Pacis*. For this work he was later hailed as the father of international law. Other jurists in the early modern period, seemingly from all corners of western Europe—Spain's Francisco de Vitoria, Oxford University's Professor of Civil Law Alberico Gentili (originally from Italy), and Samuel von Pufendorf of Germany, to name a few—had also begun to articulate principles that began to give the laws of war a modern cast. Among their most important contributions was to redefine the relationship between *jus ad bellum* and *jus in bello*. Previously, with just war theory the reigning paradigm, whatever legal protections existed under the laws of war did not extend to those deemed to be fighting an unjust war. Several writers, notably Christian von Wolff and

Emmerich de Vattel, suggested instead that the laws of war should protect all soldiers in combat, regardless of the justice of their position.[13]

Meantime, armies in the emerging nation-states of early modern Europe were starting to professionalize. Soldiers began to receive regular wages— that was by itself consequential, as their predecessors had relied on plunder as compensation for their services. Several countries adopted more comprehensive written articles of war to regulate their soldiers' behavior. England's Laws and Ordinances of Warre made infractions punishable "according to the general customs and laws of war."[14]

By the eighteenth century, warfare in Europe appeared to contemporaries to have entered a new stage. "At the present war is conducted by regular armies," said Vattel in 1758. "Ordinary people take no part and as a rule have nothing to fear from the enemy." No less a historian than Edward Gibbon described the century's wars as "temperate," a view echoed across the Atlantic by Alexander Hamilton.[15] Several factors contributed to the apparent change: the end of religious wars; economic constraints on manpower and supplies; standing armies and strong fortifications; and a shift in focus among European powers to colonies and overseas trade.[16] But if some in Europe believed that war on the continent had forever evolved into something like "games of chance in which no one risks his all," they were in for a rude awakening with the French Revolution and the Napoleonic Wars.[17]

Besides, there was a recognized category of warfare that no one could mistake for a game of any kind. These were wars to the death in which no quarter was given, no prisoners taken, and noncombatants and wounded soldiers could be slaughtered. Lawyers in the Middle Ages had a name for wars like these. They called them *bellum romanum*, in recognition of ancient Rome's reputation for ruthless military campaigns. This medieval classification applied at first to wars against peoples outside Christendom—when Charlemagne fought pagan Saxons and the Crusaders battled Muslims in the Holy Land. But once the logic of *bellum romanum* took hold—in effect legitimizing anything otherwise forbidden by the laws of war—there seemed to be no end to its usefulness. If wars to the death were justified against heathen, then why not against "rebels" and "savages"? On that basis, without the customary restraints on warfare, the English subdued the Irish, the Spanish conquistadors destroyed the Inca and Aztec empires, and British colonists warred against Native American tribes.[18]

As the European law-of-war tradition was poised between the publicists' modernizing efforts and the expansive concept of *bellum romanum*, a crucial step in the development of the modern laws of armed conflict came by way of the United States. Midway through the Civil War, President Abraham Lincoln issued General Order No. 100, *Instructions for the Government of the Armies of the United States in the Field*, a written compilation of the laws and customs of war. The need for such a code had become evident as the US Army grew from a few thousand professionals scattered across the country and its broad frontier to a military force approximately one million strong, comprised mostly of volunteers and draftees.[19]

This code was written by Francis Lieber, for whom it was named. He was well suited to the task. A German émigré who had served in the Prussian army at the close of the Napoleonic Wars, Lieber had established himself as an authority on the laws of war while delivering lectures on that subject as a professor at Columbia College in New York. Before writing the code, he had commented in public letters to the *New York Times* on some of the difficult law-of-war issues brought on by the Civil War.[20]

In looking through the Lieber Code's 157 articles, one might easily conclude that he was of two minds on the subject. In the words of John Fabian Witt, the code displayed a "tough humanitarianism."[21] It certainly was not "namby pamby," a phrase Lieber used to dismiss law-of-war theorists of the European Enlightenment, whose approach to this subject was all too gentlemanly for the former Prussian soldier. "The more vigorously wars are pursued, the better it is for humanity," he believed, but some propositions he deduced from that premise would be rejected today.[22] For instance, his code permitted the starvation of unarmed belligerents, the bombardment of civilians in cities, and the execution of prisoners of war when necessary.[23]

On the other hand, the code was infused with a basic humanitarianism that laid the groundwork for the modern laws of armed conflict. Military necessity, a guiding principle for Lieber, was broadly defined in the code but not without limit. He emphasized that "military necessity does not admit of cruelty." The code distinguished noncombatants from combatants: "the unarmed citizen is to be spared in person, property, and honour as much as the exigencies of war will admit." The intentional wounding of "wholly disabled" enemy troops was prohibited on penalty of death. Prisoners of war were to be "treated with humanity"[24] and subject to "no other intentional suffering or indignity" beyond imprisonment.[25] Torture, poison, and "wanton devastation" were explicitly prohibited.[26] "Men who take up arms," Lieber wrote, "do not cease on this account to be moral beings, responsible to one another and to God."[27]

According to Theodor Meron, the Lieber Code's "foundation in broad humanitarian principles" had "tremendous impact" on subsequent international treaties mapping out the laws of war.[28] As it turned out, this was an auspicious time for international humanitarian law on both sides of the Atlantic. The same year the Lieber Code was put into effect, the International Committee for Relief to the Wounded, forerunner of the International Committee of the Red Cross (ICRC), was founded in Geneva, Switzerland, and the first Geneva Convention was adopted in 1864. Viewed in isolation, what was achieved there was limited in several respects. The document produced was brief in comparison with subsequent treaties, its protections only covered wounded soldiers, and no more than a dozen nations signed at the conference (it was left open for others to approve later).[29]

Yet this first Geneva conference inaugurated a series of multilateral conferences.[30] The St. Petersburg Declaration of 1868 was the first international treaty to ban the use of a particular weapon, in this case an explosive bullet that made wounds more severe. Especially noteworthy was its statement on unnecessary suffering—one of the defining principles of the modern laws of armed conflict. "Arms which uselessly aggravate the sufferings of disabled men, or render their death inevitable," it said, are "contrary to the laws of humanity."[31]

Two peace conferences at The Hague around the turn of the century (1899 and 1907) focused on the means and methods of warfare. Annexed regulations forbade poisoned weapons, arms calculated to cause unnecessary suffering, pillage, attacks on undefended towns, and the improper use of a flag of truce, among other things.[32] Notwithstanding the usual bifurcation made between Hague law (means and methods of combat) and Geneva law (protection of persons), the Annex to Hague Convention IV also covered prisoners of war.[33] The Geneva Convention of 1906 enhanced Geneva's framework to safeguard wounded and sick combatants. The 1929 Geneva Conventions, the last word on this branch of the law before World War II, supplemented its predecessors with a number of protections for prisoners of war.[34]

This effort to codify the laws of war must have appeared idealistic to some, but it was at bottom a pragmatic exercise. It sprang from an understanding that people would continue to engage in wars. The goal was to regulate the conduct of warfare in order to mitigate human suffering, as treaties like the St. Petersburg Declaration of 1868 suggested ("alleviating as much as possible the calamities of war").[35]

Given what happened in the two world wars, the first eighty years of the codification movement cannot be rated an unqualified success. Undeterred, the International Committee of the Red Cross launched an initiative to revise the 1929 Geneva Conventions as World War II drew to a close.[36] Its efforts culminated in the adoption of the Geneva Conventions of 1949.

II

The four 1949 conventions built on previous iterations shown by experience to be insufficient to accomplish Geneva's fundamental purpose of protecting individuals caught up in armed conflicts. They covered wounded and sick armed forces on land (GC I), those who were wounded, sick, and shipwrecked at sea (GC II), prisoners of war (GC III), and civilians (GC IV). No international treaty has been more widely accepted, though compliance has been mixed.[37] The United States was among the original signatories, and the Senate endorsed the conventions in 1955.

Among the most important innovations in the 1949 Geneva Conventions was the approach taken for holding persons criminally liable. The conventions did not specify criminal penalties for war crimes. Indeed, the phrase "war crimes" nowhere appears in the conventions.[38] Its drafters developed a regime of what they called "grave breaches" for international conflicts including, for example, "wilful killing, torture or inhuman treatment" of persons protected by the conventions.[39] To enforce this system of grave breaches, the Geneva Conventions required nations to establish "effective penal sanctions for persons committing, or ordering to be committed, any of the grave breaches." They also imposed an affirmative obligation on nations to arrest persons who commit grave breaches and either prosecute them or extradite them to other countries for prosecution.[40]

The 1949 Geneva Conventions cover a multitude of topics relating to the conduct of war. As chapter 2 explains, President Bush sought to relieve the United States of any legal obligation under the conventions to treat detainees humanely. In doing so, he transgressed what might reasonably be considered Geneva's most basic rule—arguably the paramount value underlying modern international humanitarian law.

When the Geneva Conventions were adopted in 1949, there was precedent for viewing the humane treatment of captured individuals as a fundamental norm of warfare. This idea was abroad during the Enlightenment—a natural corollary of the overall philosophy of a common humanity. It is not surprising to find the legislators of the French Revolution expressing the sentiment in general terms. In accordance with the "principles of justice and humanity," the National Assembly of France declared in 1792, prisoners of war would be "safeguarded by the Nation" and given "special protection of the Law." Any "unjustifiable severities, or insults, violence or homicidal assaults" against enemy prisoners would be "punished by the same Laws" as if "those excesses had been committed against Frenchmen." This directive was ahead of its time; alas, too far ahead, as the conduct of the French—and their enemies—in the Revolutionary and the Napoleonic Wars would reveal.[41]

Perhaps no one in this period showed a greater commitment to this Enlightenment ideal under more trying circumstances than George Washington did during the American Revolution. It would have been easy—some might say amply justified—for General Washington to have forsaken any thought of treating the British humanely in light of their conduct. There were incendiary reports of redcoats and their Hessian allies denying quarter and slaughtering wounded American soldiers on the field in Long Island, Fort Washington, and Princeton. The account of the fighting at Drake's Farm in New Jersey was widely circulated. The British, it was reported, refused to accept the surrender of wounded and then "dashed out their brains with their muskets and ran them through with their bayonets."[42] The conditions endured by American soldiers taken prisoner were abominable—"inhuman treatment" was the phrase a congressional committee used. While British forces faced logistical problems they had not anticipated, the fact remains that nearly half of the Americans they imprisoned died while held captive, many on prison ships around New York.[43]

Washington's correspondence reveals that the treatment of Americans imprisoned by the British was an abiding concern of his throughout the war. Appealing directly to his British counterparts (General Thomas Gage, Admiral Richard Howe, and General William Howe), Washington objected to the "cruel" and "barbarous" treatment of captured Americans. He demanded that the British treat prisoners in accord with the "Rights of Humanity."[44] Though he threatened to retaliate (as permitted under contemporary understandings of the laws of war),[45] Washington admonished his own soldiers to treat British soldiers taken prisoner with humanity. He directed Colonel Benedict Arnold to treat prisoners taken on his expedition to Canada "with as much Humanity & Kindness as may be consistent with your own Safety & the publick Interest." Washington delivered the same message to the lieutenant colonel he put in charge of British privates captured in the battle of Princeton. "Treat them with humanity, and Let them have no reason to Complain of our Copying the brutal example of the Brittish Army in their Treatment of our unfortunate bretheren who have fallen into their hands."[46]

Had it not been for Washington, the Americans might well have engaged in a tit for tat with the enemy. No doubt he acted out of practical self-interest: first, in the hope that humane treatment begets humane treatment; second, with the understanding that inhumane treatment invites retaliation in kind; and third, on the view that "wanton Cruelty" is counterproductive to military objectives.[47] This was also an effort on Washington's part to shake the British from their view of Americans as rebels and traitors. In effect, by insisting that his troops be treated as soldiers, Washington was asserting that the United States was an equal sovereign nation.[48] Washington also had a broader interest in aligning the newfound republic's military practices with the Enlightenment view of human dignity. The general was no student of Enlightenment philosophy as, say, Thomas Jefferson was, but in his repeated orders and demands for humane treatment, Washington was speaking the language of the Enlightenment.

The story of the humane treatment of prisoners of war was next taken up in the American Civil War. The need for rules on this subject did not escape the notice of Francis Lieber. Article 76 of his code set forth the basic formula: prisoners shall be "treated with humanity." More detailed statements can be found elsewhere, as in Article 56, which prohibited taking revenge upon enemy prisoners by "intentional infliction of any suffering, or disgrace, by cruel imprisonment, want of food, by mutilation, death, or any barbarity."[49]

In the international conferences that followed over the next several decades, other matters such as the methods of warfare and care for the wounded took precedence over the treatment of prisoners. Yet those involved in the effort to codify the laws of war never abandoned the humane treatment of soldiers hors de combat as a basic goal. The Brussels Conference on Proposed Rules for Military Warfare in 1874 recognized prisoners as "lawful and disarmed enemies" who "must be humanely treated." This last phrase was restated in the 1907 Hague Regulations and the 1929 Geneva Conventions.[50]

So far, so good, it might be thought, but to this point in time the idea of humane treatment could be read as just that—an idea that was aspirational in nature, more of a moral obligation than a binding legal requirement. In the Napoleonic Wars, neither the French nor their enemies lived up to the standard set forth by the French National Assembly. The fact that Washington was repeatedly compelled to make demands of British generals for the sake of American prisoners speaks for itself. The Lieber Code permitted troops to kill prisoners when required for their "own salvation." It also declared prisoners liable to retaliatory measures.[51] The Brussels Conference on Proposed Rules ended without reaching a final written agreement. And whatever the Hague Regulations and the 1929 Geneva Conventions accomplished, World War II certainly exposed their limitations.

Written in the wake of that war, the 1949 Geneva Conventions were shaped to a considerable degree by what happened there. For prisoners of war in the hands of the Axis powers, the Second World War set a new low. The mortality rate for Americans in Japanese prison camps exceeded 40 percent. Among the worst prison camps for British Commonwealth soldiers was Sandakan, near Borneo. Of two thousand Australians and five hundred British imprisoned there, all but six died while imprisoned there.[52] With notable exceptions (for one, the massacre of US troops who had surrendered at Malmedy during the Battle of the Bulge), American and British prisoners of war in the European theater fared better than those in the Pacific, but the fate of Soviet soldiers was something else again. Of the 5.7 million taken prisoner by German forces, 3.3 million died.[53] And members of the resistance to Nazi occupation throughout Europe knew well what fate lay in store for them if caught by the Gestapo.

In its impact on civilians, the Second World War has no analogue in world history. The total number of people killed by war's end was fifty-five million; nearly two-thirds were civilians.[54] Many were subjected to cruelty that few would have thought possible previously. Without recounting all of the mind-numbing details, one has only to think of what took place at Nanking, Leningrad, and Warsaw, not to mention the Holocaust.

It should come as no surprise, then, that the protection of all sorts of people caught up in armed conflicts was of the utmost concern following World War II. With the adoption of the Geneva Conventions of 1949, the humane treatment of anyone not actively engaged in combat was sanctified as the core value of the laws of war.

The original Red Cross commentaries on the conventions shed light on this. The ICRC, having taken the lead in the effort to revise the 1929 Geneva Conventions, was deeply involved in the process of drafting the 1949 version. After coordinating preliminary conferences and consulting with government representatives, the ICRC put together the drafts used in the final diplomatic conference in Geneva. Its experts were on hand throughout the negotiations.[55] Once agreement was reached by the governments represented, ICRC lawyers contributed to the commentaries under the general editorship of Jean S. Pictet, the committee's director. They produced one volume for each convention, published seriatim in the decade following the conference.[56]

Evidence of the singular importance attached to humane treatment can be found in the commentaries' behind-the-scenes account of the drafting process that led to Common Article 3 ("common" because this article appears as the third article in each of the 1949 Geneva Conventions). This article requires the humane treatment of "persons taking no active part in the hostilities" in non-international conflicts (see appendix B). Its roots can be traced to a preamble drafted for the new civilian convention at the International Red Cross Conference held in Stockholm in 1948. That preamble enumerated rules that, taken to reflect "universal human law," were said to apply "at any time and in all places." One was that "individuals shall be protected against any violence to their life and limb." Another "strictly prohibited" torture "of any kind." The other rules banned summary executions and the taking of hostages.[57]

The ICRC took up the idea of having a single preamble common to all four conventions. The thinking was that it was asking too much "to expect every soldier and every civilian to know the details" of several hundred provisions, but if a preamble could be drawn up to state the "basic principle on which all the Conventions repose," then it would be possible for "anyone of good faith" to act in accordance with Geneva's requirements.[58]

The ICRC's proposed preamble began by affirming "respect for the personality and dignity of human beings" as a binding "universal principle." What followed was language that would find its way into Common Article 3. "Such a principle demands that, in time of war, all those not actively engaged in the hostilities and all those placed *hors de combat* by reason of sickness, wounds, capture, or any other circumstance, shall be given due respect and have protection from the effects of war."[59] By itself this passage drew no objections, but diplomatic conferences being what they are, this draft preamble got bogged down in a debate over additional provisions proposed by government delegates. Some insisted that the preamble should connect human rights to the "divine origin" of humankind. Others thought it should spell out sanctions for violating the conventions. Unable to resolve the impasse over these proposals, the conference ended up opening each convention with a cursory preamble that omits any reference to underlying principles.[60]

At this point, the narrative shifts to the debate over what should be done about non-international conflicts—the subject of Common Article 3. Within the Red Cross community, there was a push to apply the Geneva Conventions fully to such conflicts. That never had much chance of success, but a consensus emerged in favor of applying Geneva's basic principles to the non-international arena by stating "a minimum of humanitarian provisions."[61] To do that, the delegates looked to the draft preamble, as a side-by-side comparison with Common Article 3 reveals. Both prohibited violence, torture, the taking of hostages, and executions without judicial safeguards. In addition, the description of protected persons is almost identical. Compare the language proposed for the preamble ("in time of war, all those not actively engaged in the hostilities and all those placed *hors de combat* by reason of sickness, wounds, capture, or any other circumstance") with Common Article 3 ("persons taking no active part in the hostilities, including members of armed forces who have laid down their arms and those placed *hors de combat* by sickness, wounds, detention, or any other cause").[62]

In this way, Common Article 3—a "Convention in miniature" as it has been called—became the repository of the 1949 Geneva Conventions' central principle. "We find expressed here," the Red Cross commentary stated in reference to Common Article 3's humane treatment provision, the "fundamental principle underlying the four Geneva Conventions,"[63] elsewhere described in the commentaries as the "guiding principle common to all the Geneva Conventions,"[64] the conventions' "*raison d'être*," the "essential motive which had brought sixty-four nations together at Geneva," the "justification" for the Geneva Conventions, its "basic theme," "the *leitmotiv* of the four Geneva Conventions,"[65] and "the few essential rules of humanity which all civilized nations consider as valid everywhere and under all circumstances and as being above and outside war itself."[66]

III

Notwithstanding the considerable progress made in developing the rules and regulations governing the conduct of warfare, it may be said with some justification that the history of the laws of war is a history of the struggle to enforce them. Put another way, the chief obstacle in making the laws of war work has not been figuring out what the rules are so much as it has been in punishing those who violate them. Written codes adopted in the last 150 years have undoubtedly become more detailed, and some rules, like those concerning humane treatment, have assumed greater importance. Yet the historical record indicates that many peoples shared an intuitive understanding of what constitutes acceptable conduct in warfare. It was not entirely new when moderns said that it was wrong to use poison, kill prisoners, or destroy religious sites. What was new was the conception of the law of war as a *law* of war—a legally binding and enforceable set of rules—and what followed from that, the idea that individuals could be tried and punished for committing war crimes.

In taking that view, one is immediately met with the objection that war crimes trials can be traced well back in history. Scholars have found precedent of a sort as far back as the Peloponnesian War, though most cases cited as precursors date from the Middle Ages onward. Some concerned historical figures of note, including, for example, Sir William Wallace (the protagonist in Hollywood's *Braveheart*), who was put on trial in England in 1305. Others remain obscure, such as the case of a certain Conradin von Hohandstafen, who is sometimes described as being tried in Naples in 1268 for starting a war. Often cited is the trial of Sir Peter von Hagenbach, who was convicted in 1474 of murder and rape, among other things, for his abusive rule of an Austrian town.[67] Further advances were made in the early modern period. The Free Netherlands and Sweden were among the first to adopt articles of war that subjected soldiers to courts martial for violating them, and Spain set up tribunals to investigate the excesses of its own soldiers in its wars with the Dutch.[68]

While it may be possible to string together a handful of trials that might appear to resemble war crimes trials in some way, there is a danger in reading too much into these purported historical antecedents. One can be forgiven for having the nagging suspicion that as a general proposition war crimes trials before the twentieth century simply failed to materialize. Considering the extent of warfare and the frequent violations of the rules of war, there are few examples of anything that looks like a war crimes trial. And of those, there is room to argue over whether contemporaries regarded them as war crimes trials. Hagenbach, for example, was guilty of serious crimes, but some commentators are reluctant to classify his trial as a war crimes trial for the simple reason that there was no war at the time (others say he was in charge of a military occupation). It is true that soldiers were subject to courts martial for violating articles of war in some European nations, but these seemed more in the nature of disciplinary proceedings than war crimes trials. Hilaire McCoubrey suggests that advances in the thinking about the law of war in the early modern period were not accompanied by any "significant trials" that "could be taken to refer to war crimes *stricto sensu*."[69]

The interpretive difficulty, strange as it may seem, is that there was no clear juridical conception of war crimes as such. The recognition of customary rules of warfare did not translate into a concrete understanding that individuals who violated these customs and practices had committed crimes of war for which they should be tried. There are no contemporary records of any of these trials in which the phrase "war crimes" was used. In fact, there appears to be no record of anyone using that phrase before 1872.[70]

True, in the eighteenth century, there were suggestive commentaries on point, but they remained undeveloped. William Blackstone affirmed the government's authority to punish its own soldiers for violating the law of nations, and Vattel remarked in passing that a prisoner of war "personally guilty of some crime" could be punished by his captors.[71] By the end of the century, the set of options for responding to an enemy who violated the laws of war consisted in self-help measures—a concession by itself of the lack of enforcement machinery—designed to compel the enemy to abide by the laws of war. Essentially these were forms of retaliation, including retortion (the suspension of privileges of enemy nationals) and reprisal (the seizure of enemy property).[72]

An important step leading to the modern notion of war crimes was taken by the US Army in the war with Mexico. Confronted by Mexicans engaged in guerrilla warfare, General Winfield Scott had them brought before tribunals he called "councils of war" in the belief that their tactics violated "every rule of warfare observed by civilized nations."[73] After that conflict, the US Army abandoned Scott's terminology of "councils of war" but used military commissions from the Civil War to the Philippine Insurrection that followed the Spanish-American War. The United States was not alone in this practice. The British employed military commissions during the Boer War in South Africa.[74]

If these military commissions can be taken as a step toward the modern war crimes trial, the emphasis should remain on their preliminary nature. The wide variety of conduct brought before American military commissions as law-of-war violations indicates that there was still no clear juridical conception of war crimes as that term would be later understood. During the Civil War, the Union Army considered law-of-war violations to include noncombatants using "disloyal language," stealing horses, forging discharge papers, and sending letters of encouragement to Southerners.[75]

It might be thought that the same concerns that inspired those involved in the movement to codify the laws of war would have led them to consider war crimes prosecutions as well. They saw the problem as later generations would (with the goal of stopping people from violating the laws of war), but they had a different solution. In the view of Lieber and other jurists, the key to getting soldiers to obey the laws of war was to have those laws clearly stated and widely disseminated (hence the interest in codification). Once that happened, it was thought that there would be no need to prosecute soldiers for violating the laws of war.[76] This sentiment is best captured in a statement by Gustave Moynier, founding member of the ICRC. In 1870, he said that the "tribunal of public conscience" and the prospect of "being ostracized by civilized nations" would provide a "powerful enough deterrent."[77]

The Franco-Prussian War of that same year provided the impetus for reassessing that view, and within a decade European jurists and diplomats started thinking of violations of the laws of war as punishable crimes. The phrase "war crimes" appeared in print for the first time in an 1872 work by jurist Johann Caspar Bluntschli in reference to actions taken by the so-called franc-tireurs in that war. While Bluntschli's terminology did not catch on immediately (international lawyer Lassa Oppenheim usually receives credit for coming up with the phrase three decades later), jurists and diplomats floated various proposals edging toward war crimes accountability. In 1872, Moynier promoted the idea of having a permanent international tribunal to enforce the 1864 Geneva Convention. He also drafted a provision for the Institute of International Law's *Oxford Manual of the Laws of War on Land* (the manual was conceived as a model for domestic legislation) that required persons who violated the laws of war to be brought before a "judicial hearing" and punished appropriately. At the Brussels conference of fifteen European nations in 1874, the French representative proposed a "common penal code" governing the laws of war for nations to adopt.[78] None of these proposals came to fruition before World War I.

It was during that war that the conception of war crimes making its way through elite circles—the subject of legal commentary and diplomatic conferences—came to occupy a central place in public discourse, certainly among Allied nations. German troops, pushing their way through neutral Belgium on a strict timetable in accordance with the Schlieffen Plan, encountered unexpected resistance in that lowland country. Their response provided all that was needed for Allied propaganda, which made the most of the "rape of Belgium." False reports (German troops bayoneting babies) were given credence by what actually happened, with an estimated 6,500 Belgian civilians killed, including some taken hostage and executed in reprisals. The German army's actions were described as war crimes, and the public demanded trials of those responsible, including Kaiser Wilhelm II. Only two months had elapsed from the start of the war before the French military put three German prisoners of war on trial for pillage. Talk of war crimes continued throughout the war, especially in Great Britain, where public outrage was heightened by the Germans' execution of English nurse Edith Cavell (she admitted hiding Allied soldiers and assisting them to escape from Belgium), U-boat attacks, and Zeppelin bombings of cities in England. Under the pressure of public opinion, punishing those responsible for war crimes became a primary war aim.[79]

The first order of business taken up at the Paris peace conference was the question of war crimes. The Treaty of Versailles spelled out a twofold answer. One, Kaiser Wilhelm II, "publicly arraign[ed]" for "a supreme offence against international morality and the sanctity of treaties," was to be tried before a "special tribunal." Two, the German government was compelled to recognize the right of the victorious Allies to "bring before military tribunals" Germans accused of violating the laws of war. Under the terms of the treaty, Germany was supposed to "hand over" those identified by the Allies for trial,[80] but so great was the outcry in the defeated nation that the Allies accepted the Weimar Republic's counterproposal to have the Reichsgericht, Germany's supreme court, try its own in Leipzig.[81]

Numbers attest to how badly this came off, at least from the Allies' perspective. The Allied powers had originally identified several thousand Germans to be tried. Concern over Weimar's instability led the Allies to reduce the number to less than nine hundred, out of which came forty-five test cases. Of these, only twelve went to trial, resulting in six convictions. The sentences were lenient, and all received pardons within a few years.[82] In one of the most well-known cases, three German submariners were charged with sinking a hospital ship called the *Llandovery Castle* and shooting survivors who had made their way to lifeboats. The result: one acquittal, two convicted and later pardoned, with German newspapers hailing the "U-boat heroes" while the commander remained outside Weimar's jurisdiction. In another case, the court acquitted a general who had ordered his men to kill wounded and captured French soldiers; possibly as many as two hundred had been killed.[83] The Treaty of Versailles is known for bearing the heavy hand of those seeking retribution, but for many in the victorious Allied nations, the prosecution of German war criminals was a "scandalous failure of justice."[84] As for the Kaiser, nothing came of the demands for his trial once he had fled to the Netherlands, which refused to extradite him.[85]

As if to confirm the difficulties in enforcement, the efforts by the Allies to hold Turks responsible for killing approximately one million Armenians followed an eerily similar pattern. The treaty with the Ottoman government used some of the same language as the Treaty of Versailles (pledging to "hand over" those "responsible for the massacres"). The Allies nevertheless acquiesced in Turkey running its own trials in Constantinople. Bowing to domestic public opinion after seventeen lower-ranking officials were convicted, government officials discontinued the trials, declared a general amnesty, and named three who had been executed as martyrs.[86]

Such, then, was the state of war crimes accountability before World War II. For all the progress made in codification, there was no written provision in the Law of the Hague or the Law of Geneva for the trial and punishment of war criminals. The most that Hague Convention IV of 1907 provided was that any belligerent state "shall be responsible for all acts committed by persons forming part of its forces" and shall "be liable to pay compensation."[87] After World War I, German jurists actually cited this provision to show that war crimes trials were illegal. The Geneva Convention of 1906 politely called upon governments to take "necessary measures" to "repress" in wartime "individual acts" of "ill treatment" of sick and wounded enemy soldiers. Similar phrasing appeared in the 1929 Geneva Convention, with language that belligerent parties set up appropriate inquiries upon request and "repress" violations "as promptly as possible." Perhaps nothing better confirms the sad state of affairs than a remark made by Adolf Hitler in 1939. "Who after all," he asked his generals on the eve of Germany's invasion of Poland, "is today speaking about the destruction of the Armenians?"[88]

IV

The Nuremberg trial of principal surviving German war criminals held in the Bavarian city of that name was a breakthrough in the development of the laws of war. Looking back, the trial may seem to be the only conceivable response to Nazi atrocities. The backstory suggests otherwise.

The initial impulse for holding war crimes trials came as early as January 1942 when nine governments-in-exile from countries occupied by German forces issued the Declaration of St. James. Disavowing "acts of vengeance," the Declaration stated that punishing war criminals through "the channel of organized justice" should be one of their "principal war aims."[89] The Allied nations set up a commission to gather evidence of war crimes, but it failed to make much headway. In any event, the ultimate decision on war crimes trials was bound to fall sooner or later to Franklin D. Roosevelt, Winston Churchill, and Joseph Stalin. In November 1943, the Big Three, as they were known, announced in the Moscow Declaration their intention to punish "major criminals" by "joint decision." While this might be taken to refer to criminal trials, the wording was equivocal, leaving open the possibility of punishment without criminal proceedings.[90]

Indeed, anyone with inside information about the decision-making process probably would have bet against war crimes trials. Still smarting from what happened at Leipzig after World War I, British officials were "deeply impressed with the dangers and difficulties" of such an endeavor, and less than one month before Germany's surrender, Churchill's cabinet still held the view that "a full trial" of Nazi leaders was "out of the question." Meanwhile, the Roosevelt administration was the scene of considerable infighting. At one point, FDR endorsed the plan put forward by his treasury secretary, Henry Morgenthau Jr., who favored firing squads for those "arch-criminals of this war whose obvious guilt has generally been recognized." Countering Morgenthau was Secretary of War Henry Stimson. Although Stimson had at one point contemplated US soldiers simply shooting "Hitler and his gang," he opposed Morgenthau's proposal and pressed Roosevelt for proceedings that incorporated "the rudimentary aspects of the Bill of Rights." Further support for war crimes trials came from the French and what might seem an unlikely quarter. The Soviets supported trials, but what they had in mind was something like the Moscow purge trials of the 1930s—the point was not to determine guilt or innocence but rather to publicize guilt before execution.[91]

During the summer of 1945, representatives from the United States, Great Britain, France, and the Soviet Union hammered out their differences at meetings in London. They produced the London Charter, which established the International Military Tribunal (IMT) and defined the offenses to be tried at Nuremberg (the charter is also known as the Nuremberg Charter or the IMT Charter).[92] Given the obstacles, it was nothing short of miraculous that the four major powers reached agreement only three months after V-E Day and that the trial began in November 1945.

The proceedings lasted for one year. Four judges served on the tribunal; one from each of these Allied powers. The prosecutors hailed from those same nations. Only twenty-two defendants were put on trial there, but they were selected to represent the highest echelon of the Third Reich's war machine—civilian as well as military—including propagandists, government ministers, and Nazi party leaders. Hermann Goering, Reichsmarshall and commander of the Luftwaffe, was the prize catch as Adolf Hitler, Heinrich Himmler, and Joseph Goebbels had committed suicide. The charges included war crimes of a traditional nature along with crimes against peace and crimes against humanity. In the end, the IMT convicted nineteen defendants and sentenced twelve to death.[93]

This was the only trial before the IMT. Its legacy is mixed. In the immediate aftermath of the Nuremberg trial, war crimes trials seemingly sprang up everywhere, in marked contrast to what happened after the First World War. From 1946 to 1949, the US military tried almost two hundred defendants in a dozen additional trials at Nuremberg. The prosecution team's strategy was to single out groups of individuals implicated in different aspects of the Nazi regime's criminality, including doctors, industrialists, military leaders, members of the SS, along with judges and lawyers. In addition to these Subsequent Proceedings, as they were known, over five hundred American military tribunals convicted another 1,500 Germans.[94] The British, French, and Soviets held trials in their occupation zones, and nations that had been occupied by Germany also conducted trials. West German courts, though the old guard (judges with their own Nazi past) limited prosecutions in several respects, in the end tried thousands of Germans.[95] General Douglas MacArthur used Nuremberg as a model for the International Military Tribunal in the Far East. The proceedings there along with other trials conducted by the Allies who fought Japan convicted nearly four thousand Japanese.[96]

Yet postwar enthusiasm for war crimes trials dissipated in the face of the realpolitik interests of the Cold War.[97] Then, too, the Nuremberg trial and its progeny have always come in for their share of criticism.[98] From the first, the proceedings were vulnerable to the argument that the IMT Charter's innovative offenses like crimes against peace violated the principle of *nullum crimen sine lege, nulla poena sine lege* ("no crime without law, no punishment without law").[99] The claim that the Nuremberg trial reflected nothing more than "victor's justice" has always shadowed its legacy. That can be taken to mean either that there was no possibility of impartial judgment or that the trial applied a double standard by leaving Allied personnel unpunished for similar crimes.[100] The participation of the Soviets remains discomfiting. They could not quite embrace their counterparts' view of impartial proceedings, not to mention the irony in having a member of the Red Army rendering judgment on Germany's crimes against peace given the Soviet Union's invasions of

Poland and Finland.[101] Questions have also been raised about procedural fairness. The Nuremberg trial may hold up well enough (with the exception of defendants having no right of appeal as there was no appellate court). Other postwar trials do not fare so well. The Tokyo war crimes trial ended without a single acquittal—by itself cause for concern. Some proceedings in formerly occupied nations in Europe were clearly summary in nature. While it may be easy to brush off self-interested criticism coming from someone like Goering, it must give pause to learn that US Supreme Court Chief Justice Harlan Fiske Stone considered the Nuremberg trial a "high grade lynching party."[102]

Whatever Nuremberg's flaws, real and imagined, the trial still marks a critical point in the development of the laws of war.[103] While the break with the past may be most keenly felt with newly established offenses (crimes against peace and crimes against humanity), a good case can be made that the effect on the traditional area of the laws of war was no less significant due to the doctrine of individual criminal accountability that Nuremberg established. The meaning of that doctrine may seem obvious, but it is worth pausing over the effect of bringing its three elements together: that war criminals will be held accountable for their conduct; that they will be held accountable through the criminal process; and that criminal accountability applies to every individual. Even with the most generous interpretation given the scattered trials that preceded World War II, there was no clear expectation before Nuremberg that individuals who violated the laws of war would be tried and punished for committing criminal offenses. Nuremberg cut through the Alice-in-Wonderland logic prevailing until then (head of state immunity, superior orders defense) with a simple idea simply put. Principle I of the IMT Judgment stated that "any person" committing a crime under international law is "responsible therefor and liable to punishment." As the IMT judges explained, "crimes against international law are committed by men, not abstract entities, and only by punishing individuals who commit such crimes can the provisions of international law be enforced." No one was any longer beyond the reach of the law. Significantly, heads of state were subject to prosecution for war crimes like anyone else. The Nuremberg Charter and Judgment make this clear. In the Charter's language, "the official position of defendants, whether as Heads of State or responsible officials in Government departments, shall not be considered as freeing them from responsibility or mitigating punishment." Principle III of the Judgment stated that acting as head of state "does not relieve" one of responsibility under international law. In 1946, the UN General Assembly adopted a resolution affirming the principles articulated in the Nuremberg Charter.[104] By itself, this resolution has no legal authority, but the principles have been accepted as customary law, and the time has passed when someone could seriously claim immunity from prosecution for violating the laws of war.

V

Before turning to the Bush administration's treatment of detainees, it will be useful to examine how the Geneva Conventions applied to the war against terrorism. This issue has received a good deal of attention.[105] President Bush's position was, in brief, that the United States was "engaged in an armed conflict with al Qaeda, the Taliban, and associated forces," that those involved in the 9/11 attacks had violated the laws of war, and that the Geneva Conventions did not protect "unlawful enemy combatants," including members of the Taliban as well as Al Qaeda.[106] His interpretation was challenged on various grounds. Some critics, wary of the administration's nebulous characterization of a "global war on terror," never accepted the idea of applying the laws of war wholesale to such a conflict.[107] They believed that international human rights law (the Convention Against Torture in particular) and ordinary criminal law (the Torture Act, which criminalized acts of torture committed outside the United States) remained in effect, providing detainees in US custody with more extensive protections than they had under the Geneva Conventions.[108] Commentators also expressed skepticism over the administration's one-sided interpretation of the laws of war with the United States reaping all the benefits without incurring any obligations. Questions were raised over designating detainees as unlawful enemy combatants.[109]

President Bush's position is mistaken in several respects, but so too is the view that international humanitarian law did not apply at all. The question whether the law of war applied can be addressed step by step. Under the conventional mode of analysis, the first point to consider in applying the Geneva Conventions is the nature of the conflict. The 1949 conventions set up a deceptively simple bifurcated approach. Qualifying armed conflicts are either international or non-international. Under Common Article 2, an international conflict is an armed conflict between states bound by the conventions ("High Contracting Parties" in the wording of Common Article 2). In such a conflict, the Geneva Conventions apply in their entirety, with the exception of Common Article 3, which covers non-international conflicts.[110] The protections afforded individuals in non-international conflicts are not limited to those spelled out in Common Article 3, as it is generally understood that they are supplemented by customary international law—the unwritten rules and practices which are so widely accepted that they have legally binding effect. By the end of the twentieth century, customary international law was usually taken to embody the substance of many other provisions of the Geneva Conventions.[111] There are other possibilities that can complicate matters. Armed conflicts may have dual status as international and non-international conflicts. They may change status. Nations may be involved in actions like a border incident that fall short of a Common Article 2 conflict, and there may be riots or other internal disturbances that do not rise to the level of a Common Article 3 conflict.[112]

Applying this analytical framework yields a more nuanced interpretation than President Bush's statements suggest. While the war against terrorism as such would not qualify as an international armed conflict under the Geneva Conventions, the United States was engaged in two Common Article 2 conflicts. One was in Afghanistan. Armed conflict there began on October 7, 2001, and continued with an occupation that lasted until a new Afghan government was formed. Some commentators date the end of the occupation to June 2002, when the *loya jirga* was assembled; others to the formal establishment of the government in January 2004.[113] In either case, that did not end armed conflict there as US forces were then mired in a Common Article 3 non-international conflict with the Taliban.[114] The other Common Article 2 conflict, in Iraq, started on March 19, 2003. That conflict continued through an occupation, ending when the interim Iraqi government took over on June 28, 2004. At that point the United States became embroiled in a Common Article 3 conflict with insurgents.[115]

The United States was also engaged in a Common Article 3 conflict with Al Qaeda. So said the US Supreme Court in *Hamdan v. Rumsfeld* (2006).[116] Law-of-war experts may disagree—at least they might have hoped for something more than the cursory explanation given in the prevailing opinion in that case.[117] Nevertheless, the Court's decision is authoritative for the United States. The decision on this point hinged on the meaning of "non-international" in Common Article 3. It may be argued that "non-international" refers to internal conflicts like civil wars and that America's fight with Al Qaeda, not confined within the borders of a single nation, does not qualify. That argument is bolstered by the language of Common Article 3, which describes a non-international conflict "occurring in the territory of one of the High Contracting Parties." Further support for this position can be found in the *ICRC Commentary* on Common Article 3, with its references to "civil war," the "internal affairs of the country concerned," and the like.[118] However, Justice John Paul Stevens, writing for the *Hamdan* Court, reached a different conclusion. Construing "international" literally as "between nations," the justice read "non-international" to refer to an armed conflict that was not between nations. As Al Qaeda was not a nation, America's conflict with that terrorist organization fit that definition.[119]

At any rate, for the purposes of this inquiry, President Bush is hardly in a position to say that the laws of war did not apply at all. He called the September 11 attacks "acts of war." He said that Al Qaeda had "created a state of armed conflict" with the United States. He set up military tribunals to try foreign terrorists for "violations of the laws of war."[120] He said that they had committed "war crimes," and he insisted that the United States had "a right under the laws of war" to "detain these enemies"—the "terrorists and enemy fighters in Afghanistan, in Iraq, and other fronts of this war on terror."[121] Other administration officials also suggested that the laws of war applied. The Justice Department's Office of Legal Counsel, upon which President Bush relied so much, declared that it was "virtually self-evident" that the terrorist attacks created "an armed conflict subject to the laws of armed conflict." More circumspect was William H. Taft IV, the Bush State Department's legal advisor, who stated in 2003 that the "law of armed conflict provides the most appropriate legal framework" for the war against terrorism. Representatives from the Bush State Department provided a more technical explanation: "U.S. detention operations in Guantánamo, Afghanistan, and Iraq are part of ongoing armed conflicts and, accordingly, are governed by the law of armed conflict, which is the *lex specialis* applicable to those particular operations."[122]

Even assuming that Common Article 3 did not protect Al Qaeda and Taliban detainees in US custody, the humane treatment standard can be taken to apply under customary international law. One way to make this argument is via Additional Protocol I to the Geneva Conventions, which was adopted in 1977. Article 75 states that "persons who do not benefit from more favourable treatment" under the Geneva Conventions "shall be treated humanely in all circumstances." The article goes on to prohibit "torture of all kinds" and "outrages upon personal dignity, in particular humiliating and degrading treatment."[123] The US Senate has not approved the 1977 Additional Geneva Protocols, but most law-of-war experts agree that Article 75 reflects customary international law. Taft had an interesting statement on this, though not everyone in the Bush administration agreed with him. He said that the United States considers Article 75 as "an articulation of safeguards to which all persons in the hands of an enemy are entitled," and he stated unequivocally that terrorists "do not forfeit their right to humane treatment."[124]

In sum, while the Bush administration's conception of a "global war on terror" remains controversial, it is reasonable to conclude that, in response to the terrorist attacks of September 11, the United States detained persons in armed conflicts that were covered for some period of time by the Geneva Conventions.

It remains to be considered whether it is appropriate to evaluate President Bush's conduct regarding the treatment of detainees as a criminal offense under the laws of war. The analysis is straightforward for international conflicts. When Common Article 2 applies, the Geneva Conventions define inhuman treatment of protected persons as a prosecutable grave breach. The issue gets more complicated with Common Article 3 non-international armed conflicts. In the immediate aftermath of World War II, nations were not ready to extend the novel system of grave breaches to civil wars. As a result, none of the offenses listed in Common Article 3 when committed in non-international armed conflicts constitutes a grave breach under the Geneva Conventions.[125] For some time after the conventions were adopted in 1949, it was generally understood that individuals violating Common Article 3 could not be tried for war crimes (criminal liability would have to be based on domestic legislation). That understanding began to change with the International Criminal Tribunal for the former Yugoslavia, and the prevailing view today is that individuals can be tried for war crimes for acts committed in non-international conflicts. As Gary D. Solis said, "It is no longer correct (as it only recently was) to assert that there are no war crimes in common Article 3 non-international armed conflicts."[126] Another way to think about this would be to say that the grave breaches defined in the Geneva Conventions have become part of customary international law.[127]

Be that as it may, at the time that the administration's interrogation program was developed, US law directly addressed these issues in legislation called, appropriately enough, the War Crimes Act[128] (see appendix C). Congress, belatedly fulfilling the Geneva Conventions' mandate to establish "effective penal sanctions" for individuals committing grave breaches, adopted the War Crimes Act five years before the September 11 attacks. When the Senate approved the conventions four decades earlier, some said that existing criminal legislation satisfied this requirement.[129] That was always a dubious proposition. After all, to take one example, nothing in the federal criminal code enabled US prosecutors to indict foreign nationals who committed grave breaches against American soldiers. The 1996 version of the War Crimes Act defined any conduct that constitutes a grave breach under the Geneva Conventions as a war crime under US law, but it left for future consideration the question of whether to criminalize the acts prohibited by Common Article 3 in non-international armed conflicts.[130] Congress expanded the statute's coverage one year later to include as a war crime "any conduct" that "constitutes a violation of common Article 3."[131]

It is difficult to overstate the significance of this last statutory provision. Its meaning seems plain. As Justice Anthony M. Kennedy said in his concurring opinion in *Hamdan*, "violations of Common Article 3 are considered 'war crimes' punishable as federal offenses, when committed by or against United States nationals and military personnel." (US military personnel committing grave breaches can be prosecuted under the Uniform Code of Military Justice.)[132] In short, inhumane treatment was a war crime under US law whether the armed conflict was a Common Article 2 international conflict or a Common Article 3 non-international conflict. If Common Article 3's humane treatment standard could have been interpreted in the past—rightly or wrongly—as a laudable but nonbinding goal under the Geneva Conventions, the War Crimes Act made clear that humane treatment was a legally binding obligation under US law and that Americans violating Common Article 3's provisions were subject to prosecution for committing war crimes. In effect, Congress said that it did not matter whether an armed conflict was international or non-international—humane treatment was such a basic norm that its violation was a war crime in either case. As Bush White House aides noted (discussed in the next chapter), the penalty was substantial: any term of years (including life imprisonment) or the death penalty in case the victim died.[133]

VI

On the view that the history of the laws of war sheds light on their present significance, this chapter adopted a historical approach in order to provide a deeper explanation of what was at stake here. One lesson that might be drawn from this history is that the laws of war have been more honored in the breach than in their observance, but the difficulties in enforcing the laws of war should not detract from the striking fact that people throughout history held on to the idea that warfare should be governed by certain rules. Some rules varied in time and place; others reflected common understandings of what was acceptable in warfare. One may point to instances in past centuries suggesting an innate humanitarianism underlying customary practices, but certainly by the late nineteenth century the humanitarian impulse had emerged as a dominant force in the laws of war.

This historical survey establishes at least two points relevant to this book's inquiry. First, individuals caught up in armed conflicts are entitled to one thing at least: humane treatment. This standard emerged from the Enlightenment philosophy of the rights of humanity, was for some time put forward sporadically in favor of prisoners of war, and then blossomed into the absolute minimum required after World War II, as demonstrated by the background history of the drafting of the 1949 Geneva Conventions.

The second point concerns the Nuremberg principle of individual criminal accountability. The history of difficulties in enforcing the laws of war highlights the central importance of Nuremberg today. If it goes too far to say that war crimes accountability before World War II was nonexistent, it seems that there was no clear understanding before then that individuals who violated the laws of war ought to be punished for doing so. Nuremberg changed that. Concededly, it has remained difficult to put the principle of individual criminal accountability into effect. No doubt many would have been surprised if federal prosecutors had indicted President Bush for violating the War Crimes Act, but if it was naive to expect to see the president in the dock, this chapter has sought to explain why the accountability failure here—why abandoning the Nuremberg principle so readily—was no trifling matter.

CHAPTER TWO

The New Paradigm

On February 7, 2002, President Bush issued an order titled "Humane Treatment of al Qaeda and Taliban Detainees"[1] (see appendix A). Originally classified, the order was two pages long, single-spaced, typed on White House stationery, and styled in the form of a memorandum addressed to the top-ranking members of his national security team. This presidential memorandum should be considered an important state paper, and on a first reading it might look like a reasonable response to an unprecedented situation, something to be commended rather than condemned.

Noting that the 1949 Geneva Conventions had been designed for conventional armed forces, President Bush began with a seemingly unobjectionable statement about the laws of war. "The war against terrorism ushers in a new paradigm," he said, one that "requires new thinking in the law of war." The president then enumerated several legal issues concerning the 1949 conventions and the war against terrorism. He resolved these issues one by one in a series of crisp directives: first, the Geneva Conventions did not apply to the conflict with Al Qaeda; second, although the conventions applied to the conflict with the Taliban in Afghanistan, Taliban fighters were "unlawful combatants" who did not qualify for prisoner of war status; and third, Common Article 3 did not protect Al Qaeda or Taliban detainees. President Bush also asserted that he had the constitutional authority "to suspend Geneva as between the United States and Afghanistan," but he declined to "exercise that authority at this time."

The president added that "as a matter of policy, the United States Armed Forces shall continue to treat detainees humanely and, to the extent appropriate and consistent with military necessity, in a manner consistent with the principles of Geneva." The point he evidently sought to convey was that, even though the conventions did not apply as a matter of law, it would be US policy to conform to Geneva's principles. "Our values as a Nation," the president added, "call for us to treat detainees humanely."

With that, President Bush could say that his order should be viewed as a positive development in protecting human rights in wartime—a presidential mandate for the humane treatment of detainees beyond what the law required, in effect extending Geneva's principles to circumstances its drafters had not anticipated. Judging from the text of the memorandum, the picture that emerges is one of a deliberative decision-making process with "extensive" interagency discussions over "complex" legal issues. The president, the memorandum implied, did little more than follow the expert legal advice tendered by the government's top lawyers. President Bush made a special point of noting that he relied on the Justice Department as he worked through the questions concerning the Geneva Conventions. The phrase "I accept the legal conclusion" of the Justice Department or the US attorney general appears repeatedly in his memorandum.

A different view emerges when going beyond what was stated in this presidential memorandum and looking more deeply at the decision-making process that led to its issuance. While not everything is known, it is possible to piece together a chronology of key events from classified documents that were eventually released or leaked. Some of these primary sources, such as the Justice Department's memoranda, can make for dry reading. Yet with these documents, it is possible to reconstruct the internal discussions: the questions that were asked, the concerns that were expressed, and the strategies that were employed. In short, the legal opinions and other administration documents provide compelling evidence—on some points the only evidence available to the public—of what took place behind closed doors.

I

The initial US position on applying the Geneva Conventions in the war against terrorism was set forth not by President Bush but rather by General Tommy Franks, whom the president had entrusted to command coalition forces in Afghanistan. At the start of combat operations in October 2001, Franks had ordered his troops to comply with the 1949 conventions. If some of those captured might qualify as prisoners of war, they were to be afforded the protections of Geneva Convention III. As in previous conflicts such as the Gulf War, summary hearings were to be held if a captive's status was unclear. Those not qualifying for POW status were not necessarily released as they could be subject to prosecution under US criminal law.[2]

Not long after General Franks issued this order, administration officials began to raise questions about applying the Geneva Conventions to Taliban and Al Qaeda fighters. White House counsel Alberto Gonzales later said that he brought up that issue directly with President Bush in late October 2001. A month later, CIA lawyers distributed a draft legal memorandum that stated that a "policy decision must be made with regard to U.S. use of torture in light of our obligations under international law." This memorandum suggested that other countries "may be very unwilling to call the U.S. to task for torture when it resulted in saving thousands of lives."[3]

If President Bush had wanted expert advice on the Geneva Conventions, he had various alternatives within the administration. The State Department had experts on international law. It would have come as no surprise if Secretary of State Colin L. Powell had something to say on this subject, given his position at State and his extensive military experience (having worked his way up the ranks to chairman of the Joint Chiefs of Staff during the Gulf War). Then there were the military's lawyers known as judge advocates. Each branch of the armed services has its own Judge Advocate General's (JAG) Corps led by a two-star general (or admiral) designated, appropriately enough, the judge advocate general. Approximately four thousand judge advocates served in the military at any given moment during Bush's presidency. Their tasks ranged from litigating courts martial to providing legal advice on military operations. Some were as well versed as anyone in the US government on the practical questions of applying the laws of war.[4]

But White House insiders, evidently concerned that the government's experts on the laws of war would provide the president with answers he did not want, set up a decision-making process designed to exclude anyone who might object to the administration's emerging detention policy. According to Jack Goldsmith, White House counsel Alberto Gonzales "made it a practice" to restrict distribution of "controversial legal opinions" to a "very small group of lawyers." It was clear that the State Department was a likely source of internal dissent. Not long after September 11, the president signed a letter that required Gonzales's permission before anyone in the executive branch could submit important issues of international law to State. Once the interrogation program was underway, White House officials were "extremely concerned" that Secretary Powell would "blow his stack" if he knew "what's been going on."[5]

Instead of soliciting legal advice from the JAG Corps or State Department lawyers, the White House turned to the Justice Department's Office of Legal Counsel (OLC). While a parallel decision-making process over detainee treatment played out at all levels within the Defense Department—from a staff judge advocate at Guantánamo to Secretary of Defense Donald Rumsfeld[6]— OLC's role in the decision-making process on the Geneva Conventions cannot be overstated. On the face of it there is nothing wrong with the White House requesting advice from OLC lawyers. That office is charged with interpreting the law for the executive branch.[7] Little known by the general public for most of its history, OLC has been regarded by Washington insiders as an elite unit within the Justice Department. Chief Justice William H. Rehnquist and Justice Antonin Scalia headed the office before joining the Supreme Court. Typically consisting of two dozen lawyers, this small office has had an outsized impact over the years. OLC opinions have covered a range of issues, including major foreign policy questions (the blockade of Cuba during the Cuban Missile Crisis, for example). Despite the obvious political pressures that come with the job, OLC lawyers had previously shown that they were capable of exercising independent judgment, at least as much as might reasonably be expected.[8]

Independent judgment was not exactly what President Bush and his advisors sought, however. They wanted to exploit OLC's unique position in the federal bureaucracy.[9] The essential feature of the Office of Legal Counsel— the reason why Bush White House officials eagerly solicited its written legal advice—is that OLC opinions are considered binding on all other administrative agencies. Within the executive branch, only the attorney general and the president can overrule an OLC opinion.[10] Moreover, there may be no meaningful opportunity for congressional oversight or Supreme Court review for the simple reason that there is no guarantee that anyone outside the executive branch will see OLC opinions in a timely fashion, especially on national security matters.

The president also had a willing ally at OLC in Deputy Assistant Attorney General John Yoo, a midlevel official in the Justice Department's hierarchy. One of a handful of political appointees in that office, Yoo was a young conservative law professor who had clerked for Justice Clarence Thomas. He had established his academic reputation by writing extensively on presidential war powers.[11] That made him a natural choice for playing a leading role in developing OLC's national security portfolio. Before he left the Justice Department in 2003, Yoo prepared opinions on seemingly every legal question that came up concerning the administration's counterterrorism policies.[12]

According to the organization charts, Yoo was answerable to the attorney general as well as the assistant attorney general in charge of OLC (a post vacant for several weeks in the fall of 2001).[13] Yet he had a direct connection to the White House through an ad hoc group of five lawyers formed after the September 11 attacks. Besides Yoo, the group included Gonzales (who had been counsel to President Bush when he was governor of Texas), his deputy Timothy E. Flanigan (who had headed OLC under President George H. W. Bush), David S. Addington (counsel and later chief of staff to Vice President Dick Cheney), and Pentagon general counsel William J. Haynes II (who had been Addington's special assistant when Addington worked for Cheney at the Defense Department). They liked to call themselves the "War Council," and, meeting in Gonzales's office in the West Wing or Haynes's office at the Pentagon, they mapped out the administration's legal strategy in the war against terrorism.[14]

With Yoo in place at the Justice Department, the White House was able to take advantage of OLC's influential position without getting bogged down in the normal vetting process involving various administrative agencies.[15] His willingness to provide White House officials with the answers they wanted was so obvious that Attorney General John Ashcroft, out of Yoo's earshot, called him "Dr. Yes." That suited the White House perfectly. In the view of Jack Goldsmith (later appointed by President Bush to head the Office of Legal Counsel), obtaining OLC's "bottom line approval" was "all that mattered" to the president's close advisors.[16]

President Bush's order establishing military commissions provided an early clue of how far the White House would go to bypass the government's law-of-war experts. The question of how to prosecute those responsible for the September 11 attacks had originally been assigned to an interagency group led by Pierre-Richard Prosper, who served as the State Department's ambassador-at-large for war crimes. This group included lawyers from the military (they favored courts martial) and the Justice Department (they preferred criminal trials in the federal courts). Gonzales asked OLC about another option. Could President Bush, on his own authority, set up military commissions to try terrorists under the laws of war?[17]

OLC affirmed that he could, and Flanigan drafted an order for the president's signature. Few administration officials outside the War Council knew about the order before it was made public in mid-November. "What the hell just happened?," Secretary Powell reportedly said after learning about the military commissions from a CNN report. Neither National Security Advisor Condoleezza Rice nor Michael Chertoff (in charge of the Justice Department's Criminal Division) had advance knowledge. The military's top lawyers were kept in the dark as well.[18] Apparently Haynes felt compelled to tell Major General Tom Romig about the military commissions before President Bush issued the order, but the circumstances surrounding their exchange were unusual, given Romig's standing as the US Army's judge advocate general. Haynes did not show the general the order; he allowed Romig to designate one person to review it without taking notes or making copies. The general dispatched Colonel Lawrence Morris to do that. Taken aback by Flanigan's draft, Colonel Morris reported his misgivings to Romig who, with Morris and another JAG officer (a brigadier general), recommended several changes, but to no avail.[19]

II

While President Bush's decision on the Geneva Conventions was rationalized by OLC's legal interpretation of those treaties, it must also be seen as the product of a view of the presidency that prevailed within the Bush inner circle. To explain not only what happened but also how and why this could happen, this section explores the doctrinal building blocks underlying their understanding of presidential power.

It did not take long after the 9/11 attacks for an exceptionally broad interpretation of the president's wartime authority to make its appearance in administration documents. Within days, the White House counsel's office asked John Yoo to prepare an official OLC opinion on the "scope of the President's authority to take military action in response to the terrorist attacks." The memorandum, completed in short order by September 25, provided an overarching legal framework to justify the president's unfettered discretion over counterterrorism policies. This legal opinion was kept secret until someone posted it on the Justice Department's website three years later.[20] Although OLC would later distance itself from Yoo's work, the administration's subsequent record suggests that President Bush and his top aides never abandoned the conception of presidential power Yoo had outlined there.

The Constitution, Yoo said, put the president in "full control" of the armed forces. The logical force of his language describing the president's war powers—"inherent," "independent," "unilateral," and "plenary"—pointed to one conclusion.[21] In "the exercise of his plenary power to use military force," Yoo said, "the President's decisions are for him alone and unreviewable." He asserted that Congress cannot place "any limits on the President's determinations as to any terrorist threat, the amount of military force to be used in response, or the method, timing, and nature of the response." These were extraordinary claims to make about limited government, but they fit Yoo's preconceived notions. Years later it would emerge that he personally believed that the president had authority as commander in chief to order civilians massacred—a position at once revealing his peculiar understanding of presidential power and his lack of expertise in international humanitarian law.[22]

Yoo went on to claim that Congress and the Supreme Court concurred with the positions laid out in his memorandum, though many lawmakers and justices would have been surprised to learn of the evidence he offered in support of that dubious conclusion. Yoo said that the Court had recognized "the President's complete discretion in exercising the Commander-in-Chief power." He construed the War Powers Resolution (adopted in 1973 in an effort to circumscribe the president's war powers) and the Authorization for Use of Military Force (AUMF) that was enacted three days after the September 11 terrorist attacks as proof of "Congress's acceptance of the President's unilateral war powers" in such emergencies. He further suggested that the AUMF reflected lawmakers' "explicit agreement" that the president's authority was broad enough to encompass the preemptive use of military force—"plenary power to use force even before an attack upon the United States actually occurs, against targets and using methods of his own choosing."[23]

In the course of analyzing the scope of presidential power, Yoo said that the "centralization of authority in the President alone is particularly crucial" in war and foreign affairs "where a unitary executive can evaluate threats, consider policy choices, and mobilize national resources with a speed and energy that is far superior to any other branch."[24] The unitary executive doctrine, as it is called, was one of the principal components of the Bush conception of the presidency. President Bush often referred to his authority to supervise the unitary executive branch, and the doctrine figured prominently in his administration's efforts to deflect Congress from constraining the interrogation program. To understand President Bush's conception of presidential power in relation to the treatment of detainees, it will be helpful to take note of the doctrine's origins and development.

While adherents of the unitary executive doctrine trace its roots to the founding, the modern version began to take shape in the 1980s when Reagan conservatives sought to gain control over what they viewed as a New Deal regulatory state run amuck. In essence, the unitary executive doctrine holds in seemingly innocuous terms that the Constitution places all of the national government's executive power in the president's hands—seemingly innocuous because what that means depends on what that entails. No one disputes the idea of a unitary executive in terms of the decision to have a single person serve as president in lieu of a multimember council,[25] but those who subscribe to the doctrine these days take the idea further. Some are concerned with preserving the president's authority to remove any official performing executive functions against Congress's efforts to insulate certain executive officials. Others argue that the White House can require everyone working in the executive branch to comply with the president's policy preferences no matter what Congress stipulates. The doctrine has also been read as justification for the president's exclusive authority over all matters falling within the sphere of the executive, that neither Congress nor the judiciary can interfere with core executive functions, and that administration officials can therefore disregard legislation and judicial decisions that intrude on that sphere of constitutional authority. More broadly still, the doctrine has been coupled with an expansive reading of the president's inherent powers—powers claimed to be executive by their nature.[26] Thus, while the claim at the heart of the unitary executive doctrine that the Constitution grants the president all of the government's executive power may seem unremarkable, critics charge that, once the premise is granted, it becomes all too easy for the president to neutralize the system of checks and balances by combining exclusive presidential authority (with all that may imply for undercutting congressional oversight and judicial review) with an enlarged view of what is subject to presidential control (in foreign affairs as well as domestic policy).[27]

For those inclined to embrace the unitary executive doctrine, the history of the modern presidency showed that, contrary to the imperial presidency thesis, Congress and the courts were to blame for encroaching on the president's authority, as suggested by books like *The Fettered Presidency*.[28] The task, then, was to restore the presidency to its original constitutional status. Few in the Bush administration were more dedicated to this view than Vice President Cheney.[29] Convinced that the presidency was greatly diminished in the wake of the Vietnam War and Watergate, he described "an erosion of the powers and the ability" of the president "to do his job"—a situation he had "repeatedly" witnessed. His outlook was shaped by his experience as chief of staff to President Gerald R. Ford who, having succeeded President Richard M. Nixon, complained that the "pendulum" had swung from one extreme to the other to the point where "we have moved from an imperial Presidency to an imperiled Presidency." Cheney later served in Congress where he was a member of one of the investigative committees looking into the Iran-Contra scandal. He signed a minority report dissenting from criticism of the Reagan White House which became an early marker—a "proverbial Magna Carta" in the words of Julian Zelizer—for the unitary executive doctrine.[30]

President Bush did not have Cheney's years of experience in the nation's capital. He certainly was not immersed in the details of federal government operations like the vice president's close aide David Addington, who scoured legislation and administrative agency actions for opportunities to promote the unitary executive theory.[31] But only the president was the president, and in that capacity, he frequently cited his authority "to supervise the unitary executive branch" in official remarks when signing bills into law. These signing statements, as they are known, provide a good example of the unitary executive doctrine in action. More to the point, signing statements were an important part of President Bush's arsenal in countering congressional efforts to moderate his administration's policies on detention and interrogation.[32]

There is nothing intrinsically wrong with signing statements. Their propriety depends on how they are used. There is no problem with signing statements that are rhetorical in nature—claiming credit when signing a bill into law or clarifying how legislation would benefit particular constituencies. More complicated scenarios arise when a president uses a signing statement to interpret a statute contrary to Congress's intent.[33] The most controversial raise constitutional objections to particular provisions of a bill that the administration will not enforce or defend, even though the president signed the bill into law. Some commentators see this as inimical to the lawmaking process laid out in the Constitution on the view that, if the president considers any part of a bill unconstitutional, the remedy is to veto the entire bill and note objections in a veto message. Lawmakers would then have the opportunity to override the veto or revise the bill to accommodate White House concerns. Other analysts note that Congress has been guilty of overreach by passing urgently needed legislation with presumptively unconstitutional provisions. In those circumstances, so the argument goes, a presidential signing statement registering objections to discrete provisions of a bill is a practical response to a problem of Congress's own making.[34]

Throughout the nineteenth century, presidents rarely issued signing statements, perhaps no more than twenty-five times. President Truman, averaging sixteen a year, is usually taken to mark the start of the practice for the modern presidency. While scholars have come up with different numbers for more recent presidents, all agree that their use dramatically increased under

Ronald Reagan (250 total with 86 constitutional objections by one estimate). In keeping with the way power becomes institutionalized, George H. W. Bush (228 total, 107 constitutional objections) and Bill Clinton (381 total, 70 constitutional objections) resorted to signing statements even more frequently (again, by one estimate).[35]

President George W. Bush issued fewer signing statements than his two immediate predecessors, but no president had ever registered more constitutional objections to bills signed into law than he did. By the end of his presidency, he had amassed more than a thousand constitutional objections to 1,200 sections of bills. To take one example, he objected to over one hundred provisions in one appropriations bill on the grounds that they were "inconsistent with the constitutional authority of the President to conduct foreign affairs, command the Armed Forces, protect sensitive information, supervise the unitary executive branch, make appointments, and make recommendations to the Congress." Instead of engaging in an open debate with lawmakers over policy, the Bush White House seemed content to let his signing statements escape notice. While they were published in the Federal Register, few appreciated what was going on before journalist Charlie Savage brought President Bush's signing statements to light over five years into his administration. Savage's revelatory report noted that the president, in the belief that he was empowered to "set aside any statute" that "conflicts with his interpretation of the Constitution," had "quietly claimed the authority to disobey more than 750 laws enacted since he took office."[36]

Of particular note, President Bush used signing statements to push back on lawmakers' efforts to rein in his policy on detainees. For example, Congress required the president to report whenever the administration repurposed monies appropriated by the legislature for covert activities that had not been authorized by Congress. That would have given members of Congress some insight into the black sites. In response to the Abu Ghraib scandal, lawmakers mandated military police retraining on the Geneva Conventions' requirements for humane treatment. And when it became clear that Bush administration insiders had circumvented military lawyers in one way or another, Congress authorized the JAG Corps to provide "independent legal advice" without interference from political appointees. President Bush issued signing statements noting constitutional objections to each of these bills; the last one pointed to the authority provided OLC to "render legal opinions that bind all military and civilian attorneys in the Department of Defense."[37]

The most well-known of President Bush's signing statements dealt with the so-called Torture Ban sponsored by Senator John McCain (R-AZ). This amendment to the 2006 defense appropriations bill prohibited torture along with cruel, inhuman, and degrading treatment. The administration engaged in a long battle with Senator McCain, at first trying to dissuade him from applying the Torture Ban to the CIA, and when that failed, threatening a veto. After McCain's bill passed with veto-proof majorities in both chambers, President Bush met with the senator in the Oval Office. The president made a public show of congratulating him for making it "clear to the world that this Government does not torture." Two weeks later, at 8 p.m. on December 30 (when most likely to go unnoticed), President Bush signed the McCain Torture Ban into law with a signing statement that he would follow the law "in a manner consistent with the constitutional authority of the President to supervise the unitary executive branch and as Commander in Chief."[38]

This comment may be taken as merely asserting authority, and some commentators consider the criticism of President Bush's signing statements "overblown." Others say that the McCain Torture Ban prevented further mistreatment of detainees so that this signing statement did no harm.[39] There is some question about how well the McCain amendment actually worked to curb abusive interrogations, but the importance of this signing statement can be measured not so much in terms of its impact, more so as a declaration of intent. If nothing else, this signing statement suggests that President Bush believed that he had the authority to ignore a statute prohibiting cruel, inhuman, and degrading treatment.

Taken altogether, President Bush's signing statements show where he thought the president as unitary executive stood in relation to the other branches. What supercharged President Bush's conception of his wartime authority was how the claims he made pursuant to the unitary executive doctrine were coupled with the powers he believed he had as commander in chief. While the unitary executive provided the foundation for the administration's broad conception of presidential power, the president's inner circle seemed to regard the commander in chief clause as their ultimate ally—a constitutional jack-of-all-trades that could provide a favorable answer to any question that arose in the war against terrorism.[40] As John Yoo put it, the president's power was "at its zenith under the Constitution" when directing "military operations of the armed forces."[41]

The Constitution provides without elaboration that the president shall be "Commander in Chief of the Army and Navy of the United States" (along with state militia when in service).[42] Like other consequential constitutional provisions, this language requires interpretation. What is the scope of power granted? Is the answer to that question colored by various constitutional provisions that authorize Congress to declare war, raise and support the armed forces, make rules for their regulation, define and punish offenses against the law of nations, and prescribe rules for captures?[43]

The conventional view of the president's powers as commander in chief was based on a seemingly straightforward division of labor between the executive and the legislature. The decision whether to go to war was widely if not universally regarded as within Congress's bailiwick (a supposition sorely tested since World War II), but once lawmakers authorized the use of military force, the president was understood to have charge of how war is waged—powers so broad that Congress has no authority to interfere with the president's decisions concerning the conduct of military operations.[44]

The usual starting point for analysis—and quite often the endpoint as well—was a phrase extracted from Chief Justice Salmon P. Chase's concurring opinion in *Ex parte Milligan* (1866). He said that Congress cannot interfere with the president's "command of the forces" or "the conduct of campaigns." This wording had been repeated so often—for example, in *Hamdan v. Rumsfeld*—that it had come to represent the common sense of the matter. Even Justice Robert H. Jackson, well aware of the difficulties looming in the commander in chief clause but evidently bowing to his understanding of practical necessity, acknowledged the president's "exclusive function to command the instruments of national force." He qualified that remark with the phrase "when turned against the outside world"—an important qualification no doubt—but his statement still represents a major concession to executive power. Taken to its logical conclusion, it follows that, whatever is deemed to be within this sphere of exclusive wartime authority, the commander in chief has the final say and Congress cannot countermand the president's decisions.[45]

The obvious question, then, is what lies within the president's exclusive authority? Or, to use Chase's phrasing, what exactly constitutes the "command of the forces" and "the conduct of campaigns"? Commentators have offered various definitions: "day-to-day combat decisions"; "tactical command of military operations"; "directing where troops will go"; and "operational battlefield decisions concerning the means to be employed to achieve ends chosen by Congress."[46] As these interpretations suggest, the basic idea was that the commander in chief was in charge of the course of fighting. The more that a decision can be classified as tactical in nature and the closer it is to the battlefield, the more likely it will be seen to rest exclusively with the president.

This arrangement for keeping the legislature out of the way has some intuitive appeal. Even Congress's most enthusiastic supporters must be given pause over the prospect of lawmakers—possibly dozens or even several hundred—getting involved in the sort of decisions that go along with military command. Alexander Hamilton's oft-quoted remark is on point: "of all the cares or concerns of government, the direction of war most peculiarly demands those qualities which distinguish the exercise of power by a single hand." It requires little imagination to think of what problems might arise if members of Congress felt empowered to direct troops on the battlefield to do such things as attack at dawn or charge down that ravine—a scenario that frankly seems implausible. Even with broader strategic decisions, the legislature's involvement might reasonably be seen as a recipe for disaster. A favorite historical example is the decision to have American forces land on beaches codenamed Omaha and Utah on D-Day. Lawmakers could have surely criticized FDR if things had gone badly, but having them directly involved in that decision-making process is another matter.[47]

As commonsensical as this conventional wisdom on allocating war powers seems in the abstract, it was as if it were tailor-made for the Bush administration's interrogation program, at least as OLC made use of it. The legal memoranda, especially those written by John Yoo, showed how far presidential power could be taken based upon this notion of exclusive authority over the conduct of war. The analysis culminated in what has become known as the "commander in chief override."[48]

Yoo started from the premise that the president must have the "fullest discretion" in "commanding troops in the field." Regarding the interrogation program, the key move in the argument was to fold detainee treatment into battlefield decisions. Yoo classified "capturing, detaining, and interrogating members of the enemy" as "one of the core functions" of the commander in chief.[49] And if the president as commander in chief had "complete authority over the conduct of war" (as in take that hill), then, so the argument went, President Bush had just as much discretion—"complete discretion" in Yoo's words—to decide how to interrogate detainees.[50] In the belief that the president held a "constitutionally superior position" to the other branches of government, Yoo affirmed that "any effort by Congress to regulate the interrogation of battlefield combatants would violate the Constitution's sole vesting of the Commander-in-Chief authority in the President."[51] In a burst of what might pass for eloquence in otherwise tedious legal analysis, he wrote that Congress "may no more regulate the President's ability to detain and interrogate enemy combatants than it may regulate his ability to direct troop movements on the battlefield." Yoo seemed to like that turn of phrase, as he reiterated that Congress "can no more interfere with the President's conduct of the interrogation of enemy combatants than it can dictate strategic or tactical decisions on the battlefield."[52] Even a statute prohibiting torture was subject to the commander in chief override, as Yoo considered it "an unconstitutional infringement of the President's authority to conduct war."[53]

All of this was typical Yoo. After he left the Justice Department—and after his so-called torture memo came to light—OLC lawyers tried to distance the department from his work. But while declaring his arguments on the commander in chief clause "unnecessary," OLC never retracted the override theory.[54] Indeed, the Justice Department later reiterated that position.[55]

While the Bush administration's override theory is usually discussed as it applied to legislation, it can be viewed more broadly as justification for getting around any legal constraint that stood in the way of the president's preferred course of action. Not least of all the targets was the law of war, whether embodied in treaties or customary practices. The president, John Yoo said, has the "unilateral power" to suspend the Geneva Conventions. In the belief that the "power to override or ignore customary international law, even the law applying to armed conflict," was "an 'integral part of the President's foreign affairs power,'" Yoo claimed that the president could "exempt" military "operations from their coverage, or apply some but not all of the common laws of war to this conflict."[56]

All of this can be taken as the prelude to what might be considered the point of this exercise, at least so far as international humanitarian law was concerned: that President Bush as the commander in chief had the authority to block war crimes prosecutions. Yoo made this point repeatedly. "Executive officials," he said, cannot be prosecuted "for conducting interrogations when they were carrying out the President's Commander-in-Chief powers." The president can "preclude the trials of United States military personnel on specific charges of violations of the common laws of war." Even "if an interrogation method arguably were to violate a criminal statute, the Justice Department could not bring a prosecution because the statute would be unconstitutional as applied," as it would contravene the commander in chief clause. It is hard to overstate the significance of this line of analysis of the commander in chief's authority, as it meant, in the words of the Pentagon Working Group applying Yoo's analysis, that "specific conduct, otherwise criminal" could be rendered by the president "*not* unlawful."[57]

Yoo's principal argumentative move—categorizing detainee treatment as the equivalent of tactical battlefield decisions—built on the conventional view of the commander in chief's exclusive authority over the conduct of war. One problem with that argument is that the conventional view was susceptible to a more critical reading, as recent scholarship responding to the Bush administration's override theory suggests. In their comprehensive study of the commander in chief clause, David J. Barron and Martin S. Lederman found little historical support for the exclusive power argument. Citing numerous examples of legislation restricting what the president can do in warfare, they concluded that Congress was often an "active participant" in regulating the "conduct and organization of the armed forces and militia."[58] They pointed out that presidents had mostly accepted congressional limits on their authority over the conduct of war without raising constitutional concerns.[59] Notwithstanding an upsurge in presidential assertions of exclusive authority since the Korean War, Barron and Lederman detected nothing like an unbroken line of executive resistance to legislative constraints, even in the face of more invasive statutes and treaties.[60] Instead, they considered this modern trend notable for its inconsistency—an "inchoate jumble of often ill-defined, and occasionally contradictory, executive branch claims."[61] They conceded some "preclusive prerogative of superintendence" over the military chain of command, but what they had in mind was nothing like the Bush administration's override theory. They meant that Congress could not put individuals in charge of military operations and prevent the president from removing them.[62]

In a suggestive essay, David Luban explained how the conventional view of the president's exclusive authority over the conduct of war failed to take into account the distinctive reasons why the Constitution's commander in chief clause put the military under civilian authority. Luban constructed a classification scheme cutting across societies throughout history. For ancient heroic cultures and feudal monarchies, skill in combat served as a qualification for ruling; the purpose in unifying military and civilian leadership was to "facilitate warmaking."[63] With military dictatorships, the highest civilian office is integrated into the highest military office—the move only goes in that direction—supposedly in order to handle a crisis.[64] By contrast, the rationale for combining these offices in the United States and other liberal republics is to ensure civilian control over the armed forces—an idea given added weight in the United States when the commander in chief clause is viewed as a particular application of checks and balances; in this case with the president as a check on the military. On that reading, the reasons that may justify a leader's exclusive authority over the conduct of war in other societies do not apply here.[65]

In addition, the premise underlying the conventional view—that it is possible to distinguish between what falls in the category of the conduct of war (within the president's exclusive authority) from what lies outside it (open to congressional regulation)—breaks down upon closer scrutiny. Various line-drawing tests have been put forward over the years. Besides the obvious battlefield/nonbattlefield distinction that OLC used, some commentators have contrasted general framework legislation (permissible) from statutes addressing issues arising in a particular conflict (impermissible). It has also been suggested that Congress can enact legislation that constrains the president's scope of authority over the conduct of war before a military conflict begins while the same legislation enacted in wartime would be unconstitutional.[66]

These efforts to divide institutional responsibility raise perplexing problems, as Jules Lobel pointed out. Can Congress authorize the use of military force while stipulating that US forces refrain from launching intercontinental ballistic missiles? Can lawmakers forbid the president from introducing ground troops into a conflict? Does the exclusive authority argument render the Uniform Code of Military Justice unconstitutional to the extent that it regulates battlefield conduct? If so, would a statute criminalizing the summary execution of prisoners of war by US soldiers constitute an undue intrusion into the commander in chief's exclusive authority over the battlefield?[67]

Moreover, as the conventional approach was validated by its long history—going back to Chief Justice Chase's statement from 1866 at least—some historical clarification is in order. A close reading of his concurring opinion in context indicates that he was less willing to accede to the president's exclusive control over the conduct of war than his dictum has been taken to suggest, as Barron and Lederman noted. The *Milligan* Court had decided that the president did not have constitutional authority to establish military tribunals to try civilians in areas where civil courts were functioning. Chase agreed with that result. He said he felt compelled to write a separate concurrence because he feared that the majority opinion could be construed to mean that Congress also lacked the authority to set up military commissions.[68] Like other Republicans then, the chief justice worried about the implications such a judicial decision could have on Reconstruction legislation. His principal concern was not with shielding presidential war powers from congressional interference, but rather with recognizing the legislature's authority over the "prosecution of war." Accordingly, he stated that Congress's power "necessarily extends to all legislation essential to the prosecution of war with vigor and success." Having described legislative war powers so broadly, it appears that he felt obliged to acknowledge an exception: "except such as interferes with the command of the forces and the conduct of campaigns."[69] Possibly, he thought this stated the obvious, along the lines of Hamilton's remark that the "direction of war" requires "a single hand." One point is clear. Chase believed that decisions concerning military tribunals fell squarely within Congress's authority, and it was the president, in his view, who lacked power to establish military tribunals "without the sanction of Congress."[70] From these unlikely roots, this idea that the president has exclusive authority over the conduct of war came to have a life of its own.

As for President Bush, he surely did not read through OLC's detailed memoranda word for word, but he just as surely imbibed the basic message: that his power in the war against terrorism was "plenary," that his discretion over detainees was "unrestricted" and "complete," that any decision he made regarding military force was "unreviewable," that he had as commander in chief the authority to exempt US personnel from the Geneva Conventions and the War Crimes Act, and that he could block federal prosecutors from charging anyone involved in the interrogation program with war crimes.

III

With this expansive view of presidential power in place, the groundwork was laid to address the applicability of the Geneva Conventions directly. What was left for OLC to do was to offer an interpretation of Geneva so that the president could declare that Al Qaeda and Taliban detainees had no rights under the conventions. A key step in the decision-making process was a forty-four-page single-spaced memorandum dated November 30, 2001. Addressed to Gonzales, the memorandum recorded that he had asked about applying "certain treaties, domestic federal law, and customary international law to the armed conflict in Afghanistan," particularly regarding "the applicability of the laws of armed conflict to the conduct of the U.S. Armed Forces towards captured members of the al Qaeda terrorist group and of the Taliban militia."[71] Written by Yoo with the assistance of a career attorney named

Robert J. Delahunty, this opinion was titled "Treaties and Laws Applicable to the Conflict in Afghanistan and to the Treatment of Persons Captured by the U.S. Armed Forces in That Conflict." The arguments Yoo and Delahunty put forward here, reiterated in a slightly revised opinion that circulated within the administration two months later, provided the principal legal justification for President Bush's decision on the Geneva Conventions.[72]

When Gonzales asked OLC about "treaties, domestic federal law, and customary international law" with respect to armed conflict in Afghanistan, one might have pictured this as a run-of-the-mill request for advice on the standards governing the treatment of wartime captives. That was not really the point of Gonzales's inquiry, however. His concern was over the *applicability* of the laws of armed conflict," and whatever was contemplated at this point—around this time Haynes's office sought information about "exploitation" strategies and CIA attorneys discussed the need for a "policy decision" regarding the "U.S. use of torture in light of our obligations under international law"—the November 30 opinion was not designed as a conventional legal opinion laying out what Geneva permitted and prohibited.[73] If this opinion is any indication of the tenor of internal discussions at that time, no one in the White House was interested in expounding on the legal standards governing wartime detentions in order to follow them. The operative assumption was that there would be violations of the Geneva Conventions. The question under consideration was whether the conventions applied, or more accurately, the question was how to make sure that the Geneva Conventions did not apply.

One major concern, judging from the strained argument offered by OLC, had to do with the status of Taliban fighters under Geneva. The arguments OLC presented on this issue were among their most important, and, as evidence of the administration's internal decision-making process, among the most revealing.

The legal analysis regarding the status of the conflict with Afghanistan should have been straightforward. Once combat operations started there in October 2001, the United States was engaged in an armed conflict between "High Contracting Parties" covered by Article 2 of the Geneva Conventions. Afghanistan had ratified the 1949 conventions, as Yoo and Delahunty noted. "Some might argue," they said, that "this requires application of the Geneva Conventions to the present conflict with respect to the Taliban militia, which would then trigger the WCA [War Crimes Act]." They could also have taken note of the practice of the American military, as codified in DOD Directive

5100.77, to "comply with the law of war during all conflicts, however such conflicts are characterized."[74]

One can imagine the lawyers of the War Council batting this issue around until someone—John Yoo perhaps—came up with a novel argument based on the idea that Afghanistan was a "failed state." In academic circles, this concept had gained traction as a justification for outside intervention in countries like Somalia.[75] No one had previously applied the idea to nullify a treaty like the Geneva Conventions. Yoo would later say, apparently with a touch of pride, that OLC was "advancing the law."[76] Of course, it is one thing to try to persuade a panel of independent judges in open court to break new ground; quite another to undermine an important international treaty by making unprecedented and unopposed legal arguments in secret.

The key to OLC's analysis was presidential power; here again cast in the form of the president's "plenary constitutional power over military operations (including the treatment of captives)" and "plenary control over the conduct of foreign relations."[77] Yoo and Delahunty took the position that it was "up to the President alone" to determine whether another country was a failed state unable to fulfill its treaty commitments. There were "ample grounds" for such a presidential finding with respect to Afghanistan, they argued.[78] Outlining "the analysis that the President may wish to follow," they cited several factors, essentially going to the question of whether there was a functioning central government capable of delivering basic services and engaging in foreign relations. They were also willing to have the president rely on seemingly impromptu remarks made by his own defense secretary that the Taliban "never was a government." If the president determined that Afghanistan was a failed state that could not carry out its obligations under Geneva, then it followed for Yoo and Delahunty that Afghanistan could no longer be considered a High Contracting Party to the conventions, and the fighting with the Taliban would not qualify as an Article 2 conflict between two High Contracting Parties. Nor, Yoo and Delahunty added, could it be a non-international Common Article 3 conflict because those conflicts must take place "in the territory of one of the High Contracting Parties."[79]

The problems with this approach—the logical consequence of which would be that any nation's leader could unilaterally declare the Geneva Conventions inapplicable in countries they deemed failed states—seem too obvious to require elaboration. Perhaps wary of relying exclusively on this "failed state" theory, Yoo and Delahunty offered an alternative argument. They suggested that President Bush could "temporarily suspend" the Geneva Conventions. Again, they pointed to the president's "plenary authority"—this time his constitutional power over treaties.[80]

Even plenary power in the presidency had to do a lot of work to reach that conclusion. Yoo and Delahunty conceded that the United States had never "suspended any provision of the Geneva Conventions" to that point. Their opinion noted language in the Geneva Conventions that requires signatories to respect the conventions "*in all circumstances*" (italics in the original), but they managed to read this to permit temporary suspension. They acknowledged that the Geneva Conventions "must be regarded" as treaties of a "humanitarian character" and that international law could be read to bar the suspension of such treaties. Still Yoo and Delahunty asserted that the president could make "good faith arguments" to justify suspension (this should probably be read as arguments that could be made to appear in good faith).[81] Finally, they put OLC on record with the view that any rule that international law provided on the suspension of treaties like the Geneva Conventions had "*no bearing* on the President's constitutional powers—or on the application of the WCA" (italics in the original).[82]

For Yoo and Delahunty, the same could be said of customary international law. In the context of their argument, that branch of the law was important to consider. If their analysis on failed states or treaty suspension somehow held up, international lawyers would turn to customary international law to fill the void. Customary practice has long been a major source of the law of war. Until OLC got hold of this issue, the American military, as stated in the US Army Field Manual, recognized "unwritten or customary law of war" as "binding upon all nations."[83]

Against this, Yoo and Delahunty gave their usual answer. "Importing customary international law notions" here would constitute "a direct infringement on the President's discretion as Commander in Chief and Chief Executive to determine how best to conduct the Nation's military affairs."[84] They asserted that "any customary international law of armed conflict in no way binds, as a legal matter, the President or the operation of the U.S. Armed Forces."[85]

When these arguments first circulated more widely within the administration in an OLC draft memorandum dated January 9, 2002, they drew an immediate reaction. It was enough to lead William Howard Taft IV to dispense with whatever diplomatic niceties might be expected of the State Department's top lawyer. He wrote Yoo two days later, attached a forty-page response prepared by State's lawyers, and sent copies to Gonzales and Powell. OLC's analysis of the Geneva Conventions was "seriously flawed," Taft said; its conclusions on failed states, treaty suspension, and customary international law were "untenable." He suggested that OLC "badly confuses the distinction between states and governments in the operation of the law of treaties." OLC's "failed state" argument on Geneva, Taft noted, was "contrary to the official position of the United States, the United Nations and all other states that have considered the issue." He found OLC's claim that President Bush could suspend US obligations under the Geneva Conventions "legally flawed and procedurally impossible." Taft cited America's "unbroken record of compliance with the Geneva Conventions in our conduct of military operations over the past fifty years." He pointed out that the military had in that time "dealt with tens of thousands of detainees without repudiating its obligations under the Conventions." He expressed "no doubt we can do so here" with a "relative handful" of detainees.[86]

The attached draft State Department memorandum expanded on the "very significant" implications of such a presidential decision. Not least in importance, State argued that declaring the Geneva Conventions inapplicable would endanger US troops fighting in Afghanistan. For if that country was no longer considered a party to the conventions, the United States would have "no basis to complain" of war crimes committed against Americans posted there. State's lawyers also warned of the bad precedent such a presidential decision would set. The goal of the United States, the memorandum reminded its readers, had always been to secure "the widest possible application" of the Geneva Conventions. If the United States were "precluded from maintaining mutual treaty obligations with a 'failed State,'" that would have "far-reaching implications" for American foreign policy when dealing with "questionable governing regimes." The State Department's message was clear. With its far-flung commitments and servicemembers stationed around the world, the United States should be the last nation to undermine the Geneva Conventions.[87]

Of course, memoranda at the subcabinet level do not necessarily cross the president's desk. Was President Bush aware of the debate over Geneva within his own administration? Even if he remained oblivious of the subcabinet debate, he was undoubtedly aware of dissenting views. Secretary of State Powell arranged two meetings with the president and tried to persuade him to change his mind on Geneva. General Richard B. Myers, chairman of the Joint Chiefs of Staff, expressed his concerns to President Bush at a meeting of the National Security Council. To Myers, the question of applying the

Geneva Conventions was not primarily a legal issue. He worried about US servicemembers who might be captured by enemy forces. One can imagine the four-star US Air Force general thinking a simple reminder of those serving in the armed forces would suffice. "You have to remember," he told the president, "that as we treat them, probably so we're going to be treated." His warning was unmistakable. "We may be treated worse, but we should not give them an opening."[88]

Needless to say, this was no longer something that could be written off as a subcabinet turf war. It was clear that any decision by President Bush attempting to nullify the Geneva Conventions would have to be made over the objections of America's highest ranking military officer as well as the secretary of state, who had previously served as chairman of the Joint Chiefs of Staff.

IV

In the face of what can only be described as credible opposition, why did President Bush persist in this effort to circumvent the Geneva Conventions? Internal documents indicate that administration insiders were concerned most of all about the threat of war crimes prosecutions based on the War Crimes Act (WCA). They believed that the president could avert that threat if he declared Geneva inapplicable. By all indications, this is what led to the president's decision to nullify the Geneva Conventions.

Interestingly, OLC memoranda suggest that administration officials may have raised questions about the War Crimes Act at the earliest stages of the decision-making process. OLC's November 30 opinion examined that statute. The analysis was brief but suggestive. It reads like a preliminary overview, as if Yoo and Delahunty were getting acquainted with the legislation. A revealing footnote discussed the rule of lenity—a rule of statutory interpretation which requires courts to construe ambiguity in criminal statutes in favor of defendants. The rule of lenity has fallen out of favor, but that did not stop Yoo and Delahunty from suggesting that it could be used to block prosecutions under the WCA if applying the Geneva Conventions through this legislation was "unclear." The memorandum closed with a brief section titled, interestingly, "May a U.S. Servicemember be Tried for Violations of the Laws of War?" Given that question's focus on the armed forces, Yoo and Delahunty discussed the Uniform Code of Military Justice and customary international law. They concluded that President Bush, as commander in chief, could "preclude the trials of United States military personnel on specific charges of violations of the common laws of war."[89]

The key document in this—some might call it the smoking gun—is a Memorandum for the President purportedly written by Gonzales. It was titled "Decision Re Application of the Geneva Convention on Prisoners of War to the Conflict with Al Qaeda and the Taliban." The version leaked—dated January 25, 2002, time-stamped 3:30 p.m., and marked DRAFT—identified the White House counsel as the author, but reporters found out that Addington had written it. Gonzales later said that this "draft document" did not "represent the final advice" provided the president, but he never denied that the memorandum had been presented to him. Nor did he explain how the "final advice" given the president differed from the draft document.[90]

Even the most superficial comparison between the draft memorandum and the president's February 7 directive indicates that the arguments put forward by Gonzales and Addington found their way to President Bush. In language the president repeated, the memorandum contrasted the war against terrorism with "the traditional clash between nations adhering to the laws of war" that "formed the backdrop" for the Geneva Conventions. Gonzales and Addington said that this "new kind of war" put a "high premium" on gathering intelligence quickly from "captured" enemy forces. Here, possibly for the first time, is a reference to the "new paradigm" that, the memorandum stated, "renders obsolete Geneva's strict limitations on questioning of enemy prisoners and renders quaint some of its provisions requiring that captured enemy be afforded such things as commissary privileges, scrip (i.e., advances of monthly pay), athletic uniforms, and scientific instruments."[91]

That characterization has achieved some notoriety, but what followed merits just as much scrutiny, as Gonzales and Addington turned their attention to the "threat of domestic criminal prosecution under the War Crimes Act." They proceeded to take their readers step by step through this criminal legislation. The memorandum stated that the WCA could be applied to "U.S. officials" and that the statutory definition of war crimes included "any violation of common Article 3." Gonzales and Addington highlighted the prohibition of "outrages against personal dignity." The memorandum further explained that the War Crimes Act applied whether or not a detainee "qualifies as a POW," and it noted that the death penalty was a possible punishment.[92]

It was at this point that Addington and Gonzales offered a crucial recommendation. They suggested that the president—and only the president—

could neutralize the War Crimes Act by going directly to the source of its criminal prohibitions, that is to say, the Geneva Conventions. In the words of the memorandum: "your determination" that the conventions did not apply would "create a reasonable basis in law" that the War Crimes Act did not apply either. And, they noted, such a presidential decision "would provide a solid defense to any future prosecution."[93]

One week later, Attorney General Ashcroft sent a letter to President Bush. Ashcroft focused on one question. Given his position as the nation's chief law enforcement officer, it was an extraordinary question for him to consider, let alone discuss in a personal letter to the president. Having noted that there could be "substantial criminal liability for involved U.S. officials," the attorney general proceeded to offer a legal analysis explaining what could be done to block federal prosecutions. The solution was to be found in Supreme Court precedent that Ashcroft believed had established a fundamental distinction. On the one hand, the president could decide that Geneva did not apply because Afghanistan was a failed state unable to fulfill its commitments under that treaty. Such a decision, Ashcroft wrote, was "fully discretionary and will not be reviewed by the federal courts." He said that a presidential decision that the conventions did not apply would provide "the highest assurance" that "no court would subsequently entertain charges that American military officers, intelligence officials, or law enforcement officials violated Geneva Convention rules relating to field conduct, detention conduct or interrogation of detainees." On the other hand, if President Bush decided that the conventions applied but that members of the Taliban were "unlawful combatants" who were not protected by Geneva Convention III, that could be viewed as an executive interpretation subject to judicial review. That would not "accord American officials the same protection from legal consequences," Ashcroft said. In his view, that option carried a "higher risk" of criminal prosecution.[94]

This talk of war crimes prosecutions might be considered sufficient evidence of what is known in American jurisprudence as mens rea, which roughly translates as a guilty mind or criminal intent. To this, President Bush's close associates had an answer at the ready, which appears most clearly in the Addington/Gonzales memorandum. They were careful to point out—too careful perhaps—that any prosecutions brought under the War Crimes Act would be "unwarranted."[95] According to their memorandum, the reason for concern was not that the administration would actually violate the WCA, but rather that this legislation was susceptible to "misconstruction or misapplication" due to its "undefined" language. Addington and Gonzales pointed to its provisions criminalizing "inhuman treatment" and "outrages upon personal dignity." They thought that language made it "difficult to predict with confidence what actions might be deemed to constitute violations" of Geneva. They also expressed concern about the "motives" of "prosecutors and independent counsels" in the future.[96]

It would be interesting to learn more of the private conversations that led to the Addington/Gonzales memorandum, but it is possible to draw inferences from the documentary record in any event. The memorandum reads as if the president's advisors kept reminding themselves—with the expectation that these documents would eventually find their way into the public domain—to take every opportunity to declare war crimes prosecutions unjustified. In fact, Gonzales had OLC review the draft memorandum, and, in case anyone missed that point, OLC offered just such a recommendation: change "substantially reduces the threat of domestic criminal prosecution under the War Crimes Act" to "substantially reduces the misapplication of the War Crimes Act."[97] One may be forgiven for thinking, as with Shakespeare's *Hamlet*, that the president's advisors protested too much.

As to the substance of their complaint, it should be noted that the sort of open-ended language they found objectionable is an inescapable fact of the law (think of constitutional language like "freedom of speech" or "due process of law"). The concerns Addington and Gonzales expressed might be taken more seriously had they investigated the history surrounding the adoption of the Geneva Conventions. Or they could have consulted JAGs with relevant expertise. As for their specific concerns, defining humane treatment is not as difficult as they made it out to be. As the Red Cross commentaries suggested, the command to refrain from inhumane treatment is "simple and clear." It reflects the central purpose of the 1949 conventions. And if the words "inhumane treatment" troubled President Bush's advisors so much, what does that say about his directive that the US military treat detainees humanely?[98]

Given the interrogation regime the Bush administration put in place, it is reasonable to infer that the concern at the White House was never really about rogue prosecutors misreading the law. Rather, the concern was that federal prosecutors would understand all too well what was going on and conclude that, under any conceivable definition of Common Article 3, the administration had subjected detainees in US custody to inhumane treatment.

Interestingly, in the run-up to the president's February 7 memorandum, the State Department also recognized the "risk" of war crimes prosecutions of "U.S. civilian and military leadership and their advisers," but its lawyers thought that risk arose from a presidential decision declaring Geneva inapplicable. Their reasoning was straightforward. Without the conventions applying, Americans involved in the war effort might be more likely to engage in "conduct that would constitute a grave breach," and other parties to Geneva would have an obligation to prosecute. On the other hand, if the president left the Geneva Conventions alone, "the risk of prosecution" under the War Crimes Act was "negligible," as Taft put it. He added what many would consider the key point: "any small benefit" derived from reducing that risk "further will be purchased at the expense of the men and women in our armed forces" who could stand to lose the benefits of Geneva's protection.[99]

After Gonzales circulated the memorandum ghostwritten by Addington, Powell responded directly to the White House counsel. The secretary of state wrote that a decision that the Geneva Conventions did not apply would "reverse over a century of U.S. policy and practice in supporting the Geneva conventions and undermine the protections of the law of war for our troops." Taft reiterated the same point. "The President should know," he wrote Gonzales, that applying the conventions is "consistent" with their "plain language" and the "unvaried practice of the United States" for "over fifty years."[100] Evidently recognizing the inevitable, Powell tried to salvage what he could in a last-ditch effort. He highlighted the option that the Geneva Conventions did apply to the conflict in Afghanistan but that the Taliban did not qualify as prisoners of war. That was the position President Bush embraced in the end. It may look like the secretary of state had wrung an important concession at the last moment, but State's lawyers considered it a "hollow" victory.[101] After all, Secretary Powell had not suggested anything about dispensing with the minimum requirements of Common Article 3, but President Bush declared that important provision inapplicable as well. For all intents and purposes, the president had done everything he could to emasculate the Geneva Conventions.

V

What, then, should be made of President Bush's policy directive purportedly requiring humane treatment? In his February 7, 2002 memorandum, the president said that "our values as a Nation, values that we share with many nations in the world, call for us to treat detainees humanely, including those who are not legally entitled to such treatment." He noted that the United

States "has been and will continue to be a strong supporter of Geneva and its principles." There followed his specific order. "As a matter of policy," the president stated, "the United States Armed Forces shall continue to treat detainees humanely and, to the extent appropriate and consistent with military necessity, in a manner consistent with the principles of Geneva."[102]

While the full text of the memorandum was initially classified, it appears that public relations was an important factor behind this. On the same day President Bush signed the memorandum, the White House issued a fact sheet affirming that US policy was to treat Guantánamo detainees humanely. This fact sheet repeated the president's wording almost verbatim. Press Secretary Ari Fleischer told the White House press corps that "today President Bush affirms our enduring commitment to the important principles of the Geneva Convention." Two years later, after the story broke about prisoner abuse at Abu Ghraib, the administration declassified and released the presidential memorandum and other documents to show "the great degree of care taken in the policy-making process" and to "inform the public that the policy decisions made by the President are in keeping with the values of our nation, our Constitution, our laws, and our treaty obligations." So said White House counsel Gonzales at a press briefing responding to the scandal over Abu Ghraib. "This is very important," he said, as he made a point of quoting the president's directive on humane treatment directly "from the actual document." President Bush responded to reporters' questions about Abu Ghraib by telling them that "the message I gave our people" was that "anything we did would conform to U.S. law and would be consistent with international treaty obligations."[103]

Given OLC's interpretations of US law and treaties, this language was, to be blunt, disingenuous. So too was the president's policy mandate for humane treatment. This charade begins to unravel by taking note of who was—and, more importantly, who was not—covered by it. The policy applied to US armed forces. President Bush did not mention the CIA in his presidential memorandum, and it becomes clear from the documentary record and subsequent events that this omission was intentional. In short, the president never intended to require the CIA to comply with his policy on humane treatment.

That President Bush would take an expansive view of what the CIA could do in the war against terrorism was signaled by a classified Memorandum of Notification to the Central Intelligence Agency on September 17, 2001—when the "gloves came off" in CIA director George Tenet's account. This document, still classified, provided the agency with what the Senate Intelligence Committee described as "unprecedented authorities" to "capture and detain" terrorism suspects. The president later signed another order (also still classified) that authorized the CIA to set up secret prisons to hold "high value detainees" incommunicado. These were the "black sites" referenced in administration documents.[104]

Once the CIA got in the detention business, its officials had to figure out where to hold terrorism suspects for interrogation. Evidence of their intent to evade Geneva's requirement of humane treatment can be gleaned from efforts to locate detainees beyond the reach of legal process. One option considered—and quickly discarded—was to put them on ships sailing continuously in international waters. Another was to bring detainees to Guantánamo Naval Base, but CIA officers who inspected the newly built Camp X-Ray had concerns over its visibility (the CIA later set up a secret prison facility on the base). At one point John Bruce Jessen, a former military psychologist retained by the CIA, recommended that high priority detainees be housed in what he called an "exploitation facility." His idea was to keep detainees away from the International Committee of the Red Cross (ICRC), which monitors compliance with the Geneva Conventions.[105]

Interestingly, the distinction between law and policy underlying the president's memorandum was foreshadowed by CIA representatives in meetings with other administration lawyers in January 2002. The agency's position was that it would not be possible to obtain "actionable intelligence" if interrogators were "required to respect the limits for treatment demanded by the Geneva Conventions." Taft's notes of the meetings record that CIA lawyers suggested that, if Geneva's protections did not "apply as a matter of law" but rather "as a matter of policy," it would be "desirable to circumscribe the policy."[106]

Corroborating evidence shedding light on what was going on behind closed doors can be found in a "Memorandum for the Record" dated February 12, 2003. Marked top secret, the memorandum was not made public for eleven years. It was written by CIA general counsel Scott W. Muller out of obvious concern over the methods of interrogation. Muller recorded that it was the "consistent understanding of CIA personnel" that the policy of humane treatment stated in President Bush's February 7, 2002 memorandum was "not applicable to, was not intended to, and does not prohibit or limit CIA in the use of the type of interrogation techniques" or "impose a requirement of 'humane' treatment" on the agency. He noted that, while administration officials were "aware generally of the fact that CIA was authorized to conduct interrogations using techniques beyond those permitted" by Geneva, "no one ever suggested that there was any inconsistency between the authorized CIA conduct and the [president's] February Memo." He also memorialized a conversation he had with John Yoo, who told him that "the February Memo was not applicable to or binding on CIA." Yoo added that "the language of the memorandum had been deliberately limited to be binding only on 'the Armed Forces' which did not include the CIA." Muller also met with Gonzales and Addington, who "confirmed" that the February presidential memorandum was only applicable to the military. In another meeting that included Rice, Rumsfeld, Powell, and Cheney, Muller raised the question of an "arguable inconsistency between what CIA was authorized to do and what at least some in the international community expect in light of the Administration's public statements about 'humane treatment.'"[107]

Direct evidence of what President Bush had in mind for CIA interrogations can be found in his own description of his interaction with CIA officials. The interrogation program's first major detainee was Abu Zubaydah, captured in March 2002 in a dramatic shootout in Pakistan. President Bush by his own account "directed the team" when he was told that Zubaydah was holding back information. "We need to find out what he knows. . . . What are our options?" The president then made the fateful decision to have the CIA "take over Zubaydah's questioning" from the FBI and "move him to a secure location in another country where the Agency could have total control over his environment." President Bush also approved which enhanced interrogation techniques the CIA could use on Zubaydah. "I took a look at the list of techniques," the president wrote in his memoir, and "I approved" their use except for two that "went too far."[108]

It has also been reported that President Bush pressured the CIA's director to withhold pain medication from Zubaydah. "I said he was important," the president was said to have told Tenet, in reference to a speech he gave that described Zubaydah as one of Al Qaeda's "top operatives." "You're not going to let me lose face on this, are you?" When Tenet informed the president that Zubaydah had been given painkillers (he had been shot during his capture, and his condition was so critical that the CIA had flown a leading American surgeon to Pakistan to save his life), the president's reply, sources said, was to ask, "Who authorized putting him on pain medication?" CIA headquarters subsequently directed interrogators that gathering intelligence from Zubaydah would take "precedence" over his medical care.[109]

Any lingering question of President Bush's intent can be laid to rest by taking note of his continuing efforts to insulate the CIA's interrogation program from the other branches of government. To ensure that the agency remained exempt from any legal requirement to treat detainees humanely, the president had to take affirmative steps to counteract Congress and the Supreme Court. As previously noted, he opposed the so-called McCain Torture Ban, which prohibited inhuman treatment of anyone in US custody, including detainees held by the CIA.[110] And in his last year in office, the president vetoed a bill that would have banned the use of waterboarding along with other enhanced interrogation techniques. The White House indicated that waterboarding could still be used with the president's approval in some circumstances (an imminent attack, for example).[111] President Bush's reaction to the Supreme Court's decision in *Hamdan v. Rumsfeld* (2006) is also revealing. Contradicting the president's February 7 memorandum, the Court there held that Common Article 3 applied to the conflict with Al Qaeda. President Bush blamed the justices for putting "in question the future of the CIA program." The interrogation program was "crucial," he said, "one of the most vital tools in our war against the terrorists." The president openly expressed concern that *Hamdan* put "military and intelligence personnel" at "risk of prosecution under the War Crimes Act."[112]

Even more telling, President Bush went on to complain about Common Article 3's "vague and undefined" language. He singled out the provision prohibiting "outrages upon personal dignity" and "humiliating and degrading treatment." The president also said that "other provisions" of Common Article 3 were vague and undefined, but he did not specify which provisions he had in mind. There are only a few phrases from Common Article 3 that might be relevant: the particular acts prohibited ("cruel treatment," "torture," "mutilation," "violence to life and person," "murder of all kinds") or "humane treatment" itself.

On this point, the Red Cross commentaries on the 1949 Geneva Conventions provide pertinent background. The commentaries referred directly to "outrages upon personal dignity" and "humiliating and degrading treatment." What was vague and undefined to the president was described in the commentaries as "incompatible" with humane treatment—acts "committed frequently" during World War II which "world public opinion finds particularly revolting." The commentaries went on to explain that "lengthy definition of expressions such as 'humane treatment' or 'to treat humanely' is unnecessary, as they have entered sufficiently into current parlance to be understood." If anything, the concern at the time of the drafting the Geneva Conventions was in going into "too much detail" to define humane treatment. As stated in the commentary: "however much care were taken in establishing a list of all the forms of infliction, one would never be able to catch up with the imagination of future torturers." Recent memories of World War II provided ample evidence of the difficulty in trying to anticipate the exact form wrongdoing would take. As the commentaries stated, "the more specific and complete a list" of prohibited acts, "the more restrictive it becomes."[113]

There is, then, some irony in President Bush's efforts following *Hamdan* to "clarify the rules" for interrogations by getting Congress to enact the Military Commissions Act of 2006 in order to enumerate "specific, recognizable offenses that would be considered crimes under the War Crimes Act." Besides amending the War Crimes Act, the Military Commissions Act recognized President Bush's authority to "interpret the meaning and application of the Geneva Conventions." The president subsequently issued an executive order interpreting Common Article 3. The White House claimed that it "clarified vague terms in Common Article 3" and set forth "clear legal standards" to guide CIA officers. In fact, what the president's order made clear was that he would persist in his effort to exempt the enhanced interrogation techniques from Common Article 3's purview. The most glaring loophole was the prohibition of "willful and outrageous acts of personal abuse," which was limited to those acts "done for the purpose of humiliating or degrading the individual," with due regard for the "circumstances." In other words, the president permitted willful and outrageous acts of personal abuse so long as the purpose of such conduct was described as something like acquiring threat information rather than humiliating or degrading the detainee. Among the most forceful critics of the president's interpretation were P. X. Kelley (former commandant of the Marine Corps) and Robert F. Turner (formerly a White House lawyer for President Ronald Reagan). It is "clear to us," they wrote in a *Washington Post* op-ed titled "War Crimes and the White House," that President Bush's executive order "cannot even arguably be reconciled with America's clear duty under Common Article 3 to treat all detainees humanely." In their reading of the executive order, President Bush gave "the CIA carte blanche to engage in 'willful and outrageous acts of personal abuse'" as long as interrogators intended to "gather intelligence" or "prevent future attacks."[114]

In short, President Bush never wavered in his belief that the CIA should be relieved of any obligation, whether in law or policy, to treat detainees humanely. That leaves for consideration what the president had in mind for detainees held by the military. The exact wording in the February 7 memorandum is important to consider. He said that the armed forces shall as a matter of policy "treat detainees humanely and, to the extent appropriate and consistent with military necessity, in a manner consistent with the principles of Geneva." That statement is more problematic than it might at first appear.

One difficulty lies in the president's reference to military necessity. If this language is interpreted to qualify the Geneva Conventions' requirement to treat detainees humanely, then it contravenes Common Article 3, which states that protected persons "shall in all circumstances be treated humanely" and that enumerated acts like torture "shall remain prohibited at any time and in any place whatsoever." Common Article 3 does not permit any exceptions for military necessity or national security emergencies. In its discussion of that article's humane treatment requirement, the commentaries stated that "no possible loophole is left" and that "there can be no excuse, no attenuating circumstances."[115] There is precedent for thinking that whatever is necessary to achieve military objectives can override obligations imposed by the laws of war—a discredited minority view from the German military tradition. In international law today, military necessity means something else. The doctrine enjoins soldiers and their commanders to do no more than what is necessary to achieve their military objective. The legal obligation is twofold: (1) do not violate the laws of war and (2) do only what is necessary. The idea is that the laws of war already take practical military needs into account, as when the 1907 Hague Regulations forbid the destruction of enemy property unless "imperatively demanded by the necessities of war." Military necessity, built into the code, cannot be used to excuse violations of international humanitarian law. Allowing soldiers to determine when the rules of war must yield to military necessity, so the reasoning goes, would lead to the exception (military necessity) swallowing the rule (humane treatment, for example).[116]

Another problem has to do with President Bush's reference to the "principles of Geneva"—emphasis on "principles" instead of the law. When he said that detainees would be treated "in a manner consistent with the principles of Geneva," which principles did he have in mind?[117] The president did not say. His wording seems to contemplate that soldiers could disregard concrete provisions of the Geneva Conventions so long as they adhered to some set of unspecified principles—not exactly what was needed from a command decision for troops at all ranks in a worldwide conflict.

But the fundamental problem with President Bush's directive to the military was that this policy of humane treatment, simply because it was a policy, could never be the equivalent of a binding legal obligation, as administration lawyers had recognized from the start.[118] This had real consequences. In effect, by order of the president of the United States, Geneva's foundational rule of humane treatment was no more legally binding on US military forces than it was on the CIA.

VI

One of the most notable features of the decision-making process on interrogation policy was the extent of opposition within the administration. Nowhere were dissenting views presented more pointedly than within the armed forces.

When the Pentagon considered the use of Survival, Evasion, Resistance, Escape tactics in military interrogations, high-ranking uniformed lawyers from every branch of the armed services objected, including some of the country's foremost experts on the laws of armed conflict. Colonel John Ley, chief of the US Army's International Law Division, said that some techniques "appear to be clear violations" of the Torture Act while others cross "the line of 'humane' treatment." Alberto J. Mora, the US Navy's general counsel, similarly argued that several techniques "constituted, at a minimum, cruel and unusual treatment and, at worst, torture" in violation of "domestic and international legal norms."[119] The position of Major General Jack L. Rives, deputy judge advocate general of the US Air Force, could not be clearer. He stated that several techniques "on their face" violated domestic criminal law and military law. The Air Force expressed "serious concerns" about the "legality of many of the proposed techniques" and warned that some "could be construed as 'torture,' as that crime is defined" in the Torture Act.[120]

As it turned out, it was left to the military lawyers to articulate what else was at stake. Their various suggestions pointed to one conclusion: the Bush interrogation program failed under any standard of review—military, political, ethical, as well as legal. Major General Rives expressed concern, as others in the military did, for American troops captured in future conflicts since the administration "arguably 'lowers the bar'" for the treatment of prisoners of war. Colonel Ley pointed out the risks in a war that required public support at home and abroad. These techniques will eventually become public, Ley predicted, as he dryly noted that they "will not read well in the New York Times or the Cairo Times." Rear Admiral Michael F. Lohr, judge advocate general of the US Navy, recommended that the military ask "decision-makers directly: is this the 'right thing' for U.S. military personnel?"[121]

Law enforcement professionals in the government also opposed the interrogation program. FBI agents sent overseas got into "heated" arguments with their counterparts in the CIA and military.[122] Some of those assigned to Guantánamo recorded instances of prisoner abuse in what they called "'war crimes' case files."[123] Notwithstanding the bureau's obvious interest in investigating terrorism suspects, FBI director Robert S. Mueller III withdrew his agents from coercive interrogations. Agents in the field were instructed to "stand clear" of questionable interrogation techniques. Those same words appear in documents of the Criminal Investigation Task Force, the military's law enforcement unit that had been established in 2002 to collect evidence for cases against terrorism suspects.[124]

Despite the objections, the administration set up a labyrinthine system of prisons around the world to hold and interrogate detainees. The CIA's secret black sites included a network of subterranean interrogation cells in Thailand, the basement of a nondescript building near railroad tracks in a residential neighborhood in Bucharest, Romania, and a one-time brick factory near Kabul, Afghanistan known in the CIA as the Salt Pit. Although the CIA may not have imprisoned a large number of high-value detainees in black sites (something on the order of 119 detainees), the overall number of detainees in US custody was much larger than that.[125] According to news accounts, the military had by the end of 2005 detained over 80,000 individuals. No one knows how many held in US custody in Afghanistan, Iraq, and Guantánamo were subjected to enhanced interrogation techniques.[126] The administration also resorted to extraordinary rendition, with the CIA capturing persons around the world and, without any judicial hearing, rendering them to the intelligence services of countries like Egypt, Morocco, and Syria for interrogation. These countries had at least one thing in common: a record, previously denounced by the State Department, of torturing prisoners.[127]

The detention system was designed to avoid outside scrutiny where it mattered most. Several prisoners subjected to the most aggressive interrogations were held incommunicado by the CIA for over three years. At the agency's request, Secretary Rumsfeld ordered the Army to keep as many as one hundred "ghost detainees" at Abu Ghraib hidden from the ICRC.[128] While the prison at Guantánamo was hardly secret, the Bush administration chose the naval base to house terrorism suspects in the belief that it was beyond the jurisdiction of American courts. Administration lawyers seized on the odd status of Guantánamo—leased by the United States from Cuba after the Spanish-American War—to claim that US courts could not review what happened there, even if, as the Justice Department later maintained in court, American soldiers were "summarily executing" or torturing detainees. The Bush administration considered Guantánamo a "law-free zone," in the memorable words of reporter Charlie Savage.[129]

Perhaps nothing better illustrates the way in which this attitude toward outside scrutiny made its way down the ranks than Camp Nama in Iraq, where Special Operations Task Force 6–26 remade one of Saddam Hussein's torture chambers into an interrogation room that soldiers called the "Black Room." Signs posted nearby announced the unit's modus operandi: "NO BLOOD, NO FOUL." A Defense Department official explained its meaning: "If you don't make them bleed, they can't prosecute for it." Ironically, the treatment of prisoners in the Black Room was so abusive that the CIA ordered its personnel to refrain from participating in interrogations there.[130]

No doubt the public will never know everything that took place in the Black Room, the black sites, and elsewhere within the detention system set up by the Bush administration. Enough has come to light, however, to provide some sense of what happened. Many detainees held in custody had no connection to Al Qaeda or the Taliban. Officials from coalition forces in Iraq informed the Red Cross that 70 to 90 percent of detainees placed in custody in that country were "mistakes."[131] One person held at Guantánamo was a deaf man over eighty years old. Another was probably only twelve years old when he was sent there. Yet another inmate, declared an enemy combatant by a US military tribunal, consistently maintained that he was a shepherd. His interrogators agreed; his knowledge of herding animals was as extensive as his understanding of terrorism was minimal. Yet he remained at Guantánamo for three years before he was released.[132]

The interrogation techniques in operation belied the clinical descriptions found in Bush Justice Department legal memos. For one high-value detainee who had an artificial leg due to an amputation, "stress positions" meant that interrogators removed his artificial leg and then forced him to stand with his hands shackled above his head. In Iraq in the spring of 2004, "cramped confinement" could mean a week in a cell twenty inches by four feet by four feet. Over the course of a twenty-day period of interrogation, Abu Zubaydah was placed in a box the size of a coffin for over eleven days and in a smaller box (21″ x 30″ x 30″) for twenty-nine hours.[133] One detainee was "chained to a wall in the standing position for 17 days." Water dousing turned into putting a detainee in a bathtub "filled with ice water." As for environmental controls, an FBI agent observed one Guantánamo prisoner in a room he estimated to be "well over 100 degrees" lying on the floor "almost unconscious," with "a pile of hair next to him." Apparently, the prisoner had pulled out his hair during the night.[134] At one point during the interrogation of Mohammed al-Qahtani, he had to be hospitalized after his heartbeat was recorded at thirty-five beats a minute. Susan J. Crawford, appointed by President Bush to serve as the convening authority for military commissions at Guantánamo, felt compelled to dismiss the charges against al-Qahtani because, in her words, "his treatment met the legal definition of torture."[135]

If the CIA subjected only three persons to waterboarding as the agency claimed (despite evidence to the contrary), interrogators used the waterboard over and over—183 times in the space of one month for Khalid Shaikh Mohammed—and harshly. CIA medical personnel described his waterboardings as a "series of near drownings."[136] Abu Zubaydah became "completely unresponsive" during his waterboarding with "bubbles rising through his open, full mouth." His treatment reached a point that CIA agents were in "tears and choking up" and were ready to request transfers if the interrogations continued without modification.[137]

Once the rules against using force on prisoners became muddled, experts say that it was foreseeable that events would spin out of control with thousands of detainees around the world. Prisoners were punched, kneed, choked, kicked, and beaten with pistols, rifle butts, broom handles, and chairs. Military police at Abu Ghraib Prison broke chemical lights and poured phosphoric acid on inmates. Special operations forces used stun guns to deliver electric shocks to prisoners. US servicemembers put lit cigarettes in detainees' ears. A prisoner held by the CIA was threatened with an unloaded semi-automatic handgun and a running power drill. Interrogators told Abu Zubaydah that "he would only leave in a coffin-shaped box."[138]

While some prisoners held by the CIA were subject to mock executions, it has been estimated that at least one hundred prisoners died in US custody by the spring of 2005. Military investigators considered at least twenty-seven to be possible criminal homicides. One of the victims was an Afghan taxi driver named Dilawar. Although interrogators eventually decided that he was "almost certainly innocent," soldiers had struck him in the legs so often that a military coroner likened his fatal injuries to those sustained by someone run over by a bus.[139]

VII

Given what took place in the CIA's black sites and US military prisons, it is difficult to look back on the February 7 memorandum as a presidential mandate for humane treatment, as its title was meant to suggest. In light of secret administration documents now public, it is also difficult to accede to President Bush's characterization that he really did nothing more than "accept" the Justice Department's legal advice on the Geneva Conventions. And once it became clear that the president never intended to require the CIA to comply with his stated policy on humane treatment, it is frankly impossible to view the presidential memorandum as it was portrayed by the administration—that is, as a good faith attempt to treat all prisoners "consistent with the principles of Geneva." Indeed, the presidential memorandum can be read as an implicit authorization for the CIA to violate Common Article 3's standard of humane treatment.[140]

Obviously, more was going on than President Bush let on. Among the most telling points in all this is the extent to which the White House manipulated the process of soliciting legal advice. Those most closely involved in developing detainee policy evidently sensed the need for some legal stamp of approval, preferably in writing, that would enable the administration to say, as President Bush did say, that government lawyers had "extensively" reviewed the interrogation procedures and "determined them to be lawful."[141] Nothing could serve that purpose as well as an official opinion from the Office of Legal Counsel. From the standpoint of bureaucratic maneuvering, it was a brilliant setup. The War Council provided the means to circumvent the normal interagency decision-making process. On paper, the White House counsel posed questions to OLC, which then responded, usually through John Yoo. For all intents and purposes, Yoo became the administration's principal legal advisor on matters relating to the war against terrorism. Judging from his work product, he was willing to offer any argument to justify whatever the White House sought (how often does the US attorney general mock one of his own lawyers as "Dr. Yes"?).

Of particular relevance was the novel theory he developed that the Geneva Conventions had no effect in countries the president deemed "failed states."[142] It was an odd interpretation of this major international treaty of such long standing, on its face inconsistent with Geneva's fundamental purpose. In point of fact, it did not matter to administration insiders how far-fetched the legal rationale was for getting the Geneva Conventions out of the way. What mattered to them was that the president had the raw power to declare this treaty inapplicable, given the authority he claimed under the unitary executive doctrine and the commander in chief override.

The interrogation program was a concerted plan put into effect over significant objections from within the administration. At the same time that OLC was providing legal cover, the White House had to overcome substantial opposition from elsewhere within the administration. The president withstood personal appeals from Secretary of State Powell and General Myers, who warned him that declaring Geneva inapplicable would put American troops at risk. With the interrogation program operational, FBI headquarters ordered its agents to "stand clear" of coercive interrogations; the same order was given by the military's Criminal Investigation Task Force. High-ranking uniformed lawyers used the word "torture" to describe interrogation methods approved by the president. No one reading their memoranda could come away without at least wondering whether the administration had embarked on a criminal policy.[143]

Why, then, did President Bush and his close advisors have such a keen interest in making sure the Geneva Conventions did not apply? The documentary evidence reveals their overriding concern: "substantial criminal liability" for "involved U.S. officials." The best way to mitigate the "threat of domestic criminal prosecution" under the War Crimes Act, wrote White House counsel Gonzales (with Addington), was for President Bush to use the authority of his office to declare the Geneva Conventions inapplicable.[144]

Subsequent events confirm that President Bush never had any intention of requiring the CIA to comply with his purported policy of humane treatment. When Senator McCain proposed legislation to clarify that the agency must treat detainees humanely, the White House did everything it could to block the bill from becoming law. When the Supreme Court declared Common Article 3 applicable to detainees (requiring humane treatment in "all circumstances"), the White House worked hard to negate the Court's ruling through legislation and by executive order. President Bush castigated the justices for jeopardizing the CIA's "crucial" interrogation program.[145]

What the Supreme Court had actually put in jeopardy was the administration's elaborate scheme to insulate US officials from war crimes prosecutions. The Court's decision transformed an abstract discussion into concrete terms. Previously, administration insiders could argue in the abstract about the vagueness of legal terminology like "inhumane." Now they faced the prospect of having to appear in court to defend as humane the actual treatment of detainees—the coffin-sized boxes, near drownings, forced nudity, walling, and the like.

In the guise of interpreting the Geneva Conventions for a new kind of war, President Bush achieved the same result as if he had exercised his breathtaking assertion of power to unilaterally suspend the world's most widely ratified international treaty. With Geneva out of the way, President Bush personally approved the use of what he termed an "alternative" set of interrogation techniques.[146] It was an interrogation regime that replicated the coercive techniques employed by some of America's worst enemies in the twentieth century, sometimes against US servicemembers held prisoner. For all his talk of a "New Paradigm," President Bush's actions reverted, in sum and substance, to very old paradigms of warfare that had prevailed long before anyone had ever heard of the Geneva Conventions.

CHAPTER THREE

Congress and an Unchecked Presidency

In theory, in a political system designed by its founders to rein in the abuse of power, any president inclined to authorize the torture and inhumane treatment of wartime detainees would find substantial obstacles standing in the way. Notwithstanding the various options for constraining presidential power, it seems uncontroversial to assert that, at some point and in some way, checking a president bent upon violating the law will require the intervention of the mainstays of the system of checks and balances—either Congress or the Supreme Court, if not both. The Constitution provides Congress with substantial authority to monitor and restrain the president. The Court can exercise the singular power of judicial review to declare actions taken by the president unconstitutional.

This chapter critically evaluates Congress's performance by surveying a half-dozen key points in the legislative-executive tussle over the treatment of detainees. Many commentators consider its response inadequate, though Jack Goldsmith believed lawmakers had "pushed back far harder" than "in any other war in American history."[1] It is true that the administration's interrogation policy did not go unchallenged in Congress. Yet whatever might be counted among its achievements on that score (some commentators point to the Detainee Treatment Act), this chapter argues that they came too late, that they constituted at best half-measures on the road to presidential accountability, that they were repeatedly neutralized by the Bush administration's countermeasures, and that they were in any event outweighed by a succession of failures. Given the serious nature of the criminal offenses in question, it is difficult to view the response from Capitol Hill as anything but a case study of a legislative breakdown on presidential accountability.

I

Before examining the particulars of the actions taken by Congress in response to President Bush, it will be helpful to outline how the Constitution's framers envisioned the legislative check operating against the president. The classic exposition of the constitutional theory behind the system of checks and balances can be found in *The Federalist*, per James Madison. His view was based, to his credit, on a realistic assessment of political behavior: that the difficulty in constructing a government of limited powers was rooted in human nature, that people are naturally ambitious, that they will seek power and then they will seek more power. It was this "encroaching spirit of power," in Madison's suggestive turn of phrase, that posed the ultimate danger of a "tyrannical concentration of all the powers of government in the same hands."[2]

The Madisonian solution to this problem was, on its own terms, elegant. It was clear to him that it would be impossible to stop people from seeking power. Ambition was here to stay. Nor was it possible, to Madison's way of thinking, to rely solely on separating the powers of government among the three branches. He also dismissed the idea that "parchment barriers"— written limitations spelled out in a document like the Constitution—could standing alone constrain power. Instead, the solution in his scheme was to construct the "interior structure of the government" so that the different branches of government would, "by their mutual relations, be the means of keeping each other in their proper places." To do that, it would be necessary to harness ambition to "counteract ambition" by linking (to use Madison's exact words) the "interest of the man" with the "constitutional rights of the place." That was the key to the Madisonian vision. What was needed, then, was to arm each branch with the "constitutional means and personal motives to resist encroachments" of the other branches of government.[3]

It was a compelling theory, certainly marking an advance in political thinking in its day. Yet it has been under strain for some time; indeed, from the start of government operations. The difficulties with Madison's theory become particularly apparent when considering Congress's ability to check the president. The problem can be broken down into two parts à la Madison: means and motives.

As to motives, Madison's intuition that self-interest would guide office-holders was on the mark, but he failed to anticipate how interest would operate with the intrusion of political parties onto the constitutional scene, and in a contest between party allegiance and institutional loyalty, party often prevails because that is where members of Congress perceive their interest lies. In short, with the benefit of 250 years of hindsight, it has proven difficult to tie the interests of the officeholder to the "rights of the place."[4]

That does not mean that Congress is invariably ineffective in checking presidents,[5] but rather that the legislature's ability to check the president depends on party affiliation. As it turned out, majority control of Congress aligned with President Bush during most of his presidency. The House of Representatives was solidly Republican for his first six years in office. The Senate, with a thin Democratic majority for the better part of his first two years in office, came under GOP control for the next crucial four years before Democrats regained a majority.

As to the constitutional means at Congress's disposal, lawmakers possess a formidable set of powers that can be used to constrain the chief executive—on paper at least. There is, to begin with, the most basic legislative function: Congress can circumscribe presidential power simply by enacting laws to that effect. Not to be overlooked is oversight of the executive branch and all that goes with that—committee investigations, public hearings, and subpoenas to executive officials. Some rate Congress's budgetary authority—the power of the purse—as the most potent legislative control on executive power. The Senate has the opportunity to shape executive policy through the confirmation process, whether by rejecting presidential nominees outright or extracting promises from them pending their appointment. The power of impeachment, though infrequently exercised for most of American history, may serve to moderate presidential behavior by its very existence.[6]

Yet what looks formidable in the abstract may not be so formidable in practice. It can be difficult to pass legislation going against the president's interests for several reasons, not least of all because each chamber must muster a two-thirds supermajority to override a presidential veto. Congressional oversight presents a mixed record. For every successful committee investigation, it seems another could be cited that failed to accomplish much. Not only do presidents have more say in the budgetary process than the aphorism about Congress's "power of the purse" suggests, but the history of the modern presidency illustrates the difficulties legislators can encounter when trying to use the appropriations power to reverse or modify the chief executive's decisions in war and foreign affairs. Regarding impeachment, the short answer is that it looks more like a paper tiger than it once did. Moreover, the president has a distinct advantage in shaping public opinion in competition with the multiple voices in Congress (with some members inevitably supporting the president). And with the generally recognized "primacy" of the president in foreign affairs (not to mention the rally-round-the-flag effect of national security crises), it can be difficult for lawmakers to take full advantage of these powers the Constitution granted Congress.[7]

II

Arguably, to rate Congress's effectiveness in checking President Bush on detainee treatment, one need go no further than to say that lawmakers should have stopped the president from setting up the interrogation program. So far as Congress's institutional apparatus is concerned, the most likely place for intelligence oversight of a program like this was the so-called Gang of Eight. Whether or not "gang" is a fitting description, eight accurately represents the number of lawmakers in this group, which consists of the top four members holding leadership positions (the Speaker of the House, the House minority leader, the Senate majority leader, and the Senate minority leader) along with the chair and ranking member from each chamber's intelligence committee. Congress created the Gang of Eight as an intelligence oversight mechanism after Senate hearings in the 1970s exposed CIA and FBI abuses. From its inception, the Gang of Eight was an imperfect solution to the problem of reconciling secrecy with executive accountability to the legislature. The balance was struck by requiring the intelligence community to keep this small group of lawmakers informed of covert operations. Briefings are classified, and members of the Gang of Eight are not usually at liberty to disclose what they learn to other intelligence committee members, their own legislative aides, or committee lawyers, though staffers are sometimes allowed to attend briefings. Committee members are not allowed to take notes on briefings or to copy documents.[8]

Such restrictions matter little if the CIA does not bother to adequately inform anyone in Congress. According to CIA records, agency officials briefed leading intelligence committee members about enhanced interrogation techniques in September 2002, but exactly what was told the lawmakers in attendance remains in dispute. Senator Bob Graham (D-FL) said he did not recall any discussion of waterboarding while Senator Richard C. Shelby (R-AL) maintained that the CIA had given a "full account of the techniques." In reference to a subsequent briefing, Representative Nancy Pelosi (D-CA) said that she had been informed of waterboarding and other interrogation procedures that "could be used" and that the CIA would provide further briefings "if and when they would be used." She claimed that agency officials had not told her that interrogators had already waterboarded detainees.[9]

At a meeting with the Gang of Eight the next year, CIA officers described the waterboarding of Abu Zubaydah. Congresswoman Jane Harman (D-CA) was in attendance. In a letter to CIA general counsel Scott Muller, with a copy to CIA director George Tenet, Harman stated that the briefing raised "profound policy questions." She raised probing questions about "what kind of policy review" had taken place and "whether the most senior levels of the White House have determined that these practices are consistent with the principles and policies of the United States." She then asked the key question: "Have the enhanced techniques been authorized and approved by the President?"[10]

Muller's response was evasive. He said that "a number of Executive Branch lawyers" had "participated" in making the determination that in "appropriate circumstances" these techniques were "fully consistent with US law." He added that it was not "appropriate" to "comment on issues that are a matter of policy, much less the nature and extent of Executive Branch policy deliberations." He went on to say that "it would be fair to assume that policy as well as legal matters have been addressed within the Executive Branch."[11] This exchange appears to be the closest any lawmaker came to unearthing what was going on during the early phase of the interrogation program.

III

The Abu Ghraib Prison scandal ended the secrecy surrounding the administration's interrogation program. With the passage of time, it is difficult to convey the shock of discovery when, on April 28, 2004, CBS's *60 Minutes II* broadcast photographs that provided incontestable evidence of prisoner abuse. Probably the most well-known image was of a hooded detainee hooked to electrical wires and made to stand on a box with hands outstretched upward. CBS's Dan Rather informed his audience that military guards falsely told the prisoner that he would be electrocuted if he fell off the box. Other photographs showed naked Iraqis in sexually humiliating positions. Some were stacked in a human pyramid. One soldier held a prisoner on a leash as if he were a dog. There was an unsettling photograph of an MP grinning, thumbs up, over a dead prisoner who had been placed in ice (an Iraqi general who had turned himself in to US forces only to be beaten and suffocated).[12]

Nobody wanted to defend what happened at Abu Ghraib, and administration officials quickly joined lawmakers on both sides of the aisle to condemn the abuse of prisoners there. President Bush expressed his "deep disgust."[13] The time was ripe for members of Congress to put aside partisan differences, conduct thorough investigations, and enact remedial legislation. One might have expected aggressive congressional hearings that would have left their mark in history.

The initial reaction showed some promise. On May 21, 2004, the Senate by a vote of 92–0 approved a resolution "condemning the abuse of Iraqi prisoners at Abu Ghraib" and "urging a full and complete investigation" (a similar resolution got stuck in committee in the House). One lawmaker who took the idea of a full investigation seriously was Senator John W. Warner (R-VA), chair of the Armed Services Committee. He had an unusual record of military service, beginning in the Navy during World War II, then in the Marine Corps in the Korean War, and later as secretary of the navy during the Vietnam War. The committee's goal in investigating Abu Ghraib, as Warner laid it out, was to look "up and down and sideways in the chain of command and get to the bottom" of what happened. He had the backing of key Republicans on the committee, notably Senator McCain and Senator Lindsey Graham (R-SC). For those keen on confronting the administration, the hearings began auspiciously, with Warner swearing in Secretary Rumsfeld—contrary to the customary courtesy accorded cabinet secretaries. Rumsfeld was furious.[14]

In retrospect, that may qualify as the high point of congressional scrutiny while Republicans remained in charge of Congress. It did not take long for pressure against Warner's investigation to build within GOP ranks. Some of his colleagues on the Armed Services Committee did not hesitate to express their frustration with the hearings. Senator John Cornyn (R-TX) pronounced the "collective hand-wringing" a "distraction from fighting and winning the war"—a common refrain among Republicans. Senator James M. Inhofe (R-OK) lambasted "humanitarian do-gooders" and said that "we need to talk about the good things that have been happening." Meanwhile, in the House of Representatives (more firmly in Republican control), the Armed Services Committee had only one public hearing plus one closed session.[15]

While Warner's investigation continued, it soon became clear that relevant documents and information would not be forthcoming from the administration. Nor were Republican senators inclined to push for their release. In June, the upper chamber voted mostly along party lines against a Democratic proposal to compel the administration to produce documents. Warner came under extraordinary pressure to call a halt to further public hearings. He declined, but after several Republicans on his committee threatened to strip him of his chairmanship, the tone of the investigation changed. Gone was the get-to-the-bottom-of-what-happened attitude. In its place was a willingness to let the military investigations take precedence. The committee turned its attention to preventing prisoner abuse in the future instead of placing blame for what happened in the past.[16]

Although congressional investigations into Abu Ghraib faded from view as attention turned to the 2004 election, lawmakers soon had another opportunity to examine the mistreatment of detainees. After the election, President Bush tapped White House counsel Alberto Gonzales to be attorney general. Gonzales, of course, had been in the thick of this—whether personally briefing the president on the Geneva Conventions, moderating War Council meetings, soliciting memoranda from John Yoo, or shutting out the State Department from the decision-making process. The public had been given a glimpse into his role when the so-called torture memo was leaked. Yoo's fifty-page memorandum, titled "Standards of Conduct for Interrogation under 18 U.S.C. 2340–2340A," was addressed to Gonzales. Its opening line read: "you have asked for our Office's views regarding the standards of conduct under the Convention Against Torture." In a transparent effort to boost Gonzales's chances in the Senate, OLC had shortly before his confirmation hearings released a new opinion replacing John Yoo's memorandum. It began by stating what should have needed no reminder: torture is "abhorrent both to American law and values and to international norms."[17]

Senator Patrick J. Leahy thought this confirmation hearing might be the "only remaining forum" for Congress to look into the prisoner abuse at Abu Ghraib. As it turned out, Gonzales's testimony was an exercise in obfuscation. In his opening statement, he discussed what he could not avoid discussing. The Abu Ghraib photographs "sickened and outraged me," he said, and "left a stain on our Nation's reputation." He shared the president's "resolve that torture and abuse will not be tolerated by this administration." He promised that as attorney general he would ensure that the Justice Department would "aggressively" pursue "those responsible for such abhorrent actions." Gonzales reiterated that the president had "made clear" that the United States "will not tolerate torture under any circumstances."[18]

For Gonzales to express unequivocal opposition to torture raised an obvious definitional problem, given OLC's contrived interpretations. What exactly did Gonzales mean by "torture"? When fielding questions at the hearings, the nominee was evasive (he repeatedly said he could not recall), though some of his responses were revealing. He thought Yoo's bizarre definition of torture (producing pain comparable to that experienced with "death, organ failure, or the permanent impairment of a significant body function") was "an arguable interpretation of the law."[19] Gonzales skirted the question of whether the president could "immunize from prosecution" anyone who commits "acts of torture"—a question he called "hypothetical." Senator Richard J. Durbin (D-IL) asked him whether US personnel can "legally engage in torture under any circumstances." Gonzales responded that he did not believe so, but he could not bring himself to give a definitive response. "I'd want to get back to you on that and make sure that I don't provide a misleading answer."[20] When Senator Durbin asked whether the War Crimes Act always applied to American servicemembers, Gonzales said again that he would have to "get back to you on that."[21]

The Judiciary Committee forwarded the nomination to the Senate on a party-line vote, and sixty senators voted to confirm Gonzales as attorney general.[22]

IV

Although Gonzales's testimony was less than forthcoming, senators managed to extract new information from him through written questions. He disclosed that, under the administration's interpretation of the Convention Against Torture, that treaty's prohibition of cruel, inhuman, and degrading treatment did not apply to alien detainees in US custody overseas. He also acknowledged that CIA interrogators were not bound to follow the policy on humane treatment stated in the presidential memorandum of February 7, 2002. It would be hard to overstate the significance of these revelations. Here was an official close to the president—the White House counsel no less—declaring that there was in the administration's view no legal barrier to the inhuman treatment of detainees held at Guantánamo, Abu Ghraib, and elsewhere.[23]

In this way, the congressional checks seemed to be in proper working order, as the confirmation process had unearthed this secret and novel executive legal interpretation. The question was what Congress would do about that. Enter Senator McCain who, by virtue of his independent personality and his experience (a prisoner of war tortured by the North Vietnamese), was uniquely suited to take on the president on this subject. In July 2005, he offered an amendment to the must-pass annual defense spending bill. His proposed legislation—the McCain Torture Ban—prohibited cruel, inhuman, and degrading treatment anywhere for persons in the custody or "physical control" of the US government (thus, including the CIA). It required the military to comply with the Army Field Manual on Intelligence Interrogations; the same for anyone (i.e., the CIA) conducting interrogations at US military facilities. At the time, the manual identified "acts of violence or intimidation, including physical or mental torture, threats, insults, or exposure to inhumane treatment" used in interrogation as criminal acts prohibited by the Uniform Code of Military Justice. "Such illegal acts," the manual stated, "are not authorized and will not be condoned by the US Army."[24]

The White House made no attempt to disguise its opposition to the McCain bill. Acceding to the administration's request, Senate Majority Leader Bill Frist (R-TN) delayed a vote on defense spending in order to give Vice President Dick Cheney time to lobby senators. Stalling tactics could only work so long, of course, and when funding the Defense Department was brought to the Senate floor in October, McCain reintroduced his amendment. The White House then threatened a veto (it would have been the first of the Bush presidency). The Senate responded in short order by passing McCain's bill by a veto-proof margin (90–9). The vice president then asked Senator McCain to exempt CIA interrogators, but he refused. "I don't see how you could possibly agree to legitimizing an agent of the government engaging in torture," McCain said. After the House of Representatives approved the defense spending measure with the McCain amendment 308–122 (enough to override a veto), President Bush had by all appearances finally given up. He asked McCain and Warner to join him in the Oval Office for a show of solidarity before the White House press corps. McCain's bill, adopted by Congress as part of the Detainee Treatment Act (DTA), was seen at the time as a "stinging" rebuke to the Bush administration.[25] More than that, this legislation was later heralded as a signal achievement of Congress in checking the president's interrogation program. Jack Goldsmith said that McCain's bill "stopped the CIA program in its tracks."[26]

There is more to this story than that statement suggests, however. If Goldsmith is taken to mean that Congress was effective in changing President Bush's interrogation policy, keep in mind the time it took lawmakers to pass this legislation: twenty months after the first news reports about Abu Ghraib and over three years after the CIA's first use of enhanced interrogation

methods. If the implication is that the CIA never used enhanced interrogation techniques after Congress enacted the Detainee Treatment Act, reports
suggest otherwise. In addition to a news story describing Senator McCain's
surprise upon learning that his Torture Ban had not "put a stop" to "what the
CIA was doing," the Senate Intelligence Committee later discovered that the
agency used "extensive sleep deprivation" and other enhanced interrogation
techniques as late as 2007.[27] Instead of abandoning the interrogation program, administration officials sought to keep it running. As National Security Council principals and CIA officials explored options to modify the program, OLC concluded that the revised interrogation techniques proposed by
the CIA were "consistent with the DTA" (including sleep deprivation up to
ninety-six consecutive hours), and President Bush issued an executive order
declaring that the revamped CIA program "fully complies" with Common
Article 3. The *Washington Post* reported that, with this executive order in
place, administration officials believed that detainees "could be moved immediately" into the CIA program and "subjected to techniques that go beyond
those allowed by the U.S. military."[28]

Moreover, a close examination of the McCain bill reveals significant
loopholes in its coverage. Its self-described "uniform" interrogation standards were supposedly made so by requiring everyone to adhere to the Army
Field Manual. Uniformity had its limits evidently, as CIA interrogations conducted outside military installations were exempt. (After Democrats took
control of Congress, they passed a bill requiring the CIA to comply with the
Army Field Manual wherever interrogations took place, but President Bush
vetoed it with, it must be noted, Senator McCain's support.)[29] And while the
Army Field Manual covered military interrogations under the McCain bill,
the administration retained authority to revise the manual, and what would
come of that no one in Congress could say as it was still undergoing revision
when the DTA was adopted.[30] There was reason to be skeptical. The administration had put Stephen Cambone in charge of revisions. Given his position as undersecretary of defense for intelligence, that would seem a perfectly
appropriate task for him until one recalls that Cambone held that post when
Abu Ghraib spun out of control. Indeed, it was Cambone who had sent General Geoffrey Miller, then in command of Guantánamo prison, to restructure
the interrogation procedures used at Abu Ghraib, and it was Miller who had
recommended using military police to set up aggressive interrogations. The
revised field manual (published in September 2006) ostensibly prohibited
inhumane treatment, but its Appendix M left an opening for the questionable

use of interrogation techniques like solitary confinement for an indefinite period of time, sleep deprivation for twenty hours of every 24-hour period, and sensory deprivation (goggles, blindfolds, and earmuffs).[31]

Unlike the Army Field Manual, Senator McCain's ban on cruel, inhuman, and degrading treatment was supposed to apply to the CIA everywhere, but this prohibition was not airtight. As the statutory language referred to individuals in the "custody" or "under the physical control" of the US government, nothing in the DTA prevented the CIA from rendering terrorism suspects to countries that tortured prisoners.[32] The larger problem was definitional in nature. The DTA left the meaning of "cruel, inhuman, or degrading treatment" open to interpretation—hardly a comforting prospect for anyone familiar with the Bush Justice Department's record. Although the statute incorporated the "shocks the conscience" test to evaluate interrogation techniques (grounded in a Supreme Court due process ruling that evidence obtained by having a suspect's stomach pumped to force him to vomit morphine capsules shocks the conscience), that left an opening for administration lawyers to argue, as they did, that what would shock the conscience in an ordinary police interrogation might not be so shocking in response to a serious terrorist threat.[33] Another provision in the DTA, under the heading "Consideration of Statements Derived With Coercion," is important to note. Forced on Congress by the White House in the final stages of negotiations, this provision allowed combatant status review tribunals to consider evidence "obtained as a result of coercion." While the DTA directed tribunals to assess the "probative value" of such statements, the fact remains that this provision allowed the military to use evidence obtained by coercion—a polite reference to cruel, inhuman, and degrading treatment and even torture—exactly what Senator McCain had sought to prohibit. In case these loopholes proved to be insufficient for the administration's purposes, President Bush's signing statement reserved the authority to disregard the McCain Torture Ban when he believed it necessary for national security.[34]

In addition, the question of what Congress accomplished with its legislation cannot be confined to an analysis of the McCain Torture Ban in isolation from the Detainee Treatment Act as a whole. No one interested in accountability could be pleased with other provisions that found their way into the DTA. Immediately following the prohibition on cruel, inhuman, or degrading treatment, there was a section outlining a legal defense for interrogators in case they were prosecuted or sued. Jack Goldsmith called the defense "vague," leaving the impression that it would have afforded CIA interrogators little protection in court. The text may be wordy, and defenses based on the advice of counsel may have been more difficult for interrogators to assert than many legal experts thought. Yet Congress's intent seems clear, and it is difficult to see how judges could ignore this effort to grant interrogators statutory immunity. The title of this section appears in all capital letters in the session laws: "PROTECTION OF UNITED STATES GOVERNMENT PERSONNEL ENGAGED IN AUTHORIZED INTERROGATIONS." All that was needed to invoke this defense was to run through a short checklist to show that (1) the interrogation technique was "officially authorized," (2) the technique was "determined to be lawful at the time" it was used, (3) the interrogator "did not know that the practices were unlawful," and (4) "a person of ordinary sense and understanding would not know the practices were unlawful." Essentially, any CIA interrogator could assert this defense simply by referring to relevant OLC opinions on interrogation standards and techniques. Even with the fourth element, which looks like an objective "reasonable person" standard, the DTA brought OLC opinions into consideration by stating that "good faith reliance on advice of counsel" would be an "important factor" in making that determination. Ironically, the enactment of the McCain Torture Ban by itself bolsters this legal defense, as it could be argued that Congress implicitly conceded that it was not clear that prior laws prohibited the enhanced interrogation techniques. Whether judges would have accepted this statutory advice of counsel defense remains unclear as no one involved in the interrogation program was prosecuted after Congress enacted the DTA. In that sense, the DTA may be read as accomplishing the Bush administration's purpose if it deterred prosecutors from bringing cases against interrogators. Lawmakers also saw fit to have the US government furnish interrogators with counsel and pay for their legal defense.[35]

Additionally, the DTA deprived federal courts of jurisdiction to hear claims brought by alien detainees, including those alleging mistreatment and torture. The statute did authorize the US Court of Appeals for the DC Circuit to review the decisions reached by combatant status review tribunals and military commissions, but these reviews were confined to determining whether the standards and procedures laid out by the secretary of defense complied with the law and whether the tribunal comported with those standards and procedures.[36] This was the administration's answer, with Senator Lindsey Graham sponsoring the provision, to *Rasul v. Bush* (2004), a Supreme Court decision interpreting a statute as granting federal courts jurisdiction over detainees' claims. It is worth pausing over what effect this provision had on the McCain Torture Ban. Senator McCain worked hard to clarify the rule—the rule that detainees were protected against cruel, inhuman, and degrading treatment. What he got in return for reaffirming this rule, which many observers believed was already in place, was a law depriving detainees of the opportunity to obtain a legal remedy for its violation. Four days after the DTA became law, the Bush Justice Department asked the federal courts to dismiss all pending claims brought by detainees.[37]

When all was said and done, the Bush White House appeared to have got the better of this fight. The president was in a stronger position than if Senator McCain had done nothing at all. Considering how his Torture Ban was transformed into legislation affirmatively blocking accountability for torture, one would not expect to find another such example of political jujitsu for some time to come.

V

But then Congress enacted the Military Commissions Act of 2006 (MCA) in response to *Hamdan v. Rumsfeld*, the Supreme Court decision that reaffirmed federal court jurisdiction over detainees' claims and invalidated the military commissions President Bush had established. Jack Goldsmith considered the MCA a prime example of the unprecedented pushback against a wartime president, with the commander in chief reduced to "begging" lawmakers "for permission to convene military commissions." No doubt President Bush would have preferred not to have been bothered by the Court's ruling, but the political backstory shows that begging Congress does not quite capture what transpired. This was a case in which the White House seized the opportunity presented by an unfavorable judicial decision and got Congress to do practically everything the president could have wanted, with the MCA granting "the president more power over terrorism suspects than he had before" *Hamdan* was decided, according to *New York Times* reporters.[38]

The concurring justices in *Hamdan* had pointed out that military commissions could still be used—a modified version at least—if the president got Congress involved. The administration wasted little time in drafting legislation to submit to lawmakers. Acting OLC head Steven G. Bradbury took the lead (he had prepared key legal memoranda approving enhanced interrogation techniques after John Yoo left the administration).[39] Taking full advantage of the political calendar, the White House rushed lawmakers to pass this legislation in the midst of the campaign season for congressional midterms.[40] Democrats, still mindful of past Republican attacks portraying them as soft on national security (especially during the 2002 campaign season), were disarmed from mounting an effective opposition. Senate Democrats had the numbers to filibuster, but they declined to do so. In the House, 160 Democrats voted against the legislation. That drew a swift and predictable condemnation. "It is outrageous," said House Majority Leader John Boehner (R-OH), for Democrats to "continue to oppose giving President Bush the tools he needs to protect our country." House Republicans continued to be reliable allies. Representative Duncan D. Hunter (R-CA), chair of the House Armed Services Committee, stated that they would "do what the President wants." The same could be said of most Senate Republicans, with the exception of the usual troika of McCain, Warner, and Graham, as well as Senator Susan Collins (R-ME). They were chiefly concerned with preserving Common Article 3's humane treatment requirement in US law, but, as discussed below, their negotiations with the administration did little to prevent the president from achieving his objectives.[41]

Any discussion of the Military Commissions Act can quickly devolve into the arcane details of the legislation, perhaps one measure of the administration's efforts to mask what was really going on. Before examining the MCA's broader policy implications, it should be noted that the way in which Congress authorized the president to use military tribunals was by itself a major victory for the administration. It might appear that the statute provided defendants with a comprehensive set of procedural protections, at least in comparison with the president's original order.[42] His version hardly qualifies as a model of procedural fairness, though, and while the MCA's rules were more detailed—even prolix—that does not mean they were fair.

Indeed, the MCA's peculiar rules of evidence—about which military lawyers expressed misgivings—illustrate the problems that can arise when deviating from well-established legal procedures. Prosecutors were still allowed to offer in evidence statements from interrogations conducted before the DTA was enacted that were derived from coercion (including cruel, inhuman, and degrading treatment).[43] That would be enough for some to consider the military commission proceedings qua legal proceedings irrevocably tainted. Moreover, the legislation reversed the usual burden of proof for introducing hearsay evidence and made it easier for prosecutors to use out-of-court statements that would have been rejected in general courts martial as unreliable.

For Guantánamo detainees who had been mistakenly identified as terrorists, these evidentiary rules increased the risk of wrongful convictions.[44]

In some sense, the MCA was a misnomer as this statute went well beyond addressing the conduct of military commission proceedings. For the first time, Congress embraced the use of the "unlawful enemy combatant" designation. So broad was the statutory definition that US citizens who provided financial support to terrorist organizations were included even though they would not be considered combatants—let alone unlawful enemy combatants—under international humanitarian law.[45] Lawmakers also backed the administration's efforts to put detainees beyond the reach of the federal courts (with the exception of the DC Circuit's limited and largely inconsequential review of standards and procedures).[46] Under the Detainee Treatment Act, the federal courts could not review habeas corpus claims brought by detainees held at Guantánamo. As the *Hamdan* Court construed this provision, federal judges retained jurisdiction over cases pending on the effective date of the DTA. There could be no misreading Congress's response. The MCA deprived the federal courts of jurisdiction to hear claims filed by noncitizen detainees in "all" pending or future cases "without exception," involving "any aspect" of "detention, transfer, treatment, trial, or conditions of detention."[47] The Justice Department, as it did following enactment of the DTA, sought the immediate dismissal of all pending claims in the federal court system. The MCA also stated that detainees could not invoke the Geneva Conventions as "a source of rights" against the United States or its personnel.[48] And one imagines President Bush was particularly gratified by legislative recognition of his authority to interpret "for the United States" the "meaning and application" of the Geneva Conventions. This meant that the president, with Congress's blessing, could determine whether enhanced interrogation techniques violated the Geneva Conventions. Congress added language noting that the MCA's recognition of the president's interpretive authority should not be "construed to affect the constitutional functions and responsibilities" of the legislative and judicial branches, but that throwaway line seemed to highlight the extraordinary concessions made to the nation's chief executive.[49]

Most important from an accountability standpoint was what the MCA did to the War Crimes Act. Remember that the WCA as amended in 1997 defined "any conduct" that violated Common Article 3 (including torture, inhumane treatment, outrages upon personal dignity, along with humiliating and degrading treatment) as a war crime under US law. Out of concern over the threat of war crimes prosecutions, President Bush declared in his February 7, 2002 memorandum that Common Article 3 did not protect Al Qaeda and Taliban detainees. *Hamdan* obviously upset that strategy by applying Common Article 3 to the conflict with Al Qaeda. When President Bush asked Congress to enact legislation responding to the Court's ruling, he did not conceal his concern: "Some believe our military and intelligence personnel involved in capturing and questioning terrorists could now be at risk of prosecution under the War Crimes Act."[50]

Without directly contradicting the Court by declaring Common Article 3 inapplicable, the president and Congress achieved the same result by redefining what constitutes a violation of Common Article 3 that could be considered a war crime under the WCA. Furthermore, the Military Commissions Act made this new definition retroactive to the date when Congress first amended that statute in 1997. This redefinition can be broken down into several parts. First, instead of defining a war crime to include "any conduct" proscribed by Common Article 3, Congress limited the statutory definition of war crimes to nine offenses. While these included torture and cruel or inhuman treatment, conspicuously missing from the list was the prohibition against "outrages upon personal dignity, in particular humiliating and degrading treatment."[51] Second, although cruel and inhuman treatment was still included, the MCA narrowly defined that phrase; in effect requiring a higher degree of mistreatment—closer to what many legal experts considered torture. The statutory language gets complicated and its meaning unclear. Arguably, it does not criminalize waterboarding.[52] Third, the MCA categorized degrading treatment that shocks the conscience as "an additional prohibition" rather than a prosecutable offense. Fourth, the MCA extended the legal defense established in the DTA for relying on OLC opinions to actions occurring from September 11, 2001 to the enactment of the DTA.[53] Finally, in a truly Orwellian twist, the MCA authorized the president to "take action to ensure compliance" with the prohibition against cruel, inhuman, or degrading treatment through "administrative rules and procedures."[54]

Canvassing all of these details, as necessary as that may be to provide a full picture of this statute, runs the risk of suppressing the fundamental point of what the statute did so far as presidential accountability is concerned. In effect, lawmakers at the administration's behest changed the law (the WCA) in order to shield the president and his subordinates from prosecution for violating that law.

Notwithstanding the legalese, contemporaneous reports indicate that the administration's goal was clear at the time. R. Jeffrey Smith of the *Washington*

Post reported in late July that Attorney General Gonzales had told Republican lawmakers that "a shield is needed for actions taken by U.S. personnel under a 2002 presidential order, which the Supreme Court declared illegal" (Smith's words). Before the administration's draft version of the legislation was made public, Smith reported that Common Article 3's prohibition of "outrages upon personal dignity" was "left off the list." University of Texas law professor Derek P. Jinks was quoted by Smith as saying that "it's plain that this proposal would abrogate portions of Common Article 3" and that the "entire family of techniques" used to degrade and humiliate was "not addressed in any way, shape or form." John Sifton speculated that administration officials were "probably less worried about CIA interrogators and more worried simply about their own skins."[55]

VI

While Congress mostly refrained from conducting investigations that might embarrass President Bush when Republicans were in charge (with the exception of Senator Warner's initial hearings into Abu Ghraib), that changed after Democrats wrested control of both chambers in the 2006 election. Among the various investigations that followed, two stand out. One was conducted by the Senate Armed Services Committee; the other by the Senate Intelligence Committee. While both made substantial contributions to the public's knowledge of the administration's interrogation program, their reports raise additional questions about Congress's ability to check the president.

Under the chairmanship of Senator Carl Levin (D-MI), the Senate Armed Services Committee produced a report titled "Inquiry into the Treatment of Detainees in U.S. Custody." The *Washington Post* called it Congress's "most comprehensive critique" of military interrogations. The committee's work was noteworthy for its bipartisanship (the report was endorsed by a voice vote without anyone dissenting, though not all committee members were present when the vote was taken), its point-by-point narrative of what went wrong, its rendition of military lawyers' opposition to enhanced interrogation techniques, and its clear explanation of how the administration "reverse-engineered" tactics used on American POWs in the war with Korea.[56]

Yet to those concerned about accountability, the better the report looked, the more frustrating it must have seemed. For one thing, the timing of the report's release colored what the committee accomplished.

Granted the difficulties in moving quickly in such an in-depth investigation, the fact remains that the committee did not hold public hearings on military interrogations until the summer of President Bush's final year in office. Indeed, the report was not released to the public until after President Obama was elected. That undercut the report's value in holding President Bush and his subordinates accountable. Senator Levin was left to "hope" that the "new administration" would "look for ways, where appropriate, to hold people accountable."[57]

For another thing, the committee steered clear of finding President Bush personally responsible. As one might expect with the committee's jurisdictional mandate, the focus was on the military. It should have come as no surprise, then, that the Armed Services Committee heaped blame on Secretary of Defense Rumsfeld and his aides.[58] The committee did take note of the impact of the presidential memorandum of February 7, 2002, but rather than pin the blame on President Bush for his spurious directive on humane treatment, the report reads as if he inadvertently set events in motion: that the president "open[ed] the door to considering aggressive techniques" by replacing "well-established military doctrine" with "a policy that was subject to interpretation" without providing necessary guidance on what constitutes humane treatment.[59] This language shifted responsibility from the president, as if he had been duped by subordinates or at least failed to grasp the implications of his own memorandum.

The Senate Intelligence Committee, chaired by Senator Dianne Feinstein (D-CA), produced the other report of note—the so-called torture report—in actuality the executive summary of a classified 6,700 page report.[60] Like the Armed Services Committee, the Intelligence Committee put together a narrative of striking details, but once again, it is difficult to ignore the timing of the report's publication. It is true that the Intelligence Committee ran into a series of obstacles. The CIA was less than cooperative, for example.[61] But if the Armed Services Committee's report was late when published in 2008, so much the worse was the Intelligence Committee, which publicized its findings in December 2014, nearly six years after President Bush left office.

As for the president's role, the impression one gets from reading the committee report is that he should be absolved of personal responsibility. The report portrayed the interrogation program as a rogue operation set up by the CIA. It suggested that agency officials actively deceived President Bush.[62] The committee's focus on the CIA was bound to shape its account of what went wrong, but in the effort to point out the agency's deficiencies, committee members constructed a narrative of the president's part that raises as many questions as it answers.

The Intelligence Committee's evidence was drawn from CIA records, or more to the point, the absence of anything in agency files documenting a presidential briefing on specific interrogation tactics before April 2006. In the committee's description of CIA records: "no CIA officer" had "briefed the president on the specific CIA enhanced interrogation techniques before April 2006."[63] That statement by itself cannot compel the conclusion that no one briefed the president before then; only that there was no CIA record of briefing the president on specific techniques. That leaves open several alternative explanations that caution against drawing any firm conclusion about the state of President Bush's knowledge from the mere absence of a written record in CIA files.

One is that the president received a detailed briefing from someone outside the CIA—for example, the White House counsel—and that no record of such a briefing was transmitted to the agency. The committee's factfinding does not preclude this option. In putting together its chronology, the committee relied on CIA records. It did not conduct a comprehensive review of relevant administration files or White House documents.[64] Another option is that there was a CIA briefing of the president at some level of generality consistent with the statement quoted by the committee (that there was no CIA briefing of "specific" CIA enhanced interrogation methods). Obviously, this raises the question of what was meant by "specific."

It is also difficult to rule out the possibility that CIA records were tailored to provide President Bush with "plausible deniability"; in other words, officials purposefully maintained records so that it would appear that the president was not involved as much as he was.[65] It would not be the first time that national security officials sought to shield a president with "plausible deniability" of covert operations (National Security Advisor John Poindexter introduced many Americans to that phrase when testifying in the Iran-Contra affair).[66] In fact, the Senate Intelligence Committee report provides evidence of White House officials shaping the record of the CIA's presidential briefings about the interrogation program. The committee explained that, in July 2002, CIA officials planned to brief the president directly on the enhanced interrogation techniques in order to secure his approval. They had drafted talking points that included "a brief description of the waterboard interrogation technique." The report went on to say that the CIA revised these talking points to "eliminate references to the waterboard" in response to comments made by White House counsel Gonzales. Not long thereafter, Condoleezza Rice's staff relayed to George Tenet's chief of staff that the national security advisor "had been informed that there would be no briefing of the President on this matter," but that the CIA had, in the committee's words, "policy approval" to go ahead with the enhanced interrogation techniques. One obvious question derives from this sentence's passive construction: Who informed her of that? And assuming that Gonzales was not acting on his own, who instructed him to have the references to waterboarding eliminated? So far as the CIA files go, it could have been the president himself. Indeed, records cited by the committee indicate that President Bush had "directed that he not be informed of the locations" of black sites, supposedly so that he would not "accidentally" disclose where they were.[67] While leaving these questions unanswered, the committee report noted that John Rizzo (the CIA's acting general counsel) said that President Bush was the "one senior U.S. Government national security official" who "I did not believe was knowledgeable" about the enhanced interrogation techniques—a remark that was at least speculative if not intentionally misleading.[68]

In reaching its conclusion about President Bush's knowledge of the interrogation program, the Intelligence Committee relied most of all on the CIA's account of its April 2006 briefing of the president—purportedly the first record of briefing the president on "specific" interrogation techniques. According to the agency's records, President Bush "expressed discomfort with the 'image of a detainee, chained to the ceiling, clothed in a diaper, and forced to go to the bathroom on himself.'"[69] The committee report placed a good deal of weight on this apparent expression of discomfort. The implication was that the president's reaction betrayed a lack of prior knowledge about the enhanced interrogation tactics. Yet by that time, anyone following this story in the news would not have been surprised by that image. Besides, it remains unclear why this apparent expression of discomfort should be taken to reveal much of anything about the president's understanding beforehand. President Bush could have exhibited discomfort even though he had previously known the specifics of the interrogation techniques.

Significantly, it is not as if President Bush immediately ordered the CIA to abandon the interrogation program after that briefing. To the contrary, almost exactly five months later, he gave his post-*Hamdan* speech recounting the program's successes. He exhibited no discomfort when describing the procedures as "tough" and "necessary." The president stated that the interrogation program "has been and remains one of the most vital tools in our war against the terrorists." Had the president wanted to recalibrate interrogation policy after that CIA briefing, he might have built on the *Hamdan* decision. Instead, he criticized the Supreme Court for putting the nation's security at risk and later issued an executive order that reauthorized the use of several enhanced techniques.[70]

It is also difficult to accept the committee's chronology without summarily dismissing the account President Bush provided in his memoir. While the committee report cited CIA director George Tenet's statement that "he had never spoken to the President regarding the detention and interrogation program or EITs, nor was he aware of whether the President had been briefed by his staff," President Bush gave a detailed account of how he had "authorized waterboarding on senior al Qaeda leaders."[71] He wrote that he had been "hearing reports about Zubaydah for months," that he could hear "excitement in George Tenet's voice" when the CIA director informed him about Zubaydah's capture, that he "directed the team" to "find out what he knows," that he chose to have the CIA "take over" the interrogation of Zubaydah and "move him to a secure location in another country where the Agency could have total control over his environment," that "CIA experts drew up a list of interrogation techniques," that the Justice Department "conducted a careful legal review" at "my direction," that he "took a look at the list of techniques" and eliminated two "that I felt went too far," that one technique was waterboarding, and that his understanding was that medical experts had concluded that "it did no lasting harm." President Bush reported that Tenet asked him directly (the date is not noted but it would appear to be in March 2003) "if he had permission to use enhanced interrogation techniques, including waterboarding, on Khalid Shaikh Mohammed." The president's recollection seems clear. He said that he recalled at that moment "the 2,973 people stolen from their families by al Qaeda" and his "meeting with Danny Pearl's widow" before responding, "'Damn right.'"[72]

President Bush concluded this section of his book with this statement (written, it deserves to be mentioned, four years after that 2006 CIA briefing during which he was thought to have expressed discomfort): "Had we captured more al Qaeda operatives with significant intelligence value, I would have used the program for them as well."[73]

VII

That leaves for consideration one last major weapon in Congress's arsenal: impeachment. Even though Congress never impeached President Bush, few presidents have been the subject of more impeachment talk. Fewer still have been confronted by such serious allegations.

Before examining the debate over whether to impeach President Bush, a review of impeachment basics may be useful. In language that has become familiar to many Americans, the Constitution provides that presidents can be impeached for "Treason, Bribery, or other high Crimes and Misdemeanors." On paper, impeachment ought to serve as a particularly effective means for holding presidents to account. To Alexander Hamilton, it provided an "essential check" on the executive. James Madison considered "some provision" of this sort "indispensable." This authority granted the legislature has no parallel among the checking mechanisms available to the other branches of government. When stripped to its essence, impeachment empowers Congress to "decapitate the executive branch in a single stroke," as Laurence Tribe colorfully suggested.[74]

The interpretive question that often occupies commentators concerns the definition of "high Crimes and Misdemeanors." The narrow view, which impeached presidents and their supporters have been quick to embrace (with hardly anyone else joining them), is that this requires indictable crimes.[75] The broader interpretation holds that the phrase was meant to include grave offenses against the state not necessarily spelled out in the law. That there was a larger purpose behind presidential impeachment as originally conceived can be derived from any number of statements by those who ought to know. The language of "high Crimes and Misdemeanors" was adopted at the Constitutional Convention after George Mason expressed concern that a proposal limiting impeachment to treason and bribery would not reach many "great and dangerous" offenses that "subvert the Constitution." In The Federalist, Hamilton linked impeachment with "the abuse or violation of some public trust"—"chiefly to injuries done immediately to the society itself." In lectures delivered after the Constitution was ratified, James Wilson, one of the most influential delegates at the Constitutional Convention, described impeachable offenses as "political crimes and misdemeanors."[76]

The use of the word "high" comports with these remarks. Today a reference to high crimes might be taken to differentiate a criminal offense like murder from shoplifting, but the framers plucked this word out of the history of England where it meant political crimes. In addition, the distinct remedy for committing an impeachable offense—removal from office and possible disqualification—accords with this broader purpose. As Charles L. Black Jr. said, impeachment was supposed to address executive actions that "so seriously threaten the order of political society" that it is too dangerous to permit the president to continue in power.[77]

Whether the process put in place by the Constitution adequately serves this larger purpose is open to question. Despite the trappings of law that run through the proceedings (a trial in the Senate with the Supreme Court's chief justice presiding, senators sitting in judgment under oath), presidential impeachment is steeped in politics. That was by design. The Constitution's framers put elected officials in charge instead of judges as some delegates had proposed. The hope, Michael Gerhardt explained, was that members of Congress could look beyond their "short-term" partisan interests. The difficulty in pulling that off was not unanticipated. Hamilton admitted that the "greatest danger" was that the outcome would be decided "more by the comparative strength of parties than by the real demonstrations of innocence or guilt."[78]

To prevent Congress from ousting presidents without sufficient justification, the framers set a high bar to convict—too high perhaps. Technically, impeachment refers to the vote taken in the House of Representatives. A simple majority there can forward the case to the Senate for trial (comparable in that sense to an indictment in the criminal process). As history has shown, that does not present an insuperable obstacle, though it has been rare. Despite picking up the pace in the last fifty years, the House has so far averaged one president impeached per century. The first was Andrew Johnson (1868), followed by Bill Clinton (1998), and then Donald Trump, who was twice accorded that distinction (2019 and 2021). Of course, impeachment figured significantly in the Watergate scandal, but the proceedings only got as far as the House Judiciary Committee, which had approved three articles of impeachment. Before a vote could be taken on the House floor, the Supreme Court ordered President Nixon to release subpoenaed tape recordings of conversations he had with his aides. Once the so-called "smoking gun" tape revealed clear evidence of obstruction of justice, Nixon faced certain impeachment, and he resigned.[79]

The real stumbling block in the impeachment process is securing a conviction in the Senate. That requires a two-thirds vote. This supermajority requirement, Hamilton explained, provided "security to innocence" as "complete" as could be desired. Yet in the framers' effort to guard against "factious spirit," the bar has been set so high that the Senate has never been able to muster the votes to convict an impeached president. The closest the Senate ever came was in the trial of Andrew Johnson, a Union Democrat who became president after Lincoln's assassination. Seven senators defected from Republican ranks to vote to acquit, leaving the final tally one shy of the two-thirds required (35–19).[80]

Against that background, consider what happened—and what did not happen—with President Bush. By the end of his presidency, the typical list of possible impeachment charges ranged from warrantless domestic surveillance to the administration's inadequate response to Hurricane Katrina. The mistreatment of detainees was often mentioned, but the focal point of concern was the run-up to the invasion of Iraq, in particular the charge that President Bush intentionally misled Americans in order to convince them that Iraq possessed weapons of mass destruction and had links to Al Qaeda and the September 11 attacks.[81]

It should come as no surprise that impeachment was a nonevent while Republicans controlled the House of Representatives during the first six years of the Bush presidency. During the president's first term, calls for his impeachment were sporadic. An early entrant in the impeachment drive was former US attorney general Ramsey Clark. He was an unlikely candidate to elicit broad support, however, as he had, after serving in President Lyndon B. Johnson's administration, come to the defense of a number of unpopular figures in public and in court (Slobodan Milosevic, for example). Two years later, Ralph Nader, running as an independent presidential candidate, said President Bush should be impeached for deceiving Americans about Iraq to justify going to war. Around that same time, Nixon's former White House counsel John Dean described the Bush administration's secrecy and deception in a book titled *Worse Than Watergate*, with the obvious implication. The "I" word came up on Capitol Hill, though at one remove from the president, when Representative Charles Rangel (D-NY) offered a resolution to impeach Defense Secretary Rumsfeld for his part in the invasion of Iraq and, more to the point in this book, for "rejecting United States compliance with the Geneva Convention."[82]

It might be thought that President Bush's election win in November 2004 would have quelled what little movement there was to impeach him, at least for some time, but within a few months of his second inauguration, public opinion polls had ominous implications for the president. In June 2005, a Zogby poll recorded 42 percent of Americans in favor of impeachment if President

Bush had deceived the country to garner support for the Iraq war (up to 53 percent five months later). Correlate that with a *Washington Post*–ABC News survey also in June that found that 52 percent believed that the administration had "intentionally misled" the public in making its case for war.[83]

The disclosure of warrantless wiretapping in December 2005 turned out to be critical. John Dean said these revelations provided clear evidence of an impeachable offense. Former congresswoman Elizabeth Holtzman, who had served on the House Judiciary Committee during Watergate, wrote an article for *The Nation* (with a book published later) that identified the violation of the Foreign Intelligence Surveillance Act along with the president's false and misleading appeals to invade Iraq among his chief impeachable offenses. Journalists like *Harper's* editor Lewis H. Lapham added their voices to an emerging subgenre of books and articles calling for impeachment. Growing sentiment in favor of impeachment was summed up by Michelle Goldberg in *Salon*: "The I-Word Goes Public."[84]

Of course, if impeachment were to become a reality, Congress would have to take action. Yet six months before the November elections in 2006, Nancy Pelosi (D-CA), presumptive speaker of the House if the Democrats won a majority, declared impeachment of the president "off the table." She was able to keep most members of her caucus in line, but not everyone. The award for the best effort on Capitol Hill to impeach President Bush has to go to Congressman Dennis Kucinich (D-OH). He offered an impeachment resolution with thirty-five articles of impeachment that ran the gamut, from failing to equip US soldiers with appropriate armor to obstructing the investigation into the September 11 attacks. He also offered a slim version with one article of impeachment that charged the president with deceiving Congress in order to fraudulently obtain an authorization to use military force. Opposed by the Democratic leadership, both resolutions were referred to the Judiciary Committee, where nothing further was done.[85]

Some Americans were no doubt disappointed that no resolution calling for the impeachment of President Bush got a hearing in Congress. For many, the logic seemed straightforward: President Bush had committed high crimes and misdemeanors, and it was up to Congress to discharge its constitutional responsibilities. While this book finds little to commend regarding lawmakers' actions on detainee treatment, it takes the view that impeachment was not the accountability device of choice to respond to President Bush's violations of the Geneva Conventions.

The critical fact that cannot be ignored is that the Senate would have acquitted President Bush. That does not necessarily mean that his impeachment would have constituted an accountability failure. The question is whether a vote to impeach in the House followed by an acquittal in the Senate would have registered as a plus on the accountability ledger.

There may have been a time when a majority vote in the House of Representatives to impeach a president by itself would have provided some measure of accountability. Yet given President Bush's personality, it seems doubtful that he would have been chagrined. He probably would have written off the House vote as a partisan effort. Worse yet, he could have portrayed his acquittal in the Senate as a vindication of his policies, including detainee treatment. President Clinton's response to his impeachment is illustrative. Despite the Senate's vote of forty-five voting guilty on perjury and fifty guilty on obstruction of justice, not to mention the embarrassing details revealed about his behavior, Clinton said that he was "not ashamed" that "they impeached me." He managed to read his impeachment trial as "one of the major chapters in my defeat of the revolution Mr. Gingrich led."[86]

Moreover, a House impeachment followed by a Senate acquittal may have consequences for presidential accountability going beyond President Bush's case. The risk lies in a succession of impeachments ending in acquittal, which could render impeachment even more ineffective than it already is. The process could become normalized to the point that presidents who are impeached can more easily dismiss the charges brought against them as standard Washington politics. What in the past had been regarded as an awesome duty weighing on members of Congress—visible in the reaction of members of the House Judiciary Committee during Watergate when they voted on articles of impeachment—becomes a political sideshow. Lawmakers might be deterred from contemplating the impeachment of a president even when they would be eminently justified in doing so.

Suppose, on the other hand, that the Senate somehow mustered the votes to convict President Bush in an impeachment trial. In that event, lawmakers would have faced a complicated political situation. Removing President Bush from office would have elevated Vice President Cheney to the presidency. At the time, he was seen to be more of the culprit behind the administration's detainee treatment policy than the president was. If the idea behind the impeachment of President Bush was that he had to be removed without delay to prevent any further recourse to enhanced interrogation techniques during the remainder of his term, it can be argued that the situation would have been worse with Cheney heading the administration. In short, instead of having a straight-line impeachment of one president, one impeachment would have required two, and it is easy to imagine how much political resistance impeaching both top Republicans would have engendered with Speaker Pelosi next in the line of succession.

The other problem is that, with multiple charges circulating, the impact of convicting President Bush for violating the Geneva Conventions may have been diluted. As the various calls for impeachment suggest, the argument for impeaching President Bush was best positioned not by singling out a particular offense but rather by describing a pattern of misconduct subversive of the Constitution. Despite the public outcry over Abu Ghraib, it seems likely that the trial and the news coverage would have focused on the run-up to the war with Iraq, possibly with substantial interest in the domestic surveillance violations as well. Taken altogether, the issue of impeaching President Bush was more nuanced than some commentators suggested.

Whether Congress failed simply because it did not impeach him, or, in the view taken here, whether impeachment would have been of doubtful utility in holding President Bush accountable for violating the Geneva Conventions, this episode brings up the question of whether the impeachment process is doomed to failure as an accountability device for US presidents.[87]

The experience of state governments and other countries may shed some light on this. Almost every state has an impeachment process, though numerous states have additional remedies for dealing with wayward governors such as recall elections. Several governors have been convicted in impeachment proceedings. Others have been compelled to resign with impeachment imminent. Among the most famous governors impeached was Huey Long of Louisiana, though he was not removed from office (1929). His was the last gubernatorial impeachment until the Arizona state legislature impeached and ousted Governor Evan Mecham in 1988 for obstructing justice and diverting public funds to his own auto dealerships. The same fate awaited Illinois governor Rod R. Blagojevich for soliciting campaign contributions in exchange for official acts and for attempting to sell the Senate seat that Barack Obama had occupied. In more recent memory, a sex scandal forced Alabama governor Robert Bentley to resign before he could be impeached, and New York governor Andrew Cuomo resigned rather than risk impeachment after charges of sexual harassment accumulated.[88]

As for countries around the world, approximately 90 percent with a presidential system have impeachment procedures. Often these are similar to the bifurcated impeachment process in the United States with the initial determination on whether to impeach the nation's leader in one governmental institution (other countries rely on courts, constitutional councils, and cabinets as well as legislators) and the decision to convict and remove in another. In the last three decades or so, over 200 impeachment proposals have been filed around the world, with some countries ranking well above average (including Nigeria, South Korea, Ecuador, and Brazil). Roughly 10 percent led to presidents leaving office, half of these through convictions.[89] To take one example, South Korean president Park Geun Hye was found to have made official decisions in consultation with a confidant—something of a shaman or fortuneteller—who in turn had extorted business corporations and government leaders by trading on her close relationship with the president. Impeachment became the instrument to effectuate the will of the people as the country reached a crisis point with the president linked to this "fundamentally unacceptable" form of governing.[90] Interestingly, while the two-thirds vote required for conviction has thus far presented an insurmountable barrier in the United States (putting aside the likely outcome in Watergate had Nixon gone to trial in the Senate), that threshold has not prevented other countries from removing presidents from office through impeachment proceedings. In fact, over seventy countries set more onerous requirements than the United States does, such as a two-thirds vote on the initial question on whether to impeach or three-fourths to convict.[91]

In sum, impeachment in the United States is an unwieldy accountability mechanism to respond to presidential misconduct. For anyone who thought that President Bush had clearly committed high crimes and misdemeanors, the failure of the House of Representatives to initiate an impeachment inquiry may be taken as further proof that impeachment does not work in this country. Yet the debate over impeaching President Bush demonstrates that, for lawmakers who thought he should be removed from office, the decision was more complex than a simple binary determination of whether or not he had committed high crimes and misdemeanors. An acquittal in the Senate probably would have undermined accountability. A conviction, assuming the impossible, might have accomplished less than might be thought to hold the president responsible for the mistreatment of detainees, especially with several other charges that might well have diverted the public's attention. In any event, removing President Bush from office would have put Vice President Cheney in charge—clearly an unsatisfactory outcome for anyone concerned about the Bush administration's interrogation program.

VIII

President Bush may not have got everything he sought from lawmakers, but he seemed to get the better of Congress at every turn.

A good case can be made that the legislative branch, to be considered an effective check on the executive, should have prevented President Bush from launching his interrogation program. The Gang of Eight was set up to monitor intelligence activities. Sadly, there is not much to say about what this handful of lawmakers did, except that it proved all too easy for the CIA to turn aside one prescient congressional inquiry related to the treatment of detainees. Once the interrogation program was put in place, congressional oversight was lacking for years, despite the public outcry over Abu Ghraib and the damning evidence about prisoner abuse brought to light by the news media. Of the initial congressional investigations into what happened there, the response of the committees in the House of Representatives was obviously deficient. More interesting is what happened in the Senate. There is no reason to doubt that Senator Warner, as chairman of the Senate Armed Services Committee, was committed to conducting a full investigation. The fact that some of his Republican colleagues were able to neutralize his inquiry speaks for itself. By the time the public was given detailed results of a thorough congressional investigation into military interrogations (the Senate Armed Services Committee report of 2008), Barack Obama had been elected president. And for all the obstacles overcome by the Senate Intelligence Committee, its torture report—or, more accurately, the heavily redacted executive summary—can be faulted for its questionable assessment of the president's involvement in the interrogation program.

As for legislation, it is tempting to conclude that lawmakers did more harm than good. Indeed, one might say that the only question that remains open for debate is whether the Detainee Treatment Act or the Military Commissions Act provides better evidence of the Bush administration's success in turning the legislative check on its head. With the DTA, the White House managed to hijack a bill designed to prevent cruel, inhuman, and degrading treatment and turn it into legislation that made it more difficult to hold individuals accountable for doing that. It is difficult to avoid the conclusion that the president and his allies outmaneuvered Senator McCain and his allies. The MCA was notable for ratifying key elements of the Bush interrogation program. Congress endorsed the administration's use of the "unlawful enemy combatant" designation, allowed evidence to be used that was obtained through cruel, inhuman, and degrading treatment, declared that detainees cannot invoke the Geneva Conventions as a source of rights, stripped federal courts of jurisdiction over cases brought by detainees, and, of all things, recognized President Bush as the ultimate authority for the United States in interpreting the Geneva Conventions.

While these results may be explained in part by the party composition of Congress, lawmakers interested in genuine oversight and accountability were also hampered by the institutional mismatch between the president and Congress. In a nutshell, President Bush was able to exploit the legislative process. He forced compromises, delayed investigations, withheld material information, took advantage of the crisis atmosphere, and shaped the narrative for public consumption as against the multiple voices coming out of the legislature. Finally, Congress was unable to make use of impeachment, even though that once-promising remedy was specifically designed to address serious abuses of power in the executive (and the judiciary). It was, in a constitutional sense, a fitting summation of a presidency unchecked by legislative power.

It must be conceded that members of Congress did try to rein in another branch of government, but legislative pushback came not against the president, but rather against the Supreme Court.

CHAPTER FOUR

The Court versus the Commander in Chief

The Supreme Court has achieved an exalted position in the American system of government: umpire between nation and states; final arbiter of the higher law of the Constitution; last refuge to protect individuals disfavored by the majority; guardian of the rights of all Americans. With that in mind, it might be thought that the nation's highest court was uniquely positioned to challenge a president who was holding individuals incommunicado and denying them judicial hearings of any sort in the midst of credible reports of mistreatment and torture.

When the Court began to entertain cases brought by detainees, the justices showed promise that they were equal to the task. As they affirmed the rights of detainees to be heard in federal court in one case after another, sophisticated Court watchers had reason to view their decisions as substantial checks on executive power. Some were considered landmarks in Supreme Court history. *Hamdan v. Rumsfeld*, Senator Patrick Leahy said, was a "triumph for our constitutional system of checks and balances." Walter Dellinger called it the "most important decision on presidential power and the rule of law ever." When *Boumediene v. Bush* was decided in 2008, it was likewise described as one of "the Court's most important modern statements on the separation of powers." The federal judiciary was thought to be among "the most effective actors in actually changing the course of executive policy since September 11." The contrast with Congress seemed clear. "It was the justices, not Congress," Howard Ball wrote, "who told the president that he can't do whatever he wants to do in his battles against terrorists" and restored "some sort of constitutional checks-and-balance equilibrium."[1]

While there is something to be said for what the justices did, this chapter argues that the Supreme Court's war-on-terror decisions accomplished less than early returns suggested. Analysts such as Sanford Levinson, Jenny S. Martinez, Kim Lane Scheppele, and Stephen I. Vladek have expressed similar reservations.[2] In taking a close look at these cases in the context of this inquiry into presidential accountability, this chapter highlights several features of the pattern that emerged. First, the Court had difficulty overcoming inherent institutional handicaps when taking on the president. Second, when it came to issuing direct orders to a wartime president, the justices, sensitive to national security crisis atmospherics, preferred to work by hint and suggestion rather than by command. Third, even with rights central to Anglo-American law at stake, the justices were inclined to take the minimum response thought necessary, a practice that opened the door for continued executive resistance. Fourth, the Court was overwhelmed by presidential countermeasures, particularly when the administration got Congress and the lower federal courts to counteract Supreme Court rulings. And fifth, it proved difficult for the justices to give priority to accountability—even when the judiciary provided a natural forum in civil litigation—over executive claims about upsetting the national security policymaking process. What this episode suggests, simply put, is that the Supreme Court has a hard time contending with a wartime president bent on testing the limits of the law.

I

The Supreme Court's war-on-terrorism decisions came against the backdrop of a long history of decisions on executive power. When the Constitution was adopted, it was not clear what authority, if any, the justices had over the executive branch. While the framers provided Congress with ample means to contend with an unruly president (putting aside whether the legislature has capitalized on its opportunities to do so), they left the Supreme Court more or less on its own. The question of whether federal courts had the power of judicial review to declare executive actions unconstitutional was taken up in *Marbury v. Madison* (1803). Actually, that issue was not presented on the facts of that case, which concerned an act of Congress, but that did not stop Chief Justice John Marshall from claiming the authority in dicta. Since then, the Court has done quite nicely in enlarging its powers over all aspects of American life—to the point that some observers refer to the third branch as an "imperial judiciary."[3]

Among the cases of judicial review over presidents, several of the most important have addressed questions concerning war powers.[4] The result of the Supreme Court's ventures in this area has been a hodgepodge of decisions not necessarily known for logical consistency. For example, the *Prize Cases* (1863) confirmed President Lincoln's authority to impose a blockade on the Confederacy, but the justices were not so accommodating three years later in *Ex parte Milligan* (1866). There the Court disapproved of a presidential proclamation that authorized military tribunals to try civilians anywhere in the country, even where civil courts were still operating.[5] That decision, along with its ringing language declaring the Constitution "a law for rulers and people, equally in war and in peace," was seriously undermined—one might say scuttled—by *Ex parte Quirin* (1942), which upheld the military tribunal set up by President Franklin Roosevelt to try German saboteurs captured within the United States (while civil courts remained open).[6] A similar imperative to go along with a wartime president ("the power to protect must be commensurate with the threatened danger") appears to have motivated a majority of justices to acquiesce in the mass internment of Japanese Americans in *Korematsu v. United States* (1944), but on the same day the Court held in *Ex parte Endo* (1944) that the military lacks authority to deny a "concededly loyal" Japanese American citizen "unconditional release."[7]

Although it may be hard to extract a legal principle that neatly reconciles these decisions, there is a detectable pattern, with judicial deference the norm and pushback the exception. The question naturally arises as to what leads the Court to do one and not the other. One common explanation is that the justices are emboldened to give greater scrutiny to the president's wartime actions as the national security threat diminishes, with *Milligan*, decided a year after Appomattox, as exhibit A. While it is possible to think of practical reasons for such a course of action, that explanation standing alone is hardly satisfactory as a matter of legal principle.[8]

Another clue to the justices' thinking is that they like to factor actions taken by Congress into their constitutional analysis of executive wartime actions. Justice Robert H. Jackson's concurring opinion in *Youngstown Sheet & Tube Co. v. Sawyer* (1952) is often cited for this institutionalist approach.[9] *Youngstown* arose in the midst of the Korean War. President Truman, concerned about an impending nationwide strike by steelworkers, directed his secretary of commerce to assume control of major steel plants. A majority of justices, impressed by the fact that Congress had in the Taft-Hartley Act rejected governmental takeovers of industries to resolve labor disputes, held the so-called steel seizure unconstitutional. Justice Jackson, on the view that the president's war powers fluctuate in "disjunction or conjunction" with congressional action, put forward a tripartite framework for analysis, with the president's authority at its maximum when grounded in express or implied legislative authorization, at its "lowest ebb" when repugnant to legislation, and in a middle "zone of twilight" when Congress is silent (in which case Justice Jackson recommended a pragmatic approach).[10]

II

Against that background, with judicial deference in wartime the general rule, the Supreme Court's encounters with the Bush administration's counterterrorism policies came as something of a surprise at first. One cannot help but notice the tone taken by Justice Sandra Day O'Connor writing for the Court in *Hamdi v. Rumsfeld* (2004): "We have long since made clear that a state of war is not a blank check for the President when it comes to the rights of the Nation's citizens."[11] She was no less emphatic when rebutting the administration's contentions about judicial authority: "We necessarily reject the Government's assertion that separation of powers principles mandate a heavily circumscribed role for the courts in such circumstances."[12] She added that "as critical as the Government's interest may be in detaining those who actually pose an immediate threat to the national security of the United States during ongoing international conflict, history and common sense teach us that an unchecked system of detention carries the potential to become a means for oppression and abuse of others who do not present that sort of threat."[13] As the decision in *Hamdi* was announced two months after the first reports about Abu Ghraib, her statement that "indefinite detention for the purpose of interrogation is not authorized" looks like a stern warning to the administration. On the same day the Court issued its ruling in *Hamdi*, Justice Stevens, dissenting in *Rumsfeld v. Padilla* (2004), also made a point of noting that detention may not be "justified by the naked interest in using unlawful procedures to extract information."[14]

What the Court actually decided in *Hamdi v. Rumsfeld* was something less than what the rhetoric promised, however. *Hamdi* was among the first batch of war-on-terrorism cases to reach the Supreme Court. It was also one of the most important. Yaser Esam Hamdi was captured in Afghanistan in December 2001 and taken to Guantánamo. When his interrogators discovered that he was a US citizen (born in Louisiana), the Defense Department transferred him to a naval brig in Norfolk, Virginia and then to one in Charleston, South Carolina. Getting out of Guantánamo did nothing to enhance his access to counsel, however, as Hamdi was not allowed to consult a lawyer for two years. His case got into the federal courts in June 2002 when his father filed a petition in his behalf. In the ensuing litigation, the Defense Department submitted a nine-paragraph declaration that stated that Hamdi had traveled to Afghanistan and had affiliated with the Taliban militia.[15]

The Supreme Court's decision in *Hamdi* can be broken down into three propositions: (1) the president has the "authority to detain citizens" who, alleged to have fought the United States in Afghanistan, "qualify as 'enemy combatants'"; (2) the government's determination of enemy combatant status for citizen detainees must accord with due process; and (3) the process that is "constitutionally due to a citizen who disputes his enemy-combatant status" consists of "notice of the factual basis for his classification" and a "fair opportunity to rebut the Government's factual assertions before a neutral decision-maker."[16]

Given the way the justices split in deciding this case, the plurality opinion written by Justice O'Connor was controlling. On the question of whether the president can designate an American citizen as an enemy combatant, the justice's opinion betrays a willingness on the part of the plurality to find something—seemingly anything—to justify presidential authority to do so. The chief obstacle standing in the way was the Non-Detention Act, enacted by Congress in 1971 to prevent anything like the internment of Japanese American citizens during World War II. It states that "no citizen shall be imprisoned or otherwise detained by the United States except pursuant to an Act of Congress." Thus, in order to detain Hamdi in accordance with the Non-Detention Act, President Bush needed statutory authorization. In Justice O'Connor's view, the Authorization for Use of Military Force (AUMF) adopted by Congress shortly after September 11, 2001 served that purpose. Yet the only way the AUMF could be read to authorize the detention of American citizens was by giving a generous reading of its language empowering the president to use "all necessary and appropriate force." As Justice David Souter pointed out in a separate opinion, nothing suggested that lawmakers had the detention of US citizens in mind when they enacted that legislation.[17] Indeed, if the language of the AUMF is interpreted freely—as Justice O'Connor had done—it might be argued contrary to her position that the word "appropriate" limits what the president can do. In other words, the president can do what is necessary so long as it is also appropriate, and the detention of US citizens in violation of the rights of the accused guaranteed in the Bill of Rights does not qualify as such.

If the *Hamdi* Court can be said to have pushed back against the president on any question, it was its ruling requiring due process, as Justice O'Connor held that the government must afford due process to US citizens classified as enemy combatants. Yet the process the Court was willing to accept was so minimal—the justice herself described it as "this basic process"—that it is reasonable to ask whether Hamdi or any US citizen for that matter really won anything substantial from the Court's ruling.[18] Justice O'Connor purportedly adopted a balancing approach, weighing Hamdi's "most elemental of liberty interests" against "weighty and sensitive" governmental interests. As her analysis unfolds, however, it becomes clear that the balance favors the government. Recognizing the "uncommon potential" of combatant status proceedings "to burden the Executive at a time of ongoing military conflict," she outlined several alternatives to reduce that burden.[19] She countenanced the use of hearsay evidence even though the chaotic conditions on the ground in Afghanistan (cash bounties) should have raised questions about the use of hearsay against those captured, who might, after all, be innocent (as some were).[20] Justice O'Connor also invited the government to employ a rebuttable presumption in its favor once it had produced "credible evidence" that the detainee was an enemy combatant. "The Constitution would not be offended," she announced, if that determination were based on a presumption "in favor of the Government's evidence." In shifting the burden on the detainee to prove that he was not an enemy combatant, Justice O'Connor gave no indication that she recognized the difficulty Afghans and other nationals falsely accused of fighting the United States might encounter in obtaining evidence, likely from outside the United States, while in US custody. Finally, Justice O'Connor said in dicta that the government could use "appropriately authorized and properly constituted" military tribunals to determine whether an individual was an enemy combatant, even though the only military tribunals set up to that point were those established by the president, and their procedures were constitutionally suspect.[21]

Moreover, for all of Justice O'Connor's strong language about the judiciary's role in constraining presidential power, it is possible to extract from her opinion a series of premises that went a long way to endorsing the administration's detention policy. Some may appear obvious, innocuous, or inconsequential, but when taken together, they gave judicial imprimatur to broad authority in the president to detain individuals in the war against terrorism. The following premises can be deduced from her opinion: first, that the Court would regard the war against terrorism as just that—a war, with all that entailed for tilting the balance in favor of executive claims of wartime power as against civil liberties; second, that "detention to prevent a combatant's return to the battlefield" was a "fundamental incident of waging war";[22] third, that President Bush had statutory authority to designate US citizens as enemy combatants (his authority affirmed without rejecting the administration's questionable definition of enemy combatants);[23] fourth, that the president may have constitutional authority to do the same (the plurality opinion left that unanswered);[24] fifth, that those designated enemy combatants by the president were subject to military detention;[25] sixth, that there was no automatic prohibition against indefinite detention "for the duration of the relevant conflict" (though Justice O'Connor, besides noting that indefinite detention "for the purpose of interrogation" was not authorized, reserved the authority to revisit that issue if the war against terrorism turned out to be "entirely unlike" previous conflicts);[26] seventh, that individuals the president designates as enemy combatants do not have a right to jury trial;[27] eighth, that military tribunals might be used to determine combatant status;[28] and ninth, that all of the above applies to US citizens, at least those involved in the fighting in Afghanistan, as "there is no bar to this Nation's holding one of its own citizens as an enemy combatant."[29]

Add to that one other point: the Supreme Court never saw fit to deny the president the authority to designate American citizens arrested within the United States as enemy combatants who would then be subject to indefinite military detention. The case of José Padilla raised that issue. Arrested in May 2002 at Chicago O'Hare International Airport, Padilla was initially held as a material witness for the federal grand jury investigation in New York looking into the September 11 terrorist attacks. Attorney General Ashcroft told the public that Padilla was involved in an Al Qaeda plot to detonate a radioactive dirty bomb in the United States. Such an accusation was bound to attract attention, but the government never charged Padilla with that. One month after his arrest, with a pending motion to vacate the material witness warrant (filed by the lawyer appointed to represent him), President Bush issued an order that stated that it was "consistent with U.S. law and the laws of war" to detain Padilla as an enemy combatant. Padilla was placed in military custody, where he was held in solitary confinement for over three years (incommunicado for almost two). He claimed that he was tortured.[30]

Padilla may not have been a particularly sympathetic character, but as he was an American citizen, it seemed that the Supreme Court would have to address the broader issue of the president's authority to hold citizens arrested in the United States in indefinite military detention without court review. The justices never clearly answered that question. When Padilla's case first came before the Court, a majority ducked the issue by holding that his lawyers had filed his claim in the wrong court—in New York (where he was originally held) instead of South Carolina (where he was in military custody). By the time his case had worked its way up to the Supreme Court again, the justices declined to review it. The government had argued that his military detention had become moot because the administration had transferred him out of military custody to face criminal charges in US district court. Some critics believed that the administration moved Padilla in order to avoid further scrutiny from the Supreme Court.[31]

III

At the heart of the claim that the Supreme Court effectively checked President Bush is a trio of decisions involving alien detainees held at Guantánamo: *Rasul v. Bush* (2004), *Hamdan v. Rumsfeld* (2006), and *Boumediene v. Bush* (2008).[32] Some say these enemy combatant cases represent an unprecedented level of judicial interference with the commander in chief's authority over the conduct of war.[33] Yet upon closer scrutiny of what the Court actually decided as well as when and how its rulings were put into effect, the administration appears to have come off quite well. For one thing, it forced the justices to return to the threshold jurisdictional issue once and again. That alone substantially delayed relief for detainees. For another thing, the administration thwarted implementation of these decisions with the help of Congress and lower federal courts.[34]

The enemy combatant cases are important for many reasons; one is that they tested the scope of the writ of habeas corpus. Latin for "bring forth the body," habeas corpus is a legal instrument to determine the lawfulness of someone's imprisonment. When a judge issues the writ, the government is supposed to release the individual from custody if it is unable to produce evidence that justifies continued detention. Originating in England, habeas corpus was incorporated into American colonial law. That the Constitution's framers assumed the writ of habeas corpus in operation is suggested by the oblique reference in the suspension clause, which declared that habeas corpus shall not be suspended "unless when in Cases of Rebellion or Invasion the public Safety may require it." Since the nation's founding, Congress has enacted supplemental legislation authorizing the federal courts to hear habeas petitions.[35]

Habeas corpus may not seem like much—a procedural device that can lead at most to a judicial inquiry looking into the legality of detention. Yet the writ is widely recognized as a fundamental check on arbitrary executive action. Its "root principle," Justice William J. Brennan once said, is that the government "must always be accountable to the judiciary for a man's imprisonment." One measure of the importance placed on habeas corpus to the scheme of liberty in the United States is that Congress has rarely approved its suspension.[36]

This was the context for the cases coming out of Guantánamo. While the security benefits derived from its remote location may have factored into the administration's decision to use the naval base to hold detainees, it appears that the choice of Guantánamo was driven more than anything else by legal considerations. The overriding concern, frankly stated in an OLC memorandum titled "Possible Habeas Jurisdiction over Aliens Held in Guantánamo Bay, Cuba," was over "potential legal exposure." If detainees were able to bring habeas petitions before the federal courts, OLC lawyers warned, judges could look into any number of issues, including the legality of detainee treatment under the Geneva Conventions, the use of military commissions, and even the legal justification for the war in Afghanistan.[37]

Guantánamo seemed to administration lawyers to be as good a place as any to try to block the judiciary from hearing habeas claims brought by detainees. Their reasoning was based on *Johnson v. Eisentrager* (1950). There, the Supreme Court held that federal courts had no jurisdiction over habeas petitions filed by German prisoners of war following World War II. They had been captured in China (where they had been providing intelligence to Japanese forces), tried for war crimes before a US military commission in Nanking (for continuing these activities after Germany had surrendered), and then imprisoned in Landsberg Prison in occupied Germany. The Supreme Court noted that the German prisoners had never been within the "sovereign" territory of the United States or the "territorial jurisdiction" of the federal courts. This language of sovereignty piqued the interest of Bush administration lawyers because of Guantánamo's peculiar history. Under the lease agreement with Cuba signed after the Spanish-American War, the United States had the right to exercise "complete jurisdiction and control" over Guantánamo while Cuba retained "ultimate sovereignty."[38]

OLC lawyers recognized the "litigation risk" in this strategy.[39] As it turned out, making the leap from *Eisentrager* to Guantánamo was a step several justices were unwilling to take, as a majority on the Court asserted federal court jurisdiction over the Guantánamo detainees' habeas petitions in *Rasul, Hamdan,* and *Boumediene.* This is what has led some analysts to conclude that the Supreme Court demonstrated—on this issue at least—that the third branch of government was capable of keeping the second in check.

Yet the fact that the Court had to address the jurisdictional issue repeatedly is an important clue of what was really going on with these cases. So long as the justices got stuck on this threshold issue—one which they were compelled to address three times in five years—detainees' claims that their detention was unlawful remained unresolved. Put another way, assessing what the Supreme Court accomplished in these cases depends on how victory for the administration is defined. If the question is whether the Justice Department convinced the Court to refrain from exercising jurisdiction, then the administration lost. It becomes more difficult to reach that conclusion if the question is framed differently, as in whether detainees were held for years while the justices grappled with the jurisdictional issue.

As for the delay, little more need be said than that it took the Court too long to resolve the jurisdictional question. While many litigants encounter frustrating delays in the federal judicial system, justice delayed in habeas proceedings is especially problematic. The reason is obvious. Assuming a person is wrongfully imprisoned, delay inevitably detracts from the writ's effect. It is an essential characteristic of habeas corpus that the writ be timely granted. As Justice Stephen G. Breyer pointed out, habeas is supposed to be an "effective *and speedy* instrument."[40] Yet by the time the Court decided that Guantánamo detainees had a constitutional right to file habeas petitions, some had been held in US custody for six years.[41]

Admittedly, delay is to some degree a natural outgrowth of the deliberative character of the judicial process. It can take years for a case to make its way through the multitiered federal court system before reaching the highest court. Consider the case of *Rasul v. Bush* (2004). The detainees filed habeas petitions in February 2002, not long after they had been brought to Guantánamo. Later that year, they got their case before a federal district judge only to lose there. On appeal, the US Court of Appeals for the DC Circuit affirmed the lower court's ruling. That decision was rendered in March 2003. At the end of that year, the Supreme Court justices agreed to take the case. They heard oral arguments in April 2004 and handed down their decision two months later.[42] There was nothing unusual about this timeline; indeed, the *Rasul* detainees were fortunate with such a schedule.

Nor was there anything particularly unusual about the justices' expressions of judicial self-restraint. Judges routinely espouse a minimalist philosophy of judicial decision-making that holds that no more should be decided in a case than what is necessary. As a corollary, it is often said that courts should avoid constitutional questions when a decision resting on statutory grounds will suffice.[43] Justice O'Connor embraced this approach in *Hamdi* when she said that "we do not reach the question" of the president's constitutional authority because "Congress has in fact authorized" the detention. Likewise, Justice Stevens in *Rasul* and *Hamdan* upheld federal court jurisdiction based on the habeas statute.[44]

What the justices had not anticipated, it seems, was the extent to which the administration would squeeze every conceivable advantage out of the opportunity the judicial process presented. What followed was something like a chess match consisting of moves and countermoves between the executive and the judiciary. In *Rasul*, the Supreme Court held that the habeas corpus statute (which granted federal courts the authority to entertain claims of those "in custody in violation of the Constitution or laws or treaties of the United States") provided jurisdiction to hear habeas petitions brought by foreign nationals challenging the legality of their detention at Guantánamo. As this decision was based on statutory interpretation, the obvious move for the Bush administration was to prod members of Congress to revise the statute. Lawmakers obliged with the Detainee Treatment Act, which stripped federal courts of jurisdiction over habeas claims filed by Guantánamo inmates. The Court responded in *Hamdan* by interpreting the DTA so that it did not cover pending cases like Hamdan's. The administration then got Congress to pass the Military Commissions Act, which removed pending detainee cases from the federal courts. Only then, when the MCA was challenged in *Boumediene*, did the Court reach the constitutional question of habeas jurisdiction, as Justice Kennedy ruled that this provision violated the suspension clause. By that point, President Bush was in his last year in office.[45]

If this constitutional ruling on habeas jurisdiction was late in coming, Justice Kennedy's opinion may appear at first glance to make up for the delay for several reasons. In striking down the MCA's jurisdiction-stripping provision as an "unconstitutional suspension" of habeas corpus, the Court for the first time invalidated legislation based on the suspension clause. Besides deciding that the United States had de facto sovereignty over Guantánamo, Justice Kennedy expressed concern if not outright suspicion over the executive turning "the Constitution on or off at will" by formally surrendering sovereignty and then assuming proprietary control by leasehold.[46] Unimpressed by the DTA's procedures for combatant status review, the justice held that they did not provide an "adequate and effective substitute" for habeas corpus.[47] Justice Kennedy found *Eisentrager* clearly distinguishable given the "rigorous adversarial process" afforded German prisoners of war (a war crimes trial) in comparison with the minimal procedures used at Guantánamo. He also faulted the Bush Justice Department for failing to put forward any "credible arguments" to explain why allowing the detainees' habeas claims to go forward in the federal courts would undermine the "military mission" at Guantánamo.[48]

So far as checking the president goes, the problem with *Boumediene* was not with its rulings on habeas corpus and federal court jurisdiction, but rather with implementing the decision. This was partly a problem of the Supreme Court's own making, as Justice Kennedy's opinion left significant questions for the lower federal courts to answer.

One concerned the "extent of the showing required of the Government" at a habeas hearing.[49] Justice Kennedy set forth a general standard: the court must be able to "conduct a meaningful review of both the cause for detention and the Executive's power to detain," but what qualified as a "meaningful review" was left for lower courts to determine.[50] The justice did note that the detainee must have "a meaningful opportunity" to show that the government detained him based upon an "erroneous application or interpretation" of law, but that reads more like a restatement than an explanation. Whatever advantage this standard conferred on habeas petitioners was tempered by Justice Kennedy's apparent enthusiasm for recognizing the government's "legitimate interest in protecting sources and methods of intelligence gathering" to "the greatest extent possible."[51]

Another question left unresolved was whether the federal courts had jurisdiction to entertain habeas petitions filed by detainees held at sites besides Guantánamo. This was not a hypothetical problem as the Bush administration, following the Supreme Court's decision in *Rasul*, had turned to Bagram Air Force Base in Afghanistan as an alternative to Guantánamo.[52] But while Justice Kennedy had openly worried about the executive switching the Constitution on and off by placing detainees beyond the reach of federal court jurisdiction, his opinion in *Boumediene* left this question open. The justice articulated three factors for lower courts to consider: (1) the detainee's status (and citizenship) and the process used to make that determination; (2) the places where the detainee was caught and held; and (3) the "practical obstacles" involved in determining whether the writ should issue.[53]

It is not unusual for the Supreme Court to reserve questions for the lower federal courts to address. In *Rasul*, the Court left it to lower courts to sort out "whether and what further proceedings may become necessary." Those were "matters," Justice Stevens said, that "we need not address now." Justice Kennedy expressed the same sentiment in *Boumediene* when he said that "these and the other remaining questions are within the expertise and competence of the District Court to address in the first instance."[54] Yet by the time *Boumediene* was decided, Justice Kennedy and his colleagues were on notice that the administration would do everything it could to disrupt the flow of habeas litigation. How far the Bush administration was willing to go to resist the Supreme Court's rulings in the lower federal courts became clear in the immediate aftermath of the first set of enemy combatant cases decided by the Court, which included *Rasul*. As Linda Greenhouse reported, the Justice Department responded to that decision by asking the lower courts to dismiss the habeas petitions "as if *Rasul* had not been decided."[55]

Administration lawyers found a receptive audience in the US Court of Appeals for the DC Circuit. Its role looms large in this. Congress, it will be recalled, had given the DC Circuit exclusive authority to review combatant status determinations (with review limited to whether the tribunal's determination complied with the standards and procedures set forth by the secretary of defense and whether those procedures were constitutional).[56] While judges on that circuit represented a spectrum of opinion, some were vehemently opposed to the Supreme Court's ruling in *Boumediene*. Among the most vocal was Judge Raymond A. Randolph, who had written the circuit opinion the Court had reversed. In a speech called "The Guantánamo Mess," the judge compared the justices to characters in *The Great Gatsby*. "They were careless people," said Judge Randolph, quoting F. Scott Fitzgerald. "They smashed up things" and "let other people clean up the mess they had made."[57] He was not alone in his criticism. Judge Janice Rogers Brown took note of "*Boumediene*'s airy suppositions" that "caused great difficulty for the Executive and the courts." Judge Laurence H. Silberman characterized the "whole process" initiated by *Boumediene* as a "charade."[58]

Most of the DC Circuit's thirteen judges refrained from making similar comments in public, and circuit opinions in post-*Boumediene* litigation did not always favor the government. Yet in one case after another—whether in suggestions, dicta, or clear holdings—the opinions applying *Boumediene* seemed more in line with these three judges than with Justice Kennedy. The case law tends to get complicated, but it is worth working through some key points to see how DC Circuit judges undercut *Boumediene*.

Consider how they filled in the blanks on what constitutes a "meaningful" review. Some of the decisions may seem defensible when viewed individually, but what Judge David S. Tatel said in dissent in one case can be taken as an apt summary of their collective impact: it was "hard to see what is left of the Supreme Court's command in *Boumediene* that habeas review be 'meaningful.'"[59] The standard used for the burden of proof was a potentially decisive factor given the uncertainty surrounding many individuals held at Guantánamo and the difficulty in proving their status one way or the other. Some circuit judges seemed intent on reducing the government's evidentiary burden. The "reasonable doubt" standard used in criminal cases was never in contention. Although the DC Circuit did not reject out of hand the "preponderance of evidence" standard used for civil litigation,[60] Judge Randolph questioned its use for Guantánamo habeas petitions, and Judge Silberman considered it "unrealistic" for terrorism suspects. He thought "some evidence" better, contrary to Justice O'Connor's statement in *Hamdi* that this less onerous standard was "ill suited" to initial habeas proceedings.[61] As for what evidence was admissible, the panel in *Al-Bihani v. Obama* (2010) declared the right to confront witnesses under the Sixth Amendment's confrontation clause inapplicable in these habeas proceedings and then proceeded to note that hearsay evidence was "always admissible"—the only question left to consider was its probative value. Appellate courts normally defer to the trial court's findings of fact, but the circuit panel in *Latif v. Obama* (2011) brushed aside the district court's factual findings in favor of the detainee and reviewed the case de novo. The judges there also endorsed a presumption in favor of admitting secret intelligence reports.[62]

Then there was the issue of whether *Boumediene* applied outside Guantánamo. With his three-part test, Justice Kennedy seemed to contemplate the lower courts working through this question on a case-by-case basis. The DC Circuit's opinion in *Al Maqaleh v. Gates* (2010), which declined to extend *Boumediene* to detainees held at Bagram Air Force Base, all but foreclosed its application beyond Guantánamo. While the circuit judges worked through all three factors, their analysis of the third concerning "practical obstacles" was determinative.[63] In *Boumediene*, Justice Kennedy had indicated that detention in an "active theater of war" would be important to consider when evaluating the practical obstacles to habeas relief. Noting that Afghanistan remained "a theater of war," the circuit panel asserted that allowing habeas petitions from Bagram "would hamper the war effort."[64] Although Justice Kennedy had expressed concern over the place of capture and executive manipulation, the circuit panel was not swayed by allegations made by two of the three petitioners that they had been captured outside an active theater of war (Pakistan and Thailand) and then transferred to Afghanistan. Nor was much made of the concededly inadequate process used to determine their status.[65]

In assessing the impact of this last one of the major Supreme Court's enemy combatant decisions, the first point to note, as important as it is easy to overlook, is that *Boumediene* did not free anyone immediately, as Justice Kennedy remanded the case to the lower federal courts for further proceedings.[66] Another six months went by before district courts began to issue orders for the release of detainees, but then the DC Circuit got involved. A study published in 2012 detected a dividing line in *Al-Adahi v. Obama*, a July 2010 decision by the DC Circuit. Before that case, detainees won 59 percent of their habeas petitions. Afterwards, they prevailed only once in a dozen cases covered in that study, and that one was reversed on appeal.[67] Some of the DC Circuit judges' opinions all but dared the Supreme Court to intervene, but the justices repeatedly declined to hear any more cases brought by Guantánamo detainees. These statistics seem to confirm Judge Tatel's observation that it was "hard to see what is left" of *Boumediene*'s mandate for "meaningful" habeas review.[68]

With a fuller picture of the Guantánamo enemy combatant cases—including not only what was decided, but also when the Court intervened, what was left for other institutions to sort out, and what was not followed up—one is left with the distinct impression that the justices to varying degrees were motivated by concerns over federal judicial power, especially in the face of the administration's exaggerated claims about judges interfering with the war effort. That is not to say that those in the prevailing majorities in *Rasul*, *Hamdan*, and *Boumediene* were not sympathetic to the plight of Guantánamo detainees, but, having pushed back against the administration's over-the-top attempts to curb federal court jurisdiction, the Court did not have a majority keen on continuing to battle the president.[69] Justice Kennedy in particular, a crucial vote all along, seemed to view this as a contest between the Supreme Court and the president—brought before the Court by Guantánamo detainees and having significant implications for individual liberties, to be sure—but in the main a battle over judicial power.[70]

IV

Besides the enemy combatant cases, there were other war-on-terrorism cases that reveal something of the Supreme Court's complicated relationship with executive accountability in wartime. Among the most important were civil damages lawsuits brought against Bush administration officials. As many of these lawsuits were filed for the purpose of holding President Bush's top lieutenants accountable, the way in which the Supreme Court handled them is of some importance to this book's argument.

Civil damages lawsuits against public officials occupy a specialized niche in the law. In traditional areas like contracts and torts, the main purpose in bringing a lawsuit is to obtain compensatory damages for injuries sustained. For persons with claims against the government, the Supreme Court years ago recognized such actions against "high officials" as an "important means of vindicating" their constitutional rights.[71] For some plaintiffs, the goal in filing such a lawsuit is not so much to win a large sum of money as it is to validate their rights by holding public officials accountable through the legal process.[72] Civil lawsuits can be viewed as a feasible alternative to criminal prosecutions to secure government accountability. Plaintiffs have a lower burden of proof in civil cases, and monetary awards may be perceived by the public as a more palatable remedy when compared to criminal penalties for individual officials.[73]

The issues presented in civil lawsuits relating to the Bush administration's counterterrorism policies were wide-ranging and serious. The cases brought to the judiciary's attention questions regarding warrantless arrests, indefinite detention, prisoner abuse, extraordinary rendition, torture, drone strikes, and electronic surveillance. Experienced human rights lawyers and leading law professors represented plaintiffs. The list of defendants reads like an organization chart of the administration's national security team (including the attorney general, the CIA director, the FBI director, and the defense secretary). Lawsuits were brought against key contractors such as James Mitchell and Bruce Jessen (the psychologists behind the CIA's interrogation program) and Jeppeson Dataplan (a Boeing subsidiary that organized extraordinary rendition flights).[74]

Given the state of legal doctrine before September 11, 2001, it would not have been surprising to find many of these lawsuits turned aside at the courthouse door. The sovereign immunity doctrine generally precludes suing the US government directly unless Congress provides otherwise. Legislators, judges, and prosecutors have absolute immunity from civil damages lawsuits for actions taken in the performance of their official duties (that goes for the president as well). Most other government officials have qualified immunity from civil damages actions unless they violate "clearly established" constitutional or statutory rights. Statutory alternatives are limited.[75]

Besides the obstacles peculiar to civil damages lawsuits against officials, litigants may face other hurdles in bringing a case before the federal courts, let alone the Supreme Court. Federal judges have a toolkit of doctrines that can be used to dismiss a case without reaching its merits. These doctrines derive from Article III of the Constitution, which has been read to require a justiciable case or controversy. Accordingly, litigants are supposed to present a concrete injury to avoid having judges dismiss their claims for lack of standing. Federal courts can decline to take a case that has not developed into a genuine controversy (ripeness), one in which the controversy has ended (mootness), or one that presents a "political question" not susceptible to judicial resolution and best left to the legislative and executive branches.[76] In addition, Supreme Court justices have discretionary control over most of their docket. Litigants must request the Court to review their cases by filing a petition for certiorari; the justices may decline to hear cases by denying the petition without explanation.[77]

One option that held some promise, though not without difficulties, derived from the case of *Bivens v. Six Unknown Named Agents of the Federal Bureau of Narcotics* (1971). There, the Supreme Court recognized what is called an implied right of action for constitutional violations—in that case against law enforcement officers who conducted a warrantless arrest contrary to the Fourth Amendment. The Court subsequently applied *Bivens* to gender discrimination (under the Fifth Amendment's due process clause) and prisoners' rights to adequate medical care (under the Eighth Amendment's prohibition against cruel and unusual punishment), but the justices have refrained from applying *Bivens* to other contexts since then.[78]

No one should have expected *Bivens* plaintiffs suing Bush administration officials to prevail across the board, but the end result of these lawsuits may have surprised some observers. None went to trial. Many were dismissed. There were occasional settlements, usually accompanied by the government's refusal to admit liability.[79] Most of these cases never got to the Supreme Court, and a pattern emerged from the Court's review of cert petitions. If the government prevailed in the lower courts, it was a good bet that the justices would deny certiorari. If the government lost below, the justices were more likely to agree to hear the case. On top of that, the resulting Supreme Court decisions made it more difficult for plaintiffs to bring *Bivens* civil damages suits in the future on any subject.[80]

Analysts trying to divine what lay behind the Court's rulings have Justice Kennedy to thank for a cursory and unabashedly frank explanation given in *Ziglar v. Abbasi* (2017). This *Bivens* lawsuit sought damages from Attorney General Ashcroft, FBI director Mueller, INS commissioner James Ziglar, and other officials. The FBI had arrested the plaintiffs who brought this case— Ahmer Iqbal Abbasi and five other men—in the course of its investigation following the September 11 terrorist attacks. Conceding that they had been in the United States illegally at that time, plaintiffs did not contest that they were subject to detention and processing in accordance with ordinary procedures. What they found objectionable was that they were harshly treated in a maximum security unit while detained under a "hold-until-cleared policy." The key allegation in the complaint was that the government, having no reason to suspect them of terrorist activity, treated them in this way due to a discriminatory policy for which defendants were responsible. Justice Kennedy, assuming the allegations were true, admitted that what they had endured was "tragic." Nevertheless, he held for a 4–2 majority that plaintiffs could not pursue a *Bivens* action for damages.[81]

There was in the *Ziglar* opinion the familiar refrain about judicial deference in matters of national security (courts "traditionally have been reluctant to intrude upon the authority of the Executive in military and national security affairs" without congressional sanction).[82] Concerns over judges interfering with executive decision-making in this area might seem sensible enough, but to ensure that the courts did not do that, Justice Kennedy took traditional deference to a new level. He explained how he thought the discovery process in this case would compromise national security. As the detention policy under review was "high-level executive policy" and involved "large-scale policy decisions," Kennedy believed that Abbasi's lawsuit called into question "the formulation and implementation of a general policy" and the "major elements of the Government's whole response to the September 11 attacks."[83] In his view, permitting this case to go forward would inevitably lead to an inquiry into "the whole course of the discussions and deliberations that led to the policies and governmental acts being challenged." He also pointed to the problem posed by the "burden and demand of litigation," which "might well prevent" policymakers "from devoting the time and effort required for the proper discharge of their duties." Another problem Justice Kennedy identified concerned the "risk of personal damages liability," which he thought would make it "more likely to cause an official to second-guess difficult but necessary decisions concerning national-security policy." Justice Kennedy worried that, if "high officers" faced "personal liability for damages," they "might refrain from taking urgent and lawful action in time of crisis" (pause on that word "lawful").[84] His concern, then, was not limited to the case at hand, but rather extended to what effect the lawsuit could have on "future officials."[85]

It may not go too far to say that *Ziglar* added high-ranking national security officials to those who could claim absolute immunity. In his effort to ensure that civil litigants, no matter how serious their allegations, did not interfere with national security policymaking, the justice placed top-level policymakers presumptively off limits from legal process. It is worth noting the extent to which the decision was based on Justice Kennedy's own conjecture of the implications for policymaking, as indicated by the language of "might" he repeatedly used (that the litigation burden "might well prevent them" from fulfilling their duties or that policymakers "might refrain" from taking action). Justice Breyer, for one, thought Justice Kennedy's concerns about hauling officials into court were overblown as he noted that courts had discretion to limit discovery so as not to interfere with senior officials' business.[86]

Justice Kennedy's likely rejoinder to this criticism would be that his opinion did not foreclose all legal remedies—only one mode of judicial intervention. In lieu of *Bivens* civil damages lawsuits, he pointed to injunctive relief and habeas corpus petitions as more suitable alternatives. He thought habeas provided plaintiffs with "a faster and more direct route to relief." In an ideal world, perhaps, but his suggestion overlooks the actual circumstances surrounding post-9/11 detention. Surely Justice Kennedy had not forgotten that the administration held detainees incommunicado and denied them access to counsel, not to mention the administration's blanket refusal to concede habeas jurisdiction. And if his concerns over judicial interference with national security decision-making are well taken, then having plaintiffs' lawyers seeking injunctive relief in federal district courts around the country would seem to be a prescription for exactly the sort of intrusion Justice Kennedy sought to avoid—and at precisely the most inopportune time. As Jules Lobel pointed out, it is difficult to imagine that the Supreme Court would have upheld an injunction ordering the release of dozens of individuals detained without probable cause in the days immediately following the September 11 attacks.[87]

In another consequential decision, *Ashcroft v. Iqbal* (2009), the Supreme

Court imposed more stringent requirements on the information plaintiffs must provide in their initial filings in a civil action.[88] This made it more difficult for individuals bringing lawsuits against Bush administration officials to get their cases heard in court.

Unlike the old common-law pleading rules—a trap not only for the unwary but also for experienced attorneys—the modern Federal Rules of Civil Procedure liberalized the requirements governing what a plaintiff must do to state a valid cause of action. According to the rule articulated by the Supreme Court in 1957, judges are not supposed to dismiss nonfrivolous complaints unless it is "beyond doubt" that "no set of facts" can support the allegations. The basic idea behind the modern rules of civil procedure is to allow plaintiffs to fill out the details of their claims through pretrial discovery when they can ask questions of defendants and witnesses through written interrogatories and in depositions—especially important when relevant information is in the hands of defendants. *Ashcroft v. Iqbal* might be said to have brought back the old common-law system of pleading for lawsuits having implications for national security policymaking.[89]

The lead plaintiff in *Ashcroft v. Iqbal* was Javaid Iqbal, a Pakistani national, whom the FBI mistakenly identified as a terrorism suspect "of high interest." Iqbal was held for several months in solitary confinement. He alleged that he was kicked in the stomach, punched in the face, denied adequate food (he lost forty pounds during his detention), and repeatedly subjected to strip searches, body cavity searches, and environmental manipulation (air conditioning in winter, heating in summer).[90] According to Iqbal's complaint, this was brought about by an "unconstitutional policy" that discriminated on the basis of race, religion, or national origin. He identified Attorney General Ashcroft as the "principal architect" of this policy, and he said that FBI director Mueller was "instrumental" in implementing it. The complaint stated that "the policy" of holding detainees until the FBI "cleared" them "was approved by Defendants ASHCROFT and MUELLER in discussions in the weeks after September 11, 2001." The concern raised by this complaint was not about discrete cases, but rather that there was a "pattern" of mistreatment.[91]

Once again writing for the Court, Justice Kennedy conceded that Iqbal's "account of his prison ordeal could, if proved, demonstrate unconstitutional misconduct by some governmental actors." Yet the justice considered the allegations against Ashcroft and Mueller "conclusory," and he was unwilling to give Iqbal the opportunity to prove them in court.[92] Justice Kennedy's ruling that the complaint failed to satisfy pleading standards was dressed up in the language of "plausibility." The Federal Rules of Civil Procedure require a "short and plain statement of the claim showing that the pleader is entitled to relief."[93] There was precedent for reading that to mean plausible allegations, but what plausibility meant for Justice Kennedy went beyond what the Supreme Court had previously required.[94] In his attempt to portray the allegations as insufficient, Justice Kennedy was willing to interpose what he considered "more likely explanations"—that, for example, the "arrests Mueller oversaw" were "likely lawful and justified by his non-discriminatory intent." It may be considered ironic that Justice Kennedy rejected plaintiffs' allegations as conclusory and implausible based upon his own speculative assertions. In any event, the concern driving Justice Kennedy in *Iqbal* was the same as in *Ziglar*: to afford "high-level" national security officials the latitude necessary for the "vigorous performance of their duties."[95]

While the Supreme Court in *Ziglar* and *Iqbal* made it virtually impossible for war-on-terrorism plaintiffs to bring *Bivens* lawsuits against Bush administration officials, lower federal courts contributed to plaintiffs' difficulties in holding officials accountable, perhaps most importantly by dismissing lawsuits based on a previously little-known evidentiary privilege called the state secrets privilege. The Supreme Court implicitly gave its blessing to the use of this privilege by denying certiorari in cases that presented the issue.

The story of how the state secrets privilege came to prominence in a Supreme Court case during the Cold War might lead one to consider it susceptible to abuse. *Reynolds v. United States* (1953) was a wrongful death action brought by the survivors of civilian defense contractors killed in a B-29 crash. In pretrial discovery, the plaintiffs asked the Air Force to produce the accident report. The government, noting the "highly secret mission," responded that it could not be disclosed without "seriously hampering national security" and revealing "secret military equipment."[96] The Supreme Court accepted these assertions and recognized what has become known as the state secrets privilege. The Cold War atmosphere contributed to this result, as the Court itself noted. Years later, it was discovered that there was no secret electronic equipment. All that was kept secret was evidence showing the Air Force at fault.[97]

The US government continued to invoke the state secrets privilege in the years following *Reynolds v. United States*. The privilege was used to prevent the disclosure of particular witnesses or documents, as it was in that case. In some instances the government sought to dismiss a lawsuit based on the idea that, in the words of the *Reynolds* Court, the "very subject matter of the action" constitutes a state secret.[98] There is some difference of opinion over whether the government's use of the privilege had changed after the war against terrorism began. The consensus seems to be that Justice Department lawyers in both the Bush administration and the Obama administration had invoked the privilege more frequently and had used it as a vehicle to dismiss civil damages lawsuits more often than their predecessors. Laura K. Donohue further explained that the privilege was used more extensively during the Bush presidency than commentators had realized as they failed to take into account judicial decisions that were unpublished or sealed and lawsuits that plaintiffs voluntarily dismissed.[99] Whatever one makes of the comparison between post-9/11 and previously, the use of this privilege during the war against terrorism had striking results.

Consider the case of Khalid el-Masri, a German citizen, who, mistaken for a terrorism suspect named Khalid al-Masri, was taken by the CIA to Afghanistan, where he was held in a secret prison for five months. His lawsuit sought damages from CIA director Tenet, among others. In hearings before the district judge, government lawyers claimed that there was "no way" the case could "go forward" without harming national security.[100] El-Masri replied that the Bush administration's extraordinary rendition program had been much publicized; so too the circumstances of his own case. He acknowledged that, as the case proceeded, the district judge retained discretion to undertake a more particularized review of information to determine what was privileged. On appeal, the US Court of Appeals for the Fourth Circuit concluded that no trial could be held without divulging classified information and, in particular, that "virtually any conceivable response" to the allegations "would disclose privileged information." The Supreme Court denied certiorari. No doubt it was little consolation to El-Masri to have published an op-ed column titled "I Am Not a State Secret."[101]

If El-Masri's case bore the mark of injustice, Maher Arar's has got to be one of the most horrifying, and it sums up as well as any case the futility of using civil litigation to hold executive officials accountable for their actions in national security, here involving extraordinary rendition and torture. A computer engineer with dual citizenship (Canada and Syria), Arar was erroneously linked to Al Qaeda. On his return to Canada from a vacation in Tunisia in September 2002, US authorities took him into custody at John F. Kennedy International Airport and then sent him to Syria where he was beaten with a shredded electrical cable and kept in a prison cell measuring 6′ × 7′ × 3′ for nearly one year. The Syrian government did not release him until October 2003. After returning to Canada, Arar brought a *Bivens* lawsuit seeking compensatory damages from the US attorney general, the FBI director, the secretary of the Department of Homeland Security, and other US government officials. His complaint explicitly called into question extraordinary rendition as a policy. Rejecting Arar's claim, the US Court of Appeals for the Second Circuit cited the judiciary's "limited institutional competence" to inquire into such foreign policy matters and the likelihood that any judicial inquiry into his rendition to Syria would require the examination of classified information that could not be produced in open court. The Supreme Court declined to review the Second Circuit's ruling.[102] If the circuit court's decision could be criticized for its "utter subservience to the executive branch" (so said dissenting Judge Guido Calabresi), it had the benefit of clearly stating the majority's views on holding administration officials accountable through civil litigation. "Our federal system of checks and balances provides means to consider allegedly unconstitutional executive policy," the circuit panel said, "but a private action for money damages against individual policymakers is not one of them."[103]

V

The Supreme Court certainly did not go along with everything the Bush administration sought to do in the war against terrorism. The justices' high-minded rhetoric on the limits of presidential wartime power was eye-catching. Its position on interrogation, announced shortly after the prisoner abuse at Abu Ghraib was revealed, seemed clear. As Justice O'Connor stated, "indefinite detention for the purpose of interrogation is not authorized."[104] If President Bush's reaction to the enemy combatant cases can be taken as the measure of the Court's pushback, then there was reason to believe that, despite some lapses, the justices had stepped in to check the president where Congress had failed. The truth is more nuanced than that, however.

Hamdi v. Rumsfeld, one of the first of the Supreme Court's major opinions in the war against terrorism, looks at first like a promising reversal of the traditional pattern of judicial deference in wartime. After all, the Court ordered President Bush to do something he had previously refused to do, that is, to provide due process in the status determinations of US citizens detained as enemy combatants. Before getting to the due process question, however, it is worth pausing on the prior step in the Court's analysis. By affirming the president's authority to designate American citizens as enemy combatants, the Court handed President Bush a significant victory. Far from a preordained result, it was only by an interpretive leap of imagination that Justice O'Connor was able to find statutory authorization to justify that conclusion. And once the Court reached the question of exactly what constitutes due process in Hamdi's case, the answer—a "basic process" of minimal procedures—was hardly in keeping with the grand tradition surrounding the concept of due process. While Justice O'Connor alluded to possible limitations on the president's power to detain US citizens, her opinion in *Hamdi*, when coupled with the Court's failure to address issues raised by José Padilla, left no clear line specifying when the president could or could not designate a US citizen as an enemy combatant to be held by the military indefinitely.

Then, too, for all the praise given the Supreme Court for reining in the president in the Guantánamo enemy combatant cases, there were reasons to be skeptical about their impact from the start. Whatever the justices said that may not have been to the president's liking, the fact remains that detainees were held for years without charge. It is hard to view the Supreme Court as an effective check on the president when individuals it finds entitled to file habeas petitions remain in custody for so long without any judge passing on the legality of their confinement. *Boumediene* lost much of its sting as it was implemented in the lower federal courts. To be plain, the DC Circuit undermined the Court's ruling. Judging from the Supreme Court's actions after *Boumediene*, it is reasonable to infer that some justices were motivated chiefly by their concerns over federal court jurisdiction. Once jurisdiction was established with the constitutional decision on habeas corpus in *Boumediene*, the justices' response to the Bush administration and the DC Circuit can be summed up in two words: cert. denied.[105]

The Supreme Court's handling of civil damages lawsuits seeking accountability lends credence to this skeptical view. Some of the justices were prepared to allow civil damages lawsuits against Bush administration officials to proceed. They were unable to stop a majority of their colleagues from all but eliminating any possibility of using lawsuits to that end. In the key case of *Ziglar*, Justice Kennedy admitted that what plaintiffs alleged was nothing less than "tragic," but when he finished disposing of their allegations, the *Bivens* lawsuit seemed to be nothing more than a relic from the past. If accountability was of some concern, the interest in national security policymaking proved to be of greater concern. Justice Kennedy refashioned *Bivens* doctrine so that the policymaking process trumped everything else. And while he shrugged off what he considered to be speculative assertions made by plaintiffs in *Ziglar* and *Iqbal*, lower courts accepted without evidence executive assertions of the state secrets privilege to block entire lawsuits from proceeding.[106]

In the end, one is prompted to ask what the Supreme Court accomplished in these war-on-terrorism cases. The Court left in place practically all aspects of the Bush administration's detention program. When the justices were goaded into action by the Bush Justice Department's extravagant claims of executive unilateralism in the enemy combatant cases, one can reasonably argue that the bottom line was to protect federal judicial power. When called upon to provide a forum for holding national security officials accountable, the Court responded by erecting higher barriers to civil damages lawsuits brought against public officials. And when some justices did take on the president, the ensuing battle exposed how much the Court—outmaneuvered by a relentless executive, overridden by Congress, and undermined in the lower courts—was a captive of its own judicial process.

CHAPTER FIVE

The Torture Debate

When President Bush left office, a solid majority of Americans supported the idea of investigating the "possible use of torture." According to a *USA Today/* Gallup Poll taken in January 2009, 38 percent favored a criminal inquiry; another 24 percent preferred an independent commission.[1] Yet no commission was formed, and nobody was prosecuted. If most Americans displayed an instinctive grasp that something had gone terribly wrong, which a plurality considered criminal in nature, why was no one brought to trial? Why was so little done to hold the president accountable? Or anyone in the Bush administration for that matter?

Any attempt to address the accountability question must take note of the public debate over the mistreatment of detainees. The "torture debate," as it was dubbed, lasted several years. It encompassed a variety of issues, ranging from the morality of torture to its effectiveness.[2] Accountability was an important part of the debate, not only in the back-and-forth of arguments but also in the assumptions and concerns underlying the rhetoric. Without going so far as to claim that the torture debate fully explains why no one was prosecuted, it will be suggested that the debate framed the options for accountability and, in a complex interaction between elite discourse and mass opinion, played a critical role in scotching the idea of criminal prosecutions. The torture debate also sheds light on the possibilities and limitations of relying on public opinion, the press, and the electoral process to hold the president accountable for violating the laws of war.

I

So far as it relates to accountability, the torture debate can be divided into three principal phases. The first (April 2004–January 2005) began when the

Abu Ghraib photographs became public and, as it appears in retrospect, ended with the Senate confirmation of Alberto Gonzales as attorney general. The next segment (November 2008–August 2009)—the most crucial in terms of accountability—coincided with the change of administrations. Discussion reached a high point in April 2009 when the Obama administration released several Bush Justice Department memoranda that provided the public with a detailed inside account of authorized interrogation procedures. This stage of the torture debate might be said to have come to a close four months later when Attorney General Holder launched a preliminary criminal investigation. The Senate Intelligence Committee's so-called torture report provided the impetus for the brief third phase of this debate (December 2014–January 2015).

Of course, there were other points along the way that might be singled out. Truth be told, there was talk of torturing terrorists before the Bush administration set up its interrogation program. Within weeks of the September 11 attacks, a handful of commentators mused in public about using torture. Chief among them was *Newsweek* columnist Jonathan Alter, who wrote a piece titled "Time to Think about Torture." He said he had no desire to bring out the "rubber hoses," but he wondered whether it was time to consider something—"psychological torture" was the phrase he used—to "jumpstart" the investigation of the "greatest crime in American history." Harvard law professor Alan M. Dershowitz renewed his proposal for requiring law enforcement officials to secure a "torture warrant"—something akin to search warrants—in the belief that that would provide the best hope of regulating the interrogation of terrorism suspects.[3]

In the immediate aftermath of Al Qaeda's September 11 operation, such talk was still hypothetical—a prologue to the actual torture debate which did not really begin until the public learned of prisoner abuse at Abu Ghraib. What happened then set the pattern for what followed.

In the history of presidential scandals in America, few moments can compare to the news breaking about Abu Ghraib Prison. When the photographs were first broadcast on CBS's *60 Minutes II*, Alberto Gonzales was probably not the only one at the White House to think "this is going to kill us." Also in the lead covering the story was Seymour Hersh's *New Yorker* article, which was notable for quickly sizing up what happened as torture (its title was "Torture at Abu Ghraib") and for explicitly raising the question of accountability up the chain of command (subtitled "How Far Up Does the Responsibility Go?").[4]

Yet the story of Abu Ghraib at this stage of the torture debate was one of the Bush administration holding the scandal in check. The strategy, as it appears, was threefold. First, express outrage and keep the focus on a handful of reservists working the night shift as prison guards—the "few bad apples" in the administration's account.[5] Accordingly, President Bush railed against the "disgraceful conduct by a few American troops who dishonored our country and disregarded our values," and his press secretary described the guards' actions as "appalling" and "despicable."[6] Second, deflect responsibility at the top by demanding accountability at the bottom. President Bush spoke out in favor of a "full accounting for the cruel and disgraceful abuse of Iraqi detainees." "What we believe in," Rumsfeld told the Senate Armed Services Committee, "is making sure when wrongdoing or scandal occur that they are not covered up, but exposed, investigated, publicly disclosed—and the guilty brought to justice." White House press secretary Scott McClellan said that "the President expects" that "anyone who was involved in these kind of abuses" would be "brought to justice." Gonzales similarly stated that "anyone engaged in conduct that constitutes torture will be held accountable."[7] Third, reaffirm opposition to torture in no uncertain terms, and do so repeatedly; the idea conveyed was that the mistreatment of prisoners could not possibly be official government policy. Here is what President Bush said a few weeks after the *60 Minutes* report on Abu Ghraib: "We do not condone torture. I have never ordered torture. I will never order torture. The values of this country are such that torture is not a part of our soul and our being." Then McClellan: President Bush "does not condone torture" and "he has never authorized the use of torture." And Gonzales: "The President has said we do not condone or commit torture."[8]

By midsummer, President Bush appeared to have weathered the crisis, despite the fact that within weeks of the first disclosures about Abu Ghraib someone had leaked John Yoo's "torture memo," the *Washington Post* reported that the memorandum had advised that torture "may be justified," *Newsweek* had outlined the administration's decision-making process on the Geneva Conventions in an article titled "The Roots of Torture," the *New York Times* reported that Justice Department memoranda "suggested how officials could inoculate themselves from liability by claiming that abused prisoners were in some other nation's custody"; Michael Isikoff reported that the "White House's top lawyer warned more than two years ago that U.S. officials could be prosecuted for 'war crimes'"; the *Army Times* published an editorial describing what happened at Abu Ghraib as "a failure that ran straight to the top" (in reference to the Pentagon's hierarchy); and news reports circulated with references to secret prison sites and "ghost detainees" hidden from the Red Cross. In August 2004, one of the investigative panels Rumsfeld had set up—this one headed by former defense secretary James R. Schlesinger—disclosed that there were "five cases of detainee deaths as a result of abuse by U.S. personnel during interrogations" while an additional twenty-three deaths were "still under investigation." Americans now had to face the fact that detainees in US custody had been tortured to death.[9]

They had the opportunity to do something about it in the upcoming presidential election. Yet strange as it may seem, Abu Ghraib received hardly any attention in the campaign. In June, Senator John Kerry (D-MA) said that he would establish an independent commission to look into the prisoner abuse, but for all intents and purposes that was the last time Abu Ghraib came up in any significant way on the campaign trail. The intense news coverage faded as intervening events cut into the news cycle: the seventieth anniversary of D-Day with a captivating memorial ceremony in France; President Ronald Reagan's staid funeral; the formation of an interim Iraqi government; and the publication of the 9/11 Commission report. With a month to go before Election Day, Mark Danner observed that administration officials had "struggled, so far successfully, to keep Abu Ghraib from becoming what it early on threatened to be: a scandal that could bring down many senior officials in the Department of Defense, and perhaps the administration itself."[10]

While it is difficult to reduce a multifaceted process like a presidential election to a referendum on a particular issue (despite all that was going on with the war against terrorism, the state of the economy remained a major concern for many voters), President Bush had no hesitation in pronouncing his victory "an accountability moment." He meant that he felt vindicated for going to war in Iraq and staying the course there. Yet the sentiment he expressed ironically sums up what the election meant for the Abu Ghraib Prison scandal as well: an accountability moment gone by without accountability.[11]

This first phase of the torture debate might be said to have run its course by early 2005, concluding with the Senate hearings on the nomination of Alberto Gonzales to be attorney general. It is interesting to observe the extent to which Gonzales's opening statement hewed to the administration's three-part strategy: (1) the Abu Ghraib photographs "sickened and outraged me"; (2) as attorney general, he would "aggressively pursue those responsible for such abhorrent actions"; and (3) the president had "made clear" that the

United States "will not tolerate torture under any circumstances."[12] At best Gonzales's testimony was muddled, but that may have inadvertently served the administration's purpose, leaving the public uncertain over who was to blame for Abu Ghraib. His Senate confirmation could be read as providing one answer to that question.

With continuing disclosures and analysis (courtesy of Jane Mayer's reports in the *New Yorker*, Marty Lederman's blog posts, among other things), the controversy over the treatment of detainees never died out, but the next phase of the torture debate in which accountability was of paramount concern revolved around the 2008 election of President Barack Obama and the changeover of administrations.

As Election Day neared, speculation increased that something might be done to hold members of the Bush administration accountable for the mistreatment of detainees. The focus of attention was naturally placed on the Democratic presidential candidate.[13] Barack Obama had fueled expectations with remarks he had made early in the campaign. He said that "if crimes have been committed, they should be investigated." He also intimated that high-ranking Bush administration officials could be prosecuted. "If I found out that there were high officials who knowingly, consciously broke existing laws, engaged in coverups of those crimes with knowledge forefront, then I think the basic principle of our Constitution is nobody above the law." Yet once in office, President Obama showed little interest in finding out whether crimes had been committed. Indeed, anyone parsing his campaign statements would find that he always remained mindful of political constraints. As he said during the campaign, "I would not want my first term consumed by what was perceived on the part of the Republicans as a partisan witch hunt because I think we've got too many problems to solve."[14]

With the Democrats retaining control of Congress and taking over the White House, the question of accountability began to assume more definite shape. Public discussion coalesced around a handful of alternatives.[15] One was to have a congressional investigation with public hearings—something like the famous Senate Watergate committee or Senator Frank Church's committee on intelligence activities (the Church committee had uncovered CIA assassination attempts and the FBI's effort to push Martin Luther King Jr. to suicide, among other things).[16] With increasing partisanship on Capitol Hill, however, these inquiries seemed to belong to a different age, and any chance of replicating their success appeared unlikely. Another possibility was to establish an independent commission to investigate actions taken by the

Bush administration. Such commissions have long been used in the United States; the 9/11 commission being the most well-known example from recent history. But it was the idea of a "truth commission" like South Africa's Truth and Reconciliation Commission that was put forward as the model.[17] Alternatively, some thought the Obama Justice Department should open a criminal investigation—calling to mind the work of the Watergate special prosecutor and the Iran-Contra independent counsel.[18]

Then there was the option of none of the above—a position embraced by many Republicans. They questioned the propriety of Democrats sponsoring any type of investigation of the prior administration after the 2008 election. Republicans warned the incoming administration against prosecutions, which, they said, would "criminalize policy differences"—the implication being that they would surely return the favor in the future.[19] The *Washington Post*'s Fred Hiatt thought that prosecutions by the Obama Justice Department could "trigger a debilitating, unending cycle" of political tit for tat.[20]

During the first few months of the Obama presidency, a consensus among those seeking accountability seemed to emerge in favor of an independent commission. This was touted as a middle-ground approach between doing nothing and having criminal prosecutions. The idea was to form a nonpartisan blue ribbon panel with commissioners like Senator McCain. The emphasis, according to commission supporters, would be on establishing the facts and issuing a public report. Such a commission would perforce have to be empowered to accomplish those ends, principally by having the authority to subpoena witnesses and grant them immunity. Its proponents portrayed the commission as a workable alternative without the heightened stakes that would inevitably accompany prosecutions, though some found the idea appealing precisely because it did not foreclose subsequent criminal proceedings.[21]

Hence the difficulty, given the highly charged political atmosphere. To set up an independent commission, either Congress or the president—or both working together—would have to take the necessary steps. In Congress, Representative John Conyers (D-MI) put forward a bill to empower a nine-member National Commission on Presidential War Powers and Civil Liberties to investigate detainee treatment and other actions taken by the Bush administration, but he never had the votes to pass it.[22] That left the matter in the hands of the chief executive, but the White House made no move to set up a presidential commission on torture.

So matters stood until April, arguably the most critical point in the torture debate relating to accountability. Complying with a district court order, the administration released four of the Bush Justice Department's classified legal opinions. These were the key OLC memoranda that had approved the enhanced interrogation techniques. Their descriptions of the interrogation methods left little to the imagination. Included, for example, was a detailed account of waterboarding and its associated medical risks (vomiting, aspiration, pneumonia, spasms of the larynx, emergency tracheotomy)—a description that gave credence to the view that "waterboarding was torture," as President Obama later put it.[23]

In a brief statement announcing the release of the documents, President Obama said that the Justice Department would not bring to trial CIA agents who relied in good faith on OLC's legal advice. True to form, he had made a pragmatic calculation—that the costs of criminal prosecutions outweighed the benefits. Or so he suggested when he said that "at a time of great challenges and disturbing disunity, nothing will be gained by spending our time and energy laying blame for the past." He considered the moment "a time for reflection, not retribution."[24]

One major factor in his analysis was an executive order he had issued shortly after taking office that had ended the Bush administration's interrogation program—irrevocably, he seemed to believe, as he characterized the set of interrogation methods authorized by his predecessor as "a thing of the past." No less important, in the afterglow of his historic election, President Obama and his advisors saw considerable risk in forging ahead with criminal prosecutions. Any chance he would have to soften ideological divisions would be lost, and policies unrelated to national security—healthcare reform most of all—would fall victim to the heightened partisan warfare that, they believed, was sure to follow.[25]

On the face of it, President Obama's announcement left a small opening for prosecution. If "those who carried out their duties relying in good faith upon legal advice from the Department of Justice" would not be prosecuted, then it would seem to follow that interrogators who willfully exceeded OLC's guidelines were still in legal jeopardy. So too, it might be thought, were Bush administration officials who put the interrogation policy in place and the lawyers who advised them. In the final analysis, though, President Obama's unequivocal statement that "*nothing* will be gained" by "laying blame for the past" probably should have been taken to reflect his innermost preference that, under the circumstances, criminal prosecutions should be avoided at all costs.[26] One might surmise that President Obama, who had excelled as a Harvard law student, had weighed the arguments in favor of criminal prosecution and had found them wanting, but his decision appears to have been driven most of all by a political calculus. In any event, the president's statement that "we should be looking forward and not backwards" became something of a White House mantra.[27]

As much as President Obama might have hoped to knife through the political hazards, his statement did little to tamp down the ensuing firestorm.[28] The president drew harsh criticism simply for releasing the legal memoranda. Mark Thiessen called that decision "one of the most dangerous and irresponsible acts" ever made by a wartime president (on the view that it provided the enemy with valuable information on US intelligence-gathering methods). Bush administration officials also argued that the interrogation techniques had been effective. In an op-ed in the *Wall Street Journal*, General Michael Hayden (one of President Bush's CIA directors) and Michael Mukasey (who served as attorney general under President Bush) claimed that enhanced interrogation had disrupted several "follow-on" terrorist plots. Vice President Dick Cheney made that point too, and he demanded that President Obama release other documents that Cheney said showed how effective the interrogation tactics had been.[29]

In the midst of the controversy, the White House gave mixed signals. After Rahm Emanuel, President Obama's chief of staff, told ABC's *This Week* that the president believed that "those who devised policy" should not be prosecuted, President Obama said that Attorney General Holder would decide whether to prosecute "those who formulated those legal decisions" and that he would not "prejudge" the matter. This led to headlines such as "Bush Aides May Be Prosecuted over Torture."[30] As for establishing an independent commission, President Obama at one point offered qualified support for having Congress set up a bipartisan commission ("if and when there needs to be a fuller accounting" though "I'm not suggesting that that should be done"). He was described as turning heads by "abruptly warming to the idea of a war-on-terror 'truth commission,'" but the president was said to have "rebuffed calls for a commission" in a meeting with congressional leaders two days later.[31]

While the White House displayed ambivalence, Republicans were united in opposition to prosecutions, essentially arguing that it would be unseemly for Democrats, after taking control of the White House, to sponsor criminal investigations of the prior administration. Even Senator McCain pronounced any move to prosecute a "witch hunt." The Republican position had the benefit of coinciding with what appeared to be the mainstream view taking hold among opinion makers. In a column titled "Stop Scapegoating," David

Broder conceded that the reasons given for prosecution—accountability and deterrence—sounded plausible, but he thought they merely cloaked "an unworthy desire for vengeance."[32] And while President Obama had his critics arguing against prosecutions, his announcement also frustrated those in favor of a criminal investigation. Their concern centered on the president's good-faith exception, something Jane Mayer called a "legal 'invisibility cloak'" for CIA officers. Within days of President Obama's announcement, petitions with a quarter-million signatures asked Attorney General Holder to appoint a special prosecutor.[33]

It was also at this time that some prominent commentators made explicit what appeared to be operating as an implicit assumption underlying the opposition to prosecutions. *New York Times* columnist Thomas Friedman laid out the position clearly. "We're not just talking about 'enhanced interrogations,'" he wrote, but "sheer brutality" and "homicides." Yet he came out against prosecuting "the lawyers and interrogators who implemented the policy" because "justice taken to its logical end here would likely require bringing George W. Bush, Donald Rumsfeld and other senior officials to trial, which would rip our country apart."[34] David Broder played out the scenario.

> Suppose . . . Holder or someone else starts hauling Bush administration lawyers and operatives into hearings and courtrooms.
>
> Suppose the investigators decide that the country does not want to see the former president and vice president in the dock. Then underlings pay the price while big shots go free. But at some point, if he is at all a man of honor, George W. Bush would feel bound to say: That was my policy. I was the president. If you want to indict anyone for it, indict me.
>
> Is that where we want to go? I don't think so.

Despite the general run of commentary, Gallup reported at the end of April that a "slim majority" of Americans still favored an investigation in some form (25% supported a bipartisan commission, 22% a Justice Department investigation, and 8% a congressional inquiry).[35]

So matters stood until late August 2009, when Attorney General Holder tapped career prosecutor John H. Durham to look into whether CIA interrogations that went beyond "the scope of the legal guidance" provided by OLC violated federal law. (President Bush's attorney general had previously selected Durham to investigate the CIA's destruction of ninety-two videotapes that had recorded interrogation sessions that included waterboarding.)

Although Holder cautioned that this was only a "preliminary review" that might not lead to charges, his announcement caused quite a stir.[36] There was on the one side criticism of Holder's "nakedly political, banana republic-style criminalizing of policy differences." On the other side, there were predictions of a Justice Department "whitewash." Glenn Greenwald thought Holder was moving toward "a repeat of the Abu Ghraib experience" in which a few low-ranking soldiers took the fall. *Slate*'s Dahlia Lithwick compared the decision to exclude CIA operatives who acted in good faith to the notorious Nuremberg "just following orders" defense.[37]

As it turned out, Attorney General Holder's announcement of a preliminary review marked a critical point in the torture debate. The announcement had the effect of undercutting the momentum that had been building for an independent commission. As the Durham investigation wore on, all the while conducted in secret, public attention predictably waned. In 2011, Holder announced the end of the investigation except for two cases. Each involved the death of a detainee. Another year passed before the attorney general informed the public that the Justice Department had determined not to pursue criminal charges in those cases because the "admissible evidence would not be sufficient" to convict anyone.[38]

The closure of the criminal investigation did not go unnoticed, even though Attorney General Holder made the announcement on the Thursday before Labor Day in a presidential election year, all but inviting the charge that he had timed it to avoid public scrutiny. But the central problem plaguing this investigation was not that it ended without anything to show for it so much as that it was compromised from the start. The decision to overlook any actions that were undertaken pursuant to OLC guidelines was critical. By narrowing the inquiry to unauthorized interrogations that did not conform to Bush Justice Department requirements, Holder excluded from the investigation what was really at the heart of the problem, that is, the Bush administration's entire interrogation policy. It was, by way of explanation, not the failure to follow guidelines for waterboarding that was wrong, but rather that there were any guidelines for waterboarding at all. Holder may well have believed that waterboarding constituted torture (as he said),[39] but in his official capacity as US attorney general he shielded from prosecution interrogators who waterboarded detainees in accordance with Bush Justice Department's guidelines as well as officials who had approved its use.

The third phase of America's torture debate—seemingly the last—began in December 2014, over ten years after the first disclosures about Abu Ghraib.

The catalyst this time was the Senate Intelligence Committee's publication of an executive summary of its classified report on the CIA's interrogation program. The basic story remained the same, but the committee rounded out information previously available with gruesome new details—gruesome enough to prompt John Yoo to concede that "if these things happened as they are described in the report," then some interrogators were "at risk legally" because the Bush Justice Department had not authorized the tactics they employed.[40]

Among the more interesting revelations, the Senate report recounted the observations and reservations of CIA officials at interrogation sites. The treatment of Abu Zubaydah elicited strong reactions among agency officers on the scene. According to CIA records, members of the interrogation team were "profoundly affected"—"some to the point of tears and choking up." Their "collective opinion" was that "we should not go much further."[41] In response to a cable from the field that Zubaydah's interrogation was approaching "the legal limit," José A. Rodriguez Jr., then serving as head of the agency's Counterterrorism Center, replied: "strongly urge that any speculative language as to the legality of given activities or, more precisely, judgment calls as to their legality vis-à-vis operational guidelines for this activity agreed upon and vetted at the most senior levels of the agency, be refrained from in written traffic."[42]

While reaction to the Senate report divided along partisan lines (Republicans questioning the political motives of Democratic lawmakers and the procedures they used to compile the report),[43] there was plenty of outrage over the prisoner abuse described. Yet after a decade of airing the torture question, the tone and orientation of the public debate had changed. Gone was the shock that had greeted the first disclosures about Abu Ghraib, or so it seemed. In the days immediately following the Senate torture report's release, 49 percent of those polled had come to the conclusion that the CIA had tortured detainees. Over half of all Americans (58% according to a *Washington Post*–ABC News Poll, 51% according to Pew Research) believed the CIA's interrogation methods were justified.[44] Now the issue that dominated public discussion was whether the Bush administration's coercive interrogation tactics were effective or, put another way, whether torture works.[45]

This emphasis on effectiveness was partly attributable to the Senate Intelligence Committee. This was one of the report's main points. The executive summary opened with the statement that the CIA interrogation program "was not an effective means of acquiring intelligence or gaining cooperation" from prisoners. "At no time," the report stated, "did the CIA's coercive interrogation techniques lead to the collection of imminent threat intelligence." What the CIA often got in return for its use of enhanced interrogation was "fabricated information," according to the Senate report. Of particular note for the committee's majority were the contemporaneous views of CIA officers in the field who "regularly called into question" the effectiveness of enhanced interrogation for failing to "elicit detainee cooperation or produce accurate intelligence."[46]

The Intelligence Committee's in-depth review of effectiveness was understandable. Claims about the success of the interrogation program had been part of the public conversation for some time, coming not only from the CIA but from top Bush administration officials as well. President Bush had asserted in 2006 that enhanced interrogation had yielded "information about terrorist plans we could not get anywhere else" that had "saved innocent lives by helping us stop new attacks—here in the United States and across the world." The most attention-grabbing claim on effectiveness concerned Osama bin Laden. Some had said that information gleaned from enhanced interrogations was crucial in the effort to find him, a point dramatized in the Hollywood version *Zero Dark Thirty*. Charged with oversight of the CIA, senators on the intelligence panel could reasonably believe that they were in a unique position to rebut these assertions. Doubtless it would have been difficult for committee members to leave them unchallenged by withholding information that contradicted such claims.[47]

Yet as this third phase of the torture debate played out, it seemed as if the whole controversy had been reduced to this single question of effectiveness. Committee members had certainly not lost sight of the moral and legal issues surrounding the use of torture, but what seemed to matter most was whether the Bush administration's interrogation program was effective. And whether the committee report could convince Americans that torture was ineffective was open the question. When the report was released, a majority in the country believed that the CIA's harsh tactics yielded reliable information.[48] Moreover, it was clear that the committee's findings would not go uncontested. Former top CIA officials responded to the report by placing a forceful op-ed in the *Wall Street Journal* bearing the title "CIA Interrogations Saved Lives," a point reiterated on a website called ciasavedlives.com. Republican senators on the Intelligence Committee rebutted the report's conclusion on effectiveness with specific counterexamples. They claimed that the interrogation of Abu Zubaydah had enabled the United States to foil terrorist plans to attack hotels frequented by foreigners in Pakistan. They also explained how enhanced interrogation was essential in locating Osama bin Laden. Meanwhile, John Brennan, President Obama's CIA director, issued a statement that the Bush administration's interrogation program yielded "intelligence that helped thwart attack plans, capture terrorists, and save lives."[49]

This left the general public in the difficult position of sorting through competing versions while operating from an information deficit, since the full Senate report was still classified and 7 percent of the executive summary was redacted. Some key events—especially what led to the discovery of bin Laden's courier, which in turn pointed the way to bin Laden's whereabouts— required more than a cursory reading to decipher. In addition, the explanations offered by former CIA officials as to why the committee was mistaken on the effectiveness question sounded reasonable. One of their most important contentions was that the Democratic senators exhibited little understanding of the complexity of developing intelligence about a terrorist network like Al Qaeda. John McLaughlin, who had served as the CIA's acting director during the Bush administration, suggested that the committee underestimated the importance of "accumulating detail, corroboration and levels of confidence" in intelligence analysis. In anticipation of the report's publication, José Rodriguez had criticized the committee for making post hoc judgments on the intelligence process after the "jigsaw puzzle" had been pieced together.[50]

While there was a flurry of interest in the Senate report in the nation's capital, the public's reaction around the country was comparatively muted. When the report was released, only 23 percent followed the story "very closely" (news about police violence and the economy got more attention). Nor was there any clamor for accountability resembling the extensive public discussion that took place five years earlier. True, the Torture Report reinvigorated calls for a criminal investigation—from Amnesty International, Human Rights Watch, the American Civil Liberties Union, the *New York Times* editorial board, among others—but their scattered appeals only underscored the futility of persuading anyone in power to reopen a criminal inquiry. A few months before the Senate report was released, President Obama had casually stated that "we tortured some folks." After the Intelligence Committee publicized its findings, he maintained his usual posture on accountability. He hoped that the report would not lead Americans to "refight old arguments," but rather "help us leave these techniques where they belong: in the past."[51]

The United States had reached the point where the publication of a redacted executive summary roundly criticized by one of the two major political parties constituted as much accountability as Americans could expect from their own government. Although history may record this as the moment when the last chance for prosecution slipped away, some commentators could not resist the temptation to offer self-congratulatory remarks. The country, said Thomas Friedman, deserved praise for this "act of self-examination"—yet another example of why the United States served as "a model that others want to emulate." CNN's Fareed Zakaria explained "why releasing the CIA torture report will make America stronger" while Friedman's piece was titled, without the least hint of irony, "We're Always Still Americans." In the meantime, columnist E. J. Dionne observed that, if the torture debate had made anything clear, it was that those involved in the interrogation program "would do it all over again."[52]

II

For a more in-depth understanding of how the torture debate undercut the idea of criminal accountability, it will be helpful to evaluate the major arguments offered in opposition to prosecution. These can be divided into three categories. One revolved around the political consequences of one administration prosecuting former government officials from the opposing party. Another focused on the legal obstacles prosecutors would face in bringing these cases. The third worked neatly off the other two, as it was suggested that an investigative commission provided a feasible option without the political and legal difficulties associated with criminal prosecutions.

The political argument against prosecutions was often framed around the catchphrase "criminalizing policy differences." The idea behind this was simple. If Democrats, upon taking control of the White House, used their newfound power to prosecute officials who had served in the prior administration (or CIA officers who carried out the former president's policy), not only would they be using the Justice Department for political purposes—a serious abuse of power in itself—they would also be transgressing a fundamental norm of democratic governance. To make that point, the analogy was made to Latin American authoritarian regimes, sometimes with disparaging references to "banana republics." In fact, that analogy ignored one of the great success stories of contemporary world politics: the transition from authoritarian regimes to democracies throughout Latin America that coincided with significant human rights prosecutions.[53] This comparison between Democrats seeking prosecutions and military juntas gained traction nonetheless. President Bush's advisor Karl Rove described the situation in this way. If the Obama Justice Department prosecuted Bush administration officials based on "policy differences," he said, that would be "the moral equivalent of a Latin American country run by colonels in mirrored sunglasses."[54]

Whether those making the "criminalizing policy differences" argument sincerely believed it or acted strategically to fend off prosecutions, the message was clear. Impugning the motives of anyone who favored prosecutions, the charge shifted the focus of attention from the conduct in question (the mistreatment of detainees) to the supposed political purposes of those calling for prosecution. The implication was that Bush administration officials could be prosecuted only if Democrats manipulated the criminal process, something like fitting a round peg (public policy) into a square hole (criminal law). The argument intimated that there was not even a genuine issue of criminality, as if the claims about torture and prisoner abuse were fabricated.

There were other versions of the political argument. What the more sophisticated had in common was a cost-benefit analysis: conceding that there were legitimate questions of criminality while highlighting the problems that, it was assumed, would inevitably accompany criminal proceedings. The question, then, was not simply whether the interrogation program was properly denominated as a policy choice or criminal activity, but rather what effect prosecutions would have on policymaking and the political landscape.

One variant of this concern focused on the national security policymaking process. Richard N. Haass was among the most prominent figures to articulate this view. Writing in the *Wall Street Journal*, he suggested that prosecutions could have a "chilling effect" on internal debates in subsequent administrations as government officials, anxious about being hauled into court, would avoid offering policy recommendations that might raise legal problems. Conceivably applicable to any area of public policy, the argument drew strength from its implications for national security—a field in which crises abound and officials often face a Hobson's choice, sometimes with lives at stake.[55]

Despite raising important points, this argument is still subject to criticism. Granted, it would be desirable to ensure creative brainstorming of *legal* policies, but does the concern over constructive deliberations on national security policy override all legal limits? If not, where is the line to be drawn? Torture would seem to present a clear case of what ought to be out of bounds even in internal national security discussions.

The other form of the political argument shifted the grounds of debate from criminal accountability to questions over the vitality of American democracy. Leading scholars (including Alan Dershowitz, Eric Posner, and Michael Walzer) and journalists (David Broder and Fred Hiatt) advanced this argument in some form. They did not deny that serious crimes had been committed. Posner said that "higher government officials who authorized torture (up to President Bush), violated the law," and Walzer conceded that "Bush and Cheney authorized the torture of suspected terrorists." What they argued, essentially, was that the rationale for legal accountability was overridden by concerns over the democratic process.[56]

This argument rested on a set of assumptions about how a functioning democracy operates: that the democratic system depends upon a shared willingness to accept the outcome of elections no matter who wins; that losing candidates and their supporters acquiesce in the result of an election partly because of the opportunity to prevail in the next one; that, in short, everyone must have an interest in the electoral process as an ongoing venture. Bringing prosecutions into the mix supposedly upsets this delicate balance by raising the stakes of elections so much that politicians would have, to use Walzer's words, "a very strong incentive" to do whatever it takes to win, with all that entails.[57]

This view was also based on the idea that no president can stay in office for long without ordering some action that can be portrayed as illegal. What seems to be a legitimate policy choice for some presidents can be characterized as a criminal act by political opponents. According to Walzer, presidents do this sort of thing—not the torture necessarily—but what he called "political crimes." He defined these as acts undertaken, however mistakenly, to serve the public interest. Lincoln's suspension of habeas corpus during the Civil War and Franklin Roosevelt's internment of Japanese Americans during World War II belonged in this category, in Walzer's view. He believed that presidents could be prosecuted for what he called "personal crimes" committed for individual gain (accepting bribes, for example) without putting the entire democratic system at risk. But Walzer thought that prosecuting presidents for "political crimes" was another matter. So begins a new phase in attack politics, he suggested, with future presidents unsure whether their successors will put them on trial over policy differences. "It would be very dangerous," Walzer wrote, "to start down this path."[58] Judging from the tenor of the discussion in the press—with talk of "criminal vendettas" and the like—that day was already here.[59] If these warnings about the democratic process overstated the risks at the end of the Bush presidency, the 2020 presidential election and the January 6 insurrection bears out this concern.

Yet this argument, too, is not without its difficulties. In highlighting an undoubtedly significant aspect of the American system of government (the succession of elected leaders), the argument diminishes another (the rule of law). Another problem has to do with the distinction between "political crimes" and "personal crimes" (a distinction that Posner and Dershowitz made as well as Walzer). If prosecuting presidents for political crimes presents such a grave risk to American democracy, one wonders why prosecuting presidents for personal crimes would not have the same consequences. For the issue is not so much how elite analysts would classify the president's criminal acts, but rather how the president's supporters would react. It seems reasonable to surmise that they would suspect the motives of prosecutors in cases concerning personal crimes just as much as they would in those involving political crimes. Besides, the idea of presidents committing political crimes with impunity is troubling in itself, in effect creating a public interest exception that presidents can assert as a defense in criminal cases. It would be the rare politician who would be unable to cloak his or her actions in the guise of serving the public interest. In addition, the societal harm stemming from so-called political crimes might be far worse than from personal crimes. Again, one might have thought torture an easy call.

As for those advancing the legal argument against prosecutions, it was widely agreed that the Bush Justice Department's analysis relating to detention and interrogation was flawed. That was not in question. The issue was whether cases brought to trial would have a reasonable chance of success, even with all the legal problems surrounding the interrogation program. The answer furnished by several prominent experts was that it would be practically impossible to convict those involved.

This position, which was understood to reflect the consensus among the experts,[60] was given weight not only because those espousing that view were respected authorities in the law but also because many of them had previously opposed the interrogation program. In a well-timed op-ed published in the *New York Times* days before President Obama's inauguration, Jack Balkin confidently predicted that federal prosecutors would face "enormous" legal obstacles. John L. Helgerson had compiled the devastating report on detainee abuse while serving as the CIA's inspector general (much to the dismay of many in the agency). He thought that it would be "very difficult to mount a successful prosecution in any of these cases." Retired Air Force judge advocate general Scott Silliman shared that sentiment: prosecutions would be "exceedingly difficult" from a "legal point of view." Robert Turner also questioned going down that path even though his *Washington Post* op-ed branded President Bush's 2007 executive order interpreting Common Article 3 a war crime. Marty Lederman, an influential critic of the interrogation regime whose blog posts regularly exposed deficiencies in the Bush Justice Department's analysis, offered bloggers on the left "a dissenting view on prosecuting the waterboarders." He said that it was "virtually inconceivable that *any* Department of Justice, of any party's Administration, would ever prosecute an intelligence official or contractor who had relied on OLC advice."[61]

Lawyers being lawyers, they had their reasons for reaching these conclusions. There was the usual assortment of evidentiary problems. With the passage of time, it would be increasingly difficult to gather physical evidence and medical records. Prosecutors could find it hard to sustain their burden of proof if that required testimony from President Bush's political appointees. The most knowledgeable witnesses might be the most reluctant to testify, whether out of loyalty to the Bush administration or fellow interrogators. Defendants, it was said, would "lawyer up"; some might plead the Fifth Amendment if pressed. It was also considered likely that, following the pattern of political scandals in the nation's capital, former administration officials would contest the release of documents. As for questions of law, experts warned that prosecutors would have a hard time establishing the requisite level of criminal intent. In legal circles, it was considered difficult to satisfy the "specific intent" element of the federal statute on torture. But the main problem confronting prosecutors was thought to be the advice offered by the Office of Legal Counsel, inscribed into law as a legal defense by the Detainee Treatment Act which the Military Commissions Act made retroactive to September 11, 2001. With OLC memos in hand, Bush administration officials had a "nearly airtight defense of good-faith reliance on advice of counsel," according to legal commentator Stuart Taylor.[62]

It is true that criminal proceedings would have raised complicated legal questions—too complicated to resolve in the terse commentary of newspaper op-ed pages. Yet federal prosecutors have previously scored successes in complex criminal cases. If the Watergate scandal can be taken as roughly analogous, the fact that defendants "lawyered up" did not prevent prosecutors from obtaining convictions of two attorneys general, an FBI director, and one White House counsel, among others.

On the central question concerning advice of counsel, a close examination of the legal requisites for putting on such a defense suggests that it may not be so airtight after all. There is, to begin with, more involved than for defendants to simply assert that their lawyers told them that whatever they were contemplating would not violate the law. Generally speaking, all individuals are responsible to determine whether their own conduct is lawful independently of their lawyers' advice. Defendants raising this defense must show that they fall within an exception to the ordinary rule—a rule so widely known it hardly needs to be repeated: ignorance of the law is no excuse. Reliance on advice of counsel must be reasonable and in good faith. Courts look askance on those invoking this defense when they were "put on notice to make further inquiries."[63]

As applied to the interrogation program, the least that can be said is that President Bush and his closest associates would have been in a more difficult position than CIA interrogators to interpose the advice of counsel defense in court. For one thing, the Detainee Treatment Act did not grant immunity to President Bush and administration officials or anyone else who was not engaged in "specific operational practices" involving detention and interrogation. For another thing, given the circumstances described in chapter 2 surrounding the manipulation of OLC opinions, it is difficult to see how the president and his inner circle could make a good faith claim. Besides, anyone relying on the defense of advice of counsel waives attorney-client privilege—something that in all likelihood President Bush would have been reluctant to do.[64]

As for CIA interrogators, it is easy to imagine how their lawyers would have framed the issue at trial. How, they could ask, can the Justice Department prosecute CIA agents now for using interrogation methods which DOJ lawyers had previously told them were legal. Yet on close scrutiny, it is not clear that this defense would prevail as a matter of law. Exceptions to the general rule (ignorance of the law is no excuse) are limited, and it is difficult to see how any of them applied. One goes by the name of "entrapment by estoppel." This typically involves a government official providing advice to a private citizen about constitutional rights. In one of the earliest cases, witnesses appearing before a legislative committee refused to answer questions based upon representations the committee chair made to them that they could assert their Fifth Amendment rights. They were convicted of contempt nonetheless. Finding this "the most indefensible sort of entrapment," the Supreme Court overturned their convictions.[65] Another exception is known as the "public authority" defense. Those asserting this defense do not claim that they thought their conduct was legal. To the contrary, defendants admit that they knew their conduct was illegal—an important concession in itself which, it seems clear, Bush administration officials were not prepared to make. Moreover, the claim would have to be made that OLC had the legal power to authorize unlawful conduct in the public interest (or that defendants misapprehended the scope of OLC's power), but the Office of Legal Counsel cannot authorize illegal acts, and courts have been reluctant to broaden this exception. One last possibility is the "innocent intent" defense. Unlike the other two, this is what is known as a failure of proof defense that goes to negative a required element in the prosecution's case, in this instance concerning the defendant's mental state. The classic case for invoking this defense is a drug transaction in which government officials have an informer buy illicit drugs. The problem with applying this defense is that the government officials (in this case the Office of Legal Counsel) must again have "actual authority" to authorize illegal acts—something OLC lacks.[66]

There was room for a more sophisticated analysis of both sides of this debate over criminal accountability. It must be admitted that there is no guarantee of conviction or even getting to trial, as the Justice Department investigation of selected interrogations demonstrates. The trial process is imperfect, and it seems likely that the imperfections of an ordinary trial would be magnified given the political overtones surrounding trials of high-ranking officials. On the other hand, with the popular depiction of trials in mind, it may be said with some confidence that few institutions in public affairs have the capacity to give meaning to events like trials can. Lest it be forgotten, the criminal trial is a time-honored process for assigning blame for serious violations of public law. Many of the questions about the Bush administration's interrogation program that begged attention—what exactly happened, what was right and what was wrong, and who was responsible—fall within the traditional province of criminal justice. The criminal law provides a framework to adjudicate inherently complicated questions concerning intent, justification, and excuse. Criminal trials—war crimes trials in particular—can have what might be called a cultural resonance, with defining moments crystallizing what happened and clarifying lines of responsibility.

As the political and legal arguments against prosecutions circulated, proposals to assemble an investigative commission gained favor. The idea was intuitively appealing as a workable middle-ground approach. Its advocates included prominent lawmakers, legal academics, journalists, religious leaders, former national security officials, retired military officers, and human rights activists. There is no question that they were clearly disturbed by the reports of torture. Some thought that, given the political realities, a commission would have to suffice without criminal prosecutions. Others saw the two accountability mechanisms working in tandem.[67]

Although the "prosecution versus commission" arguments in the United States resonated with the international debate over transitional justice,[68] it would not be accurate to say that commission supporters forgot America's history of investigative commissions. They pointed to the 9/11 inquiry (the National Commission on Terrorist Attacks upon the United States) and historically important panels like the Kerner Commission (the National Advisory Commission on Civil Disorders), which examined race relations and civil unrest in the 1960s.[69] Some cited the work of the Church committee on intelligence activities, even though this was a Senate select committee rather than an independent commission.[70] No matter, the point was that new facts could be brought to light, secret activities exposed, broad patterns put in perspective, and meaningful reforms set in motion—all by bringing together a group of dedicated public servants for that purpose.

Yet judging from pro-commission rhetoric, no precedent served the argument so well as developments overseas.[71] By the time this debate played out in the United States, over two dozen countries had set up special commissions to investigate human rights abuses committed by authoritarian regimes or during civil wars. One of the earliest was Argentina's National Commission on the Disappeared, which documented the cases of nearly 9,000 persons "disappeared"—killed—by the military. Other countries followed suit, including Chile, Uganda, Guatemala, and, most famously, South Africa with its Truth and Reconciliation Commission.[72] Not all of these inquiries were officially designated truth commissions, but that is how they came to be known collectively. No doubt the implicit promise held out by that umbrella term underlay its appeal: a truth commission would, by definition, get to the truth. "We need to get to the bottom of what happened—and why," Senator Leahy said. Truth was the "overarching goal," he added, and if investigative commissions from all parts of the globe could pierce the veil of authoritarian rule and the chaos of civil war to uncover the truth, then surely Americans could do no less. That, at least, was the implication of the argument.[73]

More was involved than simply finding facts. An American torture commission could do many things, its supporters claimed. It could overcome political differences, deter future administrations from committing similar abuses, and restore the nation's standing as a champion of human rights.[74]

Or, to restate the argument in more modest terms, a commission was seen as the best hope to achieve those objectives. This argument was based on an explicit comparison with criminal prosecutions. While commission supporters seemed confident that a torture commission could develop a clear historical record for the public, they worried that prosecutors working through secret grand jury proceedings might conduct extensive investigations without publicizing the results (a reasonable concern in light of the outcome of the Durham investigation). Punishing criminal conduct and getting the truth were presented as mutually exclusive alternatives. "Do we punish wrongdoing or discover the truth?," asked Jack Balkin. His answer—"we should opt for the truth"—left the impression that criminal proceedings were ill suited for that purpose. "Anyone who wants the full truth to come out," wrote David Corn, "cannot count on a special prosecutor."[75]

Although truth commissions have performed a valuable service around the world, not least of all by providing an official forum where victims can share what happened to them on their terms, the argument for an American version was not as clear-cut as its supporters suggested. Start with the logic behind the analogy to commissions abroad. The usual reason for using truth commissions elsewhere has been to facilitate the transition to a peaceful democratic society in countries emerging from civil wars or authoritarian rule. To accomplish that objective, it has seemed necessary at times to minimize or eliminate prosecutions in order to induce those who committed human rights abuses to go along with the new government. All this is sometimes couched in the language of reconciliation, as the official title of South Africa's commission suggests. While the United States obviously did not undergo a comparable transition, commission supporters seized on that language. Senator Leahy suggested that an American truth commission on torture could foster a "reconciliation process" in the United States just as South Africa's Truth and Reconciliation Commission did. Nicholas Kristof spoke of a torture commission engaging Americans in "a process of soul searching and national cleansing."[76]

The analogy still does not work. Transitional societies that have used truth commissions have typically had an extraordinary level of conflict and repression. An important purpose served by these commissions was to reconcile victims with their oppressors—distasteful as that was to many victims—because that was considered a necessary step to build a democratic government. Archbishop Desmond Tutu reported that it was "as certain as anything" that the South African apartheid government's police and military would have made peaceful change impossible had they been subject to criminal liability without any possibility of amnesty.[77] In other words, reconciliation was considered appropriate because it served this larger goal. References to reconciliation in the United States over torture were decidedly different, as the concern was over bridging differences between political opponents within an established democracy.

Then, too, the arguments advanced in support of a truth commission in place of criminal proceedings overlooked the subtleties of transitional justice in determining the mix and sequencing of accountability mechanisms.[78] In South Africa, which had emerged as the primary model for an American torture commission, prosecutions remained an important part of the equation. As the Truth and Reconciliation Commission stated, "in order to avoid any suggestion of impunity," it had "always been understood" that a "bold prosecution policy" would be pursued against persons who did not apply for amnesty.[79] And in countries where truth commissions were used in place of criminal proceedings, there were clear reasons for doing so: a domestic legal system "in shambles"; corrupt or easily intimidated judges; prosecutors lacking expertise.[80]

Besides this attenuated comparison with truth commissions abroad, the argument for an American commission was based on the assumption that it could stand apart from domestic politics. It was thought that the charge of playing politics was bound to cloud prosecutions launched by the Obama Justice Department just as any congressional investigation would become hopelessly mired in partisan bickering. By contrast, members of an independent commission could devote themselves fully to their "straightforward" mission of uncovering the truth without politics intruding. So long as those named to the commission were "universally recognized as fair-minded," the investigation would be nonpartisan, perceived as such, and the public would be likely to embrace the commission's findings.[81]

The record of earlier commissions in the United States presents a more cautionary tale. If history is any guide, the life of a commission is interwoven with politics at every stage of its existence: born of a political context, created by political actors for political purposes, in some cases to deflect accountability, and often subject to political pressures during the course of an investigation that everyone understands has political consequences.[82] As commissioners are selected by the president acting alone or in conjunction with Congress, the appointments process offers little hope of sidestepping politics. Elected officials can use their powers of appointment to shape the commission's investigation. According to Tom Kean and Lee Hamilton, chair and vice chair of the 9/11 commission, the appointments process they witnessed could not have been "more partisan."[83] The challenge to setting up a torture commission that could operate beyond politics was unintentionally foreshadowed by *New York Times* columnist Nicholas Kristof. After recommending the appointment of nonpartisan national security experts, he felt compelled to propose putting Republicans on the commission's "three most prominent" positions in order to inoculate its work against criticism from the right.[84] Yet there was no sign that Republicans would have embraced a torture commission even then, and if the commission had blamed President Bush for authorizing torture, it is hard to imagine his supporters acceding to that conclusion no matter who was on the commission.

What is left of the pro-commission argument is an assertion, seemingly taken as an article of faith by its advocates, that a truth commission would, by definition, get to the truth. Given the way commissions are usually set up in the United States, there are reasons to doubt their institutional capacity to do that, notwithstanding some notable successes. Commissions are often quickly thrown together to address the crisis of the moment. Unlike elected officials, commissioners do not have a natural power base of support to contend with the inevitable pushback from those under investigation. Ad hoc creations, commissions do not have standard operating procedures. That can affect everything a commission does, from hiring staff to conducting the investigation. Political opponents have ample opportunity to frustrate a commission's investigation. A commission depends on Congress and the president for its budget. Besides appointing commissioners sympathetic to their own views, elected officials can limit the scope of the inquiry. One of the easiest ways to undercut a commission's work is to mandate short deadlines. The 9/11 commission, which Kean and Hamilton thought was "set up to fail," was originally given an impossible deadline of eighteen months. This can present special challenges in matters of national security when classified information is sought. Politicians can limit the commission's investigative powers; in some cases, commissions were not granted powers that would seem indispensable. For example, the Tower Commission that investigated the Iran-Contra affair involving the Reagan administration was not given subpoena power to compel the testimony of witnesses, and the two figures at the center of the scandal (Lieutenant Colonel Oliver North and National Security Advisor John Poindexter) simply refused to testify.[85]

Assuming everything had fallen into place in setting up a torture commission (adequate funding, reasonable deadlines, quality appointments), it is not clear that it would have succeeded in getting to the truth of what happened. Given the experience of the past few decades, the pattern in how such investigations go has become evident. The assumption has got to be that investigators—whether from congressional committees, the Justice Department, or an independent commission—will encounter major obstacles in unearthing evidence of executive misconduct. National security information will be classified. Administration officials closest to the president—those who may have the most knowledge of what went on—will likely be among the most resistant. Executive privilege claims should be expected. Obtaining evidence will be the subject of negotiation combined with the usual investigative tools to compel individuals to testify and produce documents. Subpoenas will have to be issued, and some witnesses will have to be granted immunity.

Generally speaking, it is not clear that a commission would make the most effective use of its investigative authority. In the past, members of commissions have been reluctant to use their powers to the fullest extent, and, however dedicated the commissioners may be to their mission, some have been loath to force the issue with uncooperative presidents. What prosecutors regard as routine—issuing subpoenas, following up with contempt orders, securing public testimony under oath that is transcribed by a court reporter—members of commissions are more likely to view as "confrontational" and "punitive." As for the conditions under which witnesses testify, experience suggests that commissioners will accede to the demands of powerful public officials to testify only in private, without being sworn under oath, or without any official transcript.[86]

In the final analysis, the problem with the pro-commission argument was that it was presented to the public in idealized form. When due consideration is given to the mechanics of how commissions actually operate in the United States, there is good reason to doubt whether a torture commission would have achieved the level of accountability its proponents desired.

III

There are times in US history when civic debate captures something essential about the spirit of the nation and the state of its democracy. So it is, perversely, with the torture debate.

As far as accountability is concerned, the main phases of the debate unfolded like a tragic opera in three acts. In the opening act, genuine shock over the prisoner abuse at Abu Ghraib gave way to a public relations coup for the Bush White House. Score one for the president and his aides, who deflected calls for accountability so effectively that the issue was given no more than passing notice in the presidential campaign that followed. Act II began with an air of expectation. Could the changeover in administrations clear the way for genuine accountability? When President Obama had four Bush Justice Department's legal memoranda released in April 2009, the public had before it substantial evidence of criminality—the documentary evidence provided in the legal opinions complementing the graphic visuals recorded in the Abu Ghraib photos (not to mention earlier reports compiled by the Red Cross and the Senate Armed Services Committee, among other things). Then came the crucial plot twist. Attorney General Eric Holder launched a criminal investigation which, by excluding interrogations that adhered to OLC guidelines, was emasculated from the start. The final act, in the nature of a last-ditch effort to achieve some measure of accountability, featured the Senate Intelligence Committee's torture report. Brutality came off as a neutral characterization given what the Senate report described, but the debate by then had shifted focus to the question of torture's effectiveness. And so the drama ended, without definitive resolution, leaving the public unclear as to whether torture can be justified and, given the intelligence committee's focus on the CIA, who should bear ultimate responsibility. One thing was clear, however. Although the Senate torture report led to renewed calls for criminal prosecution, there would be no prosecutions.

The arguments offered in opposition to criminal accountability were revealing, predictable perhaps, but revealing all the same. One common thread running through them was a tendency to exaggerate. Or so it seemed. Prosecutions, by criminalizing policy differences, would turn the United States into a banana republic, cripple national security policymaking, and undermine presidential succession so much that American democracy would be imperiled. Legal experts gave prosecutors no chance of obtaining convictions based partly on criminal defenses that on close inspection were inapplicable. Conveniently overlooking the difficulties any independent commission would likely encounter, proponents of a torture commission presented the idea to the public as if it were some sort of deus ex machina.

Taking the measure of a public debate like the torture debate is not simply a matter of tallying rhetorical points scored, but also uncovering what lies beneath the rhetoric. Historians in the future may wonder what was behind the opposition to prosecutions. That there would be some difference of opinion over accountability was to be expected, but why was the idea of prosecuting *anyone* so fiercely contested? There are several possible answers to that question, ranging from the politics surrounding the torture debate to larger cultural predispositions—whether viewed as a move-on mentality or a short attention span. It also appears that it was understood at the time that any move to prosecute CIA interrogators, Justice Department lawyers, or contractors would ultimately lead up the chain of command to the Oval Office, and whether or not putting a few CIA agents on trial would have poisoned the political atmosphere as much as the Obama White House feared, no one could entertain any doubt that prosecuting President Bush would be politically explosive.

This inquiry into the torture debate began with a snapshot of the views of Americans on accountability at the time that President Obama assumed office. At that critical juncture, a majority (62%) supported accountability with a plurality (38%) in favor of criminal prosecutions.[87] Ten years of public debate about the Bush administration's treatment of detainees opened up ominous possibilities that had been foreclosed previously. In the anxious weeks following the September 11 attacks, when 83 percent of Americans thought terrorist attacks in the United States in the next several weeks likely, 53 percent opposed torturing captured terrorists, even if they had specific information about plans to attack the United States.[88] Interestingly, a majority in opposition to torture held while President Bush was in office, but that changed during the Obama administration.[89] By December 2014, 58 percent considered torture of terrorism suspects justifiable (often or sometimes), and slightly more were willing to say the CIA's treatment of suspected terrorists was justified. Another 19 percent accepted the use of torture in rare instances, while only 20 percent said that torture was never justified. In the wake of Islamic State attacks in 2016, polling showed 84 percent of Americans sharing the view that torturing terrorism suspects was justified (often, sometimes, or rarely).[90]

No wonder the notion of individual criminal accountability fell by the wayside. Now the US government could engage in torture with the support of an overwhelming majority of Americans. There was no longer any need to resort to euphemisms like "enhanced interrogation techniques." And if torture can be justified (whether often, sometimes, or rarely), why bother with prosecutions?

Conclusion

The torture debate left a number of unanswered questions in its wake. How should President Bush's actions be characterized? As policy choices, war crimes, or something in between? Were his actions really comparable to those taken by Lincoln and FDR? What, if anything, was lost by the failure to hold anyone in the Bush administration responsible for the mistreatment of detainees? What could criminal prosecutions have accomplished? Could trials have set the record straight? Established what was right and what was wrong? Determined who was ultimately responsible? And what does this accountability failure suggest about the state of the American polity?

To accuse a US president of criminal activity is serious enough. To brand anyone elected to that office a war criminal will undoubtedly strike many as extreme—the sort of hysterical rant some might attribute to radical protesters or disaffected intellectuals. In President Bush's case, the charge is not so easily dismissed. Remember it was General Taguba who said there was "no longer any doubt" whether President Bush and other administration officials had "committed war crimes." The "only question that remains to be answered," he continued, was whether they "will be held to account."[1]

By now it seems clear that President Bush will never be held accountable for violating the Geneva Conventions. Some will say it was naive to think he could have been prosecuted. Admittedly, it will never be easy to bring a president to trial, but there is more of a dilemma here—an accountability dilemma—than might appear. On the view that there was always more at stake in this episode than simply determining one president's guilt or innocence, it has been a chief purpose of this book to bring out the implications of the failure to hold President Bush personally accountable and to highlight the complexity of this presidential accountability dilemma.

The arc of this book's argument began with what might be described as a normative justification for accountability that, in this case, was grounded in the laws of war. In lieu of a strictly legal analysis of the Geneva Conventions, an effort was made to reassert the meaning and significance of the laws of war by providing a panoramic view of their development. The contemporary laws of armed conflict grew out of a basic understanding of the nature of warfare, a desire to lessen its evils, and a conviction that law can regulate force. Great temptations inevitably arise when confronting a vicious enemy in time of war, and, in that light, there is something to be gleaned from the fact that, so far as can be determined, people have always recognized rules to govern the conduct of fighting.

As for those rules most relevant to the Bush administration's interrogation program, this book has focused on one in particular. It happens to be a foundational rule of the contemporary laws of armed conflict. That is the requirement, stated in Common Article 3, that persons not actively engaged in the conduct of hostilities "shall in all circumstances be treated humanely." This principle of humanity has a history that amplifies its significance for any American president contemplating its transgression. It was George Washington, after all, who insisted that the British treat Americans taken prisoner with humanity and directed his soldiers to do the same with British prisoners. And, of course, the atrocities committed by the Axis powers in World War II confirmed the need for undeviating respect for the humanity of wartime captives and, what necessarily follows, their humane treatment.

Then there was Nuremberg, coming as it did after a long history in which the laws of war, for all the progress that was made, had lacked an efficient enforcement mechanism. Although the record of war crimes accountability since World War II has been uneven, Nuremberg signified an end to those doctrines—act of state, superior orders, head of state immunity—that enabled civilians and soldiers to violate the laws of war with impunity. The idea underlying Nuremberg was at once simple and profound: all persons are responsible for their actions, and wars, no matter how dreadful, cannot relieve individuals of their obligation to abide by governing law—in this case, the law of war. It is not without significance that the United States played a crucial role in bringing the Nuremberg principle of individual criminal accountability into being.

Having laid out how the laws of war provide an overall framework for this inquiry, the argument turned to the particulars of the decision-making process that led to the adoption of the Bush administration's interrogation program. While this book was never meant to offer a comprehensive factual account of the treatment of detainees during the Bush presidency, it was thought necessary to offer details sufficient not only to answer the famous Watergate question—what did the president know and when did he know it—but also to get at his intent. One can imagine the difficulty in probing the inner recesses of any administration to find clear proof of a president's criminal intent, especially when it comes to war crimes. In this case, it was possible to reconstruct the administration's decision-making process from classified memoranda in order to piece together evidence throwing light on what President Bush had in mind.

Although there were legitimate questions surrounding the application of the Geneva Conventions to the conflict with Al Qaeda and the Taliban, the president was not engaged in a constructive effort to revamp existing law. His interest was in relieving the United States of any legal obligation it had under the Geneva Conventions regarding the humane treatment of detainees. For anyone willing to read between the lines, the presidential memorandum of February 7, 2002 yields more clues about what the president was contemplating than he may have anticipated. Though originally classified, this document was evidently written for public consumption as an apologia, complete with its disingenuous reference to "our values as a Nation" that "call for us to treat detainees humanely." In any event, that was how the memorandum was used. In an effort to limit the damage from the Abu Ghraib scandal, the administration released the February 7 document in conjunction with a press briefing featuring White House counsel Gonzales.[2] With this memorandum in hand, administration officials could assert that President Bush had issued a directive going beyond what the law required, leaving it to attentive observers to point out that his humane treatment policy did not apply to the CIA. Among the most interesting aspects of this memorandum is President Bush's description of the administration's internal deliberations, as he subtly (perhaps not so subtly) shifted responsibility from his own agency in this matter by characterizing the legal issues as "complex," the internal deliberations as "extensive," and the decision on Geneva as fully consonant with the law. In the space of two pages, President Bush could not have stated "I accept the legal conclusion" of the Justice Department or the attorney general any more than he did.[3]

There is no need to read between the lines with other memoranda prepared by administration officials in the lead-up to the February 7 presidential directive. They show that President Bush's memorandum was not issued to ensure humane treatment, but rather out of concern, expressly stated in White House and Justice Department documents, that federal prosecutors might charge administration officials with war crimes. Attorney General Ashcroft warned President Bush that there could be "substantial criminal liability" for "involved U.S. officials." He advised the president that the best way to minimize litigation risk was for him to declare the Geneva Conventions inapplicable to the conflict in Afghanistan. Even more revealing was the draft memorandum addressed to President Bush that was ostensibly written by White House counsel Gonzales (actually the work of David Addington). They spoke of the "threat of domestic criminal prosecution under the War Crimes Act" and recommended an official presidential memorandum declaring Geneva inapplicable in order to mitigate that threat. Could Gonzales and Addington have been any clearer on this point? They said that such a presidential "determination" on the Geneva Conventions "would create a reasonable basis in law" that the War Crimes Act did not apply and would therefore "provide a solid defense to any future prosecution." They added that criminal charges would be "unwarranted." So they said.[4]

President Bush's claim that the interrogation program was lawful should be paired against statements made by other government lawyers and the actions taken by law enforcement agencies. When leading military lawyers were apprised of the enhanced interrogation methods, they used words like "cruel and unusual treatment," "torture," and "on their face" violations of US criminal law to describe them. The State Department's top lawyer criticized OLC's analysis of the Geneva Conventions as "seriously flawed."[5] FBI agents were ordered by their superiors to "stand clear" of enhanced interrogations. The same warning was given to members of the military's Criminal Investigation Task Force.[6] President Bush was certainly not aware of every objection made within his administration, but he could not have been oblivious to the significant disagreement with OLC's conclusion about the legality of the interrogation tactics he had approved.

Indeed, when President Bush referred to "extensive" internal deliberations over "complex" legal issues—as if he had relied on the government's leading international humanitarian law experts at the Pentagon and State Department—he neglected to mention the weighty opposition he personally encountered from within his own administration. Secretary of State Colin Powell lobbied the president to stop him from declaring Geneva inapplicable. The chairman of the Joint Chiefs of Staff appealed directly to President Bush out of concern that such a decision would endanger US servicemembers. "You have to remember," said General Myers, "that as we treat them, probably so we're going to be treated" or worse, "but we should not give them an opening."[7]

Additional insight into President Bush's thinking can be derived from his reaction to subsequent events. When Senator McCain put forward a bill to make it absolutely clear that the CIA could not engage in cruel, inhuman, and degrading treatment anywhere, the White House opposed his efforts. When his bill passed by wide margins, President Bush issued a signing statement asserting the authority to disregard the legislation.[8] After the Supreme Court ruled in *Hamdan* that Common Article 3 protected Al Qaeda and Taliban detainees, the president described the CIA's "crucial" interrogation program as "one of the most vital tools" in the fight against terrorists. President Bush did not conceal his concern that the Court's decision put interrogators "at risk of prosecution under the War Crimes Act." It is difficult to believe that his concern was limited to CIA and military interrogators. In what poker players might consider an obvious tell, President Bush complained about the prohibition of "outrages upon personal dignity" and "humiliating and degrading treatment." While the administration suspended the interrogation program in response to *Hamdan*, President Bush subsequently reauthorized the use of enhanced interrogation techniques and declared the revised CIA program in full compliance with Common Article 3. As if meant to highlight just how much of an ipse dixit this was, his order made the interrogator's intent dispositive by permitting "willful and outrageous acts of personal abuse" so long as they were not "done for the purpose of humiliating or degrading the individual." In his last year in office, President Bush vetoed a bill that would have prohibited waterboarding.[9]

The fact that the Bush administration was able to outmaneuver opposition within the executive branch, set up the interrogation program, and keep it running for as long as it did raises obvious questions about the system of checks and balances. On the assumption that checking the president is difficult in any event but practically impossible without either Congress or the Supreme Court intervening, this book gave special attention to these two institutions. Congress has a robust set of powers to combat the president, and the Court has cultivated the doctrine of judicial review to the point where it can play a decisive role on any issue.

It was to be expected—and in accordance with the framers' constitutional design—that actions taken by the legislature and the judiciary to check the executive would be met by presidential countermeasures. What is remarkable about this episode is not only that Congress and the Court failed to check the president at so many points, but the extent of the failure, as the administration turned practically everything the other branches did to the president's advantage, especially on the question of accountability.

That was the story of legislation relating to detainee treatment. The White House got Congress to transform the bill Senator McCain introduced (in an effort to put an end to cruel, inhuman, and degrading treatment) into the Detainee Treatment Act, which, with legal defenses built around advice of counsel, was designed to grant immunity to individuals who engaged in the conduct the senator sought to prevent. The DTA in final form did not require all CIA interrogations to comply with the Army Field Manual and left the definition of what constituted cruel, inhuman, and degrading treatment in the hands of administration officials—hardly a cheerful prospect for those concerned about the interrogation program. At the administration's behest, Congress inserted language in the DTA to deprive the federal courts of jurisdiction over Guantánamo detainees' habeas petitions. The White House also scored a major victory by pressuring lawmakers to enact the Military Commissions Act in response to the *Hamdan* decision. This legislation endorsed the administration's use of the "unlawful enemy combatant" designation, allowed evidence obtained through cruel, inhuman, and degrading treatment to be used, recognized President Bush's interpretation of the Geneva Conventions as authoritative, declared that detainees could not invoke the conventions as a source of rights in court, and made the legal defenses spelled out in the DTA retroactive to September 11, 2001. Once again, Congress stripped the federal courts of jurisdiction to hear detainees' habeas corpus petitions.

So far as accountability is concerned, what stands out most of all with the MCA are its amendments to the War Crimes Act. In an obvious ploy to eliminate any possibility of war crimes prosecutions, administration officials got Congress to redefine the criminal offenses that had been the source of so much concern at the Bush White House. Instead of a war crime including "any conduct" prohibited by Common Article 3 (as the 1997 amendments to the WCA had done), the MCA specified nine offenses that constituted war crimes. Gone was the prohibition against "outrages upon personal dignity, in particular humiliating and degrading treatment." While cruel and inhuman treatment was still included, it was narrowly defined in order to exempt the administration's enhanced interrogation techniques. In case there was any doubt of Congress's intent to shield those involved in the interrogation program from the War Crimes Act, those MCA amendments were made retroactive to the date when the 1997 amendments were adopted.[10]

Legislative oversight for the first six years of the Bush presidency was also deficient. It is tempting to conclude that if lawmakers were incapable of conducting a meaningful and timely investigation following the incontrovertible photographic evidence of prisoner abuse at Abu Ghraib, there is not much hope for oversight whenever party affiliations in Congress align with the executive as they did then. The Democrats' takeover in 2007 led to more thorough inquiries, chief among them the investigation conducted by the Senate Armed Services Committee, but the committee did not publish its report until December of the following year, after the presidential election. Another six years passed before the Senate Intelligence Committee released its torture report. Its detailed narrative of the CIA's mistreatment of detainees renewed calls for prosecutions, but its impact was undermined by the emphasis given the question of torture's effectiveness and its forgiving chronology of President Bush's involvement.

With Congress's failings, the Supreme Court had the opportunity to take the lead in checking the president. As it happened, the Court handed down several major decisions that offered the tantalizing prospect of countering the president's worst impulses. There was the rhetoric of pushback as in "indefinite detention for the purpose of interrogation is not authorized" or a state of war does not provide the president with a "blank check."[11] Nor could President Bush have been pleased with the bottom-line results, at least on a quick reading of the opinions, as *Hamdi* required due process for US citizens detained as enemy combatants, *Hamdan* invalidated the president's military tribunals and applied Common Article 3 in the process, and *Boumediene* extended the constitutional right of habeas corpus to alien detainees held at Guantánamo.

Yet seemingly for every step forward, the justices took more than one step back, and in the end the Court reverted to its usual pattern of judicial deference in wartime. Even though the *Hamdi* Court held that a US citizen detained by the military as an enemy combatant has a right to a status hearing comporting with the due process clause, the process the Court required of the executive was embarrassingly minimal. Not to be overlooked is the strained reading Justice O'Connor gave the Authorization for Use of Military Force in order to recognize the president's authority to detain US citizens without affording them a criminal trial; in this case, citizens engaged in armed conflict against the United States in Afghanistan. *Hamdan* deserves mixed reviews. On the one hand, there is no denying the significance of its decision applying Common Article 3 to detainees held at Guantánamo. On the other hand, the Court's jurisdictional decision rested on statutory grounds, leaving nothing to stop the administration from appealing to its congressional allies to amend the habeas statute in order to deprive federal courts of jurisdiction over detainees' claims. *Boumediene* may go down in history as a genuine landmark for what the majority said about habeas corpus, but the justices left implementation in the hands of DC Circuit judges who proceeded to issue one ruling after another undermining *Boumediene*'s promise. All told, detainees were held in US custody for years without having the opportunity to test the legality of their detention in court. The Supreme Court justices may have been genuinely concerned about Guantánamo, but their failure to follow up the enemy combatant cases raises the question of whether some of their number were particularly motivated to preserve federal court jurisdiction, and, once that had been accomplished, their interest in continuing the battle with the president faded.

The Court's decisions in civil damages lawsuits seeking to hold Bush administration officials accountable deserve more attention than they have received. The pattern that obtained was for the Court, per Justice Kennedy, to concede that the government's treatment of plaintiffs was "tragic," but then to make it all but impossible for the lawsuits to proceed.[12] Given the lengths to which Justice Kennedy went to insulate "high-level executive policy" from judicial review, these decisions arguably demonstrated even more than the enemy combatant cases how far the Court was willing to defer to executive claims of national security.[13]

Taken altogether, the back-and-forth on detainee treatment yields a detailed case study of the institutional handicaps Congress and the Court face when trying to counteract abuse of power in the executive branch. In Congress, so long as party loyalty trumps institutional allegiance, the political incentives for a fair share of lawmakers will be skewed against holding a president of the same party accountable. For the Supreme Court, one of the main difficulties in contesting the president lies in the nature of the judicial process. Even if the justices expedite consideration of isolated cases, the likely scenario is one in which the Court is slow to respond, its responses will be slow to develop, and at some point it will simply be too much to ask a handful of justices to keep up with the countervailing pressures that may come from lawmakers and the lower courts as well as the president.

As troubling as it is to find that a president could contravene the laws of war unchecked by either Congress or the courts, the torture debate may be more disheartening. That debate says a lot about why the United States failed to come to terms with the brutal treatment of detainees.

There is a grand tradition of public debate in this country, from the ratification of the Constitution onward. The age of oratory the like of Daniel

Webster's historic speeches has long since passed, but from slavery to same-sex marriage, Americans have debated issues confronting the nation, often in a complex interaction between elites and mass opinion, and in the process, they have worked out what America stands for.

The irony in viewing the torture debate from that perspective should not be lost on anyone. This was a sprawling debate carried on everywhere, or so it seemed, from the halls of Congress to the latest upstart blogs in social media. As the debate lasted over a decade, it seemed useful to break it down into three phases, each prompted by a catalytic event. The first began with the disclosures about Abu Ghraib (2004), the second revolved around the Obama administration's release of Bush Justice Department "torture memos" (2009), and the last accompanied the publication of the Senate torture report (2014). Notwithstanding its start-stop quality, the debate had a detectable trajectory, as nearly universal shock and disgust over Abu Ghraib gave way to growing acceptance of the use of torture and irreconcilable political divisions over accountability.[14]

Indeed, the more one takes note of the discussion of accountability in the torture debate, the more that debate looks like a referendum on accountability. And given what the public learned about the mistreatment of detainees over the course of a decade—from Abu Ghraib to the Senate torture report—there was a remarkable level of resistance to accountability in any form and to criminal prosecution in particular. The torture debate does not by itself explain why no one was prosecuted, but several aspects of that debate set the stage for that result.

To begin with, the Bush White House mounted an effective public relations campaign to fend off criticism. The strategy, which began to take shape shortly after news broke about Abu Ghraib, was to blame "a few bad apples," denounce their misconduct, and offer vague promises of accountability. Many Americans remained unconvinced, but this line of defense enabled the administration to get past a particularly vulnerable period. Then, too, while there were always political divisions over the treatment of detainees, the accountability issue devolved into a thoroughly partisan affair by the time President Obama took office. When he released classified Bush Justice Department memoranda, it was clear that any move to prosecute would face solid Republican opposition. The Obama White House appeared to succumb to pressure built around the "criminalizing policy differences" charge. Not everyone making that claim had a vested political interest in blocking criminal accountability, but some surely did. The more sophisticated version of the political argument conceded the criminality of those involved in the interrogation program but pointed to the risks prosecutions posed to the democratic process. Add to that legal experts who assured Americans that any effort to prosecute would be futile, especially given defenses based on advice of counsel. Meantime, proponents of an investigative commission, notwithstanding their interest in accountability, undercut public support for prosecutions at a critical point during the torture debate as they held out the commission as a viable accountability alternative without the Sturm und Drang of criminal proceedings. No doubt that appealed to many, though the ideal envisioned by commission proponents was harder to realize than they let on.

Words count for a lot in public debate, but what is most often of interest are the assumptions behind the arguments. In this case, the opposition to criminal accountability appears to have been rooted in the idea that the system had corrected itself so that the problem—taken in reference to the mistreatment of detainees—had been solved. This self-correction thesis, as it might be called, can be detected in various comments (implicit in President Obama's reference to a "thing of the past," for example), but no one articulated this idea more explicitly than Jack Goldsmith. The "test" of "presidential accountability in wartime," Goldsmith said, is "self-correction," which he described as "the ability of our institutions to redirect presidential wartime initiatives that do not garner the approval of the other institutions of government and of the people." That was, in Goldsmith's view, an "apt description" of what transpired. Although his book *Power and Constraint* was notable for highlighting the contributions of untraditional accountability mechanisms in checking the president, here he singled out the actions taken by Congress and the courts. In short, the constitutional machinery that was supposed to check the president had swung into action, and the Bush administration's enhanced interrogation techniques were no longer in use thanks in particular to the Detainee Treatment Act and the Supreme Court's decision in *Hamdan*. So ran the argument.[15]

This reading of the situation put the argument against criminal prosecutions in a stronger position. Instead of having to insist that there was no need for accountability, the point was that the checking mechanisms had already provided accountability. And with the problem solved, there followed an intuitive understanding of the relative costs and benefits of going forward with prosecutions. It was felt that the costs associated with criminal trials outweighed any benefits that could possibly accrue (recall President Obama's unequivocal "nothing will be gained"). And if the benefits of having prosecutions were minimal because there already had been accountability, the imagined costs were heightened considerably by the prospect of where a full-bore criminal investigation would inevitably lead. Thomas Friedman captured this sentiment when he noted that justice, if "taken to its logical end," would mean indicting the former president, and that would "rip our country apart."[16]

In the view taken in this book, the self-correction thesis is mistaken in several respects. Laying out why that is the case provides an opportunity for a final assessment of this work's major themes and its implications.

To begin with, the self-correction view rests on a deficient conception of accountability. Missing from the analysis—a glaring omission on these facts—is any acknowledgment of the need for prospective accountability. No American president should be able to set up a global network of secret prisons in order to facilitate the use of torture by US personnel—torture, it bears restating, that resulted in some number of criminal homicides. That ought to be taken as given. If the system of checks and balances had worked, there should have been fail-safe points along the way before the Bush administration put the interrogation program into effect. Given the serious offenses committed, it is tempting to conclude that prospective accountability was so important that nothing done afterwards to hold administration officials accountable could adequately compensate for the failure to prevent this misconduct from occurring in the first place.

Another way in which the self-correction thesis is misconceived is that it reduces accountability to a single question: Did the torture end? That is undoubtedly a desirable outcome, but it falls in the category of a necessary but not sufficient condition for achieving accountability. The main problem with considering this episode an accountability success story simply because the torture eventually ended is that it discounts the importance of liability in these circumstances. As an abstract proposition, it seems uncontroversial to conclude that persons who torture prisoners should be held liable for their actions. That does not mean that everyone involved in the Bush administration's interrogation program had to be prosecuted. What form liability should take (disciplinary proceedings, civil litigation, criminal prosecutions), how to assess varying degrees of culpability, what evidence individuals may offer in mitigation—questions like these deserve consideration. But to say that no one should be liable for the cruel and inhumane treatment of detainees does not comport with the concept of accountability as this book defines it or, it is argued here, with any acceptable definition of accountability.

Even if things righted themselves eventually, the self-correction thesis fails to take into account the length of time it took to get to that point. At the latest, the start date of the interrogation program can be placed in August 2002. That was when the CIA received OLC's written approval to use enhanced interrogation techniques on Abu Zubaydah.[17] Taking December 30, 2005 as the earliest possible end date (when President Bush signed the DTA into law), over three years had elapsed since the CIA's first use of enhanced interrogation methods. Given what transpired in the interim, this lapse of time was no trivial matter.

In addition, it cannot be said with confidence that the problem—the use of enhanced interrogation techniques—was solved. Even though the Bush administration's interrogation program unraveled, there is reason to be less sanguine about the future than the self-correction thesis suggests.

It is true that, upon taking office, President Obama immediately revoked the Bush administration's interrogation directives and ordered everyone to comply with the Army Field Manual. As his executive order was only as good for as long as his successors were willing to let it stand, one might draw comfort from the National Defense Authorization Act of 2016, which also banned the use of enhanced interrogation techniques.[18] While these prohibitions have held for several years, the political will to keep to this position has been less stable than some might have hoped. Through more than one election cycle, Republican presidential candidates have expressed their willingness to employ interrogation methods similar to those used by the Bush administration. That kind of talk might be dismissed as just so much bluster on the campaign trail, but it undoubtedly reflects the candidates' assessments of the views of a substantial number of Republican voters.[19] There was also a curious abortive effort during the Trump presidency to "reinstate" the Bush administration's interrogation program. A draft executive order, "Detention and Interrogation of Enemy Combatants," would have initiated a policy review geared toward reviving enhanced interrogation techniques. This idea was quickly abandoned after the document was leaked. That might be interpreted to mean that opposition to the inhumane treatment of prisoners remains strong, but the fact that such an effort was undertaken indicates that President Obama and Congress had not laid the issue to rest.[20]

Besides, to consider the problem solved, the question is not whether elected officials stopped using enhanced interrogations with the war against terrorism waning and Al Qaeda decimated, but rather whether they would refrain from similar abusive practices in the face of another national security threat that fuels public anxiety just as much. The trends in polling data on the use of torture are sobering. In the anxious weeks following 9/11, a majority of those surveyed said they opposed torturing captured terrorists, even if they had specific information about plans to attack the United States. By the time the Senate torture report was released a dozen years later, a greater number of Americans had come around to the view that torture could be justified in some circumstances, and a majority supported its use in the war against terrorism. Questions have been raised about whether the formulation of the survey questions skewed the results (respondents may have hesitated to support absolutes as in "torture is never justified"). The least that can be said is that, after a decade of public debate, Americans' stance on torture had become more complicated.[21]

Furthermore, to have congratulations all around because the United States supposedly self-corrected—that is to say, that the CIA and military stopped mistreating detainees—sidesteps the question of what effect the Bush administration's interrogation program had on other countries. Evidence suggests that the CIA's program of enhanced interrogation and extraordinary rendition had a measurable, albeit variable, impact on human rights practices in countries that cooperated with the Bush administration (by hosting black sites, for example). Averell Schmidt and Kathryn Sikkink have described this diffusion of bad practices through what they called "learning by doing." While their research uncovered no statistically significant impact in participating countries they labeled as more democratic, Schmidt and Sikkink observed a worsening in the human rights practices in more autocratic/less democratic countries. Their data showed that this continued after President Bush left office.[22]

More broadly, there is cause for concern over what effect the Bush administration's actions has had on the global norm against torture. An essential characteristic of the antitorture norm is that it is, in the language of human rights, nonderogable. Torture is absolutely prohibited. There are no exceptions. No emergencies can justify its use. Of course, no one mindful of what was going on around the world before the Bush administration's interrogation practices became public knowledge would have thought that torture was on the verge of elimination. Yet the norm itself seemed to be on solid footing. As Juan E. Mendez (the UN special rapporteur for torture from 2010 to 2016) explained this apparent inconsistency, the "moral condemnation of torture" was "truly universal" before the war against terrorism, and nations that engaged in torture "denied that they did." That obviously left something to be desired, but stability in the antitorture norm at least provided a foundation for greater compliance in the future.[23]

Bad actors around the world certainly need no encouragement to violate the torture ban. Nor do they need lessons in how to do so. Yet Mendez reported that the "example set" by the Bush administration had been "a big draw-back" in his efforts to combat torture, as he was confronted with the predictable response: "If the US tortures, why can't we do it?" Schmidt and Sikkink observed that the administration undercut the absolute prohibition by "injecting a greater degree of legal and cultural acceptance for the situational use of torture." How the Bush team manipulated the law to circumvent the norm did not go unnoticed. To take one example, Sudan "borrowed the US concept of 'illegal combatants'" to justify unlawful acts, according to foreign embassy traffic.[24]

There was in addition to the self-correction thesis a corollary view that seemed widely held if not fully articulated: that this entire affair was a historical anomaly and that President Bush's authorization of enhanced interrogation techniques, however tragic the consequences, could be written off as a temporary wartime expedient. Various ideas may be collected under this head: that the 9/11 terrorist attacks were unprecedented; that the national security crisis they brought on was sui generis; that the violation of international humanitarian law was the product of one administration's unique characteristics. There was, in short, no need to fret over other presidents tangling with the laws of war as President Bush had, for once the occasion for the abuse of power had passed, so too had the abuse of power.

This, too, is subject to question. For one thing, the terrorist threat has not gone away. Granted, it may get harder with each passing year to imagine anyone pulling off another 9/11, but the intelligence community continues to rate global terrorism a "persistent threat." The 2022 assessment from the National Director of Intelligence stated that the Islamic State and Al Qaeda "still aspire to conduct attacks in the United States" and that terrorists "remain interested" in using chemical and biological weapons. The threat of terrorist attacks will not dissipate if these groups fail to reconstitute themselves.[25]

Rather than one of a kind, the war against terrorism may offer a glimpse of what future asymmetric conflicts may look like: the absence of a well-defined battlefield; the uncertain line between criminal justice and warfare; nonstate actors located in several countries; the difficulty in distinguishing enemy forces from civilians; public anxiety over mass casualties; the understandable desire to preempt attacks; and the political pressure to do something. In such circumstances, it should come as no surprise if decisions that used to be the prerogative of soldiers in combat, officers in the field, or commanders in theater would become increasingly centralized in the White House, with presidents drawn into making decisions having law-of-war implications, as it was with President Bush, whose top national security officials met in the White House reviewing specific interrogation plans for individual detainees. It should also come as no surprise if presidents and their advisors making those law-of-war decisions are more responsive to public opinion than the uniformed military. That makes for a combustible combination in the world of national security politics. The question, then, is not how things shape up as one crisis fades, but rather whether the powers wielded by the president in response to one crisis carry over to the next. The danger is that with a perpetual state of emergency—or the perception of such—the executive abuse of power that was rationalized as a one-time necessity becomes normalized. It is tempting to conclude that with presidential power there is no such thing as a temporary wartime expedient.[26]

Consider the actions taken by President Bush's successor in the later stages of the war against terrorism. President Obama was in many respects the polar opposite of President Bush, not least of all in projecting a heartfelt commitment to the law, befitting his background as a Harvard Law alumnus who taught constitutional law. Before he was elected president, Senator Obama had raised expectations about how he would reshape counterterrorism policy. Among other things, he promised "to restore habeas corpus."[27] The flurry of executive orders issued shortly after he took office only served to heighten expectations: enhanced interrogation techniques banned; military commissions suspended; black sites shut down; and Guantánamo prison to be closed within a year. With a new special interagency group tasked with conducting a "comprehensive review" of how to handle terrorism suspects at every step from apprehension to disposition, a wholesale restructuring of detention policy seemed in the offing.[28]

Two months into Obama's presidency, Harvard law professor Noah Feldman pointed out that, judging from the Justice Department's representations in court, the new president "still claims the authority necessary to sustain almost everything his predecessor did."[29] As time went by, wholesale restructuring no longer seemed a fitting description, though there was a range of opinion over what to make of President Obama's counterterrorism policies. The military commissions resumed with some enhanced procedural protections (notably disallowing evidence obtained by torture), but critics thought they still did not comply with the requirements of the Constitution and the Geneva Conventions.[30] In lieu of adding to Guantánamo's roll of detainees, the Obama administration looked upon Bagram Air Force Base as the principal detention center in the war against terrorism, and the Justice Department convinced federal courts to deny prisoners held there any right to file habeas corpus claims.[31] Although President Obama closed the CIA's black sites, journalists discovered secret prisons still in operation: Tor Jail run by the Defense Intelligence Agency and the Joint Special Operations Command at Bagram; another in Somalia that was used by the CIA under the guise of having it run by that country's intelligence service.[32] If President Obama's most complete departure from Bush administration policies had to do with enhanced interrogation techniques, human rights critics noted troubling holdovers in the Army Field Manual's Appendix M (separation, goggles, blindfolds).[33] And when President Obama signed the National Defense Authorization Act of 2011, indefinite military detention became the law of the land, notwithstanding his stated reservations.[34]

For all this, President Obama was portrayed as institutionalizing President Bush's counterterrorism approach, a bit smugly by some on the right, but with growing frustration for those who had anticipated a clean break. The key takeaway from the commentary was that the president, by getting rid of the Bush administration's worst excesses, softening the rhetoric on presidential power, and rationalizing policy choices under more defensible interpretations of the law, had brought President Bush's core policies into the mainstream. "It seems," remarked the *Wall Street Journal's* editors, that "the Bush administration's antiterrorist architecture is gaining new legitimacy." *New York Times* reporter Peter Baker wrote that President Obama had "to some extent validated" President Bush's national security program and put it on "a more sustainable footing." The American Civil Liberties Union expressed concern that the president was setting a "new normal"—enshrining "permanently within the law" Bush policies "widely considered extreme and unlawful."[35]

These views deserve consideration. But while President Obama's overall record fell short of what many expected, lumping all of these issues together fails to account for important distinctions.[36] On some questions, the range of choices available to him was limited. Sometimes this was due to President Bush's prior decisions. Congress also disrupted President Obama's plans, most conspicuously by blocking the closure of Guantánamo. On other questions, he is more vulnerable to criticism. One issue that stands out is the use of drone strikes for targeted killing.

The "targeted killing" terminology may be offputting, though there is nothing illegitimate per se about the premeditated use of deadly force against specified individuals in warfare (unless, it should go without saying, they are in custody).[37] For some time, the American military has relied on cruise missiles and special forces for this purpose. During the war against terrorism, the United States turned to drones—unmanned aircraft piloted by remote control equipped with weapons systems (usually missiles, sometimes bombs). The United States had conducted reconnaissance with drones since the Vietnam War. Their use for targeted killing in the war against terrorism began at the start of the fighting in Afghanistan in 2001, but drones were rarely used for this purpose until President Bush's last year in office.[38]

Despite the difficulty journalists encountered in pinning down the exact number of US drone strikes and associated casualties in the war against terrorism,[39] there is no question that President Obama significantly escalated their use (partly due to technological advances). Under President Bush, the United States conducted approximately fifty drone strikes in Yemen, Pakistan, and Somalia. These killed nearly three hundred supposed terrorists and almost two hundred civilians. President Obama is believed to have authorized over 540 drone strikes in those same countries. According to one estimate, those drone attacks left 3,797 people dead, including 324 civilians. President Obama also added to the list of groups targeted. The Bush administration had deployed drones against Al Qaeda, the Taliban, and the Haqqani network. President Obama expanded the list to include Al Qaeda in the Arabian Peninsula (targeting in Yemen), Ansar-al Sharia (in Yemen), the Islamic Movement of Uzbekistan (in Pakistan), al Shabaab (in Somalia), and the Islamic State (in Iraq and Syria).[40]

To say that President Obama was deeply involved in the decision-making process involving drone strikes does not fully capture the extent of his participation. The day after he issued his executive order ending enhanced interrogation techniques, the first drone strikes of his presidency left possibly ten civilians dead (including at least four children) in Waziristan, Pakistan. He had not been engaged in the decision to launch those strikes, but from then on he assumed responsibility for giving final approval of CIA strikes in Pakistan that presented a substantial risk of civilian casualties. For some time, the president also made the final call for individuals placed on the Pentagon's "kill list" for drone strikes conducted by the Defense Department's Joint Special Operations Command in Yemen and Somalia. That list came out of a macabre interagency video conference held on Tuesdays, complete with PowerPoint, with over one hundred officials debating who should be targeted, before it was submitted for President Obama's approval.[41]

Most Americans did not take much notice of the drone strikes until President Obama's second term in office. What captured their attention was the question of whether the president could authorize strikes against US citizens.[42] As it happened, the drone strike that received the most publicity in the United States was one in Yemen from 2011 that killed Anwar al-Awlaki, a Muslim cleric who was born in New Mexico. The administration considered him an operational leader of Al Qaeda in the Arabian Peninsula and linked him to Umar Farouk Abdulmutallab, who had tried to set off a bomb on a passenger jet heading into Detroit on Christmas Day in 2009. Many Americans were not so much troubled by al-Awlaki's death, but, with a boost from Republican senators, there was mounting concern over what limited the president's power to order strikes on US citizens—at home as well as abroad.[43]

Although the use of drones to kill American citizens received the lion's share of attention in the United States, several law-of-war questions warranted scrutiny. One *jus ad bellum* issue had to do with whether the drone strikes in Pakistan, Somalia, and Yemen violated the UN Charter. In addition to citing the "inherent right" of "self-defence" recognized in Article 51 of the UN's founding document, administration officials claimed that these nations had consented to the drone strikes, thus rendering the intrusion into their territorial integrity lawful. That did not pass muster for many human rights critics, who considered the drone strikes in places where the United States was not officially engaged in armed conflict to be "extrajudicial killings" in violation of international human rights law.[44] Another problem had to do with the president's authority under domestic law. In its 2001 Authorization for Use of Military Force, Congress had coupled the broad authorization for the president's use of "all necessary and appropriate force" with language limited to groups that had been involved in the 9/11 attacks or nations that had harbored them before September 11, 2001. That led the Obama administration to justify targeting organizations like al Shabaab, which did not exist then, with a nebulous "associated forces" argument.[45]

There was also a classic *jus in bello* question concerning the principle of distinction. International humanitarian law permits targeting combatants; also civilians who directly take part in hostilities. While so-called personality strikes against individuals who were positively identified did not present a problem in this respect, the same cannot be said of "signature strikes," as they were known. The latter, started in the Bush administration's last year, targeted individuals who were not individually identified but who were considered lawful targets because their patterns of behavior showed characteristics—"signatures"—of terrorist activity. For example, every male older than grade school age carrying weapons in some remote mountainous regions of Pakistan was considered a combatant on the theory that only terrorists would fit that description in those places. Yet there were groups there that had nothing to do with the 9/11 attacks, and it was not uncommon for young men to carry rifles in those countries.[46] Another major question involved civilian casualties. Under international humanitarian law's proportionality standard, civilian loss should not be disproportionate to military objectives. Although President Obama insisted that his administration resorted to drone strikes only when there was a "near certainty that no civilians will be killed or injured," several troubling incidents have been documented, as when a sixty-eight-year-old grandmother was killed while gathering okra or when two persons who had been taken hostage by Al Qaeda were killed, including an American working as a contractor for the US Agency for International Development.[47]

In light of President Obama's drone strike program, it looks like the issue of presidential power vis-à-vis the law of war that came up with President Bush's enhanced interrogations was not so sui generis after all. The actions taken by these two presidents differ in important respects, though one can detect similar tendencies in the executive. One concerned the legal decision-making process, notwithstanding changes in OLC personnel. John Yoo was long gone, of course. In his place, at least so far as taking the lead in analyzing the drone strike issue, was Marty Lederman, whose critical analysis from outside the government had highlighted so many problems with the Bush Justice Department's legal opinions. Yet once again, OLC's work exposed the deficiencies of a process that provided something less than a full airing of complicated legal questions. Lederman, working with David Barron to determine whether the president could authorize the targeted killing of al-Awlaki, overlooked a relevant statute when they first approved this action. The foreign-murder statute, as it is known, seems clear. The killing of an American abroad by a US national is either murder or manslaughter. Perhaps drawing on the wide expertise within the government would have brought this legislation to their attention. They apparently learned of it only after Kevin Jon Heller, a law professor, posted a comment online stating that the foreign-murder statute should be "the starting point of any analysis" regarding the targeted killing of al-Awlaki.[48] Subsequent memoranda addressed that issue at some length, but that was not the end of the questions that could be raised about OLC's legal analysis. In particular, the explanation the Office of Legal Counsel offered of why the targeted killings satisfied the Fifth Amendment's due process clause makes for uncomfortable reading. It might have been better, though still discomfiting, if they had rested their argument on the idea that citizenship does not automatically shield an American who joins enemy forces. Instead, they drew an analogy from Justice O'Connor's reading of due process in *Hamdi* (for the purpose of detaining a US citizen) to conclude that the secret internal administrative review that approved the killing of al-Awlaki provided him with all the process he was due, as high-ranking officials determined that he posed a continuing and imminent threat and that his capture was infeasible. It would be interesting to know how this star chamber reasoning might have fared in adversarial proceedings before a neutral judge. Vicki Divoll, who had served as the Senate Intelligence Committee's general counsel as well as a CIA lawyer, thought OLC's analysis read like "a brief advocating for one outcome." The same, of course, was said of John Yoo's work product.[49]

Then, too, Obama administration officials were less than forthcoming with the public and the press about the drone strike program. Secrecy was the watchword, a problem that was compounded by the administration's definitional gymnastics. With the history surrounding President Bush's line that "this Government does not torture people," it might be thought that President Obama and his team would have done their utmost to avoid misleading the public.[50] Yet they had more than their fair share of half-truths about the drone program, even granting the need for some level of operational secrecy. In the summer of 2011, John Brennan, then serving as President Obama's counterterrorism director, claimed that there had not been a "single collateral death" for nearly a year because of the drones' "exceptional proficiency" and "precision"—a questionable interpretation which he later amended to say that there was no "credible evidence" of collateral deaths outside Iraq and Afghanistan in that period of time.[51] Other misstatements were more subtle, but no less troubling. Administration officials, including the president, conveyed the idea that the drone strikes were justified by imminent threats (the standard under international law), but, by their definition, members of Al Qaeda and associated terrorist groups always presented an imminent threat. Anyone in the administration who kept abreast of civilian casualties might have avoided touting the near certainty standard that President Obama recited in public statements. He also claimed that the administration "relentlessly" targeted leaders of Al Qaeda. "Relentless" may have been accurate, but Al Qaeda foot soldiers often got caught in the crosshairs. Moreover, the administration's official tally of combatants and civilians killed was always suspect, as it counted any male over grade-school age killed in a signature strike as a presumed combatant.[52]

As his first term drew to a close, President Obama expressed interest in setting up a "legal structure" for the drone program with "oversight checks"—a statement that can be read as a concession that the existing decision-making process was inadequate. Obama did put safeguards in place, but President Trump relaxed them. And while the war against terrorism faded from view for many Americans, the use of drone strikes for targeted killing did not end with President Obama. One of the most controversial since then was the killing of Iranian general Qassim Suleimani at Baghdad airport during the Trump presidency. Drone strikes decreased under President Joseph Biden (who brought back the Obama administration's oversight checking mechanisms), but there were still civilian casualties, such as the mistaken targeting that killed ten Afghans (including seven children) in the last days of the US pullout from Afghanistan. No one, incidentally, was held accountable.[53]

To round out this book's discussion, mention should be made of two fallback accountability options on the international stage. One is universal jurisdiction, whereby a nation may authorize its courts to hear cases concerning international crimes (including war crimes, crimes against humanity, and torture) without the traditional jurisdictional nexus—that is to say, even if the offense occurred outside its territory, none of the parties were nationals of that state, and there was no other direct harm to that country's interests. The underlying rationale is that these international crimes are of such paramount importance that every nation has an interest in prosecuting them. In theory, universal jurisdiction provides an opportunity to secure accountability when domestic politics make that impossible. The principle of universal jurisdiction was implicit in the 1949 Geneva Conventions, with every nation under the obligation to prosecute or extradite persons (whatever their nationality) who committed grave breaches (no matter where they occurred). Yet like other promising advances in war crimes accountability coming out of World War II, nothing much was done until the end of the twentieth century. The idea of universal jurisdiction captured worldwide attention in 1998 when a Spanish judge issued a warrant for the arrest of Augusto Pinochet, who was in England at the time, for human rights abuses committed while he ruled Chile. British police held him in custody for sixteen months, but Pinochet avoided extradition to Spain and eventually secured his release based on questionable assertions of poor health. Nevertheless, the case established a landmark precedent for the exercise of universal jurisdiction, as Great Britain's highest court adjudged that he could not claim head-of-state immunity for torture.[54]

Despite concerted efforts, little progress was made in holding Bush administration officials criminally accountable through universal jurisdiction. Donald Rumsfeld was a prime target, as human rights activists and alleged torture victims appealed mainly to France and Germany to initiate criminal proceedings against him, but authorities there declined the invitation. Italy may have come closest to holding anyone from the CIA individually accountable when a court there convicted twenty-two CIA agents (and a US Air Force colonel) for kidnapping a Muslim cleric in Milan and taking him to Egypt, where he was allegedly tortured. Technically, this was not an assertion of universal jurisdiction as the crime took place in Italy, but more broadly, the trial's value for accountability was undermined as the defendants, convicted in absentia, were never punished. President Bush's closest brush with the law occurred in 2011, when he was scheduled to speak in Geneva, Switzerland. US human rights lawyers were prepared to request that Swiss prosecutors open a preliminary criminal investigation of him once he arrived, but the Swiss Criminal Code does not allow prosecutors to start such an investigation of individuals who are not in the country at the time, and President Bush simply canceled his trip. Spain had one of the most interesting investigations, growing out of a criminal complaint filed against several Bush administration lawyers, including David Addington, Alberto Gonzales, and John Yoo. The Obama administration pressured Spanish government officials to drop the investigation, and the case was eventually closed without any trial.[55]

That leaves one last possibility to consider: the International Criminal Court (ICC). In many respects, the ICC was designed for this type of situation. Its fundamental purpose, as stated in the Rome Statute, is "to put an end to impunity" for "the most serious crimes of concern to the international community as a whole." These include war crimes, especially when "committed as part of a plan or policy."[56] Moreover, although the ICC, with authority "complementary to national criminal jurisdictions," generally cannot take a case that a nation with jurisdiction "decided not to prosecute," an exception is made when that decision "resulted from the unwillingness or inability of the State genuinely to prosecute."[57]

Under the Rome Statute, one factor used to determine such an unwillingness to prosecute is whether domestic proceedings were conducted in a manner "inconsistent with an intent" to bring those responsible "to justice."[58] That standard was arguably satisfied once Attorney General Holder ruled out prosecuting anyone who had adhered to the Bush OLC's approved interrogation procedures. In any event, a good case can be made that the Durham probe—consisting of a preliminary review, an investigation of only two cases, and no indictments—did not manifest the requisite intent. Nor do the US military's courts martial have much to offer on this point, given the understaffed investigative teams, the focus on servicemembers in the lower ranks, the small percentage of apparently culpable individuals who were prosecuted, and the pattern of lenient punishments for those convicted.[59]

Any ICC investigation of US personnel was bound to test the court's strained relationship with the United States—complicated since its inception. Although American diplomats and lawyers participated in the Rome Conference on the Establishment of an International Criminal Court in 1998, enthusiasm for the project waned in US diplomatic circles after the conference made it practically impossible for the UN Security Council's permanent members to control the ICC prosecutor's decisions. Rightly or wrongly, the concern was that US government officials and military servicemembers stationed around the world would be particularly vulnerable to politically motivated prosecutions. Although President Clinton authorized David Sheffer, the State Department's ambassador-at-large for war crimes issues, to sign the Rome Statute, he said he would not submit the treaty to the Senate until more was done to shield Americans from "unfounded charges." The Bush administration, making clear that the United States had not incurred any legal obligation pursuant to Sheffer's signature, "unsigned" the treaty.[60]

Since then, the US government's position on the ICC has been double-edged. On the one hand, the Senate has never approved the Rome Statute. Although the statute grants the court jurisdiction over Americans who commit war crimes in the territory of states parties to the statute, Congress passed the American Servicemembers Protection Act of 2002 (known by some as the "Hague Invasion Act"), which authorized the president to take "all means necessary and appropriate"—in other words, threatening military force—to free Americans held by the ICC. The Bush administration also entered into bilateral immunity agreements with other countries, including Afghanistan, to ensure that they did not hand over Americans to the ICC.[61] On the other hand, different administrations have supported the court's efforts to prosecute individuals such as those implicated in war crimes and genocide in Darfur, Sudan. Having a good working relationship with the United States is important to the ICC, which depends on other nations to fulfill its objectives. The court can issue arrest warrants, but it has no police force or soldiers to make arrests. With limited resources, its prosecutors rely on other countries to help gather evidence. The United States obviously has much to offer with its extensive surveillance and military capabilities.[62]

The ICC acquired jurisdiction to take cases growing out of the armed conflict in Afghanistan after Afghanistan acceded to the Rome Statute in 2003. Three years later, the ICC's Office of the Prosecutor (OTP), headed by Luis Moreno-Ocampo, opened a preliminary examination of war crimes and crimes against humanity committed in the course of that conflict. The prosecutor seemed particularly concerned with the Taliban's attacks on civilians, but not to the exclusion of actions taken by Afghan National Security Forces and coalition forces. It was not until 2013, with Fatou Bensouda as the new chief prosecutor at the helm, that it became clear that prisoner abuse by Americans was under scrutiny as well.[63] Another four years passed before Bensouda sought the approval of the ICC's Pre-Trial Chamber to expand the inquiry into a full investigation. OTP's report stated that there was "a reasonable basis" to believe that US military personnel and CIA officers had committed "acts of torture, cruel treatment, outrages upon personal dignity, rape and sexual violence" against detainees in Afghanistan and at CIA detention facilities in Poland, Romania, and Lithuania. The prosecutor focused on fifty-four detainees who had been held by the US military and twenty-four who had been in the custody of the CIA. There was some question of whether these relatively low numbers satisfied the Rome Statute's so-called gravity threshold that restricts ICC prosecutions to the most serious offenses, but the OTP took the position that the "gravity of the alleged crimes" was "increased" because the alleged offenses were "committed pursuant to plans or policies approved at senior levels of the US government, following careful and extensive deliberations." The ICC prosecutor also noted that there appeared to have been "no criminal investigation or prosecution of any person who devised, authorised or bore oversight responsibility" for the CIA's interrogation program.[64]

In April 2019, the Pre-Trial Chamber declined to authorize an investigation on the view that prosecutors were unlikely to prevail given the passage of time and the difficulty in securing cooperation from "relevant authorities"—reasoning that led Kevin Jon Heller to conclude that the Pre-Trial Chamber's decision "rewards" US obstruction.[65] One year later, the ICC's Appeals Chamber reversed that decision and authorized a full investigation. Afghanistan then filed for a deferral, as it had a right to do, though US officials appear to have prompted its request. The Trump administration also imposed sanctions and visa restrictions on ICC staff involved in the investigation. In September 2021, with Karim A. A. Khan serving as the prosecutor in charge, the OTP sought reauthorization to resume the inquiry with the focus on crimes committed by the Taliban and the Islamic State–Khorasan Province.[66]

What effect this long-running inquiry may have on the International Criminal Court remains to be seen. The ICC's image had been tarnished before the OTP began looking into US war crimes in Afghanistan. The ICC had few convictions to show for its two decades of operation. The disproportionate number of cases from Africa has drawn criticism. Some efforts to bring individuals to justice, like those involved in human rights violations in Kenya and Sudan, came to nothing as those countries refused to cooperate. No doubt the back-and-forth between the Pre-Trial Chamber and the Appeals Chamber followed by Prosecutor Khan's decision reinforced skepticism about the ICC's capacity to hold war criminals accountable whatever their nationality; even more so when it comes to American policymakers, let alone presidents.

All told, then, instead of providing meaningful fallback options, the ICC, along with the failed efforts to assert universal jurisdiction, seem to confirm the difficulty in holding US presidents accountable for violations of international humanitarian law. Indeed, resistance by the Obama administration to holding Bush administration officials accountable in any venue suggests how the presidency can operate as an anti-accountability force not only within the United States but beyond its borders.

Lastly, the question arises as to how the breakdown in accountability over the Bush administration's interrogation program will take its place in the history of the laws of war. The timing of such a high-profile episode of top-to-bottom impunity, coming, as it did, at such a critical juncture in the evolution of human rights accountability, provides the context to reflect on this. Following decades of stagnation on this front—the failure to follow through on the promise of Nuremberg seems embarrassing in retrospect—the advances made at the end of the twentieth century were so sweeping that the path forward seemed irreversible. With the stage set by the seminal domestic human rights prosecutions in Greece and Argentina, the ad hoc international tribunals for the former Yugoslavia and Rwanda gave added impetus to the movement to establish a permanent international court, a goal long sought by the human rights community. Universal criminal jurisdiction was still a work in progress, but the prospects had never looked better. This moment in human rights history, though, involved something more than finding ways to implement the Nuremberg principle of individual criminal accountability, as important as that was. Not everyone looked upon criminal prosecution as the best of all solutions, certainly not for every situation, but the debate over criminal accountability and its alternatives—the "truth versus justice" shorthand version of which does not adequately capture the level of sophistication presented on both sides—could be taken as further evidence that the question was no longer whether there would be human rights accountability, but rather how that could be best accomplished.

While it goes too far to portray the accountability breakdown over the mistreatment of detainees as an inflection point in the history of human rights accountability, the Bush presidency coincided with an apparent change in the overall outlook on human rights around the world. Without claiming any direct causal connection, it is interesting to find the optimism over human rights accountability that preceded the war against terrorism giving way so quickly to a pessimistic strain. At the risk of oversimplifying the nuanced readings given by scholars, a survey of the literature suggests a change in tone at least. Instead of entering an "age of human rights accountability," readers were told they were witnessing the "endtimes of human rights" or the "twilight of human rights law." There are reasons to qualify this gloomy view, as Kathryn Sikkink pointed out in her book *Evidence for Hope*.[67] That said, twenty years after the war against terrorism began, there was no dearth of human rights hot spots that seemed to confirm a bleaker perspective. One of the most obvious for international humanitarian law has got to be the way in which Russia, without manifesting any concern over war crimes accountability, has carried out its war in Ukraine, as if its military doctrine calls for violating the Geneva Conventions and the 1907 Hague Regulations at every turn.

Achieving compliance with the laws of war has always been a difficult business. The more soldiers involved, the more intense the fighting, the more existential the threat, the more transgressions on the other side, the more likely that violations will occur. No one expects a perfect record on the field of battle.

What President Bush did regarding the treatment of detainees in the war against terrorism was not comparable to a momentary lapse of troops under fire, however. His view of America's obligations under the laws of war was shaped to a considerable degree by his conception of the presidency, and in any perceived conflict between the laws of war and presidential power, there was no question which way he would turn. The result: hideaway prisons set up by executive fiat, presidential approval of a top-secret methodology of interrogation practices that had been the staple of totalitarian regimes, individuals held incommunicado and deprived of any court hearing, a president who used the levers of state power to circumvent treaty obligations in order to block prosecutors from charging administration officials with war crimes. And, when all that was brought to light, the closest the United States came to prosecuting those responsible was a dilatory criminal investigation that specifically excluded from inquiry the use of any interrogation technique authorized by the president and approved by his lawyers—no matter how cruel, inhumane, or degrading.

In the American system of government, presidential accountability is a constitutional imperative—one that is amplified by the laws of war and the ethical sensibility of the human rights revolution that followed World War II. How a nation fights its wars can be taken as a mark of its character. In the history of warfare, some have been guided by the age-old dictum that might confers right; others by the power of an idea that has its origins in the mists of time—that there are rules for the conduct of hostilities and that these rules, whether embodied in customary practices or latter-day written codes, can govern the use of force. President Bush made his choice. So too, it seems, did everyone else who had forsaken this nation's historic commitment to the laws of war by defaulting on the legal obligations of accountability.

APPENDIX A

Presidential Memorandum

THE WHITE HOUSE
WASHINGTON
February 7, 2002

MEMORANDUM FOR THE VICE PRESIDENT
THE SECRETARY OF STATE
THE SECRETARY OF DEFENSE
THE ATTORNEY GENERAL
CHIEF OF STAFF TO THE PRESIDENT
DIRECTOR OF CENTRAL INTELLIGENCE
ASSISTANT TO THE PRESIDENT FOR NATIONAL SECURITY
    AFFAIRS
CHAIRMAN OF THE JOINT CHIEFS OF STAFF

SUBJECT: Humane Treatment of al Qaeda and Taliban Detainees

1. Our recent extensive discussions regarding the status of al Qaeda and Taliban detainees confirm that the application of the Geneva Convention Relative to the Treatment of Prisoners of War of August 12, 1949 (Geneva) to the conflict with al Qaeda and the Taliban involves complex legal questions. By its terms, Geneva applies to conflicts involving "High Contracting Parties," which can only be states. Moreover, it assumes the existence of "regular" armed forces fighting on behalf of states. However, the war against terrorism ushers in a new paradigm, one in which groups with broad, international reach commit horrific acts against innocent civilians, sometimes with the direct support of states. Our Nation recognizes that

this new paradigm—ushered in not by us, but by terrorists—requires new thinking in the law of war, but thinking that should nevertheless be consistent with the principles of Geneva.

2. Pursuant to my authority as Commander in Chief and Chief Executive of the United States, and relying on the opinion of the Department of Justice dated January 22, 2002, and on the legal opinion rendered by the Attorney General in his letter of February 1, 2002, I hereby determine as follows:

   a. I accept the legal conclusion of the Department of Justice and determine that none of the provisions of Geneva apply to our conflict with al Qaeda in Afghanistan or elsewhere throughout the world because, among other reasons, al Qaeda is not a High Contracting Party to Geneva.

   b. I accept the legal conclusion of the Attorney General and the Department of Justice that I have the authority under the Constitution to suspend Geneva as between the United States and Afghanistan, but I decline to exercise that authority at this time. Accordingly, I determine that the provisions of Geneva will apply to our present conflict with the Taliban. I reserve the right to exercise this authority in this or future conflicts.

   c. I also accept the legal conclusion of the Department of Justice and determine that common Article 3 of Geneva does not apply to either al Qaeda or Taliban detainees, because, among other reasons, the relevant conflicts are international in scope and common Article 3 applies only to "armed conflict not of an international character."

   d. Based on the facts supplied by the Department of Defense and the recommendation of the Department of Justice, I determine that the Taliban detainees are unlawful combatants and, therefore, do not qualify as prisoners of war under Article 4 of Geneva. I note that, because Geneva does not apply to our conflict with al Qaeda, al Qaeda detainees also do not qualify as prisoners of war.

3. Of course, our values as a Nation, values that we share with many nations in the world, call for us to treat detainees humanely, including those who are not legally entitled to such treatment. Our Nation has been and will continue to be a strong supporter of Geneva and its principles. As a matter of policy, the United States Armed Forces shall continue to treat detainees humanely and, to the extent appropriate and consistent with military necessity, in a manner consistent with the principles of Geneva.

4. The United States will hold states, organizations, and individuals who

gain control of United States personnel responsible for treating such personnel humanely and consistent with applicable law.

5. I hereby reaffirm the order previously issued by the Secretary of Defense to the United States Armed Forces requiring that the detainees be treated humanely and, to the extent appropriate and consistent with military necessity, in a manner consistent with the principles of Geneva.

6. I hereby direct the Secretary of State to communicate my determinations in an appropriate manner to our allies, and other countries and international organizations cooperating in the war against terrorism of global reach.

[Signed George Bush]

APPENDIX B

Common Article 3

In the case of armed conflict not of an international character occurring in the territory of one of the High Contracting Parties, each Party to the conflict shall be bound to apply, as a minimum, the following provisions:

(1) Persons taking no active part in the hostilities, including members of armed forces who have laid down their arms and those placed hors de combat by sickness, wounds, detention, or any other cause, shall in all circumstances be treated humanely, without any adverse distinction founded on race, colour, religion or faith, sex, birth or wealth, or any other similar criteria.

To this end, the following acts are and shall remain prohibited at any time and in any place whatsoever with respect to the above-mentioned persons:

(a) violence to life and person, in particular murder of all kinds, mutilation, cruel treatment and torture;

(b) taking of hostages;

(c) outrages upon personal dignity, in particular humiliating and degrading treatment;

(d) the passing of sentences and the carrying out of executions without previous judgement pronounced by a regularly constituted court, affording all the judicial guarantees which are recognized as indispensable by civilized peoples.

(2) The wounded and sick shall be collected and cared for.

An impartial humanitarian body, such as the International Committee of the Red Cross, may offer its services to the Parties to the conflict.

The Parties to the conflict should further endeavor to bring into force, by means of special agreements, all or part of the other provisions of the present Convention.

The application of the preceding provisions shall not affect the legal status of the Parties to the conflict.

APPENDIX C

War Crimes Act

[1997–2006]

§ 2441. War crimes

(a) OFFENSE. —Whoever, whether inside or outside the United States, commits a war crime, in any of the circumstances described in subsection (b), shall be fined under this title or imprisoned for life or any term of years, or both, and if death results to the victim, shall also be subject to the penalty of death.

(b) CIRCUMSTANCES. —The circumstances referred to in subsection (a) are that the person committing such war crime or the victim of such war crime is a member of the Armed Forces of the United States or a national of the United States (as defined in section 101 of the Immigration and Nationality Act).

(c) DEFINITION. —As used in this section the term "war crime" means any conduct—

    (1) defined as a grave breach in any of the international conventions signed at Geneva 12 August 1949, or any protocol to such convention to which the United States is a party;

    (2) prohibited by Article 23, 25, 27, or 28 of the Annex to the Hague Convention IV, Respecting the Laws and Customs of War on Land, signed 18 October 1907;

    (3) which constitutes a violation of common Article 3 of the international conventions signed at Geneva, 12 August 1949, or any protocol to such convention to which the United States is a party and which deals with non-international armed conflict; or

(4) of a person who, in relation to an armed conflict and contrary to the
provisions of the Protocol on Prohibitions or Restrictions on the Use
of Mines, Booby-Traps and Other Devices as amended at Geneva on
3 May 1996 (Protocol II as amended on 3 May 1996), when the United
States is a party to such Protocol, willfully kills or causes serious injury
to civilians.

ABBREVIATIONS

Bush Memorandum: Memorandum from President George W. Bush to Vice President et al., "Humane Treatment of al Qaeda and Taliban Detainees," February 7, 2002

CAT: Convention Against Torture and Other Cruel, Inhuman or Degrading Treatment or Punishment, *opened for signature* December 10, 1984, S. Treaty Doc. No. 100-20, 1465 U.N.T.S. 85

DOD: Department of Defense

DOJ: Department of Justice

DTA: Detainee Treatment Act of 2005, Pub. L. No. 109–148, 119 Stat. 2739

GC I: Geneva Convention for the Amelioration of the Condition of the Wounded and Sick in Armed Forces in the Field, August 12, 1949, 6 U.S.T. 3114, 75 U.N.T.S. 31

GC II: Geneva Convention for the Amelioration of the Condition of Wounded, Sick and Shipwrecked Members of Armed Forces at Sea, August 12, 1949, 6 U.S.T. 3217, 75 U.N.T.S. 85

GC III: Geneva Convention Relative to the Treatment of Prisoners of War, August 12, 1949, 6 U.S.T. 3316, 75 U.N.T.S. 135

GC IV: Geneva Convention Relative to the Protection of Civilian Persons in Time of War, August 12, 1949, 6 U.S.T. 3516, 75 U.N.T.S. 287

Gonzales 1/25/02 Memorandum: Memorandum from Alberto R. Gonzales, Counsel to the President, "Decision Re Application of the Geneva Convention on Prisoners of War to the Conflict with Al Qaeda and the Taliban," January 25, 2002

Hague Regs.: Regulations Respecting the Laws and Customs of War on Land, Annex to Convention (IV), October 18, 1907, 36 Stat. 2277, T.S. No. 539

ICC: International Criminal Court

ICRC: International Committee of the Red Cross

ICRC Commentary I: Jean S. Pictet, *Commentary: I Geneva Convention for the Amelioration of the Condition of the Wounded and Sick in Armed Forces in the Field* (Geneva: International Committee of the Red Cross, 1952)

ICRC Commentary III: Jean de Preux, *Commentary: III Geneva Convention Relative to the Treatment of Prisoners of War* (Geneva: International Committee of the Red Cross, 1960)

ICRC Commentary IV: Jean S. Pictet, *Commentary: IV Geneva Convention Relative to the Protection of Civilian Persons in Time of War* (Geneva: International Committee of the Red Cross, 1958)

IMT: International Military Tribunal, Nuremberg

MCA: Military Commissions Act of 2006, Pub. L. No. 109–366, 120 Stat. 2600 (codified in scattered sections of titles 10, 18, 28, and 42 U.S.C.)

OLC: Office of Legal Counsel, Department of Justice

OTP: Office of the Prosecutor, ICC

PGW: *The Papers of George Washington*

SASC 2008 Report: S. Comm. on Armed Servs., 110th Cong., *Inquiry into the Treatment of Detainees in U.S. Custody* (Comm. Print 2008)

SSCI Report: S. Select Comm. on Intelligence, S. Rep. No. 113–288, *Committee Study of the Central Intelligence Agency's Detention and Interrogation Program* (2014)

Torture Act: 18 U.S.C. §§ 2340–2340A

WCA: War Crimes Act

NOTES

Introduction

1. For multiple definitions, see Gerry J. Simpson, "War Crimes: A Critical Introduction," in *The Law of War Crimes: National and International Approaches*, ed. Timothy L. H. McCormack and Gerry J. Simpson (The Hague: Kluwer Law International, 1997), 12.

2. Yoram Dinstein, *The Conduct of Hostilities under the Law of International Armed Conflict*, 3rd ed. (Cambridge: Cambridge University Press, 2016), 47. See chap. 1 for details.

3. Paul J. Springer, *America's Captives: Treatment of POWs from the Revolutionary War to the War on Terror* (Lawrence: University Press of Kansas, 2010), 139–41, 148–51; Ulrich Straus, *The Anguish of Surrender: Japanese POWs of World War II* (Seattle: University of Washington Press, 2003), 116–49.

4. US Depts. of the Army, Navy, Air Force, and Marine Corps, *Enemy Prisoners of War, Retained Personnel, Civilian Internees and Other Detainees* (Army Reg. 190–8, OPNAVINST 3461.6, AFJI 31–304, MCO 3461.1) (Washington, DC, 1997), 1–5; Dept. of the Army, *Field Manual 34-52, Intelligence Interrogation* (Washington, DC, 1992), 1–8; Dick Jackson, "Interrogation and Treatment of Detainees in the Global War on Terror," in *The War on Terror and the Laws of War: A Military Perspective*, ed. Michael W. Lewis (New York: Oxford University Press, 2009), 125–37.

5. *Weekly Comp. Pres. Doc.*, September 6, 2006, 42:1571.

6. Jane Mayer, *The Dark Side: The Inside Story of How the War on Terror Turned into a War on American Ideals* (New York: Anchor Books, 2009), 157–58, 161–62; SASC 2008 Report, 3–6.

7. Mayer, *Dark Side*, 158–60; Scott Shane and Mark Mazzetti, "In Adopting Harsh Tactics, No Look at Past Use," *New York Times*, April 22, 2009; Scott Shane, "China Inspired Interrogations at Guantánamo," *New York Times*, July 2, 2008; Scott Shane, "Soviet-Style 'Torture' Becomes 'Interrogation' in the War on Terror," *New York Times*, June 3, 2007; Albert D. Biderman, "Communist Attempts to Elicit False Confessions from Air Force Prisoners of War," *Bulletin of the New York Academy of Medicine* 33 (1957): 616–25; *Communist Interrogation, Indoctrination and Exploitation of American Military and Civilian Prisoners: Hearings before the Permanent Subcommittee on Investigations of the S. Comm. on Government Operations*, 84th Cong., 2d sess. (1956) (testimony of Dr. Harold G. Wolff and Dr. Lawrence E. Hinkle Jr.).

8. Memorandum from Steven G. Bradbury, Principal Deputy Assistant Attorney

General, OLC, DOJ, to John A. Rizzo, Senior Deputy General Counsel, CIA, "Application of 18 U.S.C. §§ 2340–2340A to Certain Techniques That May Be Used in the Interrogation of a High Value al Qaeda Detainee," May 10, 2005, 6 (hereafter cited as OLC 5/10/05 Torture Act Opinion); Memorandum from Jay S. Bybee, Assistant Attorney General, OLC, DOJ, to John Rizzo, Acting General Counsel, CIA, "Interrogation of al Qaeda Operative," August 1, 2002, 1, 4–6 (hereafter cited as OLC 8/1/02 Interrogation Opinion).

9. Mayer, *Dark Side*, 163–64.

10. Memorandum from Steven G. Bradbury, Principal Deputy Assistant Attorney General, OLC, DOJ, to John A. Rizzo, Senior Deputy General Counsel, CIA, "Application of United States Obligations under Article 16 of the Convention Against Torture to Certain Techniques That May Be Used in the Interrogation of High Value al Qaeda Detainees," May 30, 2005, 12 (hereafter cited as OLC 5/30/05 CAT Opinion).

11. OLC 5/10/05 Torture Act Opinion, 11; SSCI Report, 49, 60, 72, 77.

12. Memorandum from Steven G. Bradbury, Principal Deputy Assistant Attorney General, OLC, DOJ, to John A. Rizzo, Senior Deputy General Counsel, CIA, "Application of 18 U.S.C. §§2340–2340A to the Combined Use of Certain Techniques in the Interrogation of High Value al Qaeda Detainees," May 10, 2005, 6.

13. OLC 5/10/05 Torture Act Opinion, 10, 34.

14. Mayer, *Dark Side*, 166.

15. OLC 5/10/05 Torture Act Opinion, 9.

16. OLC 5/30/05 CAT Opinion, 15; *Field Manual 34–52*, 1–8.

17. OLC 5/10/05 Torture Act Opinion, 8–9.

18. OLC 5/30/05 CAT Opinion, 15.

19. OLC 8/1/02 Interrogation Opinion, 15; 18 U.S.C. § 2340(2)(C). Compare OLC 5/10/05 Torture Act Opinion, 43.

20. OLC 5/10/05 Torture Act Opinion, 14.

21. Ashcroft to the President, February 2, 2002, in *The Torture Papers: The Road to Abu Ghraib*, ed. Karen J. Greenberg and Joshua L. Dratel (Cambridge: Cambridge University Press, 2005), 126; Gonzales 1/25/02 Memorandum, in Greenberg and Dratel, *Torture Papers*, 119; Michael Isikoff, "Memos Reveal War Crimes Warnings," *Newsweek*, May 16, 2004.

22. Bush Memorandum, in Greenberg and Dratel, *Torture Papers*, 134–35; Jack Goldsmith, *The Terror Presidency: Law and Judgment Inside the Bush Administration* (New York: W. W. Norton, 2007), 119–20.

23. Seymour M. Hersh, "Torture at Abu Ghraib," *New Yorker*, May 10, 2004; Scott Higham and Joe Stephens, "New Details of Prison Abuse Emerge," *Washington Post*, May 21, 2004.

24. Interview with Deputy Secretary of Defense Paul Wolfowitz, Pentagon Channel, May 4, 2004; Dana Priest, "CIA Holds Terror Suspects in Secret Prisons," *Washington Post*, November 2, 2005; R. Jeffrey Smith, "Slim Legal Grounds for Torture Memos," *Washington Post*, July 4, 2004; John Barry, "A Tortured Debate," *Newsweek*, June 20, 2004.

25. Mike Allen and Dana Priest, "Memo on Torture Draws Focus to Bush," *Washington Post*, June 9, 2004; Dana Priest, "Covert CIA Program Withstands New Furor," *Washington Post*, December 30, 2005; Office of the Press Secretary, White House, "Press Briefing by White House Counsel Judge Alberto Gonzales et al.," June 22, 2004.

26. Jan Crawford Greenburg, Howard L. Rosenberg, and Ariane de Vogue, "Sources: Top Bush Advisors Approved 'Enhanced Interrogation,'" ABC News, April 9, 2008; Jan Crawford Greenburg, Howard L. Rosenberg, and Ariane de Vogue, "Bush Aware of Advisers' Interrogation Talks," ABC News, April 11, 2008.

27. George W. Bush, *Decision Points* (New York: Crown, 2010), 169; compare SSCI Report, 40.

28. Bush, *Decision Points*, 170; David Cole, "George W. Bush: Torturer-in-Chief," *The Nation*, November 10, 2010.

29. Antonio M. Taguba, preface to *Broken Laws, Broken Lives: Medical Evidence of Torture by US Personnel and Its Impact*, by Physicians for Human Rights (2008), viii.

30. The military's response might appear to be a model of zealous prosecution. Within two years after the revelations about Abu Ghraib, the Defense Department had launched 842 criminal investigations and fifty-four servicemembers had been convicted in courts martial on charges relating to prisoner abuse. Yet, according to one estimate, servicemembers who were court-martialed represented a small percentage of those involved in mistreating prisoners. In some instances, military prosecutors were unable to build cases to bring to trial. Investigations were hampered for various reasons. Understaffed investigative teams were unable to gather physical evidence and medical records. Victims were difficult to locate. Soldiers refused to testify against their comrades. Of those cases that proceeded to court martial, defendants were mostly lower-ranking soldiers. Although several officers received administrative punishments in connection with Abu Ghraib, only one was court-martialed, and that was for disobeying an order not to discuss the investigation. When prosecutors got a conviction, the punishment often appeared more lenient than the facts warranted. US Dept. of Defense, Office of the Inspector General, *Review of DoD-Directed Investigations of Detainee Abuse* (Arlington, VA, 2006), i; Center for Human Rights and Global Justice, Human Rights First, and Human Rights Watch, *By the Numbers: Findings of the Detainee Abuse and Accountability Project* (2006), 6–14; Tim Golden, "Army Faltered in Investigating Detainee Abuse," *New York Times*, May 22, 2005; Joshua E. S. Phillips, "Inside the Detainee Abuse Task Force," *The Nation*, May 13, 2011; David P. Forsythe, *The Politics of Prisoner Abuse: The United States and Enemy Prisoners after 9/11* (Cambridge: Cambridge University Press, 2011), 132–33. See also M. Cherif Bassiouni, *The Institutionalization of Torture by the Bush Administration: Is Anyone Responsible?* (Antwerp: Intersentia, 2010), 218–24.

31. Josh White and Dafna Linzer, "Ex-Contractor Guilty of Assaulting Detainee," *Washington Post*, August 18, 2006.

32. "Attorney General Eric Holder Regarding a Preliminary Review into the Interrogation of Certain Detainees," DOJ, August 24, 2009; Carrie Johnson, "Prosecutor to Probe CIA Interrogations," *Washington Post*, August 25, 2009.

33. Peter Finn and Julie Tate, "Justice Department to Investigate Deaths of Two Detainees in CIA Custody," *Washington Post*, July 1, 2011; Scott Shane, "No Charges Filed on Harsh Tactics Used by the C.I.A.," *New York Times*, August 30, 2012.

34. "Statement of Attorney General Eric Holder on Closure of Investigation into the Interrogation of Certain Detainees," DOJ, August 30, 2012.

35. Stephanie Nebehay, "Bush's Swiss Visit Off after Complaints on Torture," *Reuters*, February 5, 2011; Katherine Gallagher, "Universal Jurisdiction in Practice: Efforts to Hold

Donald Rumsfeld and Other High-Level United States Officials Accountable for Torture," *Journal of International Criminal Justice* 7 (2009): 1110.

36. Elian Peltier and Fatima Faizi, "I.C.C. Allows Afghanistan War Crimes Inquiry to Proceed, Angering U.S.," *New York Times*, March 5, 2020.

37. Jack M. Balkin, "A Body of Inquiries," *New York Times*, January 11, 2009; Jack Goldsmith, *Power and Constraint: The Accountable Presidency after 9/11* (New York: W. W. Norton, 2012), 235; Jeffrey Rosen, "A Torturous Decision," *New York Magazine*, May 1, 2009.

38. Clifford D. May, "Interrogation Tactics Weren't Torture, American Officials Shouldn't Be Prosecuted," *US News*, May 18, 2009; David S. Broder, "Stop Scapegoating: Obama Should Stand against Prosecutions," *Washington Post*, April 26, 2009; William McGurn, "Torture and the 'Truth Commission,'" *Wall Street Journal*, April 29, 2009.

39. David S. Broder, "Stop Scapegoating: Obama Should Stand against Prosecutions," *Washington Post*, April 26, 2009; *Daily Comp. Pres. Docs.*, 2009 DCPD No. 00263.

40. U.S. Const. art. I, § 3, cl. 7; Thomas Friedman, "A Torturous Compromise," *New York Times*, April 29, 2009; Andrew Sullivan, "Dear President Bush," *Atlantic*, October 2009; Andrew Sullivan, "Obama's First Problem is US War Crimes," *Sunday Times*, November 30, 2008; Michael Walzer, "Trying Political Leaders," *New Republic*, May 21, 2010. See also David Luban, *Torture, Power, and Law* (Cambridge: Cambridge University Press, 2014), 276.

41. Mark Bovens, "Analysing and Assessing Accountability: A Conceptual Framework," *European Law Journal* 13 (2007): 450–54; Richard Mulgan, "Accountability: An Ever-Expanding Concept?" *Public Administration* 78 (2000): 555–57; Jonathan G. S. Koppell, "Pathologies of Accountability: ICANN and the Challenge of 'Multiple Accountabilities Disorder,'" *Public Administration Review* 65 (2005): 95–99. Compare Ruth W. Grant and Robert O. Keohane, "Accountability and Abuses of Power in World Politics," *American Political Science Review* 99 (2005): 30 (defining accountability as only after the fact).

42. Paige Arthur, "How 'Transitions' Reshaped Human Rights: A Conceptual History of Transitional Justice," *Human Rights Quarterly* 31 (2009): 321–67; Christine Bell, "Transitional Justice, Interdisciplinarity and the State of the 'Field' or 'Non-Field,'" *International Journal of Transitional Justice* 3 (2009): 5–27.

43. Leslie Vinjamuri and Jack Snyder, "Law and Politics in Transitional Justice," *Annual Review of Political Science* 18 (2015): 303–27; Tricia D. Olsen, Leigh A. Payne, and Andrew G. Reiter, "The Justice Balance: When Transitional Justice Improves Human Rights and Democracy," *Human Rights Quarterly* 32 (2010): 980–1007; Ruti G. Teitel, "Transitional Justice Genealogy," *Harvard Human Rights Journal* 16 (2003): 69–94.

44. For various perspectives on presidential accountability, see Heidi Kitrosser, *Reclaiming Accountability: Transparency, Executive Power, and the U.S. Constitution* (Chicago: University of Chicago Press, 2015), 1–2, 15–16; Michele P. Claibourn, *Presidential Campaigns and Presidential Accountability* (Urbana: University of Illinois Press, 2011), 9–24; Bruce Buchanan, *Presidential Power and Accountability: Toward a Presidential Accountability System* (New York: Routledge, 2013).

45. Bovens, "Accountability," 463; Mulgan, "Accountability," 556.

46. Arthur M. Schlesinger Jr., *War and the American Presidency* (New York: W. W. Norton, 2004), 45; Morrison v. Olson, 487 U.S. 654, 731 (1988) (Scalia, J., dissenting).

47. The Declaration of Independence, ¶ 2; Alexander Hamilton, James Madison, and John Jay, *The Federalist*, ed. Clinton Rossiter (New York: Mentor, 1961), no. 48.

48. Quoted in Gordon S. Wood, *The Creation of the American Republic, 1776–1787* (Chapel Hill: University of North Carolina Press, 1998), 135.

49. Richard M. Pious, *The American Presidency* (New York: Basic Books, 1979), 20–21; Saikrishna Bangalore Prakash, *Imperial from the Beginning: The Constitution of the Original Executive* (New Haven: Yale University Press, 2015), 34–35; Jack N. Rakove, *The Beginnings of National Politics: An Interpretive History of the Continental Congress* (Baltimore: Johns Hopkins University Press, 1979), 283–84.

50. Wood, *Creation of the American Republic*, 137–41.

51. *The Federalist*, no. 70.

52. *The Federalist*, no. 69.

53. *The Federalist*, no. 70.

54. U.S. Const. art. I, § 3, cl. 7; *The Federalist* no. 69.

55. *The Federalist*, no. 77.

56. Arthur M. Schlesinger Jr., *The Imperial Presidency* (Boston: Houghton Mifflin, 1973), viii.

57. Dino P. Christenson and Douglas L. Kriner, *The Myth of the Imperial Presidency: How Public Opinion Checks the Unilateral Executive* (Chicago: University of Chicago Press, 2020), 210–12.

58. Thomas E. Cronin, "A Resurgent Congress and the Imperial Presidency," *Political Science Quarterly* 95 (1980): 209.

59. Arthur Schlesinger Jr., "So Much for the Imperial Presidency," *New York Times*, August 3, 1998.

60. Schlesinger, *War and the American Presidency*, 45–67; Andrew Rudalevige, *The New Imperial Presidency: Renewing Presidential Power after Watergate* (Ann Arbor: University of Michigan Press, 2005); Charlie Savage, *Takeover: The Return of the Imperial Presidency and the Subversion of American Democracy* (New York: Little, Brown, 2007).

61. Benjamin Ginsberg, *The Imperial Presidency and American Politics: Governance by Edicts and Coups* (New York: Routledge, 2022), 1–2; Gary J. Schmitt, Joseph M. Bessette, and Andrew E. Busch, eds., *The Imperial Presidency and the Constitution* (Lanham, MD: Rowman and Littlefield, 2017), 4.

62. Stephen Skowronek, *Presidential Leadership in Political Time: Reprise and Reappraisal*, 2nd ed. (Lawrence: University Press of Kansas, 2011), 156.

63. Skowronek, *Presidential Leadership in Political Time*, 155–61; Stephen Skowronek, "The Conservative Insurgency and Presidential Power: A Developmental Perspective on the Unitary Executive," *Harvard Law Review* 122 (2009): 2079–92; Richard H. Pildes, "Law and the President," *Harvard Law Review* 125 (2012): 1381–85.

64. Matthew Crenson and Benjamin Ginsberg, *Presidential Power: Unchecked and Unbalanced* (New York: W. W. Norton, 2007), 18.

65. Peter M. Shane, *Madison's Nightmare: How Executive Power Threatens American Democracy* (Chicago: University of Chicago Press, 2009), 25.

66. Bruce Ackerman, *The Decline and Fall of the American Republic* (Cambridge: Belknap Press of Harvard University Press, 2010), 188; Crenson and Ginsberg, *Presidential Power*, 367.

67. Dennis J. Hutchinson, "'The Achilles Heel' of the Constitution: Justice Jackson and the Japanese Exclusion Cases," *Supreme Court Review* (2002): 468.

68. Schlesinger, *Imperial Presidency*, ix, 127–207, 212.

69. Mariah Zeisberg, *War Powers: The Politics of Constitutional Authority* (Princeton: Princeton University Press, 2013); Stephen M. Griffin, *Long Wars and the Constitution* (Cambridge, MA: Harvard University Press, 2013); Louis Fisher, *Presidential War Power*, 3rd ed. (Lawrence: University Press of Kansas, 2013); John Yoo, *The Powers of War and Peace: The Constitution and Foreign Affairs after 9/11* (Chicago: University of Chicago Press, 2005); John Hart Ely, *War and Responsibility: Constitutional Lessons of Vietnam and Its Aftermath* (Princeton: Princeton University Press, 1993).

70. Samuel Walker, *Presidents and Civil Liberties from Wilson to Obama: A Story of Poor Custodians* (Cambridge: Cambridge University Press, 2012); Daniel Farber, ed., *Security v. Liberty: Conflicts between Civil Liberties and National Security in American History* (New York: Russell Sage Foundation, 2008). Compare Lee Epstein et al., "The Supreme Court during Crisis: How War Affects Only Non-War Cases," *New York University Law Review* 80 (2005): 1–116.

71. Gary D. Solis, *The Law of Armed Conflict: International Humanitarian Law in War*, 2nd ed. (Cambridge: Cambridge University Press, 2016), 23–25; Hilaire McCoubrey, *International Humanitarian Law: The Regulation of Armed Conflicts* (Aldershot, UK: Dartmouth, 1990), 1–2.

72. Leslie C. Green, *The Contemporary Law of Armed Conflict*, 2nd ed. (Manchester: Manchester University Press, 2000), 20–33.

73. Declaration Renouncing the Use, in Time of War, of Explosive Projectiles under 400 Grammes Weight, December 11, 1868, in *The Laws of Armed Conflicts: A Collection of Conventions, Resolutions and Other Documents*, 4th ed., ed. Dietrich Schindler and Jiri Toman (Leiden: Martinus Nijhoff, 2004), 92; Convention Respecting the Laws and Customs of War on Land, October 18, 1907, 36 Stat. 2277, T.S. No. 539.

74. William I. Hitchcock, "Human Rights and the Laws of War: The Geneva Conventions of 1949," in *The Human Rights Revolution: An International History*, ed. Akira Iriye, Petra Goedde, and William I. Hitchcock (New York: Oxford University Press, 2012), 93–112.

75. Agreement for the Prosecution and Punishment of the Major War Criminals of the European Axis and Charter of the International Military Tribunal, August 8, 1945, 59 Stat. 1544, 82 U.N.T.S. 279, art. 6; Charter of the International Military Tribunal for the Far East, January 19, 1946, amended April 26, 1946, T.I.A.S. No. 1589, 4 Bevans 20, art. 5; GC I, arts. 49, 50; GC II, arts. 50, 51; GC III, arts. 129, 130; GC IV, arts. 146, 147.

76. Statute of the International Criminal Tribunal for the Prosecution of Persons Responsible for Serious Violations of International Humanitarian Law Committed in the Territory of the Former Yugoslavia since 1991, U.N. Doc. S/RES/827 (1993), Annex, *as amended by* SC Res. 1800 (2008), reprinted in 32 I.L.M. 1159, arts. 2–5; Statute of the International Criminal Tribunal for Rwanda, U.N. Doc. S/RES/955 (1994), Annex, *as amended by* SC Res. 1534 (2004), reprinted in 33 I.L.M. 1602, arts. 2–4.

77. Rome Statute of the International Criminal Court, July 17, 1998, 2187 U.N.T.S. 90, arts. 5–8 (hereafter cited as Rome Statute); Kathryn Sikkink, *The Justice Cascade: How*

Human Rights Prosecutions Are Changing World Politics (New York: W. W. Norton, 2011), 114.

78. Steven R. Ratner, Jason S. Abrams, and James L. Bischoff, *Accountability for Human Rights Atrocities in International Law: Beyond the Nuremberg Legacy*, 3rd ed. (New York: Oxford University Press, 2009), 246–50, 350–53; Stephen Macedo, ed., *Universal Jurisdiction: National Courts and the Prosecution of Serious Crimes under International Law* (Philadelphia: University of Pennsylvania Press, 2004); Sikkink, *Justice Cascade*, 31–83.

79. Sikkink, *Justice Cascade*, 11, 96–125; Francesca Lessa and Leigh A. Payne, *Amnesty in the Age of Human Rights Accountability: Comparative and International Perspectives* (Cambridge: Cambridge University Press, 2012).

80. GC I-IV, art. 3; Bush Memorandum, in Greenberg and Dratel, *Torture Papers*, 134–35; GC I, art. 50; GC II, art. 51; GC III, art. 130; GC IV, art. 147; Convention Against Torture, art. 16; Jeremy Waldron, "Inhuman and Degrading Treatment: The Words Themselves," *Canadian Journal of Law and Jurisprudence* 23 (2010): 278.

81. Goldsmith, *Power and Constraint*, xi, 208. Goldsmith worked in the Bush administration, first as special counsel in the Defense Department and then as assistant attorney general in charge of the Justice Department's Office of Legal Counsel. In that last position he was responsible for the administration's legal positions on counterterrorism policies, including interrogation. While Goldsmith incurred the wrath of Bush insiders for withdrawing earlier Office of Legal Counsel opinions approving interrogation techniques, he explained that he did not reject the use of waterboarding at first because he did not then "affirmatively believe" that it violated the law. Goldsmith, *Terror Presidency*, 155–56.

82. Goldsmith, *Power and Constraint*, xi–xii; 38, 51–243.

Chapter 1

1. Carolyn Patty Blum, Lisa Magarrell, and Marieke Wierda, *Criminal Justice for Criminal Policy: Prosecuting Abuses of Detainees in U.S. Counterterrorism Operations* (New York: International Center for Transitional Justice, 2009), 17; Paul Krugman, "Reclaiming America's Soul," *New York Times*, April 24, 2009; Dahlia Lithwick, "Forgive Not," *New York Times*, January 11, 2009; Mark Heinrich, "Obama Reprieve for CIA Illegal: U.N. Rapporteur," *Reuters*, April 18, 2009; Convention Against Torture (CAT), art. 7; Kenneth Roth, "To Deter U.S. from Torturing Again, Those Involved Should Be Prosecuted," *Reuters* (blog), December 9, 2014; Center for Constitutional Rights, "Factsheet: Accountability and Prosecutions for Torture."

2. Richard A. Clarke, *Against All Enemies: Inside America's War on Terror* (New York: Free Press, 2004), 24; Mayer, *Dark Side*, 41–43.

3. Hague Regs., art. 22.

4. Josiah Ober, "Classical Greek Times," in *The Laws of War: Constraints on Warfare in the Western World*, ed. Michael Howard, George J. Andreopoulos, and Mark R. Shulman (New Haven: Yale University Press, 1994), 13.

5. Green, *Contemporary Law of Armed Conflict*, 21–22; Solis, *Law of Armed Conflict*, 4–5.

6. Thucydides, *History of the Peloponnesian War*, 4.97.11–12; Green, *Contemporary Law of Armed Conflict*, 21, 142.

7. Solis, *Law of Armed Conflict*, 457.

8. Green, *Contemporary Law of Armed Conflict*, 22–23.

9. Theodor Meron, *Bloody Constraint: War and Chivalry in Shakespeare* (New York: Oxford University Press, 1998), 11–15.

10. Maurice H. Keen, *The Laws of War in the Late Middle Ages* (London: Routledge and Kegan Paul, 1965), 23–44, 137–85, 247; Robert C. Stacey, "The Age of Chivalry," in Howard, Andreopoulos, and Shulman, *Laws of War*, 31–32; Maurice H. Keen, *Chivalry* (New Haven: Yale University Press, 1984), 249; G. D. Squibb, *The High Court of Chivalry: A Study of the Civil Law in England* (Oxford: Clarendon Press, 1959), 1–17, 166; Theodor Meron, *Henry's Wars and Shakespeare's Laws: Perspectives on the Law of War in the Later Middle Ages* (Oxford: Clarendon Press, 1993), 44.

11. Keen, *Laws of War*, 105, 121, 131, 190–91; Stacey, "Chivalry," 36, 38.

12. Geoffrey Parker, *The Thirty Years' War* (London: Routledge and Kegan Paul, 1984), 211; Hugo Grotius, *De Jure Belli ac Pacis*, trans. Francis W. Kelsey (Oxford: Clarendon Press, 1925), 20.

13. Gregory M. Reichberg, Henrik Syse, and Endre Begby, eds., *The Ethics of War: Classic and Contemporary Readings* (Malden, MA: Blackwell, 2006), 323–332, 371–77, 469–74, 504–17; G. I. A. D. Draper, "Grotius' Place in the Development of Legal Ideas about War," in *Hugo Grotius and International Relations*, ed. Hedley Bull, Benedict Kingsbury, and Adam Roberts (Oxford: Clarendon Press, 1992), 193–205; Stephen C. Neff, *War and the Law of Nations: A General History* (Cambridge: Cambridge University Press, 2005), 96–100.

14. Geoffrey Parker, "Early Modern Europe," in Howard, Andreopoulos, and Shulman, *Laws of War*, 45, 53–54; William H. McNeill, *The Pursuit of Power: Technology, Armed Force, and Society since A.D. 1000* (Chicago: University of Chicago Press, 1982), 140; Charles M. Clode, *Military Forces of the Crown: Their Administration and Government* (London, 1869), 1:445.

15. Vattel quoted in Gunther Rothenberg, "The Age of Napoleon," in Howard, Andreopoulos, and Shulman, *Laws of War*, 86; Gibbon quoted in Neff, *Law of Nations*, 89; *The Federalist* no. 8.

16. Parker, "Early Modern Europe," 53–55; McNeill, *Pursuit of Power*, 149, 159.

17. Quoted in Geoffrey Best, *Humanity in Warfare* (New York: Columbia University Press, 1980), 36.

18. Keen, *Laws of War*, 104; Stacey, "Chivalry," 28; Michael Howard, "Constraints on Warfare," in Howard, Andreopoulos, and Shulman, *Laws of War*, 3, 5.

19. US War Dept., General Order No. 100, *Instructions for the Government of Armies of the United States in the Field* (April 24, 1863) (hereafter cited as Lieber Code); Burrus M. Carnahan, "Lincoln, Lieber and the Laws of War: The Origins and Limits of the Principle of Military Necessity," *American Journal of International Law* 92 (1998): 214.

20. Frank Freidel, *Francis Lieber: Nineteenth-Century Liberal* (Gloucester, MA: Peter Smith, 1968), 11–17; John Fabian Witt, *Lincoln's Code: The Laws of War in American History* (New York: Free Press, 2012), 173–83; Francis Lieber, letter to the editor, *New York Times*, August 19, 1861.

21. Witt, *Lincoln's Code*, 196.

22. Witt, *Lincoln's Code*, 182; Lieber Code, art. 29.

23. Lieber Code, arts. 17, 19, 60.

24. Lieber Code, arts. 16, 22, 71, 76.

25. Lieber Code, art. 75.

26. Lieber Code, art. 16.

27. Lieber Code, art. 15.

28. Theodor Meron, *War Crimes Law Comes of Age: Essays* (Oxford: Clarendon Press, 1998), 135.

29. Convention for the Amelioration of the Condition of the Wounded for Armies in the Field, August 22, 1864, in Schindler and Toman, *Laws of Armed Conflicts*, 365–68; François Bugnion, "The International Committee of the Red Cross and the Development of International Humanitarian Law," *Chicago Journal of International Law* 5 (2004): 193; Best, *Humanity in Warfare*, 149–51; Solis, *Law of Armed Conflict*, 52.

30. The Geneva Convention of 1864, which had ten provisions, was expanded four years later, but no country signed the revised document. Green, *Contemporary Law of Armed Conflict*, 30.

31. Declaration Renouncing the Use, in Time of War, of Explosive Projectiles under 400 Grammes Weight, in Schindler and Toman, *Laws of Armed Conflicts*, 92.

32. Hague Regs., arts. 23, 25, 28.

33. Hague Regs., arts. 4–20.

34. Convention for the Amelioration of the Condition of the Wounded and Sick in Armies in the Field, July 6, 1906, arts. 1–5, in Schindler and Toman, *Laws of Armed Conflicts*, 387–88; Geneva Convention Relative to the Treatment of Prisoners of War, July 27, 1929, 118 L.N.T.S. 343, arts. 2, 5, 77–79.

35. Schindler and Toman, *Laws of Armed Conflicts*, 92.

36. Jean S. Pictet, "The New Geneva Conventions for the Protection of War Victims," *American Journal of International Law* 45 (1951): 464.

37. See Nina Tannenwald, "Assessing the Effects and Effectiveness of the Geneva Conventions," in *Do the Geneva Conventions Matter?*, ed. Matthew Evangelista and Nina Tannenwald (New York: Oxford University Press, 2017), 21–26.

38. Ratner, Abrams, and Bischoff, *Accountability*, 87.

39. GC I, art. 50; GC II, art. 51; GC III, art. 130; GC IV, 147.

40. GC I, art. 49; GC II, art. 50; GC III, art. 129; GC IV, art. 146. For offenses not identified as grave breaches, these articles require nations "to take measures necessary for the suppression of all acts contrary" to the conventions' provisions.

41. Best, *Humanity in Warfare*, 78, 125; Rothenberg, "Age of Napoleon," 86–97.

42. David Hackett Fischer, *Washington's Crossing* (New York: Oxford University Press, 2004), 377.

43. *Journals of the Continental Congress, 1774–1789*, ed. Worthington C. Ford et al. (Washington, DC, 1904–37): 7:277; John Ferling, *Almost a Miracle: The American Victory in the War of Independence* (New York: Oxford University Press, 2007), 428; Witt, *Lincoln's Code*, 21.

44. Washington to Lord Howe, January 13, 1777, in *The Papers of George Washington*, Revolutionary War Series (hereafter cited as *PGW*), ed. Dorothy Twohig, vol. 8, *January-*

March 1777, ed. Frank E. Grizzard Jr. (Charlottesville: University Press of Virginia, 1998), 58; Washington to General William Howe, January 13, 1777, *PGW*, 8:60; Washington to Gage, August 11, 1775, in *PGW*, ed. W. W. Abbot, vol. 1, *June-September 1775*, ed. Philander D. Chase (Charlottesville: University Press of Virginia, 1985), 289.

45. Washington to Gage, August 11, 1775, *PGW*, 1:290.

46. Instructions to Colonel Benedict Arnold, September 14, 1775, *PGW*, 1:458–59; Orders to Lieutenant Colonel Samuel Blachley Webb, January 8, 1777, *PGW*, 8:16.

47. Washington to Major General Adam Stephen, April 20, 1777, in *PGW*, ed. Dorothy Twohig, vol. 9, *March-June 1777*, ed. Philander D. Chase (Charlottesville: University Press of Virginia, 1999), 223.

48. Ferling, *Almost a Miracle*, 432–33; Witt, *Lincoln's Code*, 27.

49. Lieber Code, arts. 56, 75, 76.

50. Project of an International Declaration Concerning the Laws and Customs of War, art. 23, in Schindler and Toman, *Laws of Armed Conflicts*, 25; Hague Regs., art. 4; Geneva Convention Relative to the Treatment of Prisoners of War, July 27, 1929, 118 L.N.T.S. 343, art. 2.

51. Lieber Code, art. 59.

52. Stephanie Carvin, *Prisoners of America's Wars: From the Early Republic to Guantanamo* (New York: Columbia University Press, 2010), 90; Yuki Tanaka, *Hidden Horrors: Japanese War Crimes in World War II*, 2nd ed. (Lanham, MD: Rowman and Littlefield, 2018), 13.

53. Doris L. Bergen, *War and Genocide: A Concise History of the Holocaust* (Lanham, MD: Rowman and Littlefield, 2003), 157.

54. Solis, *Law of Armed Conflict*, 86.

55. Pictet, "New Geneva Conventions," 464–67.

56. *ICRC Commentary IV*, 1–2.

57. *ICRC Commentary I*, 20.

58. *ICRC Commentary I*, 21.

59. *ICRC Commentary I*, 21.

60. *ICRC Commentary I*, 22.

61. *ICRC Commentary I*, 23.

62. *ICRC Commentary I*, 21; GC I-IV, art. 3. See also David A. Elder, "The Historical Background of Common Article 3 of the Geneva Convention of 1949," *Case Western Reserve Journal of International Law* 11 (1979): 37–69.

63. *ICRC Commentary I*, 48, 52.

64. *ICRC Commentary I*, 23.

65. *ICRC Commentary I*, 21, 22, 23; *ICRC Commentary III*, 140; *ICRC Commentary IV*, 204.

66. *ICRC Commentary I*, 60. See also Protocol Additional (I) to the Geneva Conventions of August 12, 1949, and Relating to the Protection of Victims of International Armed Conflicts, June 8, 1977, 1125 U.N.T.S. 3, art. 75.

67. Georges S. Maridakis, "An Ancient Precedent to Nuremberg," *Journal of International Criminal Justice* 4 (2006): 847–52; Georg Schwarzenberger, "The Judgment of Nuremberg," *Tulane Law Review* 21 (1947): 330; M. Cherif Bassiouni, "Perspectives on International Criminal Justice," *Virginia Journal of International Law* 50 (2010): 297–98; Gregory S. Gordon, "The Trial of Peter von Hagenbach: Reconciling History, Historiog-

raphy and International Criminal Law," in *The Hidden Histories of War Crimes Trials*, ed. Kevin Jon Heller and Gerry Simpson (New York: Oxford University Press, 2013), 13–49.

68. Timothy L. H. McCormack, "From Sun Tzu to the Sixth Committee: The Evolution of an International Criminal Law Regime," in McCormack and Simpson, *Law of War Crimes*, 39; David M. Crowe, "War Crimes and Genocide in History, and the Evolution of Responsive International Law," *Nationalities Papers* 37 (2009): 761; Parker, "Early Modern Europe," 52.

69. McCormack, "International Criminal Law Regime," 38; Jordan J. Paust, "Selective History of International Tribunals and Efforts Prior to Nuremberg," *ILSA Journal of International and Comparative Law* 10 (2003): 207; Devin O. Pendas, "Orientation: War Crimes Trials in Theory and Practice from the Middle Ages to the Present," in *War Crimes Trials and Investigations: A Multi-Disciplinary Introduction*, ed. Jonathan Waterlow and Jacques Schuhmacher (Cham, Switzerland: Palgrave Macmillan, 2018), 29–38; Hilaire McCoubrey, "The Concept and Treatment of War Crimes," *Journal of Armed Conflict Law* 1 (1996): 123.

70. Daniel Marc Segesser, "'Unlawful Warfare Is Uncivilised': The International Debate on the Punishment of War Crimes, 1872–1918," *European Review of History* 14 (2007): 224 n.2.

71. William Blackstone, *Commentaries on the Laws of England* (New York: Oxford University Press, 2016), 4:68; Emmerich de Vattell, *The Law of Nations, or, Principles of the Law of Nature, Applied to the Conduct and Affairs of Nations and Sovereigns* (Philadelphia, 1817), 354.

72. Witt, *Lincoln's Code*, 128–29.

73. Witt, *Lincoln's Code*, 126; Erika Myers, "Conquering Peace: Military Commissions as a Lawfare Strategy in the Mexican War," *American Journal of Criminal Law* 35 (2008): 228–36; Carol Chomsky, "The United States–Dakota War Trials: A Study in Military Injustice," *Stanford Law Review* 43 (1990): 65.

74. David Glazier, "Precedents Lost: The Neglected History of the Military Commission," *Virginia Journal of International Law* 46 (2005): 31–56; Detlev F. Vagts, "Military Commissions: The Forgotten Reconstruction Chapter," *American University International Law Review* 23 (2008): 231–74.

75. Witt, *Lincoln's Code*, 268–69, 331.

76. Segesser, "'Unlawful Warfare,'" 216, 223. Although Lieber's code declared soldiers liable for "crimes punishable by all penal codes" such as arson and murder, his intent, judging by the reference to domestic criminal laws, was to clarify that combatant status did not confer immunity from ordinary crimes. Lieber Code, art. 47.

77. Christopher Keith Hall, "The First Proposal for a Permanent International Criminal Court," *International Review of the Red Cross* 38 (1998): 58.

78. Segesser, "'Unlawful Warfare,'" 224 n.2; Alan Kramer, "The First Wave of International War Crimes Trials: Istanbul and Leipzig," *European Review* 14 (2006): 447; Hall, "First Proposal," 59; Green, *Contemporary Law of Armed Conflict*, 289; George Manner, "The Legal Nature and Punishment of Criminal Acts of Violence Contrary to the Laws of War," *American Journal of International Law* 37 (1943): 410.

79. James F. Willis, *Prologue to Nuremberg: The Politics and Diplomacy of Punishing War Criminals of the First World War* (Westport, CT: Greenwood, 1982), 6–22, 27–28.

80. Willis, *Prologue to Nuremberg*, 68, 177.

81. Willis, *Prologue to Nuremberg*, 113–25.

82. Willis, *Prologue to Nuremberg*, 128; Gary Jonathan Bass, *Stay the Hand of Vengeance: The Politics of War Crimes Tribunals* (Princeton: Princeton University Press, 2000), 78; Howard Ball, *Prosecuting War Crimes and Genocide: The Twentieth-Century Experience* (Lawrence: University Press of Kansas, 1999), 23–24; M. Cherif Bassiouni, "World War I: 'The War to End All Wars' and the Birth of a Handicapped International Criminal Justice System," *Denver Journal of International Law and Policy* 30 (2002): 281–82.

83. Willis, *Prologue to Nuremberg*, 137–39; Kramer, "First Wave," 448; Vahakn N. Dadrian, *The History of the Armenian Genocide: Ethnic Conflict from the Balkans to Anatolia to the Caucasus* (Providence, RI: Berghahn, 1995), 392.

84. Willis *Prologue to Nuremberg*, 139.

85. Willis *Prologue to Nuremberg*, 98–112.

86. Jennifer Balint, "The Ottoman State Special Military Tribunal for the Genocide of the Armenians: 'Doing Government Business,'" in Heller and Simpson, *Hidden Histories*, 80–100; Bass, *Hand of Vengeance*, 106–46.

87. Convention Respecting the Laws and Customs of War on Land, October 18, 1907, 36 Stat. 2277, T.S. No. 539, art. 3.

88. Convention for the Amelioration of the Condition of the Wounded and Sick in Armies in the Field, July 6, 1906, art. 27, in Schindler and Toman, *Laws of Armed Conflicts*, 390; Geneva Convention for the Amelioration of the Condition of the Wounded and Sick in Armies in the Field, July 27, 1929, arts. 29, 30, in Schindler and Toman, *Laws of Armed Conflicts*, 416; Willis, *Prologue to Nuremberg*, 173.

89. Telford Taylor, *The Anatomy of the Nuremberg Trials: A Personal Memoir* (New York: Skyhorse, 2013), 24–25. Interestingly, this prompted one contemporary scholar to say that it was "axiomatic in the law of war" that "individuals are not subjects of the law of nations." Manner, "Legal Nature and Punishment of Criminal Acts," 407.

90. The Moscow Declaration, in Bradley F. Smith, ed., *The American Road to Nuremberg: The Documentary Record, 1944–1945* (Stanford: Hoover Institution Press, 1982), 13–14; Taylor, *Nuremberg Trials*, 26–29; Bass, *Hand of Vengeance*, 149–50.

91. Ball, *Prosecuting War Crimes*, 45; Taylor, *Nuremberg Trials*, 32; Smith, *American Road to Nuremberg*, 28; Bass, *Hand of Vengeance*, 153, 165, 195–99.

92. Taylor, *Nuremberg Trials*, 56–77.

93. Taylor, *Nuremberg Trials*, 165–570; Ball, *Prosecuting War Crimes*, 50–60.

94. Kevin Jon Heller, *The Nuremberg Military Tribunals and the Origins of International Criminal Law* (New York: Oxford University Press, 2011), 12, 43–105; Kim C. Priemel and Alexa Stiller, eds., *Reassessing the Nuremberg Military Tribunals: Transitional Justice, Trial Narratives, and Historiography* (New York: Berghahn, 2012).

95. Ball, *Prosecuting War Crimes*, 56–57; Matthew Lippmann, "Prosecutions of Nazi War Criminals before Post–World War II Domestic Tribunals," *University of Miami International and Comparative Law Review* 8 (1999–2000): 1–113; Axel Marschik, "The Politics of Prosecution: European National Approaches to War Crimes," in McCormack and Simpson, *Law of War Crimes*, 74; Rebecca Wittmann, "Tainted Law: The West German Judiciary and the Prosecution of Nazi War Criminals," in *Atrocities on Trial: Historical Perspectives on the Politics of Prosecuting War Crimes*, ed. Patricia Heberer and Jürgen

Matthäus (Lincoln: University of Nebraska Press, 2008), 211–29; Fritz Weinschenk, "Nazis before German Courts: The West German War Crimes Trials," *International Lawyer* 10 (1976): 515–29.

96. Madoka Futamura, *War Crimes Tribunals and Transitional Justice: The Tokyo Trial and the Nuremberg Legacy* (New York: Routledge, 2008), 52–67; Roger S. Clark, "Nuremberg and Tokyo in Contemporary Perspective," in McCormack and Simpson, *Law of War Crimes*, 184.

97. Christopher Rudolph, *Power and Principle: The Politics of International Criminal Courts* (Ithaca: Cornell University Press, 2017), 35–39.

98. See Martha Minow, *Between Vengeance and Forgiveness: Facing History after Genocide and Mass Violence* (Boston: Beacon Press, 1998), 29–47.

99. *Trial of the Major War Criminals before the International Military Tribunal, Nuremberg, November 14, 1945–October 1, 1946* (Nuremberg, 1947), 1:169.

100. Bass, *Hand of Vengeance*, 15–16; Richard Falk, "War, War Crimes, Power, and Justice: Toward a Jurisprudence of Conscience," *Transnational Law and Contemporary Problems* 21 (2013): 669–77.

101. Bass, *Hand of Vengeance*, 200–2; Elizabeth Borgwardt, "Re-examining Nuremberg as a New Deal Institution: Politics, Culture and the Limits of Law in Generating Human Rights Norms," *Berkeley Journal of International Law* 23 (2005): 442.

102. Allison Marston Danner, "Beyond the Geneva Conventions: Lessons from the Tokyo Tribunal in Prosecuting War and Terrorism," *Virginia Journal of International Law* 46 (2005): 92–94; Jonathan A. Bush, "Nuremberg: The Modern Law of War and Its Limitations," *Columbia Law Review* 93 (1993): 2082; Alpheus Thomas Mason, "Extra-Judicial Work for Judges: The Views of Chief Justice Stone," *Harvard Law Review* 67 (1953): 212.

103. Allan A. Ryan, "Nuremberg's Contributions to International Law," *Boston College International and Comparative Law Review* 30 (2007): 55; Richard Falk, "Accountability for War Crimes and the Legacy of Nuremberg," in *War Crimes and Collective Wrongdoing: A Reader*, ed. Aleksandar Jokić (Malden, MA: Blackwell, 2001), 120–21.

104. *Principles of International Law Recognized in the Charter of the International Military Tribunal and in the Judgment of the Tribunal*, U.N. GAOR, 5th Sess., Supp. No. 12, at 11, U.N. Doc. A/1316 (1950); *Trial of the Major War Criminals*, 22:466; Charter of the International Military Tribunal, art. 7, August 8, 1945, 59 Stat. 1544, 1548, 82 U.N.T.S. 279, 288; Resolution Affirming the Principles of International Law Recognized by the Charter of the Nuremberg Tribunal, G.A. Res. 95(I), U.N. GAOR, 1st Sess., pt. 2, U. N. Doc. A/64/Add. 1 (1946).

105. See, e.g., Geoffrey S. Corn, "What Law Applies to the War on Terror?" in Lewis, *War on Terror*, 9–10; Derek Jinks, "The Applicability of the Geneva Conventions to the 'Global War on Terrorism,'" *Virginia Journal of International Law* 46 (2005): 165–95.

106. Exec. Order No. 13,440, 72 Fed. Reg. 40707, 40707 (July 24, 2007); *Weekly Comp. Pres. Doc.*, September 6, 2006, 42:1570, 1573.

107. *Weekly Comp. Pres. Doc.*, June 28, 2005, 41:1079; Mary Ellen O'Connell, "The Legal Case against the Global War on Terror," *Case Western Reserve Journal of International Law* 36 (2004): 349–57; ICRC, *International Humanitarian Law and the Challenges of Contemporary Armed Conflicts* (2011), 10.

108. See, e.g., Derek Jinks, "International Human Rights Law and the War on Terrorism,"

Denver Journal of International Law and Policy 31 (2002): 58–68; Jordan J. Paust, "Human Rights on the Battlefield," *George Washington International Law Review* 47 (2015): 509–61; Cordula Droege, "Elective Affinities? Human Rights and Humanitarian Law," *International Review of the Red Cross* 90 (2008): 501–48.

109. Allison Marston Danner, "Defining Unlawful Enemy Combatants: A Centripetal Story," *Texas International Law Journal* 43 (2007): 9; George P. Fletcher and Jens David Ohlin, *Defending Humanity: When Force Is Justified and Why* (New York: Oxford University Press, 2008), 183; Jordan J. Paust, "War and Enemy Status after 9/11: Attacks on the Laws of War," *Yale Journal of International Law* 28 (2003): 332.

110. *ICRC Commentary* I, 48; Solis, *Law of Armed Conflict*, 105.

111. Jean-Marie Henckaerts, "Study on Customary International Humanitarian Law: A Contribution to the Understanding and Respect for the Rule of Law in Armed Conflict," *International Review of the Red Cross* 87 (2005): 187; Theodor Meron, "The Geneva Conventions as Customary Law," *American Journal of International Law* 81 (1987): 348–70.

112. Solis, *Law of Armed Conflict*, 161–62, 165–68.

113. Compare Helen Duffy, *The 'War on Terror' and the Framework of International Law* (Cambridge: Cambridge University Press, 2005), 256, with Solis, *Law of Armed Conflict*, 227.

114. Solis, *Law of Armed Conflict*, 227.

115. Solis, *Law of Armed Conflict*, 165; Duffy, *'War on Terror,'* 258–59.

116. 548 U.S. 557 (2006).

117. Ingrid Detter, "The Law of War and Illegal Combatants," *George Washington Law Review* 75 (2007): 1082; David Glazier, "Full and Fair by What Measure? Identifying the International Law Regulating Military Commission Procedure," *Boston University International Law Journal* 24 (2006): 58, 93–94; David Glazier, "Law of War Developments Issue Introduction," *Loyola of Los Angeles Law Review* 48 (2015): 820; Scott L. Glabe, "Conflict Classification and Detainee Treatment in the War against al Qaeda," *Army Lawyer* (June 2010): 114–15; Allen S. Weiner, "*Hamdan,* Terror, War," *Lewis and Clark Law Review* 11 (2007): 1010–12.

118. ICRC Commentary I, 39; Anthony Cullen, *The Concept of Non-International Armed Conflict in International Humanitarian Law* (Cambridge: Cambridge University Press, 2010), 49.

119. 548 U.S. at 630–31; see Jinks, "Applicability of the Geneva Conventions," 182–89.

120. *Weekly Comp. Pres. Doc.,* September 12, 2001, 37:1302; September 20, 2001, 37:1347; Military Order of November 13, 2001, 66 Fed. Reg. 57833 (November 16, 2001).

121. *Weekly Comp. Pres. Doc.,* September 6, 2006, 42:1570, 1573.

122. Memorandum from Patrick F. Philbin, Deputy Assistant Attorney General, OLC, DOJ, to Alberto R. Gonzales, Counsel to the President, "Legality of the Use of Military Commissions to Try Terrorists," November 6, 2001, 20; William H. Taft IV, "The Law of Armed Conflict after 9/11: Some Salient Features," *Yale Journal of International Law* 28 (2003): 320. The UN Security Council construed the September 11 attacks as armed attacks justifying a response under Article 51 of the UN Charter, and Congress adopted an authorization to use military force in response to the attacks. S.C. Res. 1368, U.N. Doc. S/RES/1368 (September 12, 2001); Authorization for Use of Military Force, Pub. L. No.

107–40, 115 Stat. 224 (2001); United States' Oral Response to the Questions Asked by the Committee Against Torture (May 8, 2006), https://www.state.gov/j/drl/rls/68562.htm

123. Protocol Additional to the Geneva Conventions of 12 August 1949 and Relating to the Protection of Victims of International Armed Conflicts, June 8, 1977, 1125 U.N.T.S. 3, art. 75.

124. Taft, "Law of Armed Conflict," 321–22.

125. GC I, art. 50; GC II, art. 51; GC III, art. 130; GC IV, art. 147; Dieter Fleck, "Shortcomings of the Grave Breaches Regime," *Journal of International Criminal Justice* 7 (2009): 835.

126. Prosecutor v. Tadic, IT-94-1-A, Decision on the Defence Motion for Interlocutory Appeal on Jurisdiction, October 2, 1995, ¶ 134; Solis, *Law of Armed Conflict*, 106–7.

127. Jean-Marie Henckaerts, "The Grave Breaches Regime as Customary International Law," *Journal of International Criminal Justice* 7 (2009): 689–91; Jordan J. Paust, *Beyond the Law: The Bush Administration's Unlawful Responses in the "War" on Terror* (Cambridge: Cambridge University Press, 2007), 20–23.

128. Pub. L. No. 104-192, 110 Stat. 2104 (1996) (codified as amended at 18 U.S.C. § 2441).

129. GC I, art. 49; GC II, art. 50; GC III, art. 129; GC IV, art. 146; S. Exec. Rep. No. 84-9, at 27 (1955).

130. H.R. Rep. No. 104-698, at 4–7, 9 (1996).

131. 18 U.S.C. § 2441(c)(3) (as it was codified from 1997 to 2006).

132. Hamdan v. Rumsfeld, 548 U.S. at 642 (Kennedy, J., concurring in part); Uniform Code of Military Justice, 10 U.S.C. §§ 801–946.

133. 18 U.S.C. § 2441(a). It has been noted that "some forms of cruel treatment and humiliating and degrading treatment may not deserve to be considered a war crime." Dick Jackson, Eric T. Jensen, and Robert Matsuishi, "The Law of War after the DTA, *Hamdan*, and the MCA," *Army Lawyer* (September 2007): 24.

Chapter 2

1. All quotations in this introductory section are from the Bush Memorandum, in Greenberg and Dratel, *Torture Papers*, 134–35.

2. *Final Report of the Independent Panel to Review DoD Detention Operations* (2004), 80.

3. Alberto R. Gonzales, "Waging War within the Constitution," *Texas Tech Law Review* 42 (2010): 848–49; SSCI Report, 179–80.

4. Richard P. DiMeglio, "Training Army Judge Advocates to Advise Commanders as Operational Law Attorneys," *Boston College International and Comparative Law Review* 54 (2013): 1185–1206. For backstory, see Savage, *Takeover*, 282–89.

5. Goldsmith, *Terror Presidency*, 167; Mayer, *Dark Side*, 265; SSCI Report, Findings and Conclusions, 7.

6. Philippe Sands, *Torture Team: Rumsfeld's Memo and the Betrayal of American Values* (New York: Palgrave Macmillan, 2008), 2–6, 30–34, 56–71, 181.

7. 28 U.S.C. §§ 511–13; 28 C.F.R. § 0.25 (a).

8. Memorandum, "Legal and Practical Consequences of a Blockade of Cuba," Octo-

ber 19, 1962; Harold H. Bruff, *Bad Advice: Bush's Lawyers in the War on Terror* (Lawrence: University Press of Kansas, 2009), 67–71; Goldsmith, *Terror Presidency*, 37–38; Trevor W. Morrison, "Stare Decisis in the Office of Legal Counsel," *Columbia Law Review* 110 (2010): 1448–1525; Cornelia T. L. Pillard, "The Unfulfilled Promise of the Constitution in Executive Hands," *Michigan Law Review* 103 (2005): 710–17.

9. Goldsmith, *Terror Presidency*, 170.

10. Dawn E. Johnsen, "Faithfully Executing the Laws: Internal Legal Constraints on Executive Power," *UCLA Law Review* 54 (2007): 1577.

11. John C. Yoo, "The Continuation of Politics by Other Means: The Original Understanding of War Powers," *California Law Review* 84 (1996): 167–305.

12. Bruff, *Bad Advice*, 122; Tim Golden, "A Junior Aide Had a Big Role in Terror Policy," *New York Times*, December 23, 2005.

13. Bruff, *Bad Advice*, 122.

14. Mayer, *Dark Side*, 66, 80, 150; Bruff, *Bad Advice*, 124–26.

15. Goldsmith, *Terror Presidency*, 24.

16. Scott Shane, David Johnston, and James Risen, "Secret U.S. Endorsement of Severe Interrogations," *New York Times*, October 4, 2007; Goldsmith, *Terror Presidency*, 170.

17. Savage, *Takeover*, 135; Memorandum from Patrick F. Philbin, Deputy Assistant Attorney General, OLC, DOJ, to Alberto R. Gonzales, Counsel to the President, "Legality of the Use of Military Commissions to Try Terrorists," November 6, 2001, 1.

18. Mayer, *Dark Side*, 82.

19. Savage, *Takeover*, 137–38.

20. John C. Yoo, Deputy Assistant Attorney General, OLC, DOJ, to Timothy Flanigan, Deputy Counsel to the President, "The President's Constitutional Authority to Conduct Military Operations against Terrorists and Nations Supporting Them," September 25, 2001, in Greenberg and Dratel, *Torture Papers*, 3 (hereafter cited as OLC 9/25/01 Opinion); Savage, *Takeover*, 350 n.9.

21. OLC 9/25/01 Opinion, in Greenberg and Dratel, *Torture Papers*, 5, 20, 21, 24.

22. OLC 9/25/01 Opinion, in Greenberg and Dratel, *Torture Papers*, 24; DOJ, Office of Professional Responsibility, *Investigation into the Office of Legal Counsel's Memoranda . . .* (Washington, DC, 2009), 64.

23. OLC 9/25/01 Opinion, in Greenberg and Dratel, *Torture Papers*, 5, 20–21, 23.

24. OLC 9/25/01 Opinion, in Greenberg and Dratel, *Torture Papers*, 7.

25. The constitutional rationale for the unitary executive is based on refashioning—beyond recognition some would say—Alexander Hamilton's arguments in *The Federalist*. Those in favor of the doctrine like to claim Hamilton as one of their own as he had extolled the virtues of "unity" in the presidency. He said a single chief executive could act with "decision, activity, secrecy, and dispatch"—an expression so often cited by unitary executive proponents that it has become formulaic. All the more important in wartime, Hamilton explained, when energy in the executive is "essential." Yet Hamilton offered his arguments in favor of "unity" in the executive in comparison with the rejected alternative of a multimember council—a "plurality in the executive." *The Federalist* no. 70. What he would make of the unitary executive doctrine as it has been applied in recent years remains a point in contention. Mark J. Rozell and Jeffrey P. Crouch, *The Unitary Executive Theory: A Danger to Constitutional Government* (Lawrence: University Press of Kansas, 2021), 26–27.

26. Steven G. Calabresi and Christopher S. Yoo, *The Unitary Executive: Presidential Power from Washington to Bush* (New Haven: Yale University Press, 2008), 3–21; Ryan J. Barilleaux and Christopher S. Kelley, "What Is the Unitary Executive?," in *The Unitary Executive and the Modern Presidency*, ed. Ryan J. Barilleaux and Christopher S. Kelley (College Station: Texas A&M University Press, 2010), 1–14; Stephen G. Calabresi and Kevin H. Rhodes, "The Structural Constitution: Unitary Executive, Plural Judiciary," *Harvard Law Review* 106 (1992): 1153–1216.

27. Peter M. Shane, *Democracy's Chief Executive: Interpreting the Constitution and Defining the Future of the Presidency* (Oakland: University of California Press, 2022), 3–31; Robert J. Spitzer, "Is the Constitutional Presidency Obsolete?," in *The Presidency in the Twenty-First Century*, ed. Charles W. Dunn (Lexington: University Press of Kentucky, 2011), 64–69.

28. L. Gordon Crovitz and Jeremy A. Rabkin, eds., *The Fettered Presidency: Legal Constraints on the Executive Branch* (Washington, DC: American Enterprise Institute for Public Policy Research, 1989).

29. Barton Gelman, *Angler: The Cheney Vice Presidency* (New York: Penguin, 2008), 96–99.

30. Dana Milbank, "In Cheney's Shadow, Counsel Pushes the Conservative Cause," *Washington Post*, October 11, 2004; Marvin Stone, "Presidency: Imperial or Imperiled?," *U.S. News & World Report*, January 15, 1979, 88; Julian E. Zelizer, "The Conservative Embrace of Presidential Power," *Boston University Law Review* 88 (2008): 501.

31. Dana Milbank, "In Cheney's Shadow, Counsel Pushes the Conservative Cause," *Washington Post*, October 11, 2004; Savage, *Takeover*, 236.

32. *Weekly Comp. Pres. Doc.*, March 9, 2006, 42:425.

33. Christopher S. Kelley and Brian W. Marshall, "Assessing Presidential Power: Signing Statements and Veto Threats as Coordinated Strategies," *American Politics Research* 37 (2009): 512–15; Ian Ostrander and Joel Sievert, "What's So Sinister about Presidential Signing Statements?," *Presidential Studies Quarterly* 43 (2013): 58–80.

34. Shane, *Madison's Nightmare*, 133; Walter Dellinger, "A Slip of the Pen," *New York Times*, July 31, 2006.

35. Calabresi and Yoo, *Unitary Executive*, 387; Savage, *Takeover*, 231–37; Philip J. Cooper, *By Order of the President: The Use and Abuse of Executive Direct Action* (Lawrence: University Press of Kansas, 2014), 326–44; Shane, *Madison's Nightmare*, 135; Curtis A. Bradley and Eric A. Posner, "Presidential Signing Statements and Executive Power," *Constitutional Commentary* 23 (2006): 323.

36. Kelley and Marshall, "Assessing Presidential Power," 521; Philip J. Cooper, "George W. Bush, Edgar Allan Poe, and the Use and Abuse of Presidential Signing Statements," *Presidential Studies Quarterly* 35 (2005): 521; Charlie Savage, "Obama Looks to Limit Impact of Tactic Bush Used to Sidestep New Laws," *New York Times*, March 9, 2009; *Weekly Comp. Pres. Doc.*, December 8, 2004, 40:2924; Charlie Savage, "Bush Challenges Hundreds of Laws," *Boston Globe*, April 30, 2006. See Neil Kinkopf and Peter M. Shane, "Signed under Protest: A Database of Presidential Signing Statements, 2001–2009," last modified October 2009, https://www.researchgate.net/publication/228187707_Signed_Under_Protest_A_D atabase_of_Presidential_Signing_Statements_2001-2009

37. Savage, *Takeover*, 237–38; *Weekly Comp. Pres. Doc.*, October 28, 2004, 40:2673.

38. S. Amdt. 1977, 109th Cong., 1st Sess. (2005); Eric Schmitt, "Senate Moves to Protect Military Prisoners despite Veto Threat," *New York Times*, October 6, 2005; *Weekly Comp. Pres. Doc.*, December 15, 2005, 41:1866; Josh White, "President Relents, Backs Torture Ban," *Washington Post*, December 16, 2005; Eric Schmitt, "President Backs McCain Measure on Inmate Abuse," *New York Times*, December 16, 2005; *Weekly Comp. Pres. Doc.*, December 30, 2005, 41:1919; Charlie Savage, "Bush Could Bypass New Torture Ban," *Boston Globe*, January 4, 2006; Savage, *Takeover*, 220–26.

39. Keith E. Whittington, "Much Ado about Nothing: Signing Statements, Vetoes, and Presidential Constitutional Interpretation," *William and Mary Law Review* 58 (2017): 1753; Goldsmith, *Power and Constraint*, 120.

40. Savage, *Takeover*, 124–27.

41. OLC 9/25/01 Opinion, in Greenberg and Dratel, *Torture Papers*, 5.

42. U.S. Const. art. II, § 2, cl. 1.

43. U.S. Const., art. I, § 8, cl. 10–16.

44. See David J. Barron and Martin S. Lederman, "The Commander in Chief at the Lowest Ebb—Framing the Problem, Doctrine, and Original Understanding," *Harvard Law Review* 121 (2008): 698–701.

45. Ex parte Milligan, 71 U.S. 2, 139 (1866) (Chase, C.J., concurring in the judgment); Hamdan v. Rumsfeld, 548 U.S. 557, 591–92 (2006); Youngstown Sheet & Tube Co. v. Sawyer, 343 U.S. 579, 645 (1952) (Jackson, J., concurring).

46. Ely, *War and Responsibility*, 25; Michael D. Ramsey, *The Constitution's Text in Foreign Affairs* (Cambridge, MA: Harvard University Press, 2007), 254; Michael J. Glennon, *Constitutional Diplomacy* (Princeton: Princeton University Press, 1990), 84; Philip Bobbitt, "War Powers: An Essay on John Hart Ely's *War and Responsibility: Constitutional Lessons of Vietnam and Its Aftermath*," *Michigan Law Review* 92 (1994): 1389.

47. *The Federalist* no. 74; Barron and Lederman, "Framing the Problem," 755, 760; Jules Lobel, "Conflicts between the Commander in Chief and Congress: Concurrent Power over the Conduct of War," *Ohio State Law Journal* 69 (2008): 394.

48. David Luban, "On the Commander in Chief Power," *University of Southern California Law Review* 81 (2008): 478–82.

49. Draft Memorandum from John Yoo, Deputy Assistant Attorney General, and Robert J. Delahunty, Special Counsel, OLC, DOJ, to William J. Haynes II, General Counsel, DOD, "Application of Treaties and Laws to al Qaeda and Taliban Detainees," January 9, 2002, in Greenberg and Dratel, *Torture Papers*, 75 (hereafter cited as OLC 1/9/02 Draft Memorandum); Memorandum from Jay S. Bybee, Assistant Attorney General, OLC, to Alberto R. Gonzales, Counsel to the President, "Standards of Conduct for Interrogation under 28 U.S.C. §§ 2340–2340A," August 1, 2002, in Greenberg and Dratel, *Torture Papers*, 206 (hereafter cited as OLC 8/1/02 Interrogation Standards Opinion).

50. OLC 8/1/02 Interrogation Standards Opinion, in Greenberg and Dratel, *Torture Papers*, 202.

51. OLC 8/1/02 Interrogation Standards Opinion, in Greenberg and Dratel, *Torture Papers*, 207.

52. OLC 8/1/02 Interrogation Standards Opinion, in Greenberg and Dratel, *Torture Papers*, 203, 207.

53. OLC 8/1/02 Interrogation Standards Opinion, in Greenberg and Dratel, *Torture Papers*, 173.

54. Memorandum from Daniel Levin, Acting Assistant Attorney General, OLC, DOJ, to James B. Comey, Deputy Attorney General, DOJ, "Legal Standards Applicable under 18 U.S.C. §§ 2340–2340A," December 30, 2004, 2 (hereafter cited as OLC 12/30/04 Opinion); Barron and Lederman, "Framing the Problem," 711; Luban, "Commander in Chief Power," 479.

55. DOJ, "Legal Authorities Supporting the Activities of the National Security Agency Described by the President" (Washington, DC, 2006), 28, 29; Stephen I. Vladek, "Congress, the Commander-in-Chief, and the Separation of Powers after *Hamdan*," *Transnational Law and Contemporary Problems* 16 (2007): 952–55.

56. Memorandum from Jay S. Bybee, Assistant Attorney General, OLC, DOJ, to Alberto R. Gonzales, Counsel to the President, and William J. Haynes II, General Counsel, DOD, "Application of Treaties and Laws to al Qaeda and Taliban Detainees," January 22, 2002, in Greenberg and Dratel, *Torture Papers*, 91 (hereafter cited as OLC 1/22/02 Memorandum); OLC 1/09/02 Draft Memorandum, in Greenberg and Dratel, *Torture Papers*, 75, 78.

57. OLC 8/1/02 Interrogation Standards Opinion, in Greenberg and Dratel, *Torture Papers*, 204; OLC 1/09/02 Draft Memorandum, in Greenberg and Dratel, *Torture Papers*, 78; Memorandum from John Yoo, Deputy Assistant Attorney General, OLC, DOJ, to William J. Haynes II, General Counsel, DOD, "Military Interrogation of Alien Unlawful Combatants Held outside the United States," March 14, 2003, 18; DOD, "Working Group Report on Detainee Interrogations in the Global War on Terrorism: Assessment of Legal, Historical, Policy, and Operational Considerations," April 4, 2003, in Greenberg and Dratel, *Torture Papers*, 330.

58. David J. Barron and Martin S. Lederman, "The Commander in Chief at the Lowest Ebb—a Constitutional History," *Harvard Law Review* 121 (2008): 947.

59. Barron and Lederman, "Framing the Problem," 697.

60. Barron and Lederman, "Constitutional History," 1056–99.

61. Barron and Lederman, "Constitutional History," 1099.

62. Barron and Lederman, "Framing the Problem," 769.

63. Luban, "Commander in Chief Power," 491–99, 565.

64. Luban, "Commander in Chief Power," 505–7.

65. Luban, "Commander in Chief Power," 484. See also Lobel, "Concurrent Power over the Conduct of War," 391–467.

66. Barron and Lederman, "Framing the Problem," 750–59; Ramsey, *Constitution's Text in Foreign Affairs*, 254.

67. Lobel, "Concurrent Power over the Conduct of War," 402–9, 411–12, 427; Barron and Lederman, "Framing the Problem," 754, 757–59.

68. Barron and Lederman, "Constitutional History," 1018; Milligan, 71 U.S. at 115–31; 71 U.S. at 136 (Chase, C.J., concurring in the judgment).

69. 71 U.S. at 139 (Chase, C.J., concurring in the judgment).

70. 71 U.S. at 140 (Chase, C.J., concurring in the judgment).

71. Memorandum from John C. Yoo, Deputy Assistant Attorney General, and Robert

J. Delahunty, Special Counsel, OLC, DOJ, to Alberto R. Gonzales, Counsel to the President, "Treaties and Laws Applicable to the Conflict in Afghanistan and to the Treatment of Persons Captured by U.S. Armed Forces in That Conflict," November 30, 2001, 1 (hereafter cited as OLC 11/30/01 Opinion).

72. OLC 1/9/02 Draft Memorandum, in Greenberg and Dratel, *Torture Papers*, 38–79.

73. OLC 11/30/01 *Opinion*, 1 (italics added); SSCI Report, 179; SASC 2008 Report, 3–4.

74. OLC 1/22/02 Opinion, in Greenberg and Dratel, *Torture Papers*, 90–91; DOD, Directive 5100.77, "DOD Law of War Program," December 9, 1998, ¶ 5.3.1.

75. David D. Caron, "If Afghanistan Has Failed, Then Afghanistan Is Dead: 'Failed States' and the Inappropriate Substitution of Legal Conclusion for Political Description," in *The Torture Debate in America*, ed. Karen J. Greenberg (Cambridge: Cambridge University Press, 2006), 216–17.

76. John Yoo, *War by Other Means: An Insider's Account of the War on Terror* (New York: Atlantic Monthly Press, 2006), 28.

77. OLC 11/30/01 Opinion, 12, 19.

78. OLC 11/30/01 Opinion, 20.

79. OLC 11/30/01 Opinion, 21, 26.

80. OLC 11/30/01 Opinion, 29.

81. OLC 11/30/01 Opinion, 31, 33, 35.

82. OLC 11/30/01 Opinion, 32.

83. Dept. of the Army, *Field Manual 27–10, The Law of Land Warfare* (1956), ¶ 7(c).

84. OLC 11/30/01 Opinion, 40.

85. OLC 11/30/01 Opinion, 36.

86. Memorandum from William H. Taft, IV, Legal Adviser, Department of State, to John C. Yoo, Deputy Assistant Attorney General, OLC, DOJ, "Your Draft Memorandum of January 9," January 11, 2002.

87. Department of State, "Draft Memorandum," January 11, 2002, 2, 3.

88. R. Jeffrey Smith and Dan Eggen, "Gonzales Helped Set the Course for Detainees," January 5, 2005, *Washington Post*, January 5, 2005; Mayer, *Dark Side*, 123–25; Bob Woodward, *State of Denial* (New York: Simon and Schuster, 2006), 86.

89. Office of Professional Responsibility, *Investigation*, 37, 47; OLC 11/30/01 Opinion, 3 n.4, 42, 43.

90. Gonzales 1/25/02 Memorandum, in Greenberg and Dratel, *Torture Papers*, 118; R. Jeffrey Smith and Dan Eggen, "Gonzales Helped Set the Course for Detainees," *Washington Post*, January 5, 2005; Mayer, *Dark Side*, 124; *Confirmation Hearing on the Nomination of Alberto R. Gonzales to Be Attorney General of the United States: Hearing before the Committee on the Judiciary*, 109th Cong., 1st Sess. (2005), 244.

91. Gonzales 1/25/02 Memorandum, in Greenberg and Dratel, *Torture Papers*, 119.

92. Gonzales 1/25/02 Memorandum, in Greenberg and Dratel, *Torture Papers*, 119.

93. Gonzales 1/25/02 Memorandum, in Greenberg and Dratel, *Torture Papers*, 120.

94. Ashcroft to the President, February 1, 2002, in Greenberg and Dratel, *Torture Papers*, 126, 127.

95. Gonzales 1/25/02 Memorandum, in Greenberg and Dratel, *Torture Papers*, 120.

96. Gonzales 1/25/02 Memorandum, in Greenberg and Dratel, *Torture Papers*, 119, 120; Isikoff, "Memos Reveal War Crimes Warnings."

97. Memorandum from Jay S. Bybee, Assistant Attorney General, OLC, DOJ, to Larry D. Thompson, Deputy Attorney General, DOJ, "Memorandum from Alberto Gonzales to the President on the Application of the Geneva Convention to Al Qaeda and the Taliban," January 26, 2002.

98. *ICRC Commentary I*, 48; Bush Memorandum, in Greenberg and Dratel, *Torture Papers*, 135.

99. Department of State, "Draft Memorandum," 2; Memorandum from William H. Taft IV, Legal Adviser, to Counsel to the President, "Comments on Your Paper on the Geneva Convention," February 2, 2002, in Greenberg and Dratel, *Torture Papers*, 129.

100. Memorandum from Colin L. Powell, Secretary of State, to Counsel to the President and Assistant to the President for National Security Affairs, "Draft Decision Memorandum for the President on the Applicability of the Geneva Convention to the Conflict in Afghanistan," January 26, 2002, in Greenberg and Dratel, *Torture Papers*, 123 (hereafter cited as Powell Memorandum); Taft to Counsel to the President, "Comments," in Greenberg and Dratel, *Torture Papers*, 129.

101. Powell Memorandum, in Greenberg and Dratel, *Torture Papers*, 122; John Barry, Michael Isikoff, and Michael Hirsh, "The Roots of Torture," *Newsweek*, May 24, 2004.

102. Bush Memorandum, in Greenberg and Dratel, *Torture Papers*, 135.

103. Office of the Press Secretary, White House, "Fact Sheet: Status of Detainees at Guantánamo," February 7, 2002; Office of the Press Secretary, White House, "Statement by the Press Secretary on the Geneva Convention," February 7, 2002; Office of the Press Secretary, White House, "Press Briefing by White House Counsel Judge Alberto Gonzales et al.," June 22, 2004; *Weekly Comp. Pres. Doc.*, June 10, 2004, 40:1051.

104. George Tenet with Bill Harlow, *At the Center of the Storm: My Years at the CIA* (New York: HarperCollins, 2007), 208; SSCI Report, 11; Dana Priest, "CIA Holds Terror Suspects in Secret Prisons," *Washington Post*, November 2, 2005.

105. Mayer, *Dark Side*, 145, 147; "Exploitation Draft Plan," 4.

106. Mayer, *Dark Side*, 120; Taft to Counsel to the President, "Comments," in Greenberg and Dratel, *Torture Papers*, 130.

107. Memorandum for the Record, Scott W. Muller, General Counsel, CIA, "'Humane Treatment' of CIA Detainees," February 12, 2003.

108. Bush, *Decision Points*, 168, 169.

109. Ron Suskind, *The One Percent Doctrine: Deep inside America's Pursuit of Its Enemies since 9/11* (New York: Simon and Schuster, 2006), 100; James Risen, *State of War: The Secret History of the CIA and the Bush Administration* (New York: Free Press, 2006), 22; SSCI Report, 111.

110. Savage, *Takeover*, 222.

111. *Weekly Comp. Pres. Doc.*, March 8, 2008, 44:346–47; Steven Lee Myers, "Veto of Bill on C.I.A. Tactics Affirms Bush's Legacy," *New York Times*, March 9, 2008. See also Dan Eggen, "White House Defends CIA's Use of Waterboarding in Interrogations," *Washington Post*, February 7, 2008.

112. 548 U.S. 557, 630–31 (2006); *Weekly Comp. Pres. Doc.*, September 6, 2006, 42:1572, 1574, 1575.

113. *ICRC Commentary I*, 53, 54.

114. *Weekly Comp. Pres. Doc.*, September 6, 2006, 42:1575; Military Commissions Act, § 6(a)(3)(A); Exec. Order No. 13,440, 72 Fed. Reg. 40707, 40708 (July 24, 2007); Office of the Press Secretary, White House, "President Bush Signed Executive Order," July 20, 2007; P. X. Kelley and Robert F. Turner, "War Crimes and the White House," *Washington Post*, July 26, 2007.

115. Bush Memorandum, in Greenberg and Dratel, *Torture Papers*, 135; *ICRC Commentary IV*, 38.

116. Ingrid Detter, *The Law of War*, 2nd ed. (Cambridge: Cambridge University Press, 2000), 396–97; Green, *Contemporary Law of Armed Conflict*, 122–23, 305; Hague Regs., art. 23(g).

117. Bush Memorandum, in Greenberg and Dratel, *Torture Papers*, 135.

118. Jamie Mayerfeld, *The Promise of Human Rights: Constitutional Government, Democratic Legitimacy, and International Law* (Philadelphia: University of Pennsylvania Press, 2016), 133.

119. *The Treatment of Detainees in U.S. Custody: Hearings before the Committee on Armed Services*, 110th Cong., 2nd sess. (2008), 240; Memorandum from Alberto J. Mora, General Counsel of the Navy, to Inspector General, Department of the Navy, "Statement for the Record: Office of General Counsel Involvement in Interrogation Issues," July 7, 2004, 14.

120. Memorandum from Maj. Gen. Jack L. Rives to SAF/GC, "Final Report and Recommendations of the Working Group . . . ," February 5, 2003, 1; SASC 2008 Report, 67.

121. Memorandum from Maj. Gen. Jack L. Rives to SAF/GC, "Comments on Draft Report. . . . ," February 6, 2003, 3; *Treatment of Detainees in U.S. Custody Hearings*, 240; Memorandum from Rear Admiral Michael F. Lohr to General Counsel of the Air Force, "Working Group Recommendations Relating to Interrogation of Detainees," February 6, 2003.

122. US Dept. of Justice, Office of the Inspector General, *A Review of the FBI's Involvement in and Observations of Detainee Interrogations in Guantánamo Bay, Afghanistan, and Iraq* (Washington, DC, 2008), 85; David Johnston, "At a Secret Interrogation, Dispute Flared over Tactics," *New York Times*, September 10, 2006.

123. US Dept. of Justice, *FBI's Involvement*, 207.

124. US Dept. of Justice, *FBI's Involvement*, 71–73, 75, 95, 203; SASC 2008 Report, 87.

125. SSCI Report, 14; Dana Priest and Joe Stephens, "Secret World of U.S. Interrogation," *Washington Post*, May 11, 2004; Dana Priest, "CIA Holds Terror Suspects in Secret Prisons," *Washington Post*, November 2, 2005; Adrian Levy and Kathy Scott-Clark, "'One Huge US Jail,'" *Guardian*, March 19, 2005; Mayer, *Dark Side*, 243–48.

126. Suzanne Goldenberg, "More Than 80,000 Held by US since 9/11 Attacks," *Guardian*, November 17, 2005.

127. Mayer, *Dark Side*, 101–38; David Weissbrodt and Amy Bergquist, "Extraordinary Rendition: A Human Rights Analysis," *Harvard Human Rights Journal* 19 (2006): 123–60.

128. *ICRC Report on the Treatment of Fourteen "High Value Detainees" in CIA Custody* (2007), 7; Eric Schmitt and Douglas Jehl, "Army Says C.I.A. Hid More Iraqis Than It Claimed," *New York Times*, September 10, 2004; Josh White, "Army, CIA Agreed on 'Ghost' Prisoners," *Washington Post*, March 11, 2005.

129. Joseph Margulies, *Guantánamo and the Abuse of Presidential Power* (New York: Simon and Schuster, 2006), 45–52; Gherebi v. Bush, 352 F.3d 1278, 1300 (9th Cir. 2003), *cert. granted and vacated by* 124 S. Ct. 2932 (2004); Savage, *Takeover*, 145; see also Howard Ball, *Bush, the Detainees, and the Constitution: The Battle over Presidential Power in the War on Terror* (Lawrence: University Press of Kansas, 2007), 98.

130. Eric Schmitt and Carolyn Marshall, "In Secret Unit's 'Black Room,' a Grim Portrait of U.S. Abuse," *New York Times*, March 19, 2009.

131. Mayer, *Dark Side*, 183; Mark Denbeaux et al., "Report on Guantánamo Detainees: A Profile of 517 Detainees through Analysis of Department of Defense Data," *Seton Hall Law Review* 41 (2011): 1211–29; ICRC, *Report of the International Committee of the Red Cross (ICRC) on the Treatment by the Coalition Forces of Prisoners of War. . . .* (2004), ¶ 7.

132. Charlie Savage, William Glaberson, and Andrew W. Lehren, "Classified Files Offer New Insights into Detainees," *New York Times*, April 24, 2011.

133. *ICRC Report on the Treatment*, 11; *The Report of The Constitution Project's Task Force on Detainee Treatment* (Washington, DC, 2013), 103; SSCI Report, 42; Editorial, "Medically Assisted Torture," *New York Times*, April 9, 2009.

134. SSCI Report, 50, 96; Neil A. Lewis and David Johnston, "New F.B.I. Files Describe Abuse of Iraq Inmates," *New York Times*, December 21, 2004.

135. *Constitution Project's Task Force*, 39; Margulis, *Guantánamo*, 86–88; William Glaberson, "Detainee Was Tortured, a Bush Official Confirms," *New York Times*, January 14, 2009.

136. SSCI Report, 86, 105–8.

137. SSCI Report, 43–45.

138. Maj. Gen. Antonio M. Taguba, *Article 15–6 Investigation of the 800th Military Police Brigade* (2004), 17; ICRC, *Treatment by the Coalition Forces*, ¶¶ 6, 25; Tom Lasseter, "Day 2: U.S. Abuse of Detainees Was Routine at Afghanistan Bases," *McClatchy Newspapers*, June 16, 2008; Neil A. Lewis and David Johnston, "New F.B.I. Files Describe Abuse of Iraq Inmates," *New York Times*, December 21, 2004; Eric Schmitt and Carolyn Marshall, "In Secret Unit's 'Black Room,' a Grim Portrait of U.S. Abuse," *New York Times*, March 19, 2009; CIA, Inspector General, *Special Review: Counterterrorism Detention and Interrogation Activities (September 2001–October 2003)* (2004), 42.

139. United States Army, Criminal Investigation Command, "Army Criminal Investigators Outline 27 Confirmed or Suspected Detainee Homicides . . ." (2005), 1; Tim Golden, "Years after 2 Afghans Died, Abuse Case Falters" *New York Times*, February 13, 2006.

140. Bush Memorandum, in Greenberg and Dratel, *Torture Papers*, 134.

141. *Weekly Comp. Pres. Doc.*, September 6, 2006, 42:1571.

142. OLC 1/22/02 Opinion, in Greenberg and Dratel, *Torture Papers*, 95–102.

143. Powell Memorandum, in Greenberg and Dratel, *Torture Papers*, 123; US Dept. of Justice, *FBI's Involvement*, 203; SASC 2008 Report, 67, 87.

144. Ashcroft to the President, February 1, 2002, in Greenberg and Dratel, *Torture Papers*, 126; Gonzales 1/25/02 Memorandum, in Greenberg and Dratel, *Torture Papers*, 119.

145. *Weekly Comp. Pres. Doc.*, September 6, 2006, 42:1574.

146. *Weekly Comp. Pres. Doc.*, September 6, 2006, 42:1571.

Chapter 3

1. Ball, *Detainees*, 197; Goldsmith, *Power and Constraint*, xi.

2. *The Federalist* no. 48.

3. *The Federalist* nos. 48, 51.

4. Daryl J. Levinson and Richard H. Pildes, "Separation of Parties, Not Powers," *Harvard Law Review* 119 (2006): 2317–19; Daryl J. Levinson, "Empire-Building Government in Constitutional Law," *Harvard Law Review* 118 (2005): 952.

5. Douglas L. Kriner and Eric Schickler, *Investigating the President: Congressional Checks on Presidential Power* (Princeton: Princeton University Press, 2016).

6. On neglected powers, see Josh Chafetz, "Congress's Constitution," *University of Pennsylvania Law Review* 160 (2012): 715–78.

7. Curtis A. Bradley and Trevor W. Morrison, "Historical Gloss and the Separation of Powers," *Harvard Law Review* 126 (2012): 438–47; Linda L. Fowler, *Watchdogs on the Hill: The Decline of Congressional Oversight of U.S. Foreign Relations* (Princeton: Princeton University Press, 2015) 5; Kriner and Schickler, *Investigating the President*, 3-7, 46; Geoffrey S. Corn, "The National Security Constitution: The Separation of Powers and the War on Terror," *St. John's Journal of Legal Commentary* 23 (2009): 976; First National City Bank v. Banco Nacional de Cuba, 406 U.S. 759, 767 (1972); Mark Tushnet, "Controlling Executive Power in the War on Terrorism," *Harvard Law Review* 118 (2005): 2677–78.

8. 50 U.S.C. § 3093(c)(2); see Loch K. Johnson, "Congress and Intelligence," in *Congress and the Politics of National Security*, ed. David P. Auerswald and Colton C. Campbell (Cambridge: Cambridge University Press, 2011), 121–43; Amy B. Zegart, "The Domestic Politics of Irrational Intelligence Oversight," *Political Science Quarterly* 126 (2011): 1–25.

9. SSCI Report, 38, 438; Carl Hulse, "Pelosi Says She Knew of Waterboarding by 2003," *New York Times*, May 15, 2009; David Welna, "CIA: Pelosi Knew of Interrogation in '02," NPR, May 8, 2009.

10. Harman to Muller, February 10, 2003.

11. Muller to Harman, February 28, 2003.

12. *60 Minutes II: Court Martial in Iraq* (CBS television broadcast April 28, 2004); James Risen, "G.I.'s Are Accused of Abusing Iraqi Captives," *New York Times*, April 29, 2004. See Mark Danner, *Torture and Truth: America, Abu Ghraib, and the War on Terror* (New York: New York Review Books, 2004); Richard L. Abel, *Law's Wars: The Fate of the Rule of Law in the US "War on Terror"* (Cambridge: Cambridge University Press, 2018), 45–105.

13. *Weekly Comp. Pres. Doc.*, April 30, 2004, 40:709.

14. S. Res. 356, 108th Cong., 2nd Sess. (2004); H.R. Res. 639, 108th Cong., 2nd Sess. (2004); Helen Dewar and Spencer S. Hsu, "Warner Bucks GOP Right on Probe of Prison Abuse," *Washington Post*, May 28, 2004; Douglas Jehl, "Some Iraqis Held outside Control of Top General," *New York Times*, May 17, 2004; *Review of Department of Defense Detention and Interrogation Operations: Hearings before the S. Comm. on Armed Services*, 108th Cong., 2nd sess. (2004), 4; Jonathan Mahler, "After the Imperial Presidency," *New York Times*, November 7, 2008.

15. Carl Hulse and Christopher Marquis, "G.O.P. Split over Inquiry on Prisoner Abuse," *New York Times*, May 19, 2004; Sheryl Gay Stolberg, "Warner, Courtly Republican, Guides Panel in Rough Seas," *New York Times*, May 12, 2004; Abel, *Law's Wars*, 59.

16. Editorial, "Abu Ghraib, Stonewalled," *New York Times*, June 30, 2004; Helen Dewar and Dan Morgan, "Senate Rejects Request for Abuse Documents," *Washington Post*, June 24, 2004; Eric Schmitt, "Congress's Inquiry into Abuse of Iraqi Prisoners Bogs Down," *New York Times*, July 16, 2004; Jonathan Mahler, "After the Imperial Presidency," *New York Times*, November 7, 2008.

17. Gonzales, "Waging War," 848–49; R. Jeffrey Smith and Dan Eggen, "Gonzales Helped Set the Course for Detainees," *Washington Post*, January 5, 2005; OLC 8/1/02 Interrogation Standards Opinion, in Greenberg and Dratel, *Torture Papers*, 172; Goldsmith, *Terror Presidency*, 167; OLC 12/30/04 Opinion, 1.

18. Abel, *Law's Wars*, 211; *Confirmation Hearing on the Nomination of Alberto R. Gonzales*, 14.

19. *Confirmation Hearing on the Nomination of Alberto R. Gonzales*, 131; OLC 8/1/02 Interrogation Standards Opinion, in Greenberg and Dratel, *Torture Papers*, 176.

20. *Confirmation Hearing on the Nomination of Alberto R. Gonzales*, 58, 120.

21. *Confirmation Hearing on the Nomination of Alberto R. Gonzales*, 96.

22. Eric Lichtblau, "Gonzales Is Confirmed in a Closer Vote Than Expected," *New York Times*, February 4, 2005.

23. *Confirmation Hearing on the Nomination of Alberto R. Gonzales*, 191, 226, 249, 331; Eric Lichtblau, "Gonzales Says '02 Policy on Detainees Doesn't Bind C.I.A.," *New York Times*, January 19, 2005; Savage, *Takeover*, 213.

24. S. Amdt. 1977, 109th Cong., 1st Sess. (2005); US Dept. of the Army, *Field Manual 34–52*, 1–8.

25. Eric Schmitt, "Senate Moves to Protect Military Prisoners despite Veto Threat," *New York Times*, October 6, 2005; Savage, *Takeover*, 220–23; *Weekly Comp. Pres. Doc.*, December 15, 2005, 41:1866; Josh White, "President Relents, Backs Torture Ban," *Washington Post*, December 16, 2005; Eric Schmitt, "President Backs McCain on Inmate Abuse," *New York Times*, December 16, 2005.

26. Goldsmith, *Power and Constraint*, 120.

27. R. Jeffrey Smith, "Behind the Debate, Controversial CIA Techniques," *Washington Post*, September 16, 2006; SSCI Report, 163–67.

28. SSCI Report, 157; Memorandum from Steven G. Bradbury, Principal Deputy Assistant Attorney General, OLC, DOJ, to John A. Rizzo, Acting General Counsel, CIA, "Application of the War Crimes Act, the Detainee Treatment Act, and Common Article 3 of the Geneva Conventions to Certain Techniques . . . ," July 20, 2007, 44 (hereafter cited as OLC 7/20/07 Opinion); Exec. Order No. 13,440, 72 Fed. Reg. 40707, 40708 (July 24, 2007); Karen DeYoung, "Bush Approves New CIA Methods," *Washington Post*, July 21, 2007. Bradbury's memorandum approved the use, singly or in combination, of sleep deprivation for ninety-six hours continuously (and longer periods with additional approval), dietary manipulation, facial hold, attention grasp, abdominal slap, and facial slap. OLC 7/20/07 Opinion, 44–48.

29. DTA, § 1002(a).

30. Eric Schmitt and Tim Golden, "Pentagon Plans Tighter Control of Questioning," *New York Times*, November 8, 2005; Eric Schmitt, "New Army Rules May Snarl Talks with McCain on Detainee Issue," *New York Times*, December 14, 2005.

31. James P. Pfiffner, *Power Play: The Bush Presidency and the Constitution* (Washington, DC: Brookings Institution Press, 2008), 143; US Dept. of the Army, *Field Manual 2–22.3 (FM 34–52), Human Intelligence Collector Operations* (2006), ¶¶ M-15, M-26–30; Matthew Alexander, "Torture's Loopholes," *New York Times*, January 21, 2010.

32. DTA, § 1003(a); Arsalan M. Suleman, "Detainee Treatment Act of 2005," *Harvard Human Rights Journal* 19 (2006): 262.

33. DTA, § 1003(d); Rochin v. California, 342 U.S. 165, 172 (1952); OLC 7/20/07 Opinion, 36.

34. *Weekly Comp. Pres. Doc.*, December 30, 2005, 41:1919; Charlie Savage, "Bush Could Bypass New Torture Ban," *Boston Globe*, January 4, 2006; Savage, *Takeover*, 224–26.

35. Goldsmith, *Power and Constraint*, 119; DTA, § 1004 (a), (b).

36. DTA, § 1005(e).

37. 542 U.S. 466 (2004); Linda Greenhouse, "The Mystery of Guantánamo Bay," *Berkeley Journal of International Law* 27 (2009): 12.

38. 548 U.S. 557 (2006); Goldsmith, *Power and Constraint*, 187; Scott Shane and Adam Liptak, "Detainee Bill Shifts Power to President," *New York Times*, September 30, 2006.

39. 548 U.S. at 636 (Breyer, J., concurring); 548 U.S. at 637 (Kennedy, J. concurring in part); David S. Cloud and Sheryl Gay Stolberg, "White House Bill Proposes System to Try Detainees," *New York Times*, July 26, 2006; Kate Zernike, "White House Prods Congress to Curb Detainee Rights," *New York Times*, July 13, 2006.

40. Carlos Manuel Vasquez, "The Military Commissions Act, the Geneva Conventions, and the Courts: A Critical Guide," *American Journal of International Law* 101 (2007): 74–75.

41. Savage, *Takeover*, 310, 311; Kate Zernike, "Rebuff for Bush on Terror Trials in a Senate Test," *New York Times*, September 15, 2006; Kate Zernike, "Deal Reported Near on Rights of Suspects in Terror Cases," *New York Times*, September 13, 2006.

42. Goldsmith, *Power and Constraint*, 187.

43. MCA, § 3, 10 U.S.C. § 948r (2006). Congress later barred the use of evidence from coercion regardless of date. Military Commissions Act of 2009, Pub. L. No. 111–84, § 1802, 123 Stat. 2574, 2580 (codified at 10 U.S.C. § 948r(a)).

44. MCA, 10 U.S.C. §§ 949a(b)(2)(E), 949d(f)(2)(B) (2006).

45. MCA, 10 U.S.C. § 948a(1)(A)(i) (2006).

46. MCA, § 7(a), 28 U.S.C. § 2241(e)(1); § 3, 10 U.S.C. § 950g (2006).

47. MCA, § 7(b).

48. MCA, § 5(a); see also §3, 10 U.S.C. § 948b(g) (2006).

49. MCA, § 6(a)(3).

50. 18 U.S.C. § 2441(c)(3) (as it was codified from 1997 to 2006); Bush Memorandum, in Greenberg and Dratel, *Torture Papers*, 134–35; *Weekly Comp. Pres. Doc.*, Sept. 6, 2006, 42:1574–75.

51. MCA, § 6(b)(1); 18 U.S.C. § 2441(d).

52. Michael J. Matheson, "The Amendment of the War Crimes Act," *American Journal of International Law* 101 (2007): 52.

53. MCA, §§ 6 (c), 8(b).

54. MCA, § 6(c); see Jack M. Beard, "The Geneva Boomerang: The Military Commis-

sions Act of 2006 and U.S. Counterterror Operations," *American Journal of International Law* 101 (2007): 61. The MCA was ambiguous on cruel and inhuman treatment, which the legislation identified as both a grave breach and an additional prohibition.

55. R. Jeffrey Smith, "Detainee Abuse Charges Feared," *Washington Post*, July 28, 2006; R. Jeffrey Smith, "War Crimes Act Changes Would Reduce Threat of Prosecution," *Washington Post*, August 9, 2006; John Sifton, "Criminal, Immunize Thyself," *Slate*, August 11, 2006.

56. Joby Warrick and Karen DeYoung, "Report on Detainee Abuse Blames Top Bush Officials," *Washington Post*, December 12, 2008; Scott Shane and Mark Mazzetti, "U.S. Report Blames Rumsfeld for Detainee Abuses," *New York Times*, December 12, 2008.

57. The committee held hearings on June 17 and September 25, 2008. *Treatment of Detainees in U.S. Custody Hearings*, i; Joby Warrick and Karen DeYoung, "Report on Detainee Abuse Blames Top Bush Officials," *Washington Post*, December 12, 2008.

58. SASC 2008 Report, xix, xxviii.

59. SASC 2008 Report, xiii, 3.

60. Josh Gerstein said that codes used to disguise actual names, job titles, dates, and places combined with the redaction of 7% of the executive summary's words made it impossible to "establish a chain of responsibility." Josh Gerstein, "What's Not in the Senate Torture Report," *Politico*, December 9, 2014.

61. Greg Miller and Adam Goldman, "Public Feud between CIA, Senate Panel Follows Years of Tension over Interrogation Report," *Washington Post*, March 13, 2014; Mark Mazzetti and Scott Shane, "Senate and C.I.A. Spar over Secret Report on Interrogation Program," *New York Times*, July 20, 2013.

62. SSCI Report, 22, 33, 47, 105.

63. SSCI Report, Findings and Conclusions, xv.

64. SSCI Report, 9.

65. Risen, *State of War*, 23–25.

66. Michael Poznansky, "Revisiting Plausible Deniability," *Journal of Strategic Studies* (2020): 514–15, 519–23.

67. SSCI Report, 38, 98.

68. SSCI Report, 39.

69. SSCI Report, 40.

70. *Weekly Comp. Pres. Doc.*, September 6, 2006, 42:1571, 1572, 1574–75; Exec. Order No. 13,440, 72 Fed. Reg. 40707, 40708 (July 24, 2007).

71. SSCI Report, 38–39; Bush, *Decision Points*, 169.

72. Bush, *Decision Points*, 168, 169, 170.

73. Bush, *Decision Points*, 171.

74. U.S. Const. art. II, § 4; *The Federalist* no. 66; Max Farrand, ed., *The Records of the Federal Convention of 1787*, rev. ed. (New Haven: Yale University Press, 1937), 2:65; Laurence H. Tribe, "Defining 'High Crimes and Misdemeanors': Basic Principles," *George Washington Law Review* 67 (1999): 723.

75. Frank O. Bowman III, *High Crimes and Misdemeanors: A History of Impeachment for the Age of Trump* (Cambridge: Cambridge University Press, 2019), 244; Charles L. Black Jr., *Impeachment: A Handbook* (New Haven: Yale University Press, 1974), 33–35.

76. Farrand, *Records*, 2:550; *The Federalist* no. 65; Robert Green McCloskey, ed., *The Works of James Wilson* (Cambridge, MA: Belknap Press of Harvard University Press, 1967), 1:426.

77. Gary L. McDowell, "'High Crimes and Misdemeanors': Recovering the Intentions of the Founders," *George Washington Law Review* 67 (1999): 638; Black, *Impeachment*, 39.

78. U.S. Const. art. I, § 3, cl. 6; Farrand, *Records of the Federal Convention*, 1:22, 244, 292; Michael J. Gerhardt, *The Federal Impeachment Process: A Constitutional and Historical Analysis*, 3rd ed. (Chicago: University of Chicago Press, 2019), 1; *The Federalist* no. 65.

79. Michael Les Benedict, *The Impeachment and Trial of Andrew Johnson* (New York: W. W. Norton, 1973); Richard A. Posner, *An Affair of State: The Investigation, Impeachment, and Trial of President Clinton* (Cambridge, MA: Harvard University Press, 2000); Victoria F. Nourse, *The Impeachments of Donald Trump: An Introduction to Constitutional Interpretation* (St. Paul, MN: West Academic Publishing, 2021); Keith W. Olson, *Watergate: The Presidential Scandal That Shook America* (Lawrence: University Press of Kansas, 2016), 159–65.

80. U.S. Const. art. I, § 3, cl. 6; *The Federalist* no. 66; Laurence Tribe and Joshua Matz, *To End a Presidency: The Power of Impeachment* (New York: Basic Books, 2018), 126; *Trial of Andrew Johnson. . . .* (Washington, DC: 1868), 2:486–87, 496, 497.

81. Elizabeth Holtzman, "The Impeachment of George W. Bush," *The Nation*, January 30, 2006, 11–18; Dave Lindorff and Barbara Olshansky, *The Case for Impeachment: The Legal Argument for Removing President George W. Bush from Office* (New York: Thomas Dunne, 2006).

82. "Former U.S. Attorney General Ramsey Clark Calls for Bush Impeachment," *Democracy Now!*, January 21, 2005; Thomas J. Lueck, "Nader Calls for Impeachment of Bush over the War in Iraq," *New York Times*, May 25, 2004; John W. Dean, *Worse Than Watergate: The Secret Presidency of George W. Bush* (New York: Little, Brown, 2004); Impeaching Donald Rumsfeld, Secretary of Defense, H.R. Res. 629, 108th Cong. (2004).

83. Tim Grieve, "Zogby: No Bush Speech Bounce," *Salon*, June 30, 2005; Tim Grieve, "Three More Years of Bush, A Plan for Cheney and the I-Word, Again," *Salon*, November 8, 2005; "Iraq: June 2005," *Washington Post–ABC News Poll*, June 23–26, 2005.

84. John W. Dean, "George W. Bush as the New Richard M. Nixon," *FindLaw*, December 30, 2005; Holtzman, "Impeachment," 13–14; Elizabeth Holtzman, *The Impeachment of George W. Bush: A Practical Guide for Concerned Citizens* (New York: Nation Books, 2006), 43–115; Lewis H. Lapham, "The Case for Impeachment: Why We Can No Longer Afford George W. Bush," *Harper's*, March 2006; Michelle Goldberg, "The I-Word Goes Public," *Salon*, March 3, 2006.

85. Charles Babington, "Democrats Won't Try to Impeach President," *Washington Post*, May 12, 2006; Impeaching George W. Bush, President of the United States, of High Crimes and Misdemeanors, H.R. Res. 1258, 110th Cong. (2007); Impeaching George W. Bush, President of the United States, of High Crimes and Misdemeanors, H.R. Res. 1345, 110th Cong. (2008).

86. Peter Baker, *The Breach: Inside the Impeachment and Trial of William Jefferson Clinton* (New York: Scribner, 2000), 417.

87. Compare Sanford Levinson, "Impeachment: The Case Against," *The Nation*, Feb-

ruary 12, 2007 (criticizing the Constitution's focus on criminal conduct in lieu of providing for removal for incompetence).

88. Paula D. McClain, "Arizona 'High Noon': The Recall and Impeachment of Evan Mecham," *PS: Political Science and Politics* 21 (1988): 634–38; Malcolm Gay and Susan Saulny, "Blagojevich Ousted by Illinois State Senate," *New York Times*, January 29, 2009; Alan Binder, "Robert Bentley, Alabama Governor, Resigns amid Scandal," *New York Times*, April 10, 2017; Shannon Young and Michele Bocanegra, "Andrew Cuomo Resigns amid Sexual Harassment Scandal," *Politico*, August 10, 2021.

89. Tom Ginsburg, Aziz Huq, and David Landau, "The Comparative Constitutional Law of Presidential Impeachment," *University of Chicago Law Review* 88 (2021): 117–19, 130.

90. Ginsburg, Huq, and Landau, "Comparative Constitutional Law of Presidential Impeachment," 145; Mark Turner, Seung-Ho Kwon, and Michael O'Donnell, "Making Integrity Institutions Work in South Korea: The Role of People Power in the Impeachment of President Park in 2016," *Asian Survey* 58 (2018): 898–919; Gi-Wook Shin and Rennie J. Moon, "South Korea after Impeachment," *Journal of Democracy* 28 (2017): 119–21.

91. Ginsburg, Huq, and Landau, "Comparative Constitutional Law of Presidential Impeachment," 130.

Chapter 4

1. Hamdan v. Rumsfeld, 548 U.S. 557 (2006); Boumediene v. Bush, 553 U.S. 723 (2008); Press release, office of US Senator Patrick Leahy, "Reaction of Sen. Patrick Leahy on Supreme Court's Decision in *Hamdan* Case," June 30, 2006; Walter Dellinger, "A Supreme Court Conversation: The Most Important Decision on Presidential Power. Ever.," *Slate*, June 29, 2006; Greenhouse, "Mystery of Guantánamo Bay," 18; Deborah N. Pearlstein, "Finding Effective Constraints on Executive Power: Interrogation, Detention, and Torture," *Indiana Law Journal* 81 (2006): 1290; Ball, *Detainees*, 197.

2. Sanford Levinson, "To What Extent Is Judicial Intervention a 'Hollow Hope': Reflections on the Israeli and American Judicial Experiences since 2001," *Tulsa Law Review* 47 (2011): 376–77; Jenny S. Martinez, "Process and Substance in the 'War on Terror,'" *Columbia Law Review* 108 (2008): 1013–92; Kim Lane Scheppele, "The New Judicial Deference," *Boston University Law Review* 92 (2012): 89–170; Stephen I. Vladeck, "The Passive-Aggressive Virtues," *Columbia Law Review Sidebar* 111 (2011): 125.

3. Marbury v. Madison, 5 U.S. (1 Cranch) 137, 169–71 (1803); Linda Greenhouse, "War of Secrets: Judicial Restraint; The Imperial Presidency vs. the Imperial Judiciary," *New York Times*, September 8, 2002.

4. War powers cases date from the Quasi-War with France. See note 10.

5. Prize Cases, 67 U.S. (2 Black) 635, 666–71 (1863); Ex parte Milligan, 71 U.S. (4 Wall.) 2, 127 (1866).

6. Milligan, 71 U.S. at 120; Ex parte Quirin, 317 U.S. 1 (1942). Compare Duncan v. Kahanamoku, 327 U.S. 324 (1946) (rejecting military tribunals in place of civilian courts in Hawaii).

7. Korematsu v. United States, 323 U.S. 214, 220 (1944); Ex parte Endo, 323 U.S. 283, 297, 304 (1944).

8. Clinton Rossiter, *The Supreme Court and the Commander in Chief*, exp. ed. with additional text by Richard P. Longaker (Ithaca: Cornell University Press, 1976), 128–29.

9. 343 U.S. 579, 634–55 (1952) (Jackson, J., concurring); Samuel Isaacharoff and Richard H. Pildes, "Between Civil Libertarianism and Executive Unilateralism: An Institutional Process Approach to Rights during Wartime," *Theoretical Inquiries in Law* 5 (2004): 5.

10. 343 U.S. at 586–89; 343 U.S. at 635–38 (Jackson, J., concurring). The importance that the Court would place on congressional action in evaluating presidential war powers was presaged in *Little v. Barreme*, 6 U.S. (2 Cranch) 170 (1804). The Court there invalidated President John Adams's order, issued during the Quasi-War with France, authorizing the seizure of ships sailing to and from French ports. The justices intimated that the president was within his rights to do that if Congress had not addressed the subject, but they found dispositive previous legislation limiting seizures to ships heading to those ports. See also Mark C. Rahdert, "Double-Checking Executive Emergency Power: Lessons from *Hamdi* and *Hamdan*," *Temple Law Review* 80 (2007): 455.

11. 542 U.S. 507, 536 (2004) (plurality opinion).

12. 542 U.S. at 535.

13. 542 U.S. at 530.

14. 542 U.S. at 521; Rumsfeld v. Padilla, 542 U.S. 426, 465 (2004) (Stevens, J., dissenting).

15. Hamdi, 542 U.S. at 510–14; Ball, *Detainees*, 99–103.

16. 542 U.S. at 516, 524, 533.

17. Non-Detention Act, 18 U.S.C. § 4001; Hamdi, 542 U.S. at 518; Authorization for Use of Military Force, Pub. L. No. 107–40, 115 Stat. 224; 542 U.S. at 547 (Souter, J., concurring in part, dissenting in part, and concurring in the judgment)

18. 542 U.S. at 534.

19. 542 U.S. at 529, 531, 533.

20. 542 U.S. at 533–34; Margulies, *Guantánamo*, 69.

21. 542 U.S. at 534, 538; see also Nicholas G. Green, "A 'Blank Check': Judicial Review and the War Powers in *Hamdi v. Rumsfeld*," *South Carolina Law Review* 56 (2005): 602–3.

22. 542 U.S. at 519.

23. Justice O'Connor left further definition of who could be classified as an enemy combatant to the lower courts. 542 U.S. at 522 n.1.

24. 542 U.S. at 517.

25. 542 U.S. at 516–19.

26. 542 U.S. at 521.

27. 542 U.S. at 533–38.

28. 542 U.S. at 538.

29. 542 U.S. at 519.

30. Rumsfeld v. Padilla, 542 U.S. 426, 430–32 (2004); Ball, *Detainees*, 105–8; Eric Lichtblau, "In Legal Shift, U.S. Charges Detainee in Terrorism Case," *New York Times*, November 23, 2005; Warren Richey, "'Torture Memos' Author Can't Be Sued for Harsh Interrogations, Court Rules," *Christian Science Monitor*, May 2, 2012.

31. 542 U.S. at 451; Padilla v. Hanft, 423 F.3d 386 (4th Cir. 2005), cert. denied, 547 U.S. 1062 (2006); Editorial, "The Padilla Conviction," *New York Times*, August 17, 2007.

32. 542 U.S. 466 (2004); 548 U.S. 557 (2006); 553 U.S. 723 (2008).

33. Goldsmith, *Power and Constraint*, xi; John Yoo, "The Supreme Court Goes to War," *Wall Street Journal*, June 30, 2004.

34. See Neal Devins, "Talk Loudly and Carry a Small Stick: The Supreme Court and Enemy Combatants," *University of Pennsylvania Journal of Constitutional Law* 12 (2010): 494–95.

35. U.S. Const. art. I, § 9, cl. 2; Anthony Gregory, *The Power of Habeas Corpus in America: From the King's Prerogative to the War on Terror* (Cambridge: Cambridge University Press, 2013), 44–57; Paul D. Halliday and G. Edward White, "The Suspension Clause: English Text, Imperial Contexts, and American Implications," *Virginia Law Review* 94 (2008): 575–714; Judiciary Act of 1789, ch. 20, § 14, 1 Stat. 73, 81–82; Habeas Corpus Act of 1867, ch. 28, 14 Stat. 385; 28 U.S.C. §§ 2241–55.

36. Fay v. Noia, 372 U.S. 391, 402 (1963). The Indemnity Act of 1863 ratified President Lincoln's suspensions of the writ. Act of March 3, 1863, ch. 81, § 1, 12 Stat. 755, 755. The Ku Klux Klan Act in 1871 empowered President Ulysses S. Grant to suspend the writ in parts of South Carolina. Ku Klux Klan Act of 1871, ch. 22, § 4, 17 Stat. 13, 14–15. In 1902, Congress authorized suspension of habeas corpus in the Philippines. Act of July 1, 1902, ch. 1369, § 5, 32 Stat. 691, 692. After the attack on Pearl Harbor, Hawaii's governor claimed authority to suspend habeas corpus under legislation Congress had passed. Hawaiian Organic Act of 1900, ch. 339, § 67, 31 Stat. 141, 153.

37. Patrick F. Philbin, Deputy Assistant Attorney General, OLC, DOJ, and John C. Yoo, Deputy Assistant Attorney General, OLC, DOJ, to William J. Haynes II, General Counsel, DOD, "Possible Habeas Jurisdiction over Aliens Held at Guantánamo Bay, Cuba," December 28, 2001, in Greenberg and Dratel, *Torture Papers*, 36 (hereafter cited as OLC 12/28/01 Opinion); Yoo, *War by Other Means*, 142.

38. Johnson v. Eisentrager, 339 U.S. 763, 778 (1950); Margulies, *Guantánamo*, 49–50.

39. OLC 12/28/01 Opinion, in Greenberg and Dratel, *Torture Papers*, 29.

40. Boumediene v. Bush, 549 U.S. 1328, 1330 (2007) (mem.) (Breyer, J., dissenting from denial of certiorari) (italics in the original).

41. Helen Duffy, "Human Rights Litigation and the 'War on Terror,'" *International Review of the Red Cross* 90 (2008): 573, 578.

42. Rasul, 542 U.S. at 471–73.

43. Ashwander v. Tennessee Valley Authority, 297 U.S. 288, 347 (1936) (Brandeis, J., concurring). Compare Owen Fiss, "The Perils of Minimalism," *Theoretical Inquiries in Law* 9 (2008): 646.

44. Hamdi, 542 U.S. at 517; Rasul, 542 U.S. at 484; Hamdan, 548 U.S. at 575–84. See Trevor W. Morrison, "The Middle Ground in Judicial Review of Enemy Combatant Detentions," *Willamette Law Review* 45 (2009): 453–71.

45. Rasul, 542 U.S. at 484; DTA, § 1005(e); Hamdan, 548 U.S. at 572–84; MCA, § 7; Boumediene, 553 U.S. at 732. On habeas cases, see Richard L. Abel, *Law's Trials: The Performance of Legal Institutions in the US "War on Terror"* (Cambridge: Cambridge University Press, 2018), 322–430.

46. 553 U.S. at 733, 755, 765.

47. 553 U.S. at 733, 792.

48. 553 U.S. at 767, 769.

49. 553 U.S. at 787.

50. 553 U.S. at 783.

51. 553 U.S. at 779, 796.

52. Tim Golden and Eric Schmitt, "A Growing Afghan Prison Rivals Bleak Guantánamo," *New York Times,* February 26, 2006.

53. 553 U.S. at 766.

54. 542 U.S. at 485; 553 U.S. at 796.

55. Greenhouse, "Mystery of Guantánamo Bay," 10; Seth P. Waxman, "The Combatant Detention Trilogy through the Lenses of History," in *Terrorism, the Laws of War, and the Constitution,* ed. Peter Berkowitz (Stanford, CA: Hoover Institution Press, 2005), 34.

56. DTA, § 1005(e); MCA, § 3.

57. A. Raymond Randolph, "The Guantánamo Mess," in *Confronting Terror: 9/11 and the Future of American National Security,* ed. Dean Reuter and John Yoo (New York: Encounter Books, 2011), 241.

58. Latif v. Obama, 666 F.3d 746, 764 (D.C. Cir. 2011), *cert. denied,* 132 S. Ct. 2741 (2012) (originally classified and reissued at 677 F.3d 1175 (D.C. Cir. 2012)); Esmail v. Obama, 639 F.3d 1075, 1078 (D.C. Cir. 2011) (Silberman, J., concurring). Justice Brett Kavanaugh, on the DC Circuit at the time, played a role in undermining *Boumediene.* Stephen I. Vladek, "The D.C. Circuit after *Boumediene," Seton Hall Law Review* 41 (2011): 1455–56; Editorial, "Reneging on Justice at Guantánamo," *New York Times,* November 19, 2011.

59. Latif v. Obama, 666 F.3d at 779 (Tatel, J., dissenting).

60. Al-Bihani v. Obama, 590 F.3d 866, 878 (D.C. Cir. 2010), *cert. denied,* 131 S. Ct. 1814 (2012).

61. Al-Adahi v. Obama, 613 F.3d 1102, 1104–5 (D.C. Cir. 2010), *cert. denied,* 131 S. Ct. 1001 (2011); Esmail v. Obama, 639 F.3d at 1078 (Silberman, J., concurring); Hamdi, 542 U.S. at 537.

62. Al-Bihani, 590 F.3d at 879; Latif v. Obama, 666 F.3d at 748, 748–55.

63. Boumediene, 553 U.S. at 766; Al Maqaleh v. Gates, 605 F.3d 84, 97 (D.C. Cir. 2010).

64. 553 U.S. at 770; 605 F.3d at 97, 98 (quoting Johnson v. Eisentrager).

65. 553 U.S. at 765; 605 F.3d at 87, 96.

66. 553 U.S. at 798.

67. 613 F.3d 1102 (D.C. Cir. 2010); Mark Denbeaux et al., "No Hearing Habeas: D.C. Circuit Restricts Meaningful Review" (Seton Hall University School of Law Center for Policy and Research, May 1, 2012), 1, 4.

68. Latif v. Obama, 666 F.3d at 779 (Tatel, J., dissenting).

69. Jules Lobel, "Victory without Success?—the Guantánamo Litigation, Permanent Preventive Detention, and Resisting Injustice," *Journal of Law and Society* 14 (2013): 131.

70. Stephen I. Vladek, "*Boumediene's* Quiet Theory: Access to Courts and the Separation of Powers," *Notre Dame Law Review* 84 (2009): 2111; Devins, "Supreme Court and Enemy Combatants," 527; Emily Calhoun, "The Accounting: Habeas Corpus and Enemy Combatants," *University of Colorado Law Review* 79 (2008): 113.

71. Harlow v. Fitzgerald, 457 U.S. 800, 809 (1982).

72. See James E. Pfander, *Constitutional Torts and the War on Terror* (New York: Oxford University Press, 2017), 146–57.

73. Stephen I. Vladek, "The Torture Report and the Accountability Gap," *Georgetown Journal of International Affairs* 16 (Summer/Fall 2015): 179–80.

74. See, e.g., Mohamed v. Jeppesen Dataplan, Inc., 614 F.3d 1071 (9th Cir. 2010) (en banc), *cert. denied*, 131 S. Ct. 2442 (2011).

75. Louis Fisher, *In the Name of National Security: Unchecked Presidential Power and the* Reynolds *Case* (Lawrence: University Press of Kansas, 2006), 4–18; Jeremy Travis, "Rethinking Sovereign Immunity after *Bivens*," *New York University Law Review* 57 (1982): 599; Harlow, 457 U.S. at 807, 818. Among statutory alternatives, the Federal Tort Claims Act provides a remedy against federal officials who commit state-law torts while acting within the scope of their employment by substituting the US government as defendant. 28 U.S.C. §§ 1346 (b), 2671-2680. To take one example of its limitations, there is no Federal Tort Claims Act remedy for torts committed in foreign territory. United States v. Spelar, 338 U.S. 217 (1949).

76. U.S. Const. art. III, § 2.

77. Steven M. Shapiro et al., *Supreme Court Practice: For Practice in the Supreme Court of the United States*, 10th ed. (Arlington, VA: Bloomberg BNA, 2013), 239–41.

78. 403 U.S. 388 (1971); Davis v. Passman, 442 U.S. 228 (1979); Carlson v. Green, 446 U.S. 14 (1980); Pfander, *Constitutional Torts*, 20–24; see Hartman v. Moore, 547 U.S. 250, 256 (2006) (dictum) (First Amendment).

79. Nina Bernstein, "U.S. to Pay $1.2 Million to 5 Detainees over Abuse Lawsuit," *New York Times*, November 3, 2009; Abel, *Law's Trials*, 465.

80. Susan N. Herman, *Taking Liberties: The War on Terror and the Erosion of American Democracy* (New York: Oxford University Press, 2011), 205.

81. 137 S. Ct. 1843, 1852, 1853, 1869 (2017).

82. 137 S. Ct. at 1861.

83. 137 S. Ct. at 1860, 1861, 1862.

84. 137 S. Ct. at 1860, 1861, 1863.

85. 137 S. Ct. at 1860.

86. 137 S. Ct. at 1860, 1863; 137 S. Ct. at 1883–84 (Breyer, J., dissenting).

87. Ziglar, 137 S. Ct. at 1863; Jules Lobel, "*Ziglar v. Abbasi* and the Demise of Accountability," *Fordham Law Review* 86 (2018): 2153; see also Ziglar, 137 S. Ct. at 1884 (Breyer, J., dissenting).

88. 556 U.S. 662, 677-87 (2009).

89. Conley v. Gibson, 355 U.S. 41, 45 (1957); Stephen B. Burbank and Stephen N. Subrin, "Litigation and Democracy: Restoring a Realistic Prospect of Trial," *Harvard Civil Rights–Civil Liberties Law Review* 46 (2011): 407.

90. 556 U.S. at 667–68; 556 U.S. at 688–89 (Souter, J., dissenting); Warren Richey, "Who's at Fault for Harsh Antiterror Tactics?," *Christian Science Monitor*, Dec. 9, 2008.

91. 556 U.S. at 666, 680, 681; Editorial, "Accountability and the Court," *New York Times*, December 10, 2008.

92. 556 U.S. at 666, 681.

93. 556 U.S. at 678; Fed. R. Civ. P. 8(a)(2).

94. Peter Laumann, "*Ashcroft v. Iqbal* and Binding International Law: Command Responsibility in the Context of War Crimes and Human Rights Abuses," *University of Pennsylvania Journal of Law and Social Change* 16 (2013): 181.

95. 556 U.S. at 681, 682, 686.

96. United States v. Reynolds, 345 U.S. 1, 4, 5 (1953).

97. United States v. Reynolds, 345 U.S. at 10–11; Erin M. Stilp, "The Military and State-Secrets Privilege: The Quietly Expanding Power," *Catholic University Law Review* 55 (2006): 844.

98. 345 U.S. at 11 n.26.

99. Christina E. Wells, "State Secrets and Executive Accountability," *Constitutional Commentary* 26 (2010): 637; Amanda Frost, "The State Secrets Privilege and Separation of Powers," *Fordham Law Review* 75 (2007): 1939–40; Scott Shane, "Invoking Secrets Privilege Becomes a More Popular Legal Tactic by U.S.," *New York Times*, June 4, 2006; Dana Priest, "Secrecy Privilege Invoked in Fighting Ex-Detainee's Lawsuit," *Washington Post*, May 13, 2006; Laura K. Donohue, "The Shadow of State Secrets," *University of Pennsylvania Law Review* 159 (2010): 87. Compare Robert M. Chesney, "State Secrets and the Limits of National Security Litigation," *George Washington Law Review* 75 (2007): 1299–1308 (arguing that the Bush administration had not used the privilege differently).

100. Dana Priest, "Secrecy Privilege Invoked in Fighting Ex-Detainee's Lawsuit," *Washington Post*, May 13, 2006.

101. El-Masri v. United States, 479 F.3d 296, 308, 310 (4th Cir. 2007), *cert. denied*, 552 U.S. 947 (2007); Khaled El-Masri, "I Am Not a State Secret," *Los Angeles Times*, March 3, 2007.

102. Arar v. Ashcroft, 585 F.3d 559, 575–77 (2d Cir. 2009) (en banc), *cert. denied*, 560 U.S. 978 (2010).

103. Arar, 585 F.3d at 630 (Calabresi, J., dissenting); 585 F.3d at 574.

104. 542 U.S. at 521.

105. Stephen I. Vladek, "The Long War, the Federal Courts, and the Necessity/Legality Paradox," *University of Richmond Law Review* 43 (2009): 913–17; Editorial, "The Court Retreats on Habeas," *New York Times*, June 14, 2012.

106. 137 S. Ct. at 1869.

Chapter 5

1. USA Today/Gallup Poll, January 30–February 1, 2009. A *Washington Post*–ABC News survey conducted in January 2009 found 50% in support of an investigation with 47% opposed. Jon Cohen, "On Torture," *Behind the Numbers* (blog), *Washington Post*, January 21, 2009.

2. Sanford Levinson, ed., *Torture: A Collection* (Oxford: Oxford University Press, 2004).

3. Jonathan Alter, "Time to Think about Torture," *Newsweek*, November 4, 2001; Jim Rutenberg, "Torture Seeps into Discussion by News Media," *New York Times*, November 5, 2001; Alan M. Dershowitz, "Is There a Torturous Road to Justice?," *Los Angeles Times*, November 8, 2001.

4. *60 Minutes II: Court Martial in Iraq* (CBS television broadcast April 28, 2004); Mayer, *Dark Side*, 260; Hersh, "Torture at Abu Ghraib."

5. Paul Wolfowitz, deputy secretary of defense, interview by Pentagon Channel, May 4, 2004.

6. *Weekly Comp. Pres. Doc.*, May 24, 2004, 40:947; Office of the Press Secretary, White House, "Press Briefing by Scott McClellan," June 15, 2004.

7. *Weekly Comp. Pres. Doc.*, May 10, 2004, 40:850; *Detention and Interrogation Operations: Hearings before the Committee on Armed Services*, 11; Office of the Press Secretary, White House, "Press Briefing by Scott McClellan," May 26, 2004; "Press Briefing by White House Counsel Judge Alberto Gonzales et al.," June 22, 2004.

8. *Weekly Comp. Pres. Doc.*, June 22, 2004, 40:1131; "Press Briefing by Scott McClellan," June 22, 2004; "Press Briefing by White House Counsel," June 22, 2004.

9. Dana Priest and R. Jeffrey Smith, "Memo Offered Justification for Use of Torture," *Washington Post*, June 8, 2004; John Barry, Michael Isikoff, and Michael Hirsh, "The Roots of Torture," *Newsweek*, May 24, 2004; Neil A. Lewis, "Justice Memos Explained How to Skip Prisoner Rights," *New York Times*, May 21, 2004; Isikoff, "War Crimes Warnings"; Editorial, "A Failure of Leadership at the Highest Levels," *Army Times*, May 17, 2004; Dana Priest and Joe Stephens, "Secret World of U.S. Interrogation," *Washington Post*, May 11, 2004; *Final Report*, 13; Danner, *Torture and Truth*, 48.

10. Glen Johnson, "Kerry Vows Independent Panel on Abuse," *Boston Globe*, June 16, 2004; James W. Ceaser and Andrew E. Busch, *Red over Blue: The 2004 Elections and American Politics* (Lanham, MD: Rowman and Littlefield, 2005), 113–14; Jared Del Rosso, *Talking about Torture: How Political Discourse Shapes the Debate* (New York: Columbia University Press, 2015), 62; Danner, *Torture and Truth*, 40. See also Lisa Hajjar, *Torture: A Sociology of Violence and Human Rights* (New York: Routledge, 2013), 9–10.

11. Paul R. Abramson, John H. Aldrich, and David W. Rohde, "The 2004 Presidential Election: The Emergence of a Permanent Majority?," *Political Science Quarterly* 120 (2005): 40; Jim VandeHei and Michael A. Fletcher, "Bush Says Election Ratified Iraq Policy," *Washington Post*, January 16, 2005.

12. *Confirmation Hearing on the Nomination of Alberto R. Gonzales*, 14.

13. Mark Benjamin, "Would Obama Prosecute the Bush Administration for Torture?," *Salon*, August 4, 2008.

14. Will Bunch, "Obama Would Ask His AG to 'Immediately Review' Potential of Crimes in Bush White House," Attytood, *Philadelphia Inquirer*, April 14, 2008.

15. Scott Shane, "To Investigate or Not: Four Ways to Look Back at Bush," *New York Times*, February 22, 2009.

16. Mickey Edwards, "A Truth Commission? It's a Start," *Politico*, March 16, 2009; Loch K. Johnson, *A Season of Inquiry Revisited: The Church Committee Confronts America's Spy Agencies* (Lawrence: University Press of Kansas, 2015), 41–49, 126–28.

17. Lance Cole, "Special National Investigative Commissions: Essential Powers and Procedures (Some Lessons from the Pearl Harbor, Warren Commission, and 9/11 Commission Investigations)," *McGeorge Law Review* 41 (2009): 1–61; Jonathan Simon, "Parrhesiastic Accountability: Investigatory Commissions and Executive Power in an Age of Terror," *Yale Law Journal* 114 (2005): 1428–30; Philip Rucker, "Leahy Proposes Panel to Investigate Bush Era," *Washington Post*, February 10, 2009.

18. Katy J. Harriger, *The Special Prosecutor in American Politics*, 2nd ed. (Lawrence: University Press of Kansas, 2000).

19. Margaret Talev and William Douglas, "Pressure Grows on Obama to Call for Inter-

rogation Panel," *McClatchy Newspapers*, August 23, 2009; Andy Barr, "McCain: Obama Starting 'Witch Hunt,'" *Politico*, April 23, 2009; Eric Etheridge, "Is Cheney Winning the Torture Debate?," Opinionator, *New York Times*, April 23, 2009.

20. Fred Hiatt, "Time for a Souter-O'Connor Commission," *Washington Post*, August 30, 2009.

21. Patrick Leahy, "The Case for a Truth Commission," *Time*, February 19, 2009; Nicholas D. Kristof, "Putting Torture behind Us," *New York Times*, January 29, 2009; Editorial, "Interrogations and Prosecution," *Washington Post*, July 27, 2009; Mark Benjamin, "Would Obama Prosecute the Bush Administration for Torture?," *Salon*, August 4, 2008; Pamela Hess, "Obama Urged to Create Special Detainee Commission," *Associated Press*, February 18, 2009; Andrew Sullivan, "Obama's First Problem Is US War Crimes," *Sunday Times* (London), November 30, 2008; Human Rights Watch, "Accountability for Torture," May 13, 2009.

22. H.R. 104, 111th Cong. (2009); Josh Gerstein, "'Truth Commission' Hurdles Remain," *Politico*, April 21, 2009.

23. OLC 5/10/05 Torture Act Opinion, 14; *Daily Comp. Pres. Docs.*, 2009 DCPD No. 00305, 5.

24. *Daily Comp. Pres. Docs.*, 2009 DCPD No. 00263, 2.

25. *Daily Comp. Pres. Docs.*, 2009 DCPD No. 00263, 1; Exec. Order No. 13,491, 74 Fed. Reg. 4893 (January 27, 2009); David Johnston and Charlie Savage, "Obama Reluctant to Look into Bush Programs," *New York Times*, January 12, 2009; David M. Herszenhorn and Carl Hulse, "Obama Resisting Push for Interrogation Panel," *New York Times*, April 24, 2009.

26. *Daily Comp. Pres. Docs.*, 2009 DCPD No. 00263, 2.

27. *Daily Comp. Pres. Docs.*, 2009 DCPD No. 00277, 5; David Johnston and Charlie Savage, "Obama Reluctant to Look into Bush Programs," *New York Times*, January 12, 2009; Josh Gerstein, "'Truth Commission' Hurdles Remain," *Politico*, April 21, 2009. Foreign prosecutions might have been considered a viable alternative without roiling American politics, but the Obama administration blocked foreign investigations as well. Michael Slackman, "Officials Pressed Germans on Kidnapping by C.I.A.," *New York Times*, December 9, 2010.

28. Peter Baker and Scott Shane, "Pressure Grows to Investigate Interrogations," *New York Times*, April 21, 2009.

29. Ewen MacAskill, "Obama: Bush Aides May Be Prosecuted over Torture," *Guardian*, April 21, 2009; Michael Hayden and Michael B. Mukasey, "The President Ties His Own Hands on Terror," *Wall Street Journal*, April 17, 2009; Shailagh Murray, "A Commission on Enhanced Interrogation? Obama Rebuffs Idea," *Washington Post*, April 23, 2009; Michael D. Shear, "Cheney Says Current Policies Put More Americans at Risk," *Washington Post*, May 22, 2009.

30. Rahm Emanuel, interview by George Stephanopoulos, *This Week*, ABC, April 19, 2009; *Daily Comp. Pres. Docs.*, 2009 DCPD No. 00277, 5; Ewen MacAskill, "Bush Aides May Be Prosecuted over Torture," *Guardian*, April 21, 2009.

31. *Daily Comp. Pres. Docs.*, 2009 DCPD No. 00277, 5; Josh Gerstein, "'Truth Commission' Hurdles Remain," *Politico*, April 21, 2009; Shailagh Murray and Paul Kane, "Obama Rejects Truth Panel," *Washington Post*, April 24, 2009.

32. Andy Barr, "McCain: Obama Starting 'Witch Hunt,'" *Politico*, April 23, 2009; David

Broder, "Stop Scapegoating: Obama Should Stand against Prosecutions," *Washington Post*, April 26, 2009.

33. Jane Mayer, "Thoughts on the Levin Report," *New Yorker*, April 21, 2009; "Obama Reprieve for CIA Illegal: U.N. Rapporteur," *Reuters*, April 21, 2009; American Civil Liberties Union, "Broad Coalition of Advocacy Groups Present Attorney General with Petition," news release, April 23, 2009.

34. Thomas L. Friedman, "A Torturous Compromise," *New York Times*, April 29, 2009.

35. David Broder, "Stop Scapegoating: Obama Should Stand against Prosecutions," *Washington Post*, April 26, 2009; Jeffrey M. Jones, "Slim Majority Wants Bush-Era Interrogations Investigated," Gallup, April 27, 2009. According to an NBC/*Wall Street Journal* survey, 33% supported a criminal investigation with 61% opposed. Study #6094, April 23–26, 2009. David Forsythe read this to mean that a "clear majority" was "opposed to prosecutions." Forsythe, *Politics of Prisoner Abuse*, 203 n.23. It would be helpful to know if those supporting a commission inquiry or congressional investigations would have accepted prosecutions as an alternative if their favored option did not materialize.

36. "Statement by Attorney General Michael B. Mukasey Regarding the Opening of an Investigation into the Destruction of Videotapes by CIA Personnel," DOJ, January 2, 2008; "Attorney General Eric Holder Regarding a Preliminary Review into the Interrogation of Certain Detainees," DOJ, August 24, 2009.

37. Andrew C. McCarthy, "Eric Holder's Hidden Agenda," *National Review Online*, August 28, 2009; Glenn Greenwald, "Eric Holder Announces Investigation Based on Abu Ghraib Model," *Salon*, August 24, 2009; Liz Halloran, "CIA Probe Not Enough to Please Disaffected Liberals," *NPR*, August 26, 2009; Dahlia Lithwick, "Halfway There," *Slate*, August 25, 2009.

38. "Statement of the Attorney General Regarding Investigation into the Interrogation of Certain Detainees," DOJ, June 30, 2011; Ken Dilanian, "Most CIA Interrogation Cases Won't Be Pursued," *Los Angeles Times*, July 1, 2011; "Statement of Attorney General Eric Holder on Closure of Investigation into the Interrogation of Certain Detainees," DOJ, August 30, 2012; Scott Shane, "No Charges Filed on Harsh Tactics Used by the C.I.A.," *New York Times*, August 30, 2012. On Holder's statement, see Luban, *Torture, Power, and Law*, 280–82.

39. David Stout, "Holder Tells Senators Waterboarding Is Torture," *New York Times*, January 15, 2009.

40. John Yoo, interview by Fareed Zakaria, *Fareed Zakaria GPS*, CNN, December 14, 2014.

41. SSCI Report, 44.

42. SSCI Report, 43.

43. Scott Shane, "Political Divide about C.I.A. Torture Remains after Senate Report's Release," *New York Times*, December 9, 2014.

44. Adam Goldman and Peyton Craighill, "New Poll Finds Majority of Americans Think Torture Was Justified after 9/11 Attacks," *Washington Post*, December 16, 2014; "A Majority of Americans Support Harsh CIA Interrogations, Poll Finds," *Washington Post*, December 17, 2014; Pew Research Center, "About Half See CIA Interrogation Methods as Justified," December 15, 2014.

45. On effectiveness, see Luban, *Torture, Power, and Law*, 300–2.

46. SSCI Report, xi.

47. *Weekly Comp. Pres. Doc.*, September 6, 2006, 42:1570–71, 1572; Scott Shane and Charlie Savage, "Bin Laden Raid Revives Debate on Value of Torture," *New York Times*, May 3, 2011; José A. Rodriguez Jr., "The Path to Osama bin Laden's Death Didn't Start with Obama," *Washington Post*, April 30, 2012; Frank Bruni, "Bin Laden, Torture and Hollywood," *New York Times*, December 9, 2012.

48. Sarah Dutton et al., "Most Americans Consider Waterboarding to Be Torture: Poll," *CBS News*, December 15, 2014.

49. George J. Tenet et al., "CIA Interrogations Saved Lives," *Wall Street Journal*, December 10, 2014; Gregory Korte, "Former CIA Directors Launch Rebuttal Campaign," *USA Today*, December 9, 2014; SSCI Report, Minority Views of Vice Chairman Chambliss et al., 573–629; Jonathan Topaz, "GOP Senators Defend CIA in Alternate Report," *Politico*, December 9, 2014; "Statement from Director Brennan on the SSCI Study on the Former Detention and Interrogation Program," CIA, December 9, 2014; Juliet Eilperin, "CIA Director Rebuts Report, Says Interrogation Techniques 'Saved Lives,'" *Washington Post*, December 9, 2014.

50. John McLaughlin, "Senate Intelligence Report Distorts the CIA's Success at Foiling Terrorist Plots," *Washington Post*, December 9, 2014; José A. Rodriguez Jr., "I Ran the CIA Interrogation Program. No Matter What the Senate Report Says, I Know It Worked," *Washington Post*, April 4, 2014.

51. Pew Research Center, "CIA Interrogation Methods," 2; Oliver Laughland, "CIA Report: 'Torture Is a Crime and Those Responsible Must Be Brought to Justice,'" *Guardian*, December 10, 2014; Editorial, "Prosecute Torturers and Their Bosses," *New York Times*, December 22, 2014; David Jackson, "Obama: 'We Tortured Folks,'" *USA Today*, August 1, 2014; *Daily Comp. Pres. Docs.*, 2014 DCPD No. 00913, 1.

52. Thomas L. Friedman, "We're Always Still Americans," *New York Times*, December 10, 2014; Fareed Zakaria, "Why Releasing the CIA Torture Report Will Make America Stronger," *Washington Post*, December 11, 2014; E. J. Dionne Jr., "Reactions to the CIA Report Suggest That Many Involved Would Do It All Over Again," *Washington Post*, December 10, 2014.

53. Sikkink, *Justice Cascade*, 148–50; Kathryn Sikkink and Carrie Booth Walling, "The Impact of Human Rights Trials in Latin America," *Journal of Peace Research* 44 (2007): 427–45.

54. Steve Benen, "'Colonels in Mirrored Sunglasses,'" *Washington Monthly*, April 22, 2009; Eric Etheridge, "Is Cheney Winning the Torture Debate?," Opinionator, *New York Times*, April 23, 2009; Philip Rucker, "Leahy Proposes Panel to Investigate Bush Era," *Washington Post*, February 10, 2009.

55. Richard N. Haass, "The Interrogation Memos and the Law," *Wall Street Journal*, May 1, 2009.

56. Eric Posner, "Why Obama Won't Prosecute Torturers," *Slate*, December 9, 2014; Walzer, "Trying Political Leaders"; David S. Broder, "Why Holder Is Wrong," *Washington Post*, September 3, 2009; Alan M. Dershowitz, "Indictments Are Not the Best Revenge," *Wall Street Journal*, September 12, 2008; Fred Hiatt, "Time for a Souter-O'Connor Commission," *Washington Post*, August 30, 2009.

57. Walzer, "Trying Political Leaders."

58. Walzer, "Trying Political Leaders."

59. David Broder, "Stop Scapegoating: Obama Should Stand against Prosecutions," *Washington Post*, April 26, 2009; Roger Cohen, "No Time for Retribution," *New York Times*, April 23, 2009.

60. Charlie Savage, "Any Indictment of Interrogation Policy Makers Would Face Several Hurdles," *New York Times*, April 23, 2009.

61. Jack M. Balkin, "A Body of Inquiries," *New York Times*, January 11, 2009; David Johnston and Mark Mazzetti, "Hurdles Stand in Way of Prosecuting Abuses," *New York Times*, August 26, 2009; Marisa Taylor, "Did Bush Officials Commit War Crimes? Maybe, but Trials Aren't Likely," *McClatchy Newspapers*, December 19, 2008; P. X. Kelley and Robert F. Turner, "War Crimes and the White House," *Washington Post*, July 26, 2007; Marty Lederman, "A Dissenting View on Prosecuting the Waterboarders," *Balkinization* (blog), February 8, 2008 (italics in the original).

62. DTA, §1004(a); Rosen, "Torturous Decision"; David Corn, "The Problem with a Special Prosecutor," *Mother Jones*, April 27, 2009; Stuart Taylor Jr., "The Truth about Torture," *Newsweek*, July 12, 2008.

63. Joshua Dressler, *Understanding Criminal Law*, 4th ed. (Newark, NJ: LexisNexis, 2006), 177; "The Immunity-Conferring Power of the Office of Legal Counsel," *Harvard Law Review* 121 (2008): 2094.

64. DTA, §1004(a); "Immunity-Conferring Power," 2094, 2095.

65. Raley v. Ohio, 360 U.S. 423, 438 (1959). The Court held similarly in a First Amendment case in which a protester was convicted for demonstrating near a courthouse even though he obeyed directions given him by the chief of police. Cox v. Louisiana, 379 U.S. 559 (1965); "Immunity-Conferring Power," 2092–96.

66. "Immunity-Conferring Power," 2096–2101.

67. Leahy, "Case for a Truth Commission"; Cole, "Torturer-in-Chief"; Rosa Brooks, "Bush Can Get Away with It," *Los Angeles Times*, July 31, 2008; Pamela Hess, "Obama Urged to Create Special Detainee Commission," *Associated Press*, February 18, 2009; Margaret Talev and William Douglas, "Pressure Grows on Obama to Call for Interrogation Panel," *McClatchy Newspapers*, August 24, 2009; Mark Benjamin, "How to Build a Torture Commission," *Salon*, March 4, 2009; Scott Horton, "Justice after Bush: Prosecuting an Outlaw Administration," *Harper's*, December 2008.

68. See, e.g., M. Cherif Bassiouni, ed., *Post-Conflict Justice* (Ardsley, NY: Transnational, 2002); Robert I. Rotberg and Dennis Thompson, eds., *Truth v. Justice: The Morality of Truth Commissions* (Princeton: Princeton University Press, 2000).

69. For historical background, see Cole, "Investigative Commissions," 1–62; Stephen R. Ross, Raphael A. Prober, and Gabriel K. Gillett, "The Rise and Permanence of Quasi-Investigative Legislative Commissions," *Journal of Law and Politics* 27 (2012): 415–57.

70. Leahy, "Case for a Truth Commission."

71. Nicholas D. Kristof, "The Truth Commission," *New York Times*, July 6, 2008; Leahy, "Case for a Truth Commission"; Andrew Sullivan, "Obama's First Problem Is US War Crimes," *Sunday Times* (London), November 30, 2008.

72. See Onur Bakiner, *Truth Commissions: Memory, Power, and Legitimacy* (Philadelphia: University of Pennsylvania Press, 2016), 114–84.

73. Leahy, "Case for a Truth Commission"; Mark Benjamin, "Would Obama Prosecute the Bush Administration for Torture?," *Salon*, August 4, 2008.

74. Nicholas D. Kristof, "The Truth Commission," *New York Times*, July 6, 2008; Thomas R. Pickering and William S. Sessions, "Moving Forward by Looking Back," *Washington Post*, March 23, 2009.

75. Jack M. Balkin, "A Body of Inquiries," *New York Times*, January 11, 2009; Corn, "Special Prosecutor."

76. Patrick Leahy, "Restoring Trust in the Justice System: The Senate Judiciary Committee's Agenda in the 111th Congress" (Marver Bernstein Lecture, Georgetown University, Washington, DC, February 9, 2009); Nicholas D. Kristof, "The Truth Commission," *New York Times*, July 6, 2008.

77. Desmond Tutu, *No Future without Forgiveness* (New York: Doubleday, 1999), 20.

78. Naomi Roht-Arriaza and Javier Mariezcurrena, eds., *Transitional Justice in the Twenty-First Century: Beyond Truth versus Justice* (Cambridge: Cambridge University Press, 2006).

79. Truth and Reconciliation Commission, *Truth and Reconciliation Commission of South Africa Report* (Cape Town, South Africa, 2003), 6:595.

80. Priscilla B. Hayner, *Unspeakable Truths: Transitional Justice and the Challenge of Truth Commissions*, 2nd ed. (New York: Routledge, 2011), 9.

81. Leahy, "Case for a Truth Commission."

82. Kenneth Kitts, *Presidential Commissions and National Security: The Politics of Damage Control* (Boulder: Lynne Rienner, 2006).

83. Thomas H. Kean and Lee H. Hamilton, *Without Precedent: The Inside Story of the 9/11 Commission* (New York: Alfred A. Knopf, 2006), 20.

84. Nicholas D. Kristof, "Putting Torture behind Us," *New York Times*, January 29, 2009.

85. Kean and Hamilton, *9/11 Commission*, 14; Kitts, *Presidential Commissions*, 123, 171.

86. Richard Ben-Veniste, *The Emperor's New Clothes: Exposing the Truth from Watergate to 9/11* (New York: Thomas Dunne, 2009), 223; Cole, "Investigative Commissions," 36–60.

87. *USA Today*/Gallup poll, January 30–February 1, 2009.

88. David W. Moore, "Public Overwhelmingly Backs Bush in Attacks on Afghanistan," Gallup, October 8, 2001; Gallup, "War on Terrorism," http://www.gallup.com/poll/5257/war-terrorism.aspx

89. Paul Gronke and Darius Rejali, "U.S. Public Opinion on Torture, 2001–2009," *PS* 43 (2010): 437.

90. "Majority Says CIA Harsh Interrogations Justified," *Washington Post*–ABC News Poll, December 11–14, 2014; Ipsos Public Affairs, "Ipsos Poll Conducted for Reuters," March 28, 2016. On changing attitudes, see Peter Miller, Paul Gronke, and Darius Rejali, "Torture and Public Opinion: The Partisan Dimension," in *Examining Torture: Empirical Studies of State Repression*, ed. Tracy Lightcap and James P. Pfiffner (New York: Palgrave

Macmillan, 2014), 11–41; John Ip, "Two Narratives of Torture," *Northwestern Journal of International Human Rights* 7 (2009): 39.

Conclusion

1. Taguba, preface to *Broken Laws, Broken Lives: Medical Evidence of Torture by US Personnel and Its Impact*, by Physicians for Human Rights (2008), viii.

2. Bush Memorandum, in Greenberg and Dratel, *Torture Papers*, 135.

3. Bush Memorandum, in Greenberg and Dratel, *Torture Papers*, 134.

4. Ashcroft to the President, February 1, 2002, in Greenberg and Dratel, *Torture Papers*, 126; Gonzales 1/25/02 Memorandum, in Greenberg and Dratel, *Torture Papers*, 119, 120.

5. Mora to Inspector General, "Interrogation Issues," 14; Rives to SAF/GC, "Working Group," 1; SASC 2008 Report, 67; Taft to Yoo, "Your Draft Memorandum."

6. US Dept. of Justice, *FBI's Involvement*, 203; SASC 2008 Report, 87.

7. Woodward, *State of Denial*, 86–87.

8. Charlie Savage, "Bush Could Bypass New Torture Ban," *Boston Globe*, January 4, 2006.

9. *Weekly Comp. Pres. Doc.*, September 6, 2006, 42:1572, 1574, 1575; Exec. Order No. 13,440, 72 Fed. Reg. 40707, 40708 (July 24, 2007); P. X. Kelley and Robert F. Turner, "War Crimes and the White House," *Washington Post*, July 26, 2007; *Weekly Comp. Pres. Doc.*, March 8, 2008, 44:346–47.

10. MCA, § 6(b); 18 U.S.C. § 2441(d).

11. Hamdi, 542 U.S. at 521, 536.

12. Ziglar, 137 S. Ct. at 1869.

13. 137 S. Ct. at 1860.

14. Dahlia Lithwick, "We're All Torturers Now," *Slate*, April 25, 2009.

15. Goldsmith, *Power and Constraint*, 209.

16. *Daily Comp. Pres. Docs.*, 2009 DCPD No. 00263; Thomas L. Friedman, "A Torturous Compromise," *New York Times*, April 29, 2009; Luban, *Torture, Power, and Law*, 276.

17. OLC 8/1/02 Interrogation Opinion.

18. Exec. Order No. 13,491, 74 Fed. Reg. 4893 (January 27, 2009); National Defense Authorization Act for Fiscal Year 2016, Pub. L. No. 114–92, § 1045(a), 129 Stat. 725, 977.

19. Philip Elliott, "Jeb Bush Is Not the Only 2016 Candidate Open to Torture," *Time*, August 14, 2015; 2015; Jenna Johnson, "Trump Says 'Torture Works,' Backs Waterboarding and 'Much Worse,'" *Washington Post*, February 17, 2016.

20. "Sean Spicer: Draft Order on Interrogation Methods 'Is Not a White House Document,'" CBS News, January 25, 2017; Mark Mazzetti and Charlie Savage, "Leaked Draft of Executive Order Could Revive C.I.A. Prisons," *New York Times*, January 25, 2017.

21. Gallup, "War on Terrorism"; "Majority Says CIA Harsh Interrogations Justified," *Washington Post*–ABC News Poll.

22. Averell Schmidt and Kathryn Sikkink, "Partners in Crime: An Empirical Evaluation of the CIA Rendition, Detention, and Interrogation Program," *Perspectives on Politics* 16 (2018): 1018–27.

23. Amnesty International, *Torture in 2014: 30 Years of Broken Promises* (London:

Amnesty International, 2014), 10; UN Office of the High Commissioner on Human Rights, "'If the US Tortures, Why Can't We Do It?'"—UN Expert Says Moral High Ground Must Be Recovered," December 11, 2014; Nick Cumming-Bruce, "Torture Fight Set Back by U.S. Failure to Prosecute, U.N. Official Says," *New York Times*, December 11, 2014.

24. UN Office of the High Commissioner on Human Rights, "'If the US Tortures, Why Can't We Do It?'"—UN Expert Says Moral High Ground Must Be Recovered," December 11, 2014; Averell Schmidt and Kathryn Sikkink, "Breaking the Ban? The Heterogeneous Impact of US Contestation of the Torture Norm," *Journal of Global Security Studies* 4 (2019): 110–11, 118; Lisa Hajjar, "The Counterterrorism War Paradigm versus International Humanitarian Law: The Legal Contradictions and Global Consequences of the US 'War on Terror,'" *Law and Social Inquiry* 44 (2019): 928–29.

25. US Office of the Director of National Intelligence, *Annual Threat Assessment of the U.S. Intelligence Community* (2022), 25, 26.

26. Sanford Levinson and Jack M. Balkin, "Constitutional Dictatorship: Its Dangers and Design," *Minnesota Law Review* 94 (2010): 1836; Sanford Levinson, "Constitutional Norms in a State of Permanent Emergency," *Georgia Law Review* 40 (2006): 737.

27. Elizabeth White, "Obama Says Gitmo Facility Should Close," *Washington Post*, June 24, 2007.

28. Exec. Order No. 13,493, 74 Fed. Reg. 4901 (January 27, 2009).

29. Noah Feldman, "A Prison of Words," *New York Times*, March 19, 2009.

30. David Glazier, "Destined for an Epic Fail: The Problematic Guantánamo Military Commissions," *Ohio State Law Journal* 75 (2014): 903–67.

31. Al Maqaleh v. Gates, 605 F.3d 84 (D.C. Cir. 2010).

32. Lisa Hajjar, *The War in Court: Inside the Long Fight against Torture* (Oakland: University of California Press, 2022), 229; Constitution Project, *The Report of the Constitution Project's Task Force on Detainee Treatment* (Washington, DC, 2013), 328; Jeremy Scahill, "The CIA's Secret Sites in Somalia," *The Nation*, August 1, 2011; Alyssa J. Rubin, "Afghans Detail U.S. Detention in 'Black Jail,'" *New York Times*, November 29, 2009.

33. Constitution Project, *Report of the Constitution Project's Task Force*, 23.

34. National Defense Authorization Act for Fiscal Year 2012, Pub. L. No. 112–81, § 1021, 125 Stat. 1298, 1562; *Daily Comp. Pres. Docs.*, 2011 DCPD No. 00978, 1–2.

35. Charlie Savage, "Obama's War on Terror May Resemble Bush's in Areas," *New York Times*, February 18, 2009; Peter Baker, "Even as Wars Fade, Obama Maintains Bush's Data Mining," *New York Times*, June 6, 2013; ACLU, *Establishing a New Normal: National Security, Civil Liberties, and Human Rights under the Obama Administration* (2010), 2.

36. Stephen I. Vladek, "The Unreviewable Executive: *Kiyemba, Maqaleh*, and the Obama Administration," *Constitutional Commentary* 26 (2010): 604–6.

37. Jelena Pejic, "Extraterritorial Targeting by Means of Armed Drones: Some Legal Implications," *International Review of the Red Cross* 96 (2014): 69.

38. Solis, *Law of Armed Conflict*, 546–47; Tom Bowman, "The Rise of the Drone, and the Thorny Questions That Have Followed," *NPR*, September 8, 2016; Rosa Brooks, "Drones and the International Rule of Law," *Ethics and International Affairs* 28 (2014): 89.

39. Columbia Law School Human Rights Clinic, *Counting Drone Strike Deaths* (New York, 2012), 4–6.

40. Mikah Zenko, "Final Drone Strike Data" (blog), Council on Foreign Relations, January 20, 2017; Kerstin Fisk and Jennifer M. Ramos, "Introduction: The Preventive Force Continuum," in *Preventive Force: Drones, Targeted Killing, and the Transformation of Contemporary Warfare*, ed. Kerstin Fisk and Jennifer M. Ramos (New York: New York University Press, 2016), 8; David E. Sanger, "Cyber, Drones, and Secrecy," in *Understanding Cyber Conflict: Fourteen Analogies*, ed. George Perkovich and Ariel E. Levite (Washington, DC: Georgetown University Press, 2017), 63.

41. Daniel Klaidman, *Kill or Capture: The War on Terror and the Soul of the Obama Presidency* (Boston: Houghton Mifflin Harcourt, 2012), 39–40; Jo Becker and Scott Shane, "Secret 'Kill List' Proves a Test of Obama's Principles and Will," *New York Times*, May 29, 2012; Scott Shane, "Election Spurred a Move to Codify U.S. Drone Policy," *New York Times*, November 25, 2012; Karen DeYoung, "Secrecy Defines Obama's Drone War," *Washington Post*, December 19, 2011.

42. H. Jefferson Powell, *Targeting Americans: The Constitutionality of the U.S. Drone War* (New York: Oxford University Press, 2016), xvii.

43. Charlie Savage, *Power Wars: Inside Obama's Post-9/11 Presidency* (New York: Little, Brown, 2015), 227–28, 230, 235; Lisa Hajjar, "Anatomy of the US Targeted Killing Policy," *Middle East Report* 264 (2012): 13–16; Klaidman, *Kill or Capture*, 216; Jo Becker and Scott Shane, "Secret 'Kill List' Proves a Test of Obama's Principles and Will," *New York Times*, May 29, 2012.

44. UN Charter, art. 51; Harold Hongju Koh, legal advisor, US Dept. of State, "The Obama Administration and International Law" (speech at the Annual Meeting of the American Society of International Law, Washington, DC, March 25, 2010); David Glazier, "The Drone: It's in the Way That You Use It," in Fisk and Ramos, *Preventive Force*, 160–61; Mary Ellen O'Connell, "Unlawful Killing with Combat Drones: A Case Study of Pakistan, 2004–2009," in *Shooting to Kill: Socio-Legal Perspectives on the Use of Lethal Force*, ed. Simon Bronitt, Miriam Gani, and Saskia Hufnagel (Oxford, UK: Hart, 2012), 280; Philip Alston, "Study on Targeted Killings," Addendum to Report of the Special Rapporteur on Extrajudicial, Summary or Arbitrary Executions, U.N. Doc. A/HRC/14/24/Add. 6 (2010), 25.

45. Charlie Savage, "White House Tightens Rules on Counterterrorism Drone Strikes," *New York Times*, October 7, 2022; Glazier, "Drone," 146–47; Pejic, "Extraterritorial Targeting," 83.

46. Protocol Additional to the Geneva Conventions of 12 August 1949 and Relating to the Protection of Victims of International Armed Conflicts, June 8, 1977, 1125 U.N.T.S. 3, arts. 48, 51(3); Glazier, "Drone," 153–54; Kevin Jon Heller, "'One Hell of a Killing Machine': Signature Strikes and International Law," *Journal of International Criminal Justice* 11 (2013): 97–109.

47. Protocol Additional to the Geneva Conventions of 12 August 1949 and Relating to the Protection of Victims of International Armed Conflicts, June 8, 1977, 1125 U.N.T.S. 3, art. 51(5); *Daily Comp. Pres. Docs.*, 2013 DCPD No. 00361, 6; Amnesty International, *"Will I Be Next?" US Drone Strikes in Pakistan* (London: Amnesty International, 2013), 14, 18, 23, 28, 30, 56; Human Rights Watch, *"Between a Drone and Al-Qaeda": The Civilian Cost of US Targeted Killings in Yemen* (New York: Human Rights Watch, 2013); Peter Baker, "Obama

Apologizes after Drone Kills American and Italian Held by Qaeda," *New York Times*, April 23, 2015.

48. 18 U.S.C. § 1119; Kevin Jon Heller, "Let's Call Killing al-Awlaki What It Is—Murder," *Opinio Juris*, April 8, 2010, https://opiniojuris.org/2010/04/08/lets-call-killing-al-awlaki-what-it-is-murder/; Savage, *Power Wars*, 233–39, 249–50.

49. Glazier, "Drone," 154–55; US DOJ, White Paper, "Lawfulness of a Lethal Operation Directed against a U.S. Citizen Who Is a Senior Operational Leader of Al-Qa'ida or an Associated Force," Draft, November 8, 2011, 5–9; Charlie Savage and Scott Shane, "Memo Cites Legal Basis for Killing U.S. Citizens in Al Qaeda," *New York Times*, February 5, 2013; Charlie Savage, "Secret U.S. Memo Made Legal Case to Kill a Citizen," *New York Times*, October 9, 2011; Vicki Divoll, "Drone Strikes: What's the Law?," *Los Angeles Times*, February 17, 2013.

50. *Weekly Comp. Pres. Doc.*, October 5, 2007, 43:1312.

51. Scott Shane, "C.I.A. Is Disputed on Civilian Toll in Drone Strikes," *New York Times*, August 12, 2011; Karen DeYoung, "Secrecy Defines Obama's Drone War," *Washington Post*, December 19, 2011.

52. *Daily Comp. Pres. Docs.*, 2013 DCPD No. 00361, 6; *Daily Comp. Pres. Docs.*, 2016 DCPD No. 00226, 17; Eric Holder, US Att'y Gen., DOJ, speech at Northwestern University School of Law, Evanston, IL, March 5, 2012.

53. Scott Shane, "Election Spurred a Move to Codify U.S. Drone Policy," *New York Times*, November 25, 2012; Greg Jaffe and Karen DeYoung, "Trump Wants to Relax Rules Governing Drone Strikes," *Washington Post*, March 14, 2017; Charlie Savage, "Trump's Secret Rules for Drone Strikes Outside War Zones Are Disclosed," *New York Times*, May 1, 2021; Michael Crowley, Falih Hassan, and Eric Schmitt, "U.S. Strike in Iraq Kills Qassim Suleimani, Commander of Iranian Forces," *New York Times*, January 2, 2020; Charlie Savage, "White House Tightens Rules on Counterterrorism Drone Strikes," *New York Times*, October 7, 2022; Eric Schmitt, "No U.S. Troops Will Be Punished for Deadly Kabul Strike, Pentagon Chief Decides," *New York Times*, January 13, 2021.

54. Roger O'Keefe, "Universal Jurisdiction: Clarifying the Basic Concept," *Journal of International Criminal Justice* 2 (2004): 745; Ratner, Abrams, and Bischoff, *Accountability*, 178–79; Lisa Hajjar, "Universal Jurisdiction as Praxis: An Option to Pursue Legal Accountability for Superpower Torturers," in *When Governments Break the Law: The Rule of Law and the Prosecution of the Bush Administration*, ed. Austin Sarat and Nasser Hussain (New York: New York University Press, 2010), 97; GC I, art. 49; GC II, art. 50; GC III, art. 129; GC IV, art. 146; Richard A. Falk, "Assessing the Pinochet Litigation: Whither Universal Jurisdiction?," in Macedo, *Universal Jurisdiction*, 97–120.

55. Gallagher, "Universal Jurisdiction," 1100–1114; Rachel Donadio, "Italy Convicts 23 Americans, Most Working for C.I.A., of Abducting Muslim Cleric," *New York Times*, November 5, 2009; Peter Finn, "Bush Cancels Swiss Trip as Foes Call for Protests, Torture Prosecution," *Washington Post*, February 6, 2011; Craig Whitlock, "European Nations May Investigate Bush Officials over Prisoner Treatment," *Washington Post*, April 22, 2009; Hajjar, "Universal Jurisdiction," 106–9.

56. Rome Statute, arts. 5, 8(1); Jamie Mayerfeld, "Who Shall Be the Judge? The United States, the International Criminal Court, and the Global Enforcement of Human Rights," *Human Rights Quarterly* 25 (2003): 98–104.

57. Rome Statute, pmbl., arts. 1, 17(1)(b).

58. Rome Statute, art. 17(2)(c).

59. See note 30 in introduction.

60. *Is a U.N. International Criminal Court in the U.S. National Interest? Hearing before the Subcommittee on International Operations of the Committee on Foreign Relations*, 105th Cong., 2d sess. (1998); *Weekly Comp. Pres. Doc.*, December 31, 2000, 37:4; John R. Bolton, Under Secretary of State for Arms Control and International Security Affairs, to UN Secretary-General Kofi Annan, May 6, 2002, https://2001-2009.state.gov/r/pa/prs/ps /2002/9968.htm; William A. Schabas, "United States Hostility to the International Criminal Court: It's All about the Security Council," *European Journal of International Law* 15 (2004): 714–19.

61. Rome Statute, art. 12(2); Pub. L. No. 107-206, § 2008, 116 Stat. 820, 905 (2002) (codified at 22 U.S.C. § 7427); Attila Bogdan, "The United States and the International Criminal Court: Avoiding Jurisdiction through Bilateral Agreements in Reliance on Article 98," *International Criminal Law Review* 8 (2008): 1–54. See also Daniel Krcmaric, letter, "Does the International Criminal Court Target the American Military?," *American Political Science Review* (2022): 1–7, https://doi.org/10.1017S0003055422000478

62. Krcmaric, "International Criminal Court," 2.

63. David Bosco, "Is the ICC Investigating Crimes by U.S. Forces in Afghanistan?," *Foreign Policy*, May 15, 2014, https://foreignpolicy.com/2014/05/15/is-the-icc-investigati ng-crimes-by-u-s-forces-in-afghanistan/

64. ICC, OTP, *Report on Preliminary Examination Activities (2016)*, November 14, 2016, ¶ 224; Rome Statute, art. 17(1) (d); ICC, OTP, Public Redacted Version of "Request for Authorisation of an Investigation Pursuant to Article 15," ICC-02/17–7-Red, November 20, 2017, ¶¶ 4, 49, 189, 219, 328.

65. Decision Pursuant to Article 15 of the Rome Statute on the Authorisation of an Investigation into the Situation in the Islamic Republic of Afghanistan, ICC-02/17–33, Pre-Trial Chamber II, April 12, 2019, ¶ 94; Kevin Jon Heller, "One Word for the PTC on the Interests of Justice: Taliban," *Opinio Juris*, April 13, 2019, http://opiniojuris.org/2019/04/13 /one-word-for-the-ptc-on-the-interests-of-justice-taliban/

66. Judgment on the Appeal Against the Decision on the Authorisation of an Investigation into the Situation on the Islamic Republic of Afghanistan, ICC-02/17–138, March 5, 2020, ¶ 79; Kyra Wigard and Guissou Jahangiri, "The International Criminal Court and Afghanistan: A Tale of Misunderstandings and Misinformation," *Journal of International Criminal Justice* 20 (2022): 216 n.57; Exec. Order No. 13,928, 85 Fed. Reg. 36139 (June 15, 2020); "Statement of the Prosecutor of the ICC, Karim A. A. Khan, QC," September 27, 2021.

67. Lessa and Payne, *Age of Human Rights Accountability*; Stephen Hopgood, *The Endtimes of Human Rights* (Ithaca: Cornell University Press, 2013); Eric A. Posner, *The Twilight of Human Rights Law* (New York: Oxford University Press, 2014); Kathryn Sikkink, *Evidence for Hope: Making Human Rights Work in the 21st Century* (Princeton: Princeton University Press, 2017).

BIBLIOGRAPHY

Abel, Richard L. *Law's Trials: The Performance of Legal Institutions in the US "War on Terror"*. Cambridge: Cambridge University Press, 2018.

Abel, Richard L. *Law's Wars: The Fate of the Rule of Law in the US "War on Terror"*. Cambridge: Cambridge University Press, 2018.

Abramson, Paul R., John H. Aldrich, and David W. Rohde. "The 2004 Presidential Election: The Emergence of a Permanent Majority?" *Political Science Quarterly* 120 (2005): 33–57.

Ackerman, Bruce. *The Decline and Fall of the American Republic*. Cambridge, MA: Belknap Press of Harvard University Press, 2010.

Alter, Jonathan. "Time to Think about Torture." *Newsweek*, November 4, 2001.

American Civil Liberties Union. *Establishing a New Normal: National Security, Civil Liberties, and Human Rights under the Obama Administration*. New York: ACLU, 2010.

Amnesty International. *Torture in 2014: 30 Years of Broken Promises*. London: Amnesty International, 2014.

Amnesty International. *"Will I Be Next?" US Drone Strikes in Pakistan*. London: Amnesty International, 2013.

Arthur, Paige. "How 'Transitions' Reshaped Human Rights: A Conceptual History of Transitional Justice." *Human Rights Quarterly* 31 (2009): 321–67.

Baker, Peter. *The Breach: Inside the Impeachment and Trial of William Jefferson Clinton*. New York: Scribner, 2000.

Bakiner, Onur. *Truth Commissions: Memory, Power, and Legitimacy*. Philadelphia: University of Pennsylvania Press, 2016.

Balint, Jennifer. "The Ottoman State Special Military Tribunal for the Genocide of the Armenians: 'Doing Government Business.'" In *The Hidden Histories of War Crimes Trials*, edited by Kevin Jon Heller and Gerry Simpson, 77–100. New York: Oxford University Press, 2013.

Ball, Howard. *Bush, the Detainees, and the Constitution: The Battle over Presidential Power in the War on Terror*. Lawrence: University Press of Kansas, 2007.

Ball, Howard. *Prosecuting War Crimes and Genocide: The Twentieth-Century Experience*. Lawrence: University Press of Kansas, 1999.

Barilleaux, Ryan J., and Christopher S. Kelley. "What Is the Unitary Executive?" In *The Unitary Executive and the Modern Presidency*, edited by Ryan J. Barilleaux and Christopher S. Kelley, 1–14. College Station: Texas A&M University Press, 2010.

Barron, David J., and Martin S. Lederman. "The Commander in Chief at the Lowest Ebb—a Constitutional History." *Harvard Law Review* 121 (2008): 941–1112.

Barron, David J., and Martin S. Lederman. "The Commander in Chief at the Lowest Ebb—Framing the Problem, Doctrine, and Original Understanding." *Harvard Law Review* 121 (2008): 689–804.

Barry, John. "A Tortured Debate." *Newsweek*, June 20, 2004.

Barry, John, Michael Isikoff, and Michael Hirsh. "The Roots of Torture." *Newsweek*, May 24, 2004.

Bass, Gary Jonathan. *Stay the Hand of Vengeance: The Politics of War Crimes Tribunals.* Princeton: Princeton University Press, 2000.

Bassiouni, M. Cherif. *The Institutionalization of Torture by the Bush Administration: Is Anyone Responsible?* Antwerp: Intersentia, 2010.

Bassiouni, M. Cherif. "Perspectives on International Criminal Justice." *Virginia Journal of International Law* 50 (2010): 269–323.

Bassiouni, M. Cherif, ed. *Post-Conflict Justice.* Ardsley, NY: Transnational, 2002.

Bassiouni, M. Cherif. "World War I: 'The War to End All Wars' and the Birth of a Handicapped International Criminal Justice System." *Denver Journal of International Law and Policy* 30 (2002): 244–91.

Beard, Jack M. "The Geneva Boomerang: The Military Commissions Act of 2006 and U.S. Counterterror Operations." *American Journal of International Law* 101 (2007): 56–73.

Bell, Christine. "Transitional Justice, Interdisciplinarity, and the State of the 'Field' or 'Non-Field.'" *International Journal of Transitional Justice* 3 (2009): 5–27.

Benedict, Michael Les. *The Impeachment and Trial of Andrew Johnson.* New York: W. W. Norton, 1973.

Ben-Veniste, Richard. *The Emperor's New Clothes: Exposing the Truth from Watergate to 9/11.* New York: Thomas Dunne, 2009.

Bergen, Doris L. *War and Genocide: A Concise History of the Holocaust.* Lanham, MD: Rowman and Littlefield, 2003.

Best, Geoffrey. *Humanity in Warfare.* New York: Columbia University Press, 1980.

Biderman, Albert D. "Communist Attempts to Elicit False Confessions from Air Force Prisoners of War." *Bulletin of the New York Academy of Medicine* 33 (1957): 616–25.

Black, Charles L., Jr., *Impeachment: A Handbook.* New Haven: Yale University Press, 1974.

Blackstone, William. *The Oxford Edition of Blackstone: Commentaries on the Laws of England.* Edited by Wilfred Prest. Vol. 4, *Of Public Wrongs*, edited by Ruth Paley. New York, Oxford University Press, 2016.

Blum, Carolyn Patty, Lisa Magarrell, and Marieke Wierda. *Criminal Justice for Criminal Policy: Prosecuting Abuses of Detainees in U.S. Counterterrorism Operations.* New York: International Center for Transitional Justice, 2009.

Bobbitt, Philip. "War Powers: An Essay on John Hart Ely's *War and Responsibility: Constitutional Lessons of Vietnam and Its Aftermath.*" *Michigan Law Review* 92 (1994): 1364–1400.

Bogdan, Attila. "The United States and the International Criminal Court: Avoiding Jurisdiction through Bilateral Agreements in Reliance on Article 98." *International Criminal Law Review* 8 (2008): 1–54.

Borgwardt, Elizabeth. "Re-examining Nuremberg as a New Deal Institution: Politics, Culture, and the Limits of Law in Generating Human Rights Norms." *Berkeley Journal of International Law* 23 (2005): 401–62.

Bovens, Mark. "Analysing and Assessing Accountability: A Conceptual Framework." *European Law Journal* 13 (2007): 447–68.

Bowman, Frank O., III. *High Crimes and Misdemeanors: A History of Impeachment for the Age of Trump.* Cambridge: Cambridge University Press, 2019.

Bradley, Curtis A., and Eric A. Posner. "Presidential Signing Statements and Executive Power." *Constitutional Commentary* 23 (2006): 307–64.

Bradley, Curtis A., and Trevor W. Morrison. "Historical Gloss and the Separation of Powers." *Harvard Law Review* 126 (2012): 411–85.

Brooks, Rosa. "Drones and the International Rule of Law." *Ethics and International Affairs* 28 (2014): 83–103.

Bruff, Harold H. *Bad Advice: Bush's Lawyers in the War on Terror.* Lawrence: University Press of Kansas, 2009.

Buchanan, Bruce. *Presidential Power and Accountability: Toward a Presidential Accountability System.* New York: Routledge, 2013.

Bugnion, François. "The International Committee of the Red Cross and the Development of International Humanitarian Law." *Chicago Journal of International Law* 5 (2004): 191–215.

Burbank, Stephen B., and Stephen N. Subrin. "Litigation and Democracy: Restoring a Realistic Prospect of Trial." *Harvard Civil Rights–Civil Liberties Law Review* 46 (2011): 399–414.

Bush, George W. *Decision Points.* New York: Crown, 2010.

Bush, Jonathan A. "Nuremberg: The Modern Law of War and Its Limitations." *Columbia Law Review* 93 (1993): 2022–85.

Calabresi, Stephen G., and Kevin H. Rhodes. "The Structural Constitution: Unitary Executive, Plural Judiciary." *Harvard Law Review* 106 (1992): 1153–1216.

Calabresi, Steven G., and Christopher S. Yoo. *The Unitary Executive: Presidential Power from Washington to Bush.* New Haven: Yale University Press, 2008.

Calhoun, Emily. "The Accounting: Habeas Corpus and Enemy Combatants." *University of Colorado Law Review* 79 (2008): 77–136.

Carnahan, Burrus M. "Lincoln, Lieber, and the Laws of War: The Origins and Limits of the Principle of Military Necessity." *American Journal of International Law* 92 (1998): 213–31.

Caron, David D. "If Afghanistan Has Failed, Then Afghanistan Is Dead: 'Failed States' and the Inappropriate Substitution of Legal Conclusion for Political Description." In *The Torture Debate in America*, edited by Karen J. Greenberg, 214–22. Cambridge: Cambridge University Press, 2006.

Carvin, Stephanie. *Prisoners of America's Wars: From the Early Republic to Guantanamo.* New York: Columbia University Press, 2010.

Ceaser, James W., and Andrew E. Busch. *Red over Blue: The 2004 Elections and American Politics.* Lanham, MD: Rowman and Littlefield, 2005.

Center for Human Rights and Global Justice, Human Rights First, and Human Rights

Watch. *By the Numbers: Findings of the Detainee Abuse and Accountability Project.*
2006.

Chafetz, Josh. "Congress's Constitution." *University of Pennsylvania Law Review* 160 (2012):
715–78.

Chesney, Robert M. "State Secrets and the Limits of National Security Litigation." *George
Washington Law Review* 75 (2007): 1249–1332.

Chomsky, Carol. "The United States–Dakota War Trials: A Study in Military Injustice."
Stanford Law Review 43 (1990): 13–98.

Christenson, Dino P., and Douglas L. Kriner. *The Myth of the Imperial Presidency: How
Public Opinion Checks the Unilateral Executive.* Chicago: University of Chicago Press,
2020.

CIA, Inspector General. *Special Review: Counterterrorism Detention and Interrogation Activities (September 2001–October 2003).* 2004.

Claibourn, Michele P. *Presidential Campaigns and Presidential Accountability.* Urbana:
University of Illinois Press, 2011.

Clark, Roger S. "Nuremberg and Tokyo in Contemporary Perspective." In McCormack and
Simpson, *Law of War Crimes,* 171–87.

Clarke, Richard A. *Against All Enemies: Inside America's War on Terror.* New York: Free
Press, 2004.

Clode, Charles M. *Military Forces of the Crown: Their Administration and Government.* 2
vols. London, 1869.

Cole, David. "George W. Bush: Torturer-in-Chief." *The Nation,* November 10, 2010.

Cole, Lance. "Special National Investigative Commissions: Essential Powers and Procedures (Some Lessons from the Pearl Harbor, Warren Commission, and 9/11 Commission Investigations)." *McGeorge Law Review* 41 (2009): 1–61.

Columbia Law School Human Rights Clinic. *Counting Drone Strike Deaths.* New York,
2012.

Constitution Project. *The Report of The Constitution Project's Task Force on Detainee Treatment.* Washington, DC, 2013.

Continental Congress. *Journals of the Continental Congress, 1774–1789.* Edited by Worthington C. Ford et al. 34 vols. Washington, DC, 1904–37.

Cooper, Philip J. *By Order of the President: The Use and Abuse of Executive Direct Action.*
Lawrence: University Press of Kansas, 2014.

Cooper, Philip J. "George W. Bush, Edgar Allan Poe, and the Use and Abuse of Presidential
Signing Statements." *Presidential Studies Quarterly* 35 (2005): 515–32.

Corn, David. "The Problem with a Special Prosecutor." *Mother Jones,* April 27, 2009.

Corn, Geoffrey S. "The National Security Constitution: The Separation of Powers in the
War on Terror." *St. John's Journal of Legal Commentary* 23 (2009): 973–77.

Corn, Geoffrey S. "What Law Applies to the War on Terror?" In *The War on Terror and
the Laws of War: A Military Perspective,* edited by Michael W. Lewis, 1–36. New York:
Oxford University Press, 2009.

Crenson, Matthew, and Benjamin Ginsberg. *Presidential Power: Unchecked and Unbalanced.* New York: W. W. Norton, 2007.

Cronin, Thomas E. "A Resurgent Congress and the Imperial Presidency." *Political Science
Quarterly* 95 (1980): 209–37.

Crovitz, L. Gordon, and Jeremy A. Rabkin, eds. *The Fettered Presidency: Legal Constraints on the Executive Branch*. Washington, DC: American Enterprise Institute for Public Policy Research, 1989.

Crowe, David M. "War Crimes and Genocide in History, and the Evolution of Responsive International Law." *Nationalities Papers* 37 (2009): 757–806.

Cullen, Anthony. *The Concept of Non-International Armed Conflict in International Humanitarian Law*. Cambridge: Cambridge University Press, 2010.

Dadrian, Vahakn N. *The History of the Armenian Genocide: Ethnic Conflict from the Balkans to Anatolia to the Caucasus*. Providence, RI: Berghahn, 1995.

Danner, Allison Marston. "Beyond the Geneva Conventions: Lessons from the Tokyo Tribunal in Prosecuting War and Terrorism." *Virginia Journal of International Law* 46 (2005): 83–130.

Danner, Allison Marston. "Defining Unlawful Enemy Combatants: A Centripetal Story." *Texas International Law Journal* 43 (2007): 1–14.

Danner, Mark. *Torture and Truth: America, Abu Ghraib, and the War on Terror*. New York: New York Review of Books, 2004.

Dean, John W. *Worse Than Watergate: The Secret Presidency of George W. Bush*. New York: Little, Brown, 2004.

Del Rosso, Jared. *Talking About Torture: How Political Discourse Shapes the Debate*. New York: Columbia University Press, 2015.

Denbeaux, Mark, Jonathan Hafetz, Sara Ben-David, Nicholas Stratton, and Lauren Winchester. "No Hearing Habeas: D.C. Circuit Restricts Meaningful Review." Seton Hall University School of Law Center for Policy and Research. May 1, 2012.

Denbeaux, Mark, Joshua Denbeaux, David Gratz, John Gregorek, Matthew Darby, Shana Edwards, Shane Hartman, Daniel Mann, Megan Sassaman, and Helen Skinner. "Report on Guantánamo Detainees: A Profile of 517 Detainees through Analysis of Department of Defense Data." *Seton Hall Law Review* 41 (2011): 1211–29.

Detter, Ingrid. *The Law of War*. 2nd ed. Cambridge: Cambridge University Press, 2000.

Detter, Ingrid. "The Law of War and Illegal Combatants." *George Washington Law Review* 75 (2007): 1049–1104.

Devins, Neal. "Talk Loudly and Carry a Small Stick: The Supreme Court and Enemy Combatants." *University of Pennsylvania Journal of Constitutional Law* 12 (2010): 491–528.

DiMeglio, Richard P. "Training Army Judge Advocates to Advise Commanders as Operational Law Attorneys." *Boston College International and Comparative Law Review* 54 (2013): 1185–1206.

Dinstein, Yoram. *The Conduct of Hostilities under the Law of International Armed Conflict*. 3rd ed. Cambridge: Cambridge University Press, 2016.

Donohue, Laura K. "The Shadow of State Secrets." *University of Pennsylvania Law Review* 159 (2010): 77–216.

Draper, G. I. A. D. "Grotius' Place in the Development of Legal Ideas about War." In *Hugo Grotius and International Relations*, edited by Hedley Bull, Benedict Kingsbury, and Adam Roberts, 177–208. Oxford: Clarendon Press, 1992.

Dressler, Joshua. *Understanding Criminal Law*. 4th ed. Newark, NJ: LexisNexis, 2006.

Droege, Cordula. "Elective Affinities? Human Rights and Humanitarian Law." *International Review of the Red Cross* 90 (2008): 501–48.

Duffy, Helen. "Human Rights Litigation and the 'War on Terror.'" *International Review of the Red Cross* 90 (2008): 573–97.

Duffy, Helen. *The 'War on Terror' and the Framework of International Law*. Cambridge: Cambridge University Press, 2005.

Elder, David A. "The Historical Background of Common Article 3 of the Geneva Convention of 1949." *Case Western Reserve Journal of International Law* 11 (1979): 37–69.

Ely, John Hart. *War and Responsibility: Constitutional Lessons of Vietnam and Its Aftermath*. Princeton: Princeton University Press, 1993.

Emanuel, Rahm. Interview by George Stephanopoulos. *This Week*, ABC, April 19, 2009.

Epstein, Lee, Daniel E. Ho, Gary King, and Jeffrey E. Siegel. "The Supreme Court during Crisis: How War Affects Only Non-War Cases," *New York University Law Review* 80 (2005): 1–116.

Falk, Richard. "Accountability for War Crimes and the Legacy of Nuremberg." In *War Crimes and Collective Wrongdoing: A Reader*, edited by Aleksandar Jokić, 113–36. Malden, MA: Blackwell, 2001.

Falk, Richard A. "Assessing the Pinochet Litigation: Whither Universal Jurisdiction?" In *Universal Jurisdiction: National Courts and the Prosecution of Serious Crimes under International Law*, edited by Stephen Macedo, 97–120. Philadelphia: University of Pennsylvania Press, 2004.

Falk, Richard. "War, War Crimes, Power, and Justice: Toward a Jurisprudence of Conscience." *Transnational Law and Contemporary Problems* 21 (2013): 667–84.

Farber, Daniel, ed. *Security v. Liberty: Conflicts between Civil Liberties and National Security in American History*. New York: Russell Sage Foundation, 2008.

Farrand, Max, ed. *The Records of the Federal Convention of 1787*. Rev. ed. 4 vols. New Haven: Yale University Press, 1937.

Ferling, John. *Almost a Miracle: The American Victory in the War of Independence*. New York: Oxford University Press, 2007.

Fischer, David Hackett. *Washington's Crossing*. New York: Oxford University Press, 2004.

Fisher, Louis. *In the Name of National Security: Unchecked Presidential Power and the Reynolds Case*. Lawrence: University Press of Kansas, 2006.

Fisher, Louis. *Presidential War Power*. 3rd ed. Lawrence: University Press of Kansas, 2013.

Fisk, Kerstin, and Jennifer M. Ramos. "Introduction: The Preventive Force Continuum." In *Preventive Force: Drones, Targeted Killing, and the Transformation of Contemporary Warfare*, edited by Kerstin Fisk and Jennifer M. Ramos, 1–29. New York: New York University Press, 2016.

Fiss, Owen. "The Perils of Minimalism." *Theoretical Inquiries in Law* 9 (2008): 643–64.

Fleck, Dieter. "Shortcomings of the Grave Breaches Regime." *Journal of International Criminal Justice* 7 (2009): 833–54.

Fletcher, George P., and Jens David Ohlin. *Defending Humanity: When Force Is Justified and Why*. New York: Oxford University Press, 2008.

Forsythe, David P. *The Politics of Prisoner Abuse: The United States and Enemy Prisoners after 9/11*. Cambridge: Cambridge University Press, 2011.

Fowler, Linda L. *Watchdogs on the Hill: The Decline of Congressional Oversight of U.S. Foreign Relations*. Princeton: Princeton University Press, 2015.

Freidel, Frank. *Francis Lieber: Nineteenth-Century Liberal*. Gloucester, MA: Peter Smith, 1968.

Frost, Amanda. "The State Secrets Privilege and Separation of Powers." *Fordham Law Review* 75 (2007): 1931–64.

Futamura, Madoka. *War Crimes Tribunals and Transitional Justice: The Tokyo Trial and the Nuremberg Legacy*. New York: Routledge, 2008.

Gallagher, Katherine. "Universal Jurisdiction in Practice: Efforts to Hold Donald Rumsfeld and Other High-Level United States Officials Accountable for Torture." *Journal of International Criminal Justice* 7 (2009): 1087–1116.

Gelman, Barton. *Angler: The Cheney Vice Presidency*. New York: Penguin, 2008.

Gerhardt, Michael J. *The Federal Impeachment Process: A Constitutional and Historical Analysis*. 3rd ed. Chicago: University of Chicago Press, 2019.

Ginsberg, Benjamin. *The Imperial Presidency and American Politics: Governance by Edicts and Coups*. New York: Routledge, 2022.

Ginsburg, Tom, Aziz Huq, and David Landau. "The Comparative Constitutional Law of Presidential Impeachment." *University of Chicago Law Review* 88 (2021): 81–164.

Glabe, Scott L. "Conflict Classification and Detainee Treatment in the War against al Qaeda." *Army Lawyer* (June 2010): 112–16.

Glazier, David. "Destined for an Epic Fail: The Problematic Guantánamo Military Commissions." *Ohio State Law Journal* 75 (2014): 903–67.

Glazier, David. "The Drone: It's in the Way That You Use It." In *Preventive Force: Drones, Targeted Killing, and the Transformation of Contemporary Warfare*, edited by Kerstin Fisk and Jennifer M. Ramos, 142–69. New York: New York University Press, 2016.

Glazier, David. "Full and Fair by What Measure? Identifying the International Law Regulating Military Commission Procedure." *Boston University International Law Journal* 24 (2006): 55–122.

Glazier, David. "Law of War Developments Issue Introduction." *Loyola of Los Angeles Law Review* 48 (2015): 815–28.

Glazier, David. "Precedents Lost: The Neglected History of the Military Commission." *Virginia Journal of International Law* 46 (2005): 5–81.

Glennon, Michael J. *Constitutional Diplomacy*. Princeton: Princeton University Press, 1990.

Goldsmith, Jack. *Power and Constraint: The Accountable Presidency after 9/11*. New York: W. W. Norton, 2012.

Goldsmith, Jack. *The Terror Presidency: Law and Judgment Inside the Bush Administration*. New York: W. W. Norton, 2007.

Gonzales, Alberto R. "Waging War within the Constitution." *Texas Tech Law Review* 42 (2010): 843–91.

Gordon, Gregory S. "The Trial of Peter von Hagenbach: Reconciling History, Historiography and International Criminal Law." In *The Hidden Histories of War Crimes Trials*, edited by Kevin Jon Heller and Gerry Simpson, 13–49. New York: Oxford University Press, 2013.

Grant, Ruth W., and Robert O. Keohane. "Accountability and Abuses of Power in World Politics." *American Political Science Review* 99 (2005): 29–43.

Green, Leslie C. *The Contemporary Law of Armed Conflict*. 2nd ed. Manchester: Manchester University Press, 2000.

Green, Nicholas G. "A 'Blank Check': Judicial Review and the War Powers in *Hamdi v. Rumsfeld*." *South Carolina Law Review* 56 (2005): 581–606.

Greenberg, Karen J., and Joshua L. Dratel, eds. *The Torture Papers: The Road to Abu Ghraib*. New York: Cambridge University Press, 2005.

Greenhouse, Linda. "The Mystery of Guantánamo Bay." *Berkeley Journal of International Law* 27 (2009): 1–21.

Gregory, Anthony. *The Power of Habeas Corpus in America: From King's Prerogative to the War on Terror*. Cambridge: Cambridge University Press, 2013.

Griffin, Stephen M. *Long Wars and the Constitution*. Cambridge, MA: Harvard University Press, 2013.

Gronke, Paul, and Darius Rejali. "U.S. Public Opinion on Torture, 2001–2009." *PS* 43 (2010): 437–44.

Grotius, Hugo. *De Jure Belli ac Pacis*. Translated by Francis W. Kelsey. Oxford: Clarendon Press, 1925.

Hajjar, Lisa. "Anatomy of the US Targeted Killing Policy." *Middle East Report* 264 (2012): 10–17.

Hajjar, Lisa. "The Counterterrorism War Paradigm versus International Humanitarian Law: The Legal Contradictions and Global Consequences of the US 'War on Terror.'" *Law and Social Inquiry* 44 (2019): 922–56.

Hajjar, Lisa. *Torture: A Sociology of Violence and Human Rights*. New York: Routledge, 2013.

Hajjar, Lisa. "Universal Jurisdiction as Praxis: An Option to Pursue Legal Accountability for Superpower Torturers." In *Governments Break the Law: The Rule of Law and the Prosecution of the Bush Administration*, edited by Austin Sarat and Nasser Hussain, 87–120. New York: New York University Press, 2010.

Hajjar, Lisa. *The War in Court: Inside the Long Fight against Torture*. Oakland: University of California Press, 2022.

Hall, Christopher Keith. "The First Proposal for a Permanent International Criminal Court." *International Review of the Red Cross* 38 (1998): 57–74.

Halliday, Paul D., and G. Edward White. "The Suspension Clause: English Text, Imperial Contexts, and American Implications." *Virginia Law Review* 94 (2008): 575–714.

Hamilton, Alexander, James Madison, and John Jay. *The Federalist*. Edited by Clinton Rossiter. New York: Mentor, 1961.

Harriger, Katy J. *The Special Prosecutor in American Politics*. 2nd ed. Lawrence: University Press of Kansas, 2000.

Hayner, Priscilla B. *Unspeakable Truths: Transitional Justice and the Challenge of Truth Commissions*. 2nd ed. New York: Routledge, 2011.

Heller, Kevin Jon. *The Nuremberg Military Tribunals and the Origins of International Criminal Law*. New York: Oxford University Press, 2011.

Heller, Kevin Jon. "'One Hell of a Killing Machine': Signature Strikes and International Law." *Journal of International Criminal Justice* 11 (2013): 89–119.

Henckaerts, Jean-Marie. "The Grave Breaches Regime as Customary International Law." *Journal of International Criminal Justice* 7 (2009): 683–701.

Henckaerts, Jean-Marie. "Study on Customary International Humanitarian Law: A Contribution to the Understanding and Respect for the Rule of Law in Armed Conflict." *International Review of the Red Cross* 87 (2005): 175–212.

Herman, Susan N. *Taking Liberties: The War on Terror and the Erosion of American Democracy.* New York: Oxford University Press, 2011.

Hersh, Seymour M. "Torture at Abu Ghraib." *New Yorker*, May 10, 2004.

Hitchcock, William I. "Human Rights and the Laws of War: The Geneva Conventions of 1949." In *The Human Rights Revolution: An International History*, edited by Akira Iriye, Petra Goedde, and William I. Hitchcock, 93–112. New York: Oxford University Press, 2012.

Holder, Eric. Speech at Northwestern University School of Law, Evanston, Illinois, March 5, 2012.

Holtzman, Elizabeth. "The Impeachment of George W. Bush." *The Nation*, January 30, 2006.

Holtzman, Elizabeth. *The Impeachment of George W. Bush: A Practical Guide for Concerned Citizens.* New York: Nation Books, 2006.

Hopgood, Stephen. *The Endtimes of Human Rights.* Ithaca: Cornell University Press, 2013.

Horton, Scott. "Justice after Bush: Prosecuting an Outlaw Administration." *Harper's*, December 2008.

Howard, Michael. "Constraints on Warfare." In Howard, Andrepoulos, and Shulman, *Laws of War*, 1–11.

Howard, Michael, George J. Andrepoulos, and Mark R. Shulman, eds. *The Laws of War: Constraints on Warfare in the Western World.* New Haven: Yale University Press, 1994.

Human Rights Watch. *"Between a Drone and Al-Qaeda": The Civilian Cost of US Targeted Killings in Yemen.* New York: Human Rights Watch, 2013.

Hutchinson, Dennis J. "'The Achilles Heel' of the Constitution: Justice Jackson and the Japanese Exclusion Cases." *Supreme Court Review* (2002): 455–94.

"The Immunity-Conferring Power of the Office of Legal Counsel." *Harvard Law Review* 121 (2008): 2086–2109.

Independent Panel to Review DoD Detention Operations. *Final Report of the Independent Panel to Review DoD Detention Operations.* Arlington, VA, 2004.

International Committee of the Red Cross. *ICRC Report on Treatment of Fourteen "High Value Detainees" in CIA Custody.* 2007.

International Committee of the Red Cross. *International Humanitarian Law and the Challenges of Contemporary Armed Conflicts.* 2011.

International Committee of the Red Cross. *Report of the International Committee of the Red Cross (ICRC) on the Treatment by the Coalition Forces of Prisoners of War.* 2004.

Ip, John. "Two Narratives of Torture." *Northwestern Journal of International Human Rights* 7 (2009): 35–77.

Isaacharoff, Samuel, and Richard H. Pildes. "Between Civil Libertarianism and Executive Unilateralism: An Institutional Process Approach to Rights during Wartime." *Theoretical Inquiries in Law* 5 (2004): 1–45.

Isikoff, Michael. "Memos Reveal War Crimes Warnings." *Newsweek*, May 16, 2004.

Jackson, Dick. "Interrogation and Treatment of Detainees in the Global War on Terror." In *The War on Terror and the Laws of War: A Military Perspective*, edited by Michael W. Lewis, 125–59. New York: Oxford University Press, 2009.

Jackson, Dick, Eric T. Jensen, and Robert Matsuishi. "The Law of War after the DTA, *Hamdan*, and the MCA." *Army Lawyer* (September 2007): 19–27.

Jinks, Derek. "The Applicability of the Geneva Conventions to the 'Global War on Terrorism.'" *Virginia Journal of International Law* 46 (2005): 165–95.

Jinks, Derek. "International Human Rights Law and the War on Terrorism." *Denver Journal of International Law and Policy* 31 (2002): 58–68.

Johnsen, Dawn E. "Faithfully Executing the Laws: Internal Legal Constraints on Executive Power." *UCLA Law Review* 54 (2007): 1559–1611.

Johnson, Loch K. "Congress and Intelligence." In *Congress and the Politics of National Security*, edited by David P. Auerswald and Colton C. Campbell, 121–43. Cambridge: Cambridge University Press, 2011.

Johnson, Loch K. *A Season of Inquiry Revisited: The Church Committee Confronts America's Spy Agencies*. Lawrence: University Press of Kansas, 2015.

Kean, Thomas H., and Lee H. Hamilton. *Without Precedent: The Inside Story of the 9/11 Commission*. New York: Alfred A. Knopf, 2006.

Keen, Maurice H. *Chivalry*. New Haven: Yale University Press, 1984.

Keen, Maurice H. *The Laws of War in the Late Middle Ages*. London: Routledge and Kegan Paul, 1965.

Kelley, Christopher S., and Brian W. Marshall. "Assessing Presidential Power: Signing Statements and Veto Threats as Coordinated Strategies." *American Politics Research* 37 (2009): 508–33.

Kinkopf, Neil, and Peter M. Shane. "Signed under Protest: A Database of Presidential Signing Statements, 2001–2009." Last modified October 2009. https://www.researchgate.net/publication/228187707_Under_Protest_A_Database_of_Presidential_Signing_St atements_2001-2009

Kitrosser, Heidi. *Reclaiming Accountability: Transparency, Executive Power, and the U.S. Constitution*. Chicago: University of Chicago Press, 2015.

Kitts, Kenneth. *Presidential Commissions and National Security: The Politics of Damage Control*. Boulder: Lynne Rienner, 2006.

Klaidman, Daniel. *Kill or Capture: The War on Terror and the Soul of the Obama Presidency*. Boston: Houghton Mifflin Harcourt, 2012.

Koh, Harold Hongju. "The Obama Administration and International Law." Speech at the Annual Meeting of the American Society of International Law, Washington, DC, March 25, 2010.

Koppell, Jonathan G. S. "Pathologies of Accountability: ICANN and the Challenge of 'Multiple Accountabilities Disorder.'" *Public Administration Review* 65 (2005): 94–108.

Kramer, Alan. "The First Wave of International War Crimes Trials: Istanbul and Leipzig." *European Review* 14 (2006): 441–55.

Krcmaric, Daniel. Letter, "Does the International Criminal Court Target the American Military?" *American Political Science Review* (2022): 1–7, https://doi.org/10.1017S00030 55422000478

Kriner, Douglas L., and Eric Schickler. *Investigating the President: Congressional Checks on Presidential Power*. Princeton: Princeton University Press, 2016.

Lapham, Lewis H. "The Case for Impeachment: Why We Can No Longer Afford George W. Bush." *Harper's*, March 2006.

Laumann, Peter. "*Ashcroft v. Iqbal* and Binding International Law: Command Responsibility in the Context of War Crimes and Human Rights Abuses." *University of Pennsylvania Journal of Law and Social Change* 16 (2013): 181–201.

Leahy, Patrick. "The Case for a Truth Commission." *Time*, February 19, 2009.

Leahy, Patrick. "Restoring Trust in the Justice System: The Senate Judiciary Committee's Agenda in the 111th Congress." Marver Bernstein Lecture, Georgetown University, Washington, DC, February 9, 2009.

Lessa, Francesca, and Leigh A. Payne. *Amnesty in the Age of Human Rights Accountability: Comparative and International Perspectives.* Cambridge: Cambridge University Press, 2012.

Levinson, Daryl J. "Empire-Building Government in Constitutional Law." *Harvard Law Review* 118 (2005): 915–72.

Levinson, Daryl J., and Richard H. Pildes. "Separation of Parties, Not Powers." *Harvard Law Review* 119 (2006): 2312–86.

Levinson, Sanford. "Constitutional Norms in a State of Permanent Emergency." *Georgia Law Review* 40 (2006): 699–751.

Levinson, Sanford. "Impeachment: The Case Against." *The Nation.* February 12, 2007.

Levinson, Sanford, ed. *Torture: A Collection.* Oxford: Oxford University Press, 2004.

Levinson, Sanford. "To What Extent Is Judicial Intervention a 'Hollow Hope': Reflections on the Israeli and American Judicial Experiences since 2001." *Tulsa Law Review* 47 (2011): 363–78.

Levinson, Sanford, and Jack M. Balkin. "Constitutional Dictatorship: Its Dangers and Design." *Minnesota Law Review* 94 (2010): 1789–1866.

Lindorff, Dave, and Barbara Olshansky. *The Case for Impeachment: The Legal Argument for Removing President George W. Bush from Office.* New York: Thomas Dunne, 2006.

Lippman, Matthew. "Prosecutions of Nazi War Criminals before Post–World War II Domestic Tribunals." *University of Miami International and Comparative Law Review* 8 (1999–2000): 1–113.

Lobel, Jules. "Conflicts between the Commander in Chief and Congress: Concurrent Power over the Conduct of War." *Ohio State Law Journal* 69 (2008): 391–467.

Lobel, Jules. "Victory without Success?—the Guantánamo Litigation, Permanent Preventive Detention, and Resisting Injustice." *Journal of Law and Society* 14 (2013): 121–66.

Lobel, Jules. "*Ziglar v. Abbasi* and the Demise of Accountability." *Fordham Law Review* 86 (2018): 2149–66.

Luban, David. "On the Commander in Chief Power." *University of Southern California Law Review* 81 (2008): 477–569.

Luban, David. *Torture, Power, and Law.* Cambridge: Cambridge University Press, 2014.

Macedo, Stephen, ed. *Universal Jurisdiction: National Courts and the Prosecution of Serious Crimes under International Law.* Philadelphia: University of Pennsylvania Press, 2004.

Manner, George. "The Legal Nature and Punishment of Criminal Acts of Violence Contrary to the Laws of War." *American Journal of International Law* 37 (1943): 407–35.

Margulies, Joseph. *Guantánamo and the Abuse of Presidential Power.* New York: Simon and Schuster, 2006.

Maridakis, Georges S. "An Ancient Precedent to Nuremberg." *Journal of International Criminal Justice* 4 (2006): 847–52.

Marschik, Axel. "The Politics of Prosecution: European National Approaches to War Crimes." In McCormack and Simpson, *Law of War Crimes*, 65–101.

Martinez, Jenny S. "Process and Substance in the 'War on Terror.'" *Columbia Law Review* 108 (2008): 1013–92.

Mason, Alpheus Thomas. "Extra-Judicial Work for Judges: The Views of Chief Justice Stone." *Harvard Law Review* 67 (1953): 193–216.

Matheson, Michael J. "The Amendment of the War Crimes Act." *American Journal of International Law* 101 (2007): 48–55.

Mayer, Jane. *The Dark Side: The Inside Story of How the War on Terror Turned into a War on American Ideals*. New York: Anchor Books, 2009.

Mayer, Jane. "Thoughts on the Levin Report." *New Yorker*, April 21, 2009.

Mayerfeld, Jamie. *The Promise of Human Rights: Constitutional Government, Democratic Legitimacy, and International Law*. Philadelphia: University of Pennsylvania Press, 2016.

Mayerfeld, Jamie. "Who Shall Be the Judge? The United States, the International Criminal Court, and the Global Enforcement of Human Rights." *Human Rights Quarterly* 25 (2003): 93–129.

McClain, Paula D. "Arizona 'High Noon': The Recall and Impeachment of Evan Mecham." *PS: Political Science and Politics* 21 (1988): 628–38.

McCloskey, Robert Green, ed. *The Works of James Wilson*. 2 vols. Cambridge, MA: Belknap Press of Harvard University Press, 1967.

McCormack, Timothy L. H. "From Sun Tzu to the Sixth Committee: The Evolution of an International Criminal Law Regime." In McCormack and Simpson, *Law of War Crimes*, 31–63.

McCormack, Timothy L. H., and Gerry J. Simpson, eds. *The Law of War Crimes: National and International Approaches*. The Hague: Kluwer Law International, 1997.

McCoubrey, Hilaire. "The Concept and Treatment of War Crimes." *Journal of Armed Conflict Law* 1 (1996): 121–39.

McCoubrey, Hilaire. *International Humanitarian Law: The Regulation of Armed Conflicts*. Aldershot, UK: Dartmouth, 1990.

McDowell, Gary L. "'High Crimes and Misdemeanors': Recovering the Intentions of the Founders." *George Washington Law Review* 67 (1999): 626–49.

McNeill, William H. *The Pursuit of Power: Technology, Armed Force, and Society since A.D. 1000*. Chicago: University of Chicago Press, 1982.

Meron, Theodor. *Bloody Constraint: War and Chivalry in Shakespeare*. New York: Oxford University Press, 1998.

Meron, Theodor. "The Geneva Conventions as Customary Law." *American Journal of International Law* 81 (1987): 348–70.

Meron, Theodor. *Henry's Wars and Shakespeare's Laws: Perspectives on the Law of War in the Later Middle Ages*. Oxford: Clarendon Press, 1993.

Meron, Theodor. *War Crimes Law Comes of Age: Essays*. Oxford: Clarendon Press, 1998.

Miller, Peter, Paul Gronke, and Darius Rejali. "Torture and Public Opinion: The Partisan

Dimension." In *Examining Torture: Empirical Studies of State Repression*, edited by Tracy Lightcap and James P. Pfiffner, 11–41. New York: Palgrave Macmillan, 2014.

Minow, Martha. *Between Vengeance and Forgiveness: Facing History after Genocide and Mass Violence*. Boston: Beacon Press, 1998.

Morrison, Trevor W. "The Middle Ground in Judicial Review of Enemy Combatant Detentions." *Willamette Law Review* 45 (2009): 453–71.

Morrison, Trevor W. "Stare Decisis in the Office of Legal Counsel." *Columbia Law Review* 110 (2010): 1448–1525.

Mulgan, Richard. "Accountability: An Ever-Expanding Concept?" *Public Administration* 78 (2000): 555–73.

Myers, Erika. "Conquering Peace: Military Commissions as a Lawfare Strategy in the Mexican War." *American Journal of Criminal Law* 35 (2008): 201–40.

Neff, Stephen C. *War and the Law of Nations: A General History*. Cambridge: Cambridge University Press, 2005.

Nourse, Victoria F. *The Impeachments of Donald Trump: An Introduction to Constitutional Interpretation*. St. Paul, MN: West Academic Publishing, 2021.

Ober, Josiah. "Classical Greek Times." In Howard, Andrepoulos, and Shulman, *Laws of War*, 12–26.

O'Connell, Mary Ellen. "The Legal Case against the Global War on Terror." *Case Western Reserve Journal of International Law* 36 (2004): 349–57.

O'Connell, Mary Ellen. "Unlawful Killing with Combat Drones: A Case Study of Pakistan, 2004–2009." In *Shooting to Kill: Socio-Legal Perspectives on the Use of Lethal Force*, edited by Simon Bronitt, Miriam Gani, and Saskia Hufnagel, 263–91. Oxford, UK: Hart, 2012.

O'Keefe, Roger. "Universal Jurisdiction: Clarifying the Basic Concept." *Journal of International Criminal Justice* 2 (2004): 735–60.

Olsen, Tricia D., Leigh A. Payne, and Andrew G. Reiter. "The Justice Balance: When Transitional Justice Improves Human Rights and Democracy." *Human Rights Quarterly* 32 (2010): 980–1007.

Olson, Keith W. *Watergate: The Presidential Scandal That Shook America*. Lawrence: University Press of Kansas, 2016.

Ostrander, Ian, and Joel Sievert. "What's So Sinister about Presidential Signing Statements?" *Presidential Studies Quarterly* 43 (2013): 58–80.

Parker, Geoffrey. "Early Modern Europe." In Howard, Andrepoulos, and Shulman, *Laws of War*, 40–58.

Parker, Geoffrey. *The Thirty Years' War*. London: Routledge and Kegan Paul, 1984.

Paust, Jordan J. *Beyond the Law: The Bush Administration's Unlawful Responses in the "War" on Terror*. Cambridge: Cambridge University Press, 2007.

Paust, Jordan J. "Human Rights on the Battlefield." *George Washington International Law Review* 47 (2015): 509–61.

Paust, Jordan J. "Selective History of International Tribunals and Efforts Prior to Nuremberg." *ILSA Journal of International and Comparative Law* (2003): 207–13.

Paust, Jordan J. "War and Enemy Status after 9/11: Attacks on the Laws of War." *Yale Journal of International Law* 28 (2003): 325–35.

Pearlstein, Deborah N. "Finding Effective Constraints on Executive Power: Interrogation, Detention, and Torture." *Indiana Law Journal* 81 (2006): 1255–95.

Pejic, Jelena. "Extraterritorial Targeting by Means of Armed Drones: Some Legal Implications." *International Review of the Red Cross* 96 (2014): 67–106.

Pendas, Devin O. "Orientation: War Crimes Trials in Theory and Practice from the Middle Ages to the Present." In *War Crimes Trials and Investigations: A Multi-Disciplinary Introduction*, edited by Jonathan Waterlow and Jacques Schuhmacher, 23–58. Cham, Switzerland: Palgrave Macmillan, 2018.

Pfander, James E. *Constitutional Torts and the War on Terror.* New York: Oxford University Press, 2017.

Pfiffner, James P. *Power Play: The Bush Presidency and the Constitution.* Washington, DC: Brookings Institution Press, 2008.

Phillips, Joshua E. S. "Inside the Detainee Abuse Task Force." *The Nation*, May 13, 2011.

Pictet, Jean S. *Commentary: I Geneva Convention for the Amelioration of the Condition of the Wounded and Sick in Armed Forces in the Field.* Geneva: International Committee of the Red Cross, 1952.

Pictet, Jean S. *Commentary: IV Geneva Convention Relative to the Protection of Civilian Persons in Time of War.* Geneva: International Committee of the Red Cross, 1958.

Pictet, Jean S. "The New Geneva Conventions for the Protection of War Victims." *American Journal of International Law* 45 (1951): 462–75.

Pildes, Richard H. "Law and the President." *Harvard Law Review* 125 (2012): 1381–1424.

Pillard, Cornelia T. L. "The Unfulfilled Promise of the Constitution in Executive Hands." *Michigan Law Review* 103 (2005): 676–758.

Pious, Richard M. *The American Presidency.* New York: Basic Books, 1979.

Posner, Eric A. *The Twilight of Human Rights Law.* New York: Oxford University Press, 2014.

Posner, Richard A. *An Affair of State: The Investigation, Impeachment, and Trial of President Clinton.* Cambridge, MA: Harvard University Press, 2000.

Powell, H. Jefferson. *Targeting Americans: The Constitutionality of the U.S. Drone War.* New York: Oxford University Press, 2016.

Poznansky, Michael. "Revisiting Plausible Deniability." *Journal of Strategic Studies* (2020): 511–33.

Prakash, Saikrishna Bangalore. *Imperial from the Beginning: The Constitution of the Original Executive.* New Haven: Yale University Press, 2015.

Preux, Jean de. *Commentary: III Geneva Convention Relative to the Treatment of Prisoners of War.* Geneva: International Committee of the Red Cross, 1960.

Priemel, Kim C., and Alexa Stiller, eds. *Reassessing the Nuremberg Military Tribunals: Transitional Justice, Trial Narratives, and Historiography.* New York: Berghahn, 2012.

Rahdert, Mark C. "Double-Checking Executive Emergency Power: Lessons from *Hamdi* and *Hamdan*." *Temple Law Review* 80 (2007): 451–88.

Rakove, Jack N. *The Beginnings of National Politics: An Interpretive History of the Continental Congress.* Baltimore: Johns Hopkins University Press, 1979.

Ramsey, Michael D. *The Constitution's Text in Foreign Affairs.* Cambridge, MA: Harvard University Press, 2007.

Randolph, A. Raymond. "The Guantánamo Mess." In *Confronting Terror: 9/11 and the Future of American National Security*, edited by Dean Reuter and John Yoo, 241–61. New York: Encounter Books, 2011.

Ratner, Steven R., Jason S. Abrams, and James L. Bischoff. *Accountability for Human Rights Atrocities in International Law: Beyond the Nuremberg Legacy*. 3rd ed. New York: Oxford University Press, 2009.

Reichberg, Gregory M., Henrik Syse, and Endre Begby, eds. *The Ethics of War: Classic and Contemporary Readings*. Malden, MA: Blackwell, 2006.

Risen, James. *State of War: The Secret History of the CIA and the Bush Administration*. New York: Free Press, 2006.

Roht-Arriaza, Naomi, and Javier Mariezcurrena, eds. *Transitional Justice in the Twenty-First Century: Beyond Truth versus Justice*. Cambridge: Cambridge University Press, 2006.

Rona, Gabor. "Interesting Times for International Humanitarian Law: Challenges from the 'War on Terror.'" *Fletcher Forum of World Affairs* 27 (2003): 55–74.

Rosen, Jeffrey. "A Torturous Decision." *New York Magazine*, May 3, 2009.

Ross, Stephen R., Raphael A. Prober, and Gabriel K. Gillett. "The Rise and Permanence of Quasi-Investigative Legislative Commissions." *Journal of Law and Politics* 27 (2012): 415–57.

Rossiter, Clinton. *The Supreme Court and the Commander in Chief*. Exp. ed. with additional text by Richard P. Longaker. Ithaca: Cornell University Press, 1976.

Rotberg, Robert I., and Dennis Thompson, eds. *Truth v. Justice: The Morality of Truth Commissions*. Princeton: Princeton University Press, 2000.

Rothenberg, Gunther. "The Age of Napoleon." In Howard, Andrepoulos, and Shulman, *Laws of War*, 86–97.

Rozell, Mark J., and Jeffrey P. Crouch. *The Unitary Executive Theory: A Danger to Constitutional Government*. Lawrence: University Press of Kansas, 2021.

Rudalevige, Andrew. *The New Imperial Presidency: Renewing Presidential Power after Watergate*. Ann Arbor: University of Michigan Press, 2005.

Rudolph, Christopher. *Power and Principle: The Politics of International Criminal Courts*. Ithaca: Cornell University Press, 2017.

Ryan, Allan A. "Nuremberg's Contributions to International Law." *Boston College International and Comparative Law Review* 30 (2007): 55–89.

Sands, Philippe. *Torture Team: Rumsfeld's Memo and the Betrayal of American Values*. New York: Palgrave Macmillan, 2008.

Sanger, David E. "Cyber, Drones, and Secrecy." In *Understanding Cyber Conflict: Fourteen Analogies*, edited by George Perkovich and Ariel E. Levite, 61–78. Washington, DC: Georgetown University Press, 2017.

Savage, Charlie. *Power Wars: Inside Obama's Post-9/11 Presidency*. New York: Little, Brown, 2015.

Savage, Charlie. *Takeover: The Return of the Imperial Presidency and the Subversion of American Democracy*. New York: Little, Brown, 2007.

Scahill, Jeremy. "The CIA's Secret Sites in Somalia." *The Nation*, August 1, 2011.

Schabas, William A. "United States Hostility to the International Criminal Court: It's All about the Security Council." *European Journal of International Law* 15 (2004): 701–20.

Scheppele, Kim Lane. "The New Judicial Deference." *Boston University Law Review* 92 (2012): 89–170.

Schindler, Dietrich, and Jiri Toman, eds. *The Laws of Armed Conflicts: A Collection of Conventions, Resolutions and Other Documents.* 4th ed. Leiden: Martinus Nijhoff, 2004.

Schlesinger, Arthur M., Jr. *The Imperial Presidency.* Boston: Houghton Mifflin, 1973.

Schlesinger, Arthur M., Jr. *War and the American Presidency.* New York: W. W. Norton, 2004.

Schmidt, Averell, and Kathryn Sikkink. "Breaking the Ban? The Heterogeneous Impact of US Contestation of the Torture Norm." *Journal of Global Security Studies* 4 (2019): 105–22.

Schmidt, Averell, and Kathryn Sikkink. "Partners in Crime: An Empirical Evaluation of the CIA Rendition, Detention, and Interrogation Program." *Perspectives on Politics* 16 (2018): 1014–33.

Schmitt, Gary J., Joseph M. Bessette, and Andrew E. Busch, eds. *The Imperial Presidency and the Constitution.* Lanham, MD: Rowman and Littlefield, 2017.

Schwarzenberger, Georg. "The Judgment of Nuremberg." *Tulane Law Review* 21 (1947): 329–61.

Segesser, Daniel Marc. "'Unlawful Warfare Is Uncivilised': The International Debate on the Punishment of War Crimes, 1872–1918." *European Review of History* 14 (2007): 215–34.

Shane, Peter M. *Democracy's Chief Executive: Interpreting the Constitution and Defining the Future of the Presidency.* Oakland: University of California Press, 2022.

Shane, Peter M. *Madison's Nightmare: How Executive Power Threatens American Democracy.* Chicago: University of Chicago Press, 2009.

Shapiro, Steven M., Kenneth S. Geller, Timothy S. Bishop, Edward A. Hartnett, and Dan Himmelfarb. *Supreme Court Practice: For Practice in the Supreme Court of the United States.* 10th ed. Arlington, VA: Bloomberg BNA, 2013.

Shin, Gi-Wook, and Rennie J. Moon. "South Korea after Impeachment." *Journal of Democracy* 28 (2017): 117–31.

Sikkink, Kathryn. *Evidence for Hope: Making Human Rights Work in the 21st Century.* Princeton: Princeton University Press, 2017.

Sikkink, Kathryn. *The Justice Cascade: How Human Rights Prosecutions Are Changing World Politics.* New York: W. W. Norton, 2011.

Sikkink, Kathryn, and Carrie Booth Walling. "The Impact of Human Rights Trials in Latin America." *Journal of Peace Research* 44 (2007): 427–45.

Simon, Jonathan. "Parrhesiastic Accountability: Investigatory Commissions and Executive Power in an Age of Terror." *Yale Law Journal* 114 (2005): 1419–57.

Simpson, Gerry J. "War Crimes: A Critical Introduction." In McCormack and Simpson, *Law of War Crimes,* 1–30.

Skowronek, Stephen. "The Conservative Insurgency and Presidential Power: A Developmental Perspective on the Unitary Executive." *Harvard Law Review* 122 (2009): 2070–2103.

Skowronek, Stephen. *Presidential Leadership in Political Time: Reprise and Reappraisal.* 2nd ed. Lawrence: University Press of Kansas, 2011.

Smith, Bradley F., ed. *The American Road to Nuremberg: The Documentary Record, 1944–1945*. Stanford, CA: Hoover Institution Press, 1982.

Solis, Gary D. *The Law of Armed Conflict: International Humanitarian Law in War*. 2nd ed. Cambridge: Cambridge University Press, 2016.

Spitzer, Robert J. "Is the Constitutional Presidency Obsolete?" In *The Presidency in the Twenty-First Century*, edited by Charles W. Dunn, 55–82. Lexington: University Press of Kentucky, 2011.

Springer, Paul J. *America's Captives: Treatment of POWs from the Revolutionary War to the War on Terror*. Lawrence: University Press of Kansas, 2010.

Squibb, G. D. *The High Court of Chivalry: A Study of the Civil Law in England*. Oxford: Clarendon Press, 1959.

Stacey, Robert C. "The Age of Chivalry." In Howard, Andrepoulos, and Shulman, *Laws of War*, 27–39.

Stilp, Erin M. "The Military and State-Secrets Privilege: The Quietly Expanding Power." *Catholic University Law Review* 55 (2006): 831–65.

Straus, Ulrich. *The Anguish of Surrender: Japanese POWs of World War II*. Seattle: University of Washington Press, 2003.

Suleman, Arsalan M. "Detainee Treatment Act of 2005." *Harvard Human Rights Journal* 19 (2006): 257–65.

Sullivan, Andrew. "Dear President Bush." *Atlantic*, October 2009.

Suskind, Ron. *The One Percent Doctrine: Deep inside America's Pursuit of Its Enemies since 9/11*. New York: Simon and Schuster, 2006.

Taft, William H., IV. "The Law of Armed Conflict after 9/11: Some Salient Features." *Yale Journal of International Law* 28 (2003): 319–23.

Taguba, Antonio M. *Article 15-6 Investigation of the 800th Military Police Brigade*. 2004.

Taguba, Antonio M. Preface to *Broken Laws, Broken Lives: Medical Evidence of Torture by US Personnel and Its Impact*, by Physicians for Human Rights, viii. 2008.

Tanaka, Yuki. *Hidden Horrors: Japanese War Crimes in World War II*. 2nd ed. Lanham, MD: Rowman and Littlefield, 2018.

Tannenwald, Nina. "Assessing the Effects and Effectiveness of the Geneva Conventions." In *Do the Geneva Conventions Matter?*, edited by Matthew Evangelista and Nina Tannenwald, 1–34. New York: Oxford University Press, 2017.

Taylor, Telford. *The Anatomy of the Nuremberg Trials: A Personal Memoir*. New York: Skyhorse, 2013.

Teitel, Ruti G. "Transitional Justice Genealogy." *Harvard Human Rights Journal* 16 (2003): 69–94.

Tenet, George, with Bill Harlow. *At the Center of the Storm: My Years at the CIA*. New York: HarperCollins, 2007.

Travis, Jeremy. "Rethinking Sovereign Immunity after *Bivens*." *New York University Law Review* 57 (1982): 597–668.

Trial of Andrew Johnson . . . 3 vols. Washington, DC: 1868.

Trial of the Major War Criminals before the International Military Tribunal, Nuremberg, November 14, 1945–October 1, 1946. 42 vols. Nuremberg, Germany, 1947–49.

Tribe, Laurence H. "Defining 'High Crimes and Misdemeanors': Basic Principles." *George Washington Law Review* 67 (1999): 712–34.

Tribe, Laurence H., and Joshua Matz. *To End a Presidency: The Power of Impeachment.* New York: Basic Books, 2018.

Truth and Reconciliation Commission. *Truth and Reconciliation Commission of South Africa Report.* 7 vols. Cape Town, South Africa, 1998–2003.

Turner, Mark, Seung-Ho Kwon, and Michael O'Donnell. "Making Integrity Institutions Work in South Korea: The Role of People Power in the Impeachment of President Park in 2016." *Asian Survey* 58 (2018): 898–919.

Tushnet, Mark. "Controlling Executive Power in the War on Terrorism." *Harvard Law Review* 118 (2005): 2673–82.

Tutu, Desmond. *No Future without Forgiveness.* New York: Doubleday, 1999.

US Dept. of Defense, Office of the Inspector General. *Review of DoD-Directed Investigations of Detainee Abuse.* Arlington, VA, 2006.

US Dept. of Justice, Office of Professional Responsibility. *Investigation into the Office of Legal Counsel's Memoranda Concerning Issues Relating to the Central Intelligence Agency's Use of "Enhanced Interrogation Techniques" on Suspected Terrorists.* Washington, DC, 2009.

US Dept. of Justice, Office of the Inspector General. *A Review of the FBI's Involvement in and Observations of Detainee Interrogations in Guantánamo Bay, Afghanistan, and Iraq.* Washington, DC, 2008.

US Dept. of the Army. *Field Manual 27–10, The Law of Land Warfare.* Washington, DC, 1956.

US Dept. of the Army. *Field Manual 2–22.3 (FM 34–52), Human Intelligence Collector Operations.* Washington, DC, 2006.

US Dept. of the Army. *Field Manual 34-52, Intelligence Interrogation.* Washington, DC, 1992.

US Depts. of the Army, Navy, Air Force, and Marine Corps. *Enemy Prisoners of War, Retained Personnel, Civilian Internees and Other Detainees* (Army Reg. 190-8, OPNAVINST 3461.6, AFJI 31–304, MCO 3461.1). Washington, DC, 1997.

US Office of the Director of National Intelligence. *Annual Threat Assessment of the U.S. Intelligence Community.* 2022.

US War Dept. General Order No. 100, *Instructions for the Government of Armies of the United States in the Field.* April 24, 1863.

Vagts, Detlev F. "Military Commissions: The Forgotten Reconstruction Chapter." *American University International Law Review* 23 (2008): 231–74.

Vasquez, Carlos Manuel. "The Military Commissions Act, the Geneva Conventions, and the Courts: A Critical Guide." *American Journal of International Law* 101 (2007): 73–98.

Vattell, Emmerich de. *The Law of Nations, or, Principles of the Law of Nature, Applied to the Conduct and Affairs of Nations and Sovereigns.* Philadelphia, 1817.

Vinjamuri, Leslie, and Jack Snyder. "Law and Politics in Transitional Justice." *Annual Review of Political Science* 18 (2015): 303–27.

Vladek, Stephen I. "*Boumediene*'s Quiet Theory: Access to Courts and the Separation of Powers." *Notre Dame Law Review* 84 (2009): 2107–50.

Vladek, Stephen I. "Congress, the Commander-in-Chief, and the Separation of Powers after *Hamdan.*" *Transnational Law and Contemporary Problems* 16 (2007): 933–64.

Vladek, Stephen I. "The D.C. Circuit after *Boumediene*." *Seton Hall Law Review* 41 (2011): 1451–90.

Vladek, Stephen I. "The Long War, the Federal Courts, and the Necessity/Legality Paradox." *University of Richmond Law Review* 43 (2009): 893–926.

Vladeck, Stephen I. "The Passive-Aggressive Virtues." *Columbia Law Review Sidebar* 111 (2011): 122–40.

Vladek, Stephen I. "The Torture Report and the Accountability Gap." *Georgetown Journal of International Affairs* 16 (Summer/Fall 2015): 174–82.

Vladek, Stephen I. "The Unreviewable Executive: *Kiyemba, Maqaleh*, and the Obama Administration." *Constitutional Commentary* 26 (2010): 603–23.

Waldron, Jeremy. "Inhuman and Degrading Treatment: The Words Themselves." *Canadian Journal of Law and Jurisprudence* 23 (2010): 269–86.

Walker, Samuel. *Presidents and Civil Liberties from Wilson to Obama: A Story of Poor Custodians*. Cambridge: Cambridge University Press, 2012.

Walzer, Michael. "Trying Political Leaders." *New Republic*, May 21, 2010.

Washington, George. *The Papers of George Washington*. Revolutionary War Series. Edited by W. W. Abbot, Dorothy Twohig, Philander D. Chase, et al. 30 vols. to date. Charlottesville: University of Virginia Press, 1985–.

Waxman, Seth P. "The Combatant Detention Trilogy through the Lenses of History." In *Terrorism, the Laws of War, and the Constitution*, edited by Peter Berkowitz, 22–57. Stanford, CA: Hoover Institution Press, 2005.

Weiner, Allen S. "*Hamdan*, Terror, War." *Lewis and Clark Law Review* 11 (2007): 997–1021.

Weinschenk, Fritz. "Nazis before German Courts: The West German War Crimes Trials." *International Lawyer* 10 (1976): 515–29.

Weissbrodt, David, and Amy Bergquist. "Extraordinary Rendition: A Human Rights Analysis." *Harvard Human Rights Journal* 19 (2006): 123–60.

Wells, Christina E. "State Secrets and Executive Accountability." *Constitutional Commentary* 26 (2010): 625–50.

Whittington, Keith E. "Much Ado about Nothing: Signing Statements, Vetoes, and Presidential Constitutional Interpretation." *William and Mary Law Review* 58 (2017): 1751–91.

Wigard, Kyra, and Guissou Jahangiri. "The International Criminal Court and Afghanistan: A Tale of Misunderstandings and Misinformation." *Journal of International Criminal Justice* 20 (2022): 203–22.

Willis, James F. *Prologue to Nuremberg: The Politics and Diplomacy of Punishing War Criminals of the First World War*. Westport, CT: Greenwood, 1982.

Witt, John Fabian. *Lincoln's Code: The Laws of War in American History*. New York: Free Press, 2012.

Wittmann, Rebecca. "Tainted Law: The West German Judiciary and the Prosecution of Nazi War Criminals." In *Atrocities on Trial: Historical Perspectives on the Politics of Prosecuting War Crimes*, edited by Patricia Heberer and Jürgen Matthäus, 211–29. Lincoln: University of Nebraska Press, 2008.

Wolfowitz, Paul. Interview by Pentagon Channel, May 4, 2004.

Wood, Gordon S. *The Creation of the American Republic, 1776–1787*. Chapel Hill: University of North Carolina Press, 1998.

Woodward, Bob. *State of Denial*. New York: Simon and Schuster, 2006.

Yoo, John C. "The Continuation of Politics by Other Means: The Original Understanding of War Powers." *California Law Review* 84 (1996): 167–305.

Yoo, John. Interview by Fareed Zakaria. *Fareed Zakaria GPS*, CNN, December 14, 2014.

Yoo, John. *The Powers of War and Peace: The Constitution and Foreign Affairs after 9/11*. Chicago: University of Chicago Press, 2005.

Yoo, John. *War by Other Means: An Insider's Account of the War on Terror*. New York: Atlantic Monthly Press, 2006.

Zegart, Amy B. "The Domestic Politics of Irrational Intelligence Oversight." *Political Science Quarterly* 126 (2011): 1–25.

Zeisberg, Mariah. *War Powers: The Politics of Constitutional Authority*. Princeton: Princeton University Press, 2013.

Zelizer, Julian E. "The Conservative Embrace of Presidential Power." *Boston University Law Review* 88 (2008): 499–503.

INDEX

Abbasi, Ahmer Iqbal, 132
Abdulmutallab, Umar Farouk, 186
Abu Ghraib prison scandal: Bush administration response, 90, 143–45, 171, 177–78; congressional investigations, 54, 89–91, 101, 175; detainee treatment, 5–6, 71, 78, 80, 89–94, 113; press coverage and public reaction, 89, 111, 113, 142–44, 151, 166, 177; prosecutions, 209n30; Supreme Court decisions and, 118, 137
accountability: defined, 8–10; discourse of, 7; normative justification for, 9, 16, 25, 43, 169–70; Nuremberg principle of individual accountability, 16, 19, 38–40, 42, 44, 170, 193–94; prospective (before-the-fact), 9, 179; retrospective (after-the-fact), 9; untraditional mechanisms, 17–18. *See also* human rights accountability; presidential accountability in wartime
Addington, David S., 49, 53, 67–70, 73, 172, 190
Additional Protocol I to the Geneva Conventions, 41–42
Afghanistan: detainee sites, 78, 126, 128–29, 184; drone strikes against, 185, 188–89; "failed state" argument and, 63–64; Geneva Conventions and, 40, 45, 62–63, 70, 172; ICC and, 7, 191–93
Al-Adahi v. Obama (2010), 129
al-Awlaki, Anwar, 186–88
Al-Bihani v. Obama (2010), 128
Al Maqaleh v. Gates (2010), 128
Al Qaeda: drone strikes against, 185–87;

Geneva Conventions and, 4, 39–41, 45, 47, 61, 74, 100, 171, 173; intelligence about, 105, 153; threat of, 180, 182
al-Qahtani, Mohammed, 80
al Shabaab, 185–86
Alter, Jonathan, 142
American Civil Liberties Union, 153, 184
American Revolution, 26–27, 170
American Servicemembers Protection Act (2002), 191
Amnesty International, 153
Arar, Maher, 136–37
Argentina, 161, 193
armed forces: civilian control over, 59–60; professionalization of, 22; regulation of (*see* laws of war). *See also* Uniform Code of Military Justice; US military
Army Field Manual (US), 64, 93–95, 174, 180, 184
Army Times, 143
Articles of Confederation, 10–11
Ashcroft, John, 4–5, 49, 68, 121, 132, 134, 172
Ashcroft v. Iqbal (2009), 133–35, 139
authoritarian regimes, 1, 9, 154–55, 161–62
Authorization for Use of Military Force (AUMF), 51, 119, 175, 186, 220n122

Bagram Air Force Base (Afghanistan), 126, 128–29, 184
Balkin, Jack M., 7, 157, 162
Barron, David J., 59–60, 187
Belgium, 33–34

ABOUT THE AUTHOR

Stuart Streichler has taught law and politics at the University of Washington and as a Fulbright scholar at Tohoku University in Japan. He is the author of *Justice Curtis in the Civil War Era: At the Crossroads of American Constitutionalism*. Streichler also practiced law in Washington, DC, where, among other things, he participated in constitutional litigation before the US Supreme Court.